Collins

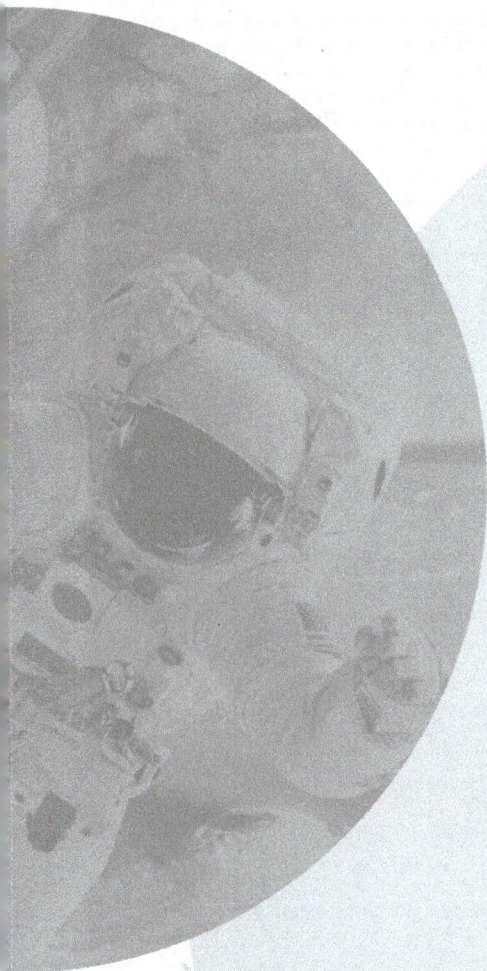

AQA KS3 Science

Teacher Guide Part 1

Ed Walsh and Tracey Baxter

HarperCollins

P U B L I S H E R S
————200————

William Collins' dream of knowledge for all began with the publication of his first book in 1819. A self-educated mill worker, he not only enriched millions of lives, but also founded a flourishing publishing house. Today, staying true to this spirit, Collins books are packed with inspiration, innovation and practical expertise. They place you at the centre of a world of possibility and give you exactly what you need to explore it.

Collins. Freedom to teach.

An imprint of HarperCollins*Publishers*
The News Building
1 London Bridge Street
London
SE1 9GF

Browse the complete Collins catalogue at
www.collins.co.uk

British Library Cataloguing in Publication Data
A catalogue record for this publication is available from the British Library.

Commissioned by Sarah Busby and Joanna Ramsay
Authors Tracey Baxter and Ed Walsh
Contributors to original material Sarah Askey, Sunetra Berry, Pat Dower, Anne Pilling and Ken Gadd
Project managed by Siobhan Brown
Copyedited by Jane Roth
Proofread by Helen Bleck
Technical review by John Ormiston
Cover design by We Are Laura
Cover images: arigato/Shutterstock, (tl) Artem Kovalenco/Shutterstock, (tr) fuyu liu/Shutterstock, (c) NikoNomad/Shutterstock, (bl) Pavel Vakhrushev/Shutterstock, (bc) robert_s/Shutterstock, (br) Sailorr/Shutterstock
Designed by Joerg Hartmannsgruber and Ken Vail Graphic Design Ltd
Illustrations by Ken Vail Graphic Design Ltd
Typeset by Ken Vail Graphic Design Ltd
Production by Rachel Weaver
Printed and bound by CPI Group (UK) Ltd, Croydon, CR0 4YY

The publishers wish to thank the following for permission to reproduce photographs and artwork. Every effort has been made to trace copyright holders and to obtain their permission for the use of copyright materials. The publishers will gladly receive any information enabling them to rectify any error or omission at the first opportunity.
Chapter 3: WS 1.3.3 (tl) ChiccoDodiFC/shutterstock, WS 1.3.3 (tr) Jarous/shutterstock, WS 1.3.3 (l) Yarik/Shutterstock, WS 1.3.3 (r) Andrei Kuzmik/Shutterstock, WS 1.3.7 (a) Orla/Shutterstock, WS 1.3.7 (b) Smileus/shutterstock, WS 1.3.7 (c) Arvind Balaraman/Shutterstock, WS 1.3.9 Tomasz Trojanowski/Shutterstock **Chapter 4:** WS 1.4.1 (l) Ilya Akinshin/Shutterstock, WS 1.4.1 (c) Venus Angel/Shutterstock, WS 1.4.1 (r) Christian Draghici/Shutterstock **Chapter 6:** WS 1.6.1 (tl) claudio zaccherini/Shutterstock, WS 1.6.1 (tc) DanielW/Shutterstock, WS 1.6.1 (tr) Sergiy Kuzmin/Shutterstock, WS 1.6.1 (cl) Darren Pullman/Shutterstock, WS 1.6.1 (c) Ruslan Ivantsov /Shutterstock, WS 1.6.1 (cr) Constantinos Loumakis/Shutterstock, WS 1.6.1 (bl) Igor Sokolov (breeze)/Shutterstock, WS 1.6.1 (bc) Oksana2010/Shutterstock, WS 1.6.1 (br) Elnur/Shutterstock **Chapter 8:** WS 1.8.9 (tl) Eric Grave/Science Photo Library, WS 1.8.9 (tr) Lebendkulturen.de/Shutterstock, WS 1.8.9 (cl) A.B. Dowsett/Science Photo Library, WS 1.8.9 (cr) GraphicsRF/shutterstock **Chapter 9:** WS 1.9.5(tl) Elena Elisseeva/Shutterstock, WS 1.9.5 (tc) Brian Maudsley/Shutterstock, WS 1.9.5 (tr) Chris2766/Shutterstock, WS 1.9.5 (bl) ESB Essentials /Shutterstock, WS 1.9.5(bc) Chungking/Shutterstock, WS 1.9.5(br) Vaide Seskauskiene/Shutterstock **Chapter 10:** WS 1.10.1 (l) Allstar Picture Library/Alamy, WS 1.10.1 (cl) Atlaspix/Shutterstock, WS 1.10.1 (cr) Featureflash Photo Agency/Shutterstock, WS 1.10.1 (r) Featureflash Photo Agency Shutterstock, WS 1.10.2 (t) Marco Govel/Shutterstock, WS 1.10.2 (b) Holbox/Shutterstock, WS 1.10.8 (tl) imtmphoto /Shutterstock, WS 1.10.8 (tr) DeymosHR /Shutterstock, WS 1.10.8 (bl) Maksim M /Shutterstock.

Contents

Contents

Introduction

Purpose of the Collins AQA Key Stage 3 Science course

This course has been developed to provide support to teachers in planning and delivering exciting, engaging and effective lessons. The overarching priorities have been to:

- meet the requirements of the National Curriculum Programme of Study and AQA KS3 Science syllabus;

- support students to make good progress in KS3 and build a firm foundation for success at KS4;

- offer ways of tracking, reporting on and responding to progress;

- support schools to deliver the KS3 course flexibly;

- address the need to challenge and engage students working at different levels of attainment;

- focus on the development of skills and processes as well as content;

- provide guidance on how learning can be managed, from initial engagement to consolidation and application.

Organisation of the Collins AQA Key Stage 3 Science course

How the lesson plans work:

Chapter introductions

These:

- give an overview of the content and skills covered in the chapter

- help in assessing prior learning and identifying misconceptions

- provide references to both the AQA KS3 Syllabus and the Programme of Study to help medium-term planning.

Learning objectives and outcomes

- Learning objectives for each topic are shared with students in the Student Book for short-term planning.

- Learning outcomes are listed; these are referred to throughout the lesson to show which activities contribute to each outcome. The outcomes are strongly rooted in the statements in the AQA KS3 Syllabus to provide detailed coverage.

These help in tracking the progress of students, identifying those making good progress and who are on the right trajectory for appropriate results at GCSE, those who are making better than expected progress and those making less progress and for whom some intervention may be needed.

Skills development

Ensuring progression in skills has underpinned the development of the course. The AQA KS3 Syllabus has a strong and clear treatment of Working Scientifically and this is used to structure the enquiry aspects of these resources. As well as ensuring that all sixteen components are covered the resources also include a range of enquiry activities based on the suggested investigations in the AQA KS3 Syllabus. These provide a good opportunity for students to develop skills and processes that will be assessed in GCSE courses.

The development of mathematical skills is a key feature of science education and is an explicit feature of GCSE courses. There are many opportunities in these resources for a wide range of skills to be introduced and reinforced; these are clearly indicated.

Students also need to be able to express themselves in writing and these skills need to be developed through KS3. Some of the questions provide an opportunity for students to work at this and demonstrate their competence; clear reference to this is given here.

Resources needed gives an overview of all the resources needed for a lesson. More detailed guidance for practicals is given in student practical sheets and technician's notes on the accompanying CD-ROM.

Common misconceptions highlight specific misconceptions for the topic.

Key vocabulary is highlighted throughout to support literacy and develop a command of key terms. These terms have been selected with reference to the core knowledge in the AQA KS3 Syllabus.

Teaching sequence

The lesson plans all use the same learning sequence. This is based on the idea that learning develops in stages during a lesson and that different parts of the lesson have different functions.

Engage This section draws students in to thinking about the ideas, and includes possible starter activities. Here students encounter ideas that will make them want to find out more.

Challenge and develop Students meet something that will challenge their existing understanding. It might be questions, ideas, demonstrations or experiments that make them realise the inadequacy of a simpler explanation.

Explain Students are encouraged to develop a good explanation and supported in capturing ideas in words or graphically. Differentiation ideas are given for students making less or more than expected progress.

Consolidate and apply Students realise how the new learning is to be consolidated and applied, including real-world applications. Again, differentiation ideas are given for students making different levels of progress.

Extend Addresses how the ideas of the topic can be extended to stretch students able to progress further.

Plenary suggestions Varied activities help in gauging student progress.

Answers All answers to Student Book questions and worksheet questions are provided.

Extra resources on the accompanying CD-ROM

Every lesson has an associated differentiated worksheet to support written work. These are provided as write-on versions with lines for student responses, and reusable versions without lines that can be used again and again to reduce photocopying costs. Practical sheets are provided to give support for planning, carrying out and analysing practical work. Technician's notes are provided to explain the materials and setup and help with planning.

Collins Connect provides digital versions of the Student Book and Teacher Packs.

Planning the learning process:
The thinking behind Collins AQA Key Stage 3 Science

Planning effective provision

Each of the lesson plans is designed to support the delivery of high quality interactive lessons. They have a common structure that is transparent, making it easy for teachers to see what is suggested and make decisions about whether to use the plan as it stands or to customise. The lessons map to the content in the Student Book which is carefully developed to cover the AQA KS3 Science syllabus. Sequences of lessons are planned to cover the requirements of the Programme of Study for Science and the AQA KS3 Science syllabus.

It is important to understand the particular approach to progress and outcomes taken by the AQA KS3 Syllabus. The traditional approach has tended to be to present students with a range of ideas and processes around a theme and then to use assessment to work out how much of this they have grasped. It is accepted that although every effort is made to give students access to a wide range of learning that for many they will leave a topic with a partial understanding. What the mastery approach in the AQA KS3 Syllabus does is to take a different approach and place greater emphasis upon a handful of key ideas. Whatever else might be part of the topic, it is these concepts that regarded as 'deal breakers'. Students should be supported to grasp these. If they know those ideas and can apply them, they are regarded as having mastered that topic. That mastery can be considered as a firm foundation for then progressing to GCSE.

The role of assessment

Assessment, of course, plays a fundamental role in mastery. A key aspect of the AQA KS3 Syllabus is that it enables teachers to prioritise certain aspects of the content and not only encourages a strong emphasis upon these in the teaching but also assumes that intervention will take place if students haven't mastered these.

The conventional model of teaching tends to use assessment at the end of a topic. This is fine if the prime purpose is to assess what has been learned but less useful if it necessary to address areas that have not been grasped (which is a key aspect of mastery). The student books include questions which can be made use of at any point.

However, support from Collins for KS3 also includes publications designed to complement the student books and teacher guides. *GCSE Science Ready Transition Tests for KS3 to GCSE* (ISBN 9780008215316) consists of sets of assessment items structured around the categories of 'Know', 'Apply' and 'Extend'. These can be used to supplement the assessment material in the student book and could be used, for example, to identify whether students have mastered the key ideas before the end of the topic. *GCSE Science Ready Intervention Tasks for KS3 to GCSE* (9780008215323) then offers a range of other learning activities that could be used to address incomplete understanding. These tasks provide ways for students to revisit key ideas without repeating actual activities.

Outstanding lesson plans

Objectives and outcomes

Learning objectives are drawn from the AQA KS3 Syllabus and based upon the concept of mastery. The Syllabus defines mastery as being 'Know + Apply'. However the Extend statements are also fully addressed, some through ideas in the text books and some through activities described in this guide. Each chapter in this book starts with a clear indication as to where everything is covered. These objectives use the stem of 'we are learning how to' as it is important that students develop abilities as opposed to just learning facts.

From these, outcomes were developed; there is a strong relationship between objectives and outcomes. Outcomes could be said to use the stem 'what I'm looking for' (in which 'I' is the teacher) and indicate the evidence the teacher should see that indicates that learning has occurred.

Skills

Each lesson has two or three focus skills selected. The three sets of skills are as follows:

- **Thinking scientifically**. These are the skills that scientists use in a variety of contexts, such as asking questions, using equations and analysing data. Although these are used in practical activities their role is much wider than that. All lessons have such a skill identified; this skill will also be reflected in the learning activities and often feature in the objectives and outcomes.

- **Working scientifically**. These skills are strongly based on the 'Working scientifically' aspect of the Programme of Study and are selected where practical activities form part of the lesson. Although students may well be developing and using a number of these skills there is usually one in particular that is highlighted. This is designed to make it easier for teachers and students to focus upon particular aspects. Over a sequence of lessons the focus will change so that all are covered over a period of time.

- **Learner development**. Science has the power to develop a wider range of skills than those which are subject specific; it also draws upon these wider skills. In every lesson one of these is focused upon and reflected in the learning activities, providing an opportunity for the lesson to be placed in the wider context of the development of the student as a learner.

The learning cycle

The main part of each lesson plan forms a common sequence as part of a 'learning cycle'. Many examples of learning cycles have since been developed; one current version is the 5E Learning Cycle, which is used in the new BSCS (Biological Sciences Curriculum Study) science programmes as well as in other texts and materials. The Collins KS3 Science sequence is derived from this and consists of the following stages:

- **Engage**, in which the teacher draws students into thinking about certain ideas. Here a student encounters ideas that will make them want to find out more.

- **Challenge and develop**, in which a student meets something that will challenge their existing understanding. It might be questions, ideas, demonstrations, experiments, etc., that make them realise the inadequacy of a simpler explanation.

- **Explain**, in which students are encouraged and supported to develop a good explanation. This draws upon the previous section and supports students to capture ideas in words or graphically.

- **Consolidate and apply**, where students realise how the new learning is to be consolidated and applied. Real-world applications are often drawn upon at this point.

- **Extend**, in which ideas can be extended by students making greater than expected progress.

Throughout, the emphasis is upon students' active learning. Authors have identified what students should be doing to engage with each phase, and the purpose of the component, as well as the nature. This is designed to present the teacher with an open, easily assimilated structure which shows what is intended at each point. A teacher wishing to substitute their own activity will therefore be supported in knowing what it should achieve to support progress. Similarly, a teacher using the plan as it is can see the reasoning behind what they are doing.

Appendix A: Strategies for encouraging discussion

Discussion is important for exploring ideas and evidence in science and for developing an understanding of concepts, as well as improving literacy. There is a wide variety of ways of organising small-group discussion. Eight of these are used extensively in the lesson plans:

- **Pair talk** This is easy to organise even in cramped classrooms. It is also ideal to promote high levels of participation and to ensure that the discussions are highly focused, especially if allied to tight deadlines. It can be used in the early stages of learning for students to recall work from a previous lesson, generate questions, work together to plan a piece of writing or take turns to tell a story. Pairs can also work as reading partners with an unfamiliar text. It is also ideal for quick-fire reflection and review, and for rehearsal of ideas before presenting them to the whole class.

- **Pairs to fours** Students work together in pairs – possibly friendship, possibly boy/girl, etc. Each pair then joins up with another pair to explain and compare ideas.

- **Listening triads** Students work in groups of three. Each student takes on the role of talker, questioner or recorder. The talker explains something, or comments on an issue, or expresses opinions. The questioner prompts and seeks clarification. The recorder makes notes and gives a report at the end of the conversation. Another time roles are changed.

- **Envoys** Once groups have carried out a task, one person from each group is selected as an 'envoy' and moves to a new group to explain and summarise, and to find out what the new group thought, decided or achieved. The envoy then returns to the original group and feeds back. This is an effective way of avoiding tedious and repetitive 'reporting back' sessions. It also puts a 'press' on the envoy's use of language and creates groups of active listeners.

- **Snowball** Individuals explore an issue briefly; then pairs discuss the issue or suggest ideas quickly; then double up to fours and continue the process into groups of eight. This allows for comparison of ideas, or to sort out the best, or to agree on a course of action. Finally, the whole class is drawn together and a spokesperson for each group of eight feeds back ideas.

- **Rainbow groups** This is a way of ensuring that students are regrouped and learn to work with a range of others. After small groups have discussed together, students are given a number or colour. Students with the same number or colour join up, making groups comprising representatives of each original group. In their new group, students take turns to report back on their group's work and perhaps begin to work on a new, combined task.

- **Jigsaw** A topic is divided into sections. In 'home' groups of four or five, students allocate a section each, and then regroup into 'expert' groups. In these groups, they work together on their chosen area, then return to original 'home' groups to report back on their area of expertise. The 'home' group is then set a task that requires the students to use the different areas of 'expertise' for a joint outcome. This requires advance planning, but is a very effective speaking and listening strategy as it ensures the participation of all students.

- **Spokesperson** Each group appoints a spokesperson. The risks of repetition can be avoided if:
  - one group gives a full feedback, and others offer additional points if not covered;
  - each group is asked in turn to offer one new point until every group 'passes';
  - groups are asked to summarise their findings on A3 sheets which are then displayed – the class is invited to compare and comment on them.

From: Literacy in Science, DfES © Crown copyright 2004

Appendix B: Starter and plenary toolkit

Authors have drawn on a varied selection of learning strategies, bringing ideas from lessons they have given or observed themselves, and drawing extensively from the following list:

- **Ideas hothouse** Ask students to work in pairs to list points about what they know about a particular idea. Then ask the pairs to join together into 4s and then 6–8s to discuss this further and to come up with an agreed list of points. Ask one person from each group to report back to the class.

- **Where's the answer?** As students enter the room, give them a card with a word written on it. Then ask a question, ask them if they think they are the answer and why.

- **What's in the picture?** Have a complex picture such as the water cycle or a photo of an industrial process concealed by rectangles, each of which can be removed in turn. Ask for suggestions as to which tile should be removed and what the partially revealed graphic shows. Encourage speculation and inference; ask for suggestions as to which tile should go next and continue until a full explanation has been produced.

- **Learning triangle** At the end of a lesson ask students to draw a large triangle with a smaller inverted triangle that just fits inside it (so they have four triangles). In the outer three ask them to think back over the lesson and identify (and write in the respective triangles):

  - Something they've seen
  - Something they've done
  - Something they've discussed
  - Then to add in the central triangle: something they've learned

- **Heads and tails** Ask each student to write a question about something from the topic on a coloured paper strip and the answer on another colour. In groups of 6–8, hand out the strips so that each pupil gets a question and an answer. One student reads out their question. The student with the right answer then reads it out, followed by their question.

- **What do I know?** Ask students to each write down one thing about the topic they are sure of, one thing they are unsure of and one thing they need to know more about, being specific. Ask them to work in groups of 5–6 to agree on group lists, ask each group to say what they decided and agree as a class about what they are confident about, what they are less sure of and what things they want to know more about. This is a good way towards the end of a topic of identifying topics for revision.

- **Freeze frame** Ask students to create a 'freeze frame' of an idea in the topic. This involves 3–4 students arranging themselves as static image and other students to suggest what it represents.

- **The big ideas** Ask students to write down three ideas they learnt during the topic. Then ask them to share their facts in groups and to compile a master list of facts, with the most important at the top. Ask for ideas to be shared and find out which other group(s) agreed.

- **Ask me a question** Ask students to write a question about something from the topic and then a mark scheme for the answer. Encourage them to come up with ones worth more than 1 or 2 marks and to try out their questions on one another.

- **Hot seat** Ask each student to think up a question, using material from the topic. Select someone to put in the hot seat, ask students to ask their question and say at the end whether the answer is correct or incorrect.

Tracking progress

In the Collins AQA KS3 Science materials there are two principle reasons for assessing students.

- To decide whether ideas have been mastered or whether intervention is necessary

- To report on progress and indicate whether students are on track to achieving targeted grades

This section focuses upon the latter.

Trajectories of Progress

Progress in KS3 Science can be represented by Trajectories of Progress based on what individual students need to achieve to be 'making good progress'. An average student who studies the material, tries the assessment activities and gains 40–70% of the marks is deemed to be progressing well. The materials enable the teacher to gather evidence, report and plan subsequent lessons. Students gaining close to full marks may need additional challenge; those scoring half marks or under may need intervention.

Some schools are using the new GCSE numbered grades to track progress throughout the secondary phase whereas others are using tracking systems based on NC levels and it may be that data from the materials in these resources has to be used to support this. As a rule of thumb, assessment data from the books can be used to inform a levels-based system as follows:

	KS3		KS4 (GCSE)	
	First part (Book 1)	Second part (Book 2)	First part	Second part
				9
			9	8
			8	7
		7	7	6
			6	5
Higher ToP: scores above 70%	7	7	5	4
	6	6	4	3
Average ToP: scores 40–70%	5	5	3	2
	4	4	2	1
Lower ToP: scores below 40%	3	3	1	

FIGURE 1 Trajectory of Progress (ToP) the Collins AQA Key Stage 3 Science progress tracking system, using old NC levels in KS3 and new GCSE grades in KS4

	KS3		KS4 (GCSE)	
	First part (Book 1)	Second part (Book 2)	First part	Second part
	9	9	9	9
	8	8	8	8
	7	7	7	7
	6	6	6	6
Higher ToP: scores above 70%	5	5	5	5
	4	4	4	4
Average ToP: scores 40–70%	3	3	3	3
	2	2	2	2
Lower ToP: scores below 40%	1	1	1	1

FIGURE 2 Trajectory of Progress (ToP) the Collins AQA Key Stage 3 Science progress tracking system, using new GCSE grades through KS3 & 4

The Collins AQA KS3 Science scheme has a number of assessment devices available to students and teachers. As well as questions in each spread which will give rise to written and spoken outcomes, there are also:

- **What you should already know** summarises ideas that students will have met previously at the start of each chapter. These provide an opportunity for discussions around prior learning so that the teacher can gauge what is already understood and plan teaching accordingly.

- **Questions** at the end of each chapter, with a balance of style and focus. The styles of questions include objective test questions, short written answers and longer responses. The focuses include knowledge and understanding, application, and evaluation. This means that responses can be analysed against these criteria as well as against area of content.

- **Checking progress** sections at the end of each chapter showing how the key ideas progress. This supports students in assessing their own progress and targeting areas they need to focus on. The teacher could get students to suggest why they've assessed themselves as they have.

Big idea	Sub-topic	Lesson	Sub-topic	Lesson
Forces	Speed	1.1 Understanding Speed 1.2 Describing journeys with distance-time graphs 1.3 Exploring journeys on distance-time graphs 1.4 Investigating the motion of a car on a ramp 1.5 Understanding relative motion	Gravity	1.6 Understanding forces 1.7 Understanding gravitational fields 1.8 Understanding mass and weight 1.9 Understanding gravity
Electromagnets	Voltage and resistance	2.1 Describing electric circuits 2.2 Understanding energy in circuits 2.3 Explaining resistance 2.4 Describing series and parallel circuits 2.5 Comparing series and parallel circuits	Current	2.3 Explaining resistance 2.4 Describing series and parallel circuits 2.5 Comparing series and parallel circuits 2.6 Investigating static charge 2.7 Explaining static charge 2.8 Understanding electric fields
Energy	Energy Costs	3.3 Looking at the cost of energy use in the home 3.5 Using electricity responsibly	Energy transfer	3.1 Understanding energy transfer by fuels and food 3.2 Comparing rates of energy transfers 3.4 Getting the electricity we need 3.6 Energy stores and transfers 3.7 Exploring energy transfers 3.8 Understanding potential energy and kinetic energy 3.9 Understanding elastic energy
Waves	Sound	4.1 Exploring sound 4.2 Describing sound 4.3 Hearing sounds 4.4 Understanding how sound travels through materials 4.5 Learning about the reflection and absorption of sound	Light	4.6 Exploring properties of light 4.7 Exploring reflection 4.8 Exploring refraction 4.9 Seeing clearly 4.10 Exploring coloured light

Big idea	Sub-topic	Lesson	Sub-topic	Lesson
Matter	Particle model	5.1 Using particles to explain matter 5.2 Understanding solids 5.3 Understanding liquids and gases 5.4 Exploring diffusion 5.5 Explaining changes of state	Separating mixtures	5.6 Separating mixtures 5.7 Exploring solutions 5.8 Understanding distillation 5.9 Exploring chromatography
Reactions	Metals and non-metals	6.1 Using metals and non-metals 6.2 Exploring the reactions of metals with acids 6.3 Understanding displacement reactions 6.4 Understanding oxidation reactions	Acids and alkalis	6.2 Exploring the reactions of metals with acids 6.5 Exploring acids 6.6 Exploring alkalis 6.7 Using indicators 6.8 Exploring neutralisation 6.9 Investigating neutralization
Earth	Earth structure	7.1 Understanding the structure of the Earth 7.2 Exploring igneous rocks 7.3 Exploring sedimentary rocks 7.4 Exploring metamorphic rocks 7.5 Understanding the rock cycle	Universe	7.6 Describing stars and galaxies 7.7 Explaining the effects of the Earth's motion 7.8 Exploring our neighbours in the Universe 7.9 Using models in science
Organisms	Movement	8.1 Exploring the human skeleton 8.2 Understanding the role of joints and muscles 8.3 Examining interacting muscles 8.4 Exploring problems with the skeletal system	Cells	8.5 Understanding organisation of organisms 8.6 Describing animal and plant cells 8.7 Understanding adaptations of cells 8.8 Exploring cells 8.9 Understanding unicellular organisms
Ecosystem	Interdependence	9.1 Understanding food webs 9.2 Understanding the effects of toxins in the environment 9.3 Exploring the importance of insects 9.4 Exploring ecological balance	Plant reproduction	9.5 Exploring flowering plants 9.5 Exploring fertilisation 9.7 Understanding how seeds are dispersed 9.8 Understanding how fruits disperse seeds

Big idea	Sub-topic	Lesson	Sub-topic	Lesson
Genes	Variation	10.1 Looking at variation 10.2 Exploring causes of variation 10.3 Considering the importance of variation	Human reproduction	10.4 Understanding the female reproductive system and fertility 10.5 Understanding the male reproductive system and fertilisation 10.6 Learning how a foetus develops 10.7 Understanding factors affecting a developing foetus 10.8 Communicating ideas about smoking in pregnancy

1.1.0 Forces: Introduction

When and how to use these pages

The Introduction in the Student Book indicates some of the ideas and skills in this topic area that students will already have met from KS2 or from previous KS3 work. It also provides an indication of what they will be studying in this chapter. *Ideas you have met before* is not intended to be a comprehensive summary of all the prior ideas, but rather to point out a few of the key ones and to support the view that scientific understanding is progressive. Even though we might be meeting contexts that are new to us, we can often use existing ideas to start to make sense of them.

In this chapter you will find out indicates some of the new ideas that the chapter will introduce. Again, it isn't a detailed summary of content. Its purpose is more to act as a 'trailer' and generate some interest.

The outcomes, then, will be: recognition of prior learning that can be built on; and interest in finding out more.

There are a number of ways this can be used. You might, for example:

- use *Ideas you have met before* as the basis for a revision lesson as you start the first new topic

- use *Ideas you have met before* as the centre of spider diagrams, to which students can add examples, experiments they might have done previously or what they found interesting

- make a note of any unfamiliar/difficult terms and return to these in the relevant lessons

- use ideas from *In this chapter you will find out* to ask students questions such as:

  - Why is this important?

  - How could it be used?

  - What might we be doing in this topic?

Overview of the chapter

This chapter covers three main ideas. The first of these is speed, and how it can be described through calculation and graphically. It builds on students' prior learning in both of these areas. Speed is then related to forces. This is a development of understanding from KS2 but extended to combining and balancing forces.

Finally, ideas about gravity are explored. Again, students are likely to have studied this previously but here it is related to the concept of fields, the relationship between mass and weight, and the context of space travel.

Obstacles to learning

Students may need extra guidance with the following terms and misconceptions:

- **Forces:** students may think that moving objects always have forces acting on them. Their experience makes it hard to accept the idea that an object which is moving will continue with the same speed and direction unless a force acts on it (Newton's First Law) because, on Earth, the forces of friction and gravity are always present. Following on from this, they may think that if an object is slowing down then either: the force that was moving it forward must be decreasing, or the opposing force must be increasing.

- They may also think that if two forces are acting on an object in opposing directions the greater force becomes the only force acting.

- **Weight and mass:** students need to grasp the idea that weight is a force with the unit newton, yet when people talk about 'weight' they often mean mass.

How the Programme of Study is covered by the Student Book

Big idea	Topic	Lesson	Programme of study reference
Forces	Speed	1.1.1 Understanding speed	Change depending on direction of force and its size Speed and the quantitative relationship between average speed, distance and time (speed = distance ÷ time)
		1.1.2 Describing journeys with distance–time graphs	The representation of a journey on a distance–time graph
		1.1.3 Exploring journeys on distance–time graphs	The representation of a journey on a distance–time graph Speed and the quantitative relationship between average speed, distance and time (speed = distance ÷ time)
		1.1.4 Investigating the motion of a car on a ramp	Relating ideas about changing speed and factors affecting it to the identification and management of variables to gather evidence and form conclusions
		1.1.5 Understanding relative motion	Relative motion: trains and cars passing one another
	Gravity	1.1.6 Understanding forces	Forces as pushes or pulls arising from the interaction between two objects Using force arrows in diagrams
		1.1.7 Understanding gravitational fields	Gravity force, weight = mass × gravitational field strength (g), on Earth g =10 N/kg, different on other planets and stars
		1.1.8 Understanding mass and weight	Explain the difference between mass and weight
		1.1.9 Understanding gravity	Understanding that weight is an effect caused by an object being in a gravitational field and that moving from one such field to another (such as various places in the solar system) causes a change in weight

How the AQA KS3 Syllabus is covered by the Student books and Teacher Guide

Speed

	Student Book	Teacher Guide
Know		
If the overall, resultant force on an object is non-zero, its motion changes and it slows down, speeds up or changes direction.	(1.6)	(1.6)
Skill		
Use the formula: speed = distance (m)/time (s) or distance-time graphs, to calculate speed.	1.1	1.1
Facts		
A straight line on a distance-time graph shows constant speed, a curving line shows acceleration.	1.2	1.2
The higher the speed of an object, the shorter the time taken for a journey.	1.1	1.1
Keywords		
Speed: How much distance is covered in how much time.	1.1	1.1
Average speed: The overall distance travelled divided by overall time for a journey.	1.1	1.1
Relative motion: Different observers judge speeds differently if they are in motion too, so an object's speed is relative to the observer's speed.	1.5	1.5
Acceleration: How quickly speed increases or decreases.	1.2, 1.3	1.2, 1.3
Apply		
Illustrate a journey with changing speed on a distance-time graph, and label changes in motion.	1.2	1.2
Describe how the speed of an object varies when measured by observers who are not moving, or moving relative to the object.	1.5	1.5
Extend		
Suggest how the motion of two objects moving at different speeds in the same direction would appear to the other.	1.5	1.5
Predict changes in an object's speed when the forces on it change.	1.6	1.6

Gravity

	Student Book	Teacher Guide
Know		
Mass and weight are different but related. Mass is a property of the object; weight depends upon mass but also on gravitational field strength.	1.8	1.8
Every object exerts a gravitational force on every other object. The force increases with mass and decreases with distance. Gravity holds planets and moons in orbit around larger bodies.	1.9	1.9
Skill: Use the formula: weight (N) = mass (kg) x gravitational field strength (N/kg).	1.7	1.7
Fact: g on Earth = 10 N/kg. On the moon it is 1.6 N/kg.	1.7	1.7
Weight: The force of gravity on an object (N).	1.7	1.7
Non-contact force: One that acts without direct contact.	1.7	1.7
Mass: The amount of stuff in an object (kg).	1.8	1.8
Gravitational field strength, g: The force from gravity on 1 kg (N/kg).	1.7	1.7
Field: The area where other objects feel a gravitational force.	1.7	1.7
Apply		
Explain unfamiliar observations where weight changes.	1.8	1.8
Draw a force diagram for a problem involving gravity.	1.7	1.7
Deduce how gravity varies for different masses and distances.	1.9	1.9
Compare your weight on Earth with your weight on different planets using the formula.	1.9	1.9
Extend		
Compare and contrast gravity with other forces.	1.9	1.9
Draw conclusions from data about orbits, based on how gravity varies with mass and distance.		1.9
Suggest implications of how gravity varies for a space mission.	1.8, 1.9	1.8, 1.9

1.1.1 Understanding speed

Lesson overview

Learning objectives

- List the factors involved in defining speed.
- Explain a simple method to measure speed.
- Use the speed formula.

Learning outcomes

- Describe a method in simple terms to find the speed of an object. [O1]
- Explain the concept of speed and demonstrate how the speed equation is derived using students' understanding of speed. [O2]
- Provide an effective explanation of the concept of speed and independently derive the equation for speed; link students' understanding of the speed equation to explain the operation of speed cameras. [O3]

Skills development

- Working scientifically: 2.1 Analyse patterns
- Developing numeracy: using formulae to perform calculations
- Developing literacy: explain differences and justify developments (Q7 & 8)

Resources needed 10 m measuring tape; stopwatches (or digital timers); mini-whiteboards; marker pens; calculators; video camera; Worksheet 1.1.1; Practical sheet 1.1.1

Key vocabulary distance, speed, average speed, unit, formula, average

Teaching and learning

Engage

- Ask the students to **recall** a car journey they have made and ask them what the speed limit was on the roads they were travelling on. Ask them to state the units. They should write a few examples of the speeds with units (miles per hour, mph). Ask them to **suggest** other units that speed may be measured in. [O1, O2, O3]

- Guide the students in deconstructing the units and stating what quantity each of them measures (distance and time). This leads them to see that speed is how far a thing has travelled in a certain time. [O1, O2, O3]

Challenge and develop

- Use a few very simple examples to illustrate the principle of speed measurement and calculation:

  - a person travels 10 km in 1 hour, so their speed is 10 km per hour (10 km/h)

  - someone else travels the same distance but it takes 2 hours, so they only travel 5 km in an hour and their speed is 5 km/h.

  After a few more simple examples, help students to identify the process. (They are dividing the distance travelled by the time it takes.) Establish that speed = distance travelled divided by time taken. [O2]

- Working outside or in a sports hall and using Practical sheet 1.1.1, the students mark out a distance of 10 m and then **collect data** by timing how long it takes to walk, jog, run and hop the 10 m distance. They can **record data** on mini-whiteboards. Prior to the activity ask them to compose a short list of suggestions that would constitute acting responsibly during the activity. [O1]

- For ease of calculation during this part of the learning, ask the students to round each measured time to the nearest second. Students then **calculate the speed** in metres per second. [O1, O2, O3]

  High demand students may be able to **suggest** how a car's speed is measured (circumference of tyres and number of turns of the wheel measures distance, or satnav tracks distance covered as the car moves).

Explain

- **Group task** Organise students into groups to **plan a presentation** of how to calculate speed, showing the reasoning behind the method. They could film themselves giving their presentations. [O1, O2, O3]

Consolidate and apply

- Students use Worksheet 1.1.1 to do further speed calculations with less convenient numbers. They should **estimate** their answers as a method of checking the calculation. [O1, O2]

    High demand students may be able to **predict** the effect that changing the diameter of a car's wheels would have on the speedometer reading (bigger diameter wheels make the speedometer under-read).

Extend

- Using the example of averaging speed cameras, ask students able to progress further to **calculate speed** when told the distance between the cameras and the time at which a car passes each of the two cameras. [O3]

Plenary suggestions

Quick quiz Set some quiz questions, such as:

- Speed is measured in …
- What equipment do you need for taking measurements to calculate speed?
- The method for calculating speed is … [O1, O2, O3]

Answers to Student Book questions

1. The distance covered in a certain time.
2. The distance covered and the time taken.
3. A
4. C, 25 m/s; D, 20 m/s
5. Speed = distance ÷ time; speed = 15 ÷ 1.5 = 10 km/h
6. 0.5 m/s
7. Calculation of average speed uses the whole distance and the total time for the journey. During a journey you need to slow down and speed up at appropriate times.
8. Drivers could slow down briefly for a camera measuring at one spot but exceed the speed limit the rest of the time. Cameras that work out the average speed over a long stretch of road will be able to tell if drivers do this.

Answers to Worksheet 1.1.1

1. a) Speed = distance travelled ÷ time taken

    b) Kilometres per hour (km/h); metres per second (m/s); miles per hour (mph)
2. a) 50 m/s b) 12 m/s c) 19 m/s d) 108 km/h, 0.3 km/s or 30 m/s e) 60 km/h, or 1 km/min f) 70 km/h
3. a) 7.5 km/h

    b) The car's speed is a lot slower than the top speed for much of the journey; this decreases the average.

    c) Victoria: 10 km/h; Laura: 17.6 km/h

    d) Laura may have been able to continue without stopping at junctions; or she may be fitter than Victoria.

1.1.2 Describing journeys with distance–time graphs

Lesson overview

Learning objectives

- Gather relevant data to describe a journey.
- Use the conventions of a distance–time graph.
- Display the data on a distance–time graph.

Learning outcomes

- Gather evidence to construct a distance–time graph. [O1]
- Construct a graph to represent a journey. [O2]
- Construct a graph to represent a more complex journey. [O3]

Skills development

- Working scientifically: 2.1 Analyse patterns
- Developing numeracy: interpret graphs
- Developing literacy: describe relationship shown on graph and convert ideas into graphical form (Q7, 8 & 9)

Resources needed dynamics trolley; ramp; wind-up toy cars; digital timers; metre rulers; graph paper; calculators; Worksheet 1.1.2; Practical sheet 1.1.2; Technician's notes 1.1.2

Common misconceptions A straight line sloping upwards on a distance–time graph indicates that speed is increasing.

Key vocabulary distance–time graph, accelerate, stationary

Teaching and learning

Engage

- Demonstrate a simple journey by rolling a dynamics trolley down a ramp, across the floor and allowing it to come to rest due to friction or when it reaches a wall. The students **describe** the journey in words. [O1]

- Ask some students to **share** their descriptions with the class. Highlight the good points, such as students recognising how speed and distance from the start position changed during the journey. [O1]

  High demand students can be encouraged to **use scientific terms** such as 'accelerate' and 'constant speed' in their descriptions, where appropriate.

Challenge and develop

- Explain to the students that they will learn to **translate** their journey descriptions into distance–time graphs. As an introduction to this, they **plot** a distance–time graph using the data in task 1 of Worksheet 1.1.2, which represents travel at a constant speed. [O2]

- Using Figures 1.1.2b and 1.1.2c in the Student Book, show the students some graphs for different simple movements. [O1, O2]

- Students **match** graphs to descriptions of different journeys in task 2 of Worksheet 1.1.2. [O1, O2]

Explain

- **Pair work** Using Practical sheet 1.1.2, the students work in pairs to **observe** the motion of a mechanical toy and **write a description** of its journey. They should **present** their evidence by **sketching** a distance–time graph. They should then annotate the graph to **explain** what the toy is doing at significant parts of the graph – for example 'The toy is released here and moves away', 'The line is straight and this shows that the toy is moving at constant speed'. Ask the students to think about the accuracy of the data they have presented, and how this might be improved. [O1, O2, O3]

High demand students may be able to **measure** the distance travelled and the time so that they can add a scale to their graph.

Consolidate and apply

- The students **analyse data** by answering questions 5–9 in the Student Book. [O2, O3]

- They use quantitative data to **plot** a distance–time graph accurately in task 3 of Worksheet 1.1.2. [O2, O3]

Extend

- Ask students able to progress further to **suggest** what a distance–time graph would look like if, after travelling some distance, someone turned around and went back to where they started. (As time passes, the distance from the start position *decreases*, so the line slopes down from left to right until it meets the *x*-axis. Note: at this stage they are not asked to consider displacement, so the line does not return to the origin.) [O3]

Plenary suggestions

Whole class discussion Select a group to **sketch** a distance–time graph on the board so that the whole class can **share** it. Members of the group ask questions to other students to test their **interpretation** and **understanding** of distance–time graphs. [O1, O2, O3]

Answers to Student Book questions

1. M/s; metres per second
2. 30 m
3. 5 m/s
4. The second line should be half as steep, indicating that half the distance is covered in the same time; 25 m in 10 s.
5. a) The object is not moving.
   b) The object is moving at a steady speed.
   c) The object is accelerating.
6. From 45 s onward (15 s).
7. The line is steeper; more distance is covered during each minute, so the bus must be moving faster.
8. Section 1 is slightly steeper than section 3; in section 3 the student was walking with a friend, so they may have been talking and therefore walking more slowly.
9. Numerical scales are not needed but students who have progressed well may be able to include them. The labels should show clearly that the student appreciates the main features of a distance–time graph: upward slope indicates movement; horizontal line indicates no movement; steep slope indicates faster speed than a less steep slope; upward curve indicates acceleration.

Answers to Worksheet 1.1.2

1. a) Straight line through the origin; *x*-axis = time; *y*-axis = distance; axes labelled; scales and units included. b) iii
2. a) vi b) iii c) ii d) v
3. a) Points plotted accurately; axes and the two curves labelled; scales and units included. Some students may consider that the changes in speed are not abrupt and will smooth out the transitions.
   b) i) Between 10 minutes and 15 minutes. ii) Between 20 minutes and 30 minutes, and after 50 minutes when the journey has ended.
   c) i) 90 minutes ii) 50 minutes
   d) Both achieved 20 km in 10 minutes; speed = distance travelled ÷ time taken = 20 ÷ 10 = 2 km/minute = 120 km/h.
   e) Car travels 80 km in 90 minutes; speed = 80 ÷ 90 = 0.89 km/minute = 53.3 km/h.
   Train travels 80 km in 50 minutes; speed = 80 ÷ 50 = 1.6 km/minute = 96 km/h.
   f) The car has to travel more slowly in town, stopping for traffic lights and in congestion. The train encounters fewer delays and only has to stop occasionally at stations.

Answers to Practical sheet 1.1.2

4, 5. Not accurate; it is difficult to judge the changes in speed; the graph shows information for motion in a straight line – the path of the car may curve.

6. Ensure the motion is along a straight track; fix a card to the car and use light gates and a datalogger/use time-lapse photography.

1.1.3 Exploring journeys on distance–time graphs

Lesson overview

Learning objectives

- Interpret distance–time graphs to learn about the journeys represented.

- Relate distance–time graphs to different situations and describe what they show.

Learning outcomes

- Explain some of the features of a distance–time graph. [O1]

- Explain what is represented on a distance–time graph. [O2]

- Explain what is represented on a more complex distance–time graph. [O3]

Skills development

- Working scientifically: 2.4 Present data

- Developing numeracy: construct graphs

- Developing literacy: interpret graphs and describe relationships (Q4 & 7)

Resources needed large sheets of paper (e.g. flip chart paper); marker pens; mini-whiteboards; video or still camera capable of time-lapse photography; objects that travel in a straight line (e.g. balls, trolleys, gliders on an air track); roll of paper to mark out regular distances; thick pen; digital timer; metre ruler; Worksheet 1.1.3; Practical sheet 1.1.3; Technician's notes 1.1.3

Common misconceptions A straight line sloping upwards on a distance–time graph indicates that speed is increasing.

Key vocabulary accelerate, stationary

Teaching and learning

Engage

- Show a video clip of a sporting activity that involves running at different speeds and stopping, such as tennis or football. Ask students to work in small groups and use a large sheet of paper to **sketch** a distance–time graph for the sporting activity. They should add captions to **describe** what the sportsperson is doing in each part of the graph. [O1, O2, O3]

- The students **compare** their graphs with those of other groups, **ask questions** and make any modifications required. [O1, O2, O3]

  High demand students should be encouraged to draw their graphs showing the sportsperson returning to their starting position.

Challenge and develop

- **Group work** If the technology is available, the students should work in groups to **collaborate effectively** to make time-lapse video/image sequences to help them to **record evidence** and **analyse** the movement of different objects, such as a ball or a trolley on a ramp. Practical sheet 1.1.3 gives instructions for this practical work and the analysis of the results. (Hint: a clearly visible scale should be placed alongside each moving object so that its position can be observed at regular time intervals.) The students use data from the time-lapse images to **plot** and **analyse** distance–time graphs. Before starting the practical activity, the students should **assess the risks**. (Hint: the main risks are from obstruction and tripping in the work area.) [O1, O2, O3]

  If you do not have access to enough suitable cameras, this activity could be carried out as a teacher demonstration in which the students are involved in making important decisions and help to record the images.

- Show a video clip of an 800 m athletics race. Ask the students to **imagine** three athletes in the race: one who sets off running fast, gets tired and finishes in 2 minutes 15 seconds; one who runs at a slightly slower pace but is able to sprint the last 50 m and finishes in 1 minute 58 seconds; and one who runs slower than the others for most of the race but then speeds up for the last 200 m and overtakes them to finish in 1 minute 48 seconds. [O2, O3]

- **Pair talk** Ask students to **discuss** the three athletes and **sketch** distance–time graphs to show the races. [O2, O3]

Explain

- The students then **explain** what the graphs show about the motion of the three athletes. [O2, O3]

High demand students could be asked to superimpose additional lines on the graph to show a 100 m sprinter in action and a marathon runner.

Consolidate and apply

- **Pair talk** Ask students to **discuss** and **interpret** the distance–time graphs and answer the questions in the Student Book. [O1, O2, O3]

- The students complete the tasks of Worksheet 1.1.3. [O1, O2, O3]

Extend

- Ask students able to progress further to **calculate** acceleration from some of the distance–time graphs in the Student Book. For example, for Figure 1.1.3b they could calculate the speed for the first and second straight-line sections. They could then estimate the time span over which the change in speed took place. Acceleration = (initial speed – final speed) ÷ time taken to change speed. In this case, the answer will be negative because the car is slowing down. [O3]

Plenary suggestions

Mini-whiteboard quiz Select students to **ask questions** of the rest of the class about the lesson, which they answer on mini-whiteboards. Students will need to be primed to ask questions that require a short answer, such as a calculation or sketching a graph. [O1, O2, O3]

Answers to Student Book questions

1. Speed = distance travelled ÷ time taken   2. The line is not straight; the slope has changed.
2. Student reads the graph and uses the speed formula correctly; speed = 3 m/s in first section; 2 m/s in second section.
3. 25 minutes 5. 43.2 km/h 6. Graph should have linear scales: x-axis = time; y-axis = distance; straight, accurate line through (0, 0) and chosen point. 7. a) B b) C   8. m/s^2
4. a) The line is extended along the same slope, and then suddenly becomes horizontal. b) The straight line curves smoothly to become horizontal underneath the horizontal section of line A. c) The line becomes shallower and then straight at an angle.

Answers to Worksheet 1.1.3

1. a) i) Where the graph is steepest ii) Where the graph curves upwards iii) Where the upward curve of the graph gets shallower iv) Where the graph is horizontal. b) The force due to gravity/weight pulls it downwards so it gets faster; once it is level on the floor, friction slows it down. c) The spaces between the images increase until the ball leaves the ramp, and then reduce again. The last two images should be very close together, or even overlapping, because the ball is hardly moving as it comes to a stop.

2. a) 4 b) 460 m c) 210 m d) The ball travels fastest as it leaves the club. After that, the forces acting are air resistance and then friction with the ground, which slow the ball down until it stops. The curves show that the speed is changing; straight lines are where speed is not changing (e.g. the horizontal sections show the ball is stationary).

3. a) For a car travelling 1 km in 1 minute, speed = distance travelled ÷ time taken = 1 km/min = 60 km/h.

   b) Car A travels at a steady speed (60 mph) for the whole journey. Car B travels at a higher speed at first (approx. 1.5 miles in 1 minute = 90 mph) and then slows for the first camera (approx. 0.1 miles in 0.2 minutes = 30 mph). It then travels at its original speed again, before slowing for the second camera. Finally, car B speeds up to its original speed. (Note: allow reasonable tolerance on reading data from the graph, but encourage precision. Also encourage students to convert speeds into 'per hour' rather than 'per minute'.) c) Driver of car A would not be convicted. Driver of car B could be convicted even though the car passes both cameras at 30 mph, because it takes approximately 0.8 minutes to travel 1 mile = 75 mph average speed between the two cameras.

Answers to Practical sheet 1.1.3

1. to 3. (students' own graphs). 4. A shorter time interval samples the data a higher number of times, so gives more information and makes the graph and analysis more accurate.

5. It allows frequent observations that could not be done by eye; the information is automatically recorded; an alternative would be light gates and a datalogger.

1.1.4 Investigating the motion of a car on a ramp

Lesson overview

Learning objectives

- To describe the motion of an object whose speed is changing.
- To devise questions that can be explored scientifically.
- To present data so that it can be analysed to answer questions.

Learning outcomes

- Plan an investigation. [O1]
- Gather evidence to answer a question. [O2]
- Use evidence to support a conclusion about how the speed of an object has changed. [O3]

Skills development

- Working scientifically: 2.11 Plan variables
- Developing numeracy: gather and present data
- Developing literacy: draw conclusions (Q8)

Resources needed For each group: ramp; marbles; toy car or trolley; support to raise height of ramp by various amounts; metre ruler; timer; Worksheet 1.1.4

Common misconceptions A constant force is needed to produce a constant speed, and therefore if the speed of an object is increasing then the force on it must be increasing too.

Key vocabulary dependent, independent, control, variable, correlation

Teaching and learning

Engage

- Show students a marble and a ramp, and say that you are going to roll the marble down the ramp. Ask them to **estimate** how far it will go from the end of the ramp. Then ask for suggestions about the variables that will influence how far it will roll. Ask students to work in small groups to **develop** a definitive list of variables. [O1]
- Draw out that the variables might include gradient of the ramp, mass of the vehicle, starting point on the ramp, surface of the ramp, and so on. [O1, O2]
- Show students a video of a roller coaster (or a log flume ride is a good example to use) and **challenge** students to come up with ideas about what determines how far and how fast it will travel. [O1, O2]

Challenge and develop

- Introduce the equipment listed above and ask students to use it to explore a question about the motion of the vehicle. Ask students to **devise** a question based on the relationship between variables. [O2]
- Ask students to **use** the sentence template: 'We are investigating to see if changing the ...... will alter the ....' to plan their enquiry. [O2]
- Ask students to **conduct the investigation**, changing one of the variables, keeping others constant and measuring an output. Students could use Worksheet 1.1.4 to help plan their investigation. [O1, O2, O3]
- Data should be **gathered, tabulated and graphed**. [O3]

Explain

- Ask students to **discuss, develop, record and share a conclusion**. This should use evidence, explain a relationship and relate what they have found to their ideas about motion. [O1, O3]

Consolidate and apply

- Students should **relate** the motion to the ideas of forces acting on the car, identifying the various forces and their contribution to the overall motion. [O1, O3]

- Students could **explain** how this is related to contexts such as roller coasters, skateboards on ramps, and so on. [O1, O3]

Extend

- Ask students to **consider** whether the relationship between variables is a pattern that has limits. In other words, if they continued to increase the independent variable, would the dependent variable continue to alter in the same way. [O2, O3]

- Ask students to **suggest** the implications of what they have found for designers of roller coasters, multi-storey car park ramps, and so on. [O3]

Plenary suggestions

- From each group conducting an experiment, ask one student to **tell** the class the question they explored and another to **state** the answer they came up with. [O1, O2, O3]

- Ask students to **compose** and be prepared to **share** sentences stating one thing they've learned about the motion of the car on the ramp. [O3]

Answers to Student Book questions

1. Gravity is causing it to accelerate.
2. Friction is causing it to decelerate.
3. In the first part of the journey gravity contributes to the motion of the car. In the second part this motion is only affected by the retarding forces of friction and air resistance.
4. a) Mass of car, friction in car wheels, air resistance of car, height of ramp, surface of ramp, starting point on ramp. b) How fast the car is travelling when it reaches the end of the ramp, how far the car goes across the level ground.
5. a) For example, 'How does the height of the ramp affect the distance the car will travel across the level ground?' b) Use the same car (to control mass, friction and air resistance), start the car from the same point on the ramp each time and don't alter the surface of the ramp.
6. Headings will be determined by whatever the independent and dependent variables are, but allow for repeat readings and the processing of those (i.e. identifying outliers and taking the mean of the remaining data).
7. For an experiment such as this, repeat readings are likely to be appropriate. The number of repeats, however, is likely to be influenced by the range of the readings.
8. Depends on graph.
9. Sketch showing positive correlation between the variables. A better graph might indicate that there's a limit to the relationship – too steep a ramp doesn't result in a long journey afterwards. At this stage we wouldn't expect a theoretical understanding of the quantitative relationship between height of ramp and speed at the end.

Answers to Worksheet 1.1.4

1. It speeds up because gravity is causing it to accelerate downhill and slows down because friction and air resistance oppose its motion on the level.
2. Mass of car, friction in the axles of the car, surface of the ramp, gradient of the ramp, starting point on the ramp, etc.
3. Car, ramp, metre ruler, timer. In addition, depending on what is being investigated: balance, different surfaces, weights, and so on.
4. Student's choice.
5. As for question 4, but the student should choose values that will make a difference and are at regular intervals.
6. Values other than those listed in the answer to 4.
7. Distance travelled from bottom of ramp.
8. Table with column headings corresponding to independent and dependent variables. Table should accommodate different values of the independent variable and allow for repeat readings of the dependent variable for each value.
9. The independent variable should go on the horizontal axis and the dependent variable on the vertical axis.
10. Answer will depend on the student's choice: if the independent variable has discrete values (e.g. ramp surface) the graph should be a bar chart, but if the value is continuous (e.g. height of starting point) it should be a line graph.

1.1.5 Understanding relative motion

Lesson overview

Learning objectives

- Describe the motion of objects in relation to each other.
- Explain the concept of relative motion.
- Apply the concept of relative motion to various situations.

Learning outcomes

- Describe a situation in which different objects are travelling at different speeds. [O1]
- Apply the concept of relative motion to a situation with two objects moving at different speeds. [O2]
- Apply the concept of relative motion to a situation with more than two objects moving at different speeds. [O3]

Skills development

- Working scientifically: 2.1 Analyse patterns
- Developing numeracy: extract and use data from graphs
- Developing literacy: explain differences and compare and contrast situations (Q5 & 6)

Resources needed A4 sheets of paper; scissors; paper clips; digital timers; metre rulers or tape measures; graph paper; mini-whiteboards; marker pens; Worksheet 1.1.5; Practical sheet 1.1.5; Technician's notes 1.1.5

Common misconceptions When a free-falling parachutist opens their parachute, they fly upwards.

Key vocabulary relative motion, relative speed

Teaching and learning

Engage

- Explore the students' ideas by showing a video clip of a parachutist when viewed from the ground and when viewed by another descending parachutist. The students **describe** the motion of the first parachutist relative to the ground (accelerating downwards until terminal velocity is reached) and the motion relative to the other parachutist (none). [O1, O2]

  High demand students may be able to **suggest** other situations in which relative motion is important – such as when police are trying to judge the speed of a car they are chasing, or when a driver is overtaking on a single carriageway road.

Challenge and develop

- Ask the students to **consider** the difference between the *absolute* speed of two objects and their *relative* speed. Use the 'Relative motion' section in the Student Book. [O2]

- The students then **make** paper models of sycamore seeds, **test** them and **collect data** of their relative motion, following the instructions on Practical sheet 1.1.5. They will need to drop the 'seeds' from a height of at least 2 m. Tell students to act responsibly and take care to avoid the risk of falling from a height. [O1, O2]

  High demand students may be able to collect additional data to compare the motion of three differently weighted model sycamore seeds. [O3]

- The students design a table to **record** their observations and **plot** a distance–time graph for their model sycamore seeds. They then **interpret** and **consider** the quality of the evidence they have collected and **suggest** what improvements could be made. Practical sheet 1.1.5 can be used to guide the analysis and evaluation of the method and the results. [O2, O3]

- Ask students to complete the tasks of Worksheet 1.1.5. They **analyse** the relative motion of vehicles travelling along a single carriageway road. [O2, O3]

Explain

- Ask the students to read the 'Journeys and collisions' section in the Student Book. Ask them to **explain** how relative speed is crucially important when considering road traffic collisions. [O1, O2, O3]

  High demand students can be asked to **suggest** steps that could be taken to reduce the risk of damage and reduce the damage caused by head-on collisions. [O2, O3]

Consolidate and apply

- Show the students a large traditional analogue clock. Ask them to **compare** the absolute and relative motion of the hands on the clock. Use the linear distance between each of the numbers on the clock face. This requires careful measurement on the clock that is used. [O1, O2]

- They **calculate** how long after 12 o'clock it takes for the minute and hour hands to reach the same position again. (Just over 65 minutes because the hour hand moves incrementally just past the '1' as the minute hand reaches the '1' having done one-and-a-bit revolutions.) [O2]

  If there is a seconds hand on the clock, high demand students can consider this in addition to the hour and minute hands. [O3]

Extend

- Ask students able to progress further to **consider** the relative speeds of light (speed ≈ 300 million m/s), sound (speed ≈ 340 m/s), a bullet from a hand gun (speed varies but take as 320 m/s) and a bullet from a high-velocity rifle (speed varies but take as 900 m/s). If they were standing watching the two guns being fired simultaneously, what would they see, hear and feel, and in what order? [O3]

Plenary suggestions

Mini-whiteboard activity The students draw axes for a distance–time graph on mini-whiteboards and then add lines to show journeys that you describe. Check their responses after each line has been added. [O2, O3]

Answers to Student Book questions

1. a) Person will travel 6 km; boat will travel 5 km. b) The jogger is 2 km/h faster than the boat. c) Backwards.
2. Speed of A = 60 km/h; speed of B = 120 km/h; relative speed of car B to car A is 60 km/h.
3. a) Car A is 2 km ahead of car B, which has not moved from the start point.

   b) Car B has been travelling for 1 min, and has covered 2 km; it is 1 km behind car A.
4. The collision speed is the combined speed of the two vehicles.
5. If you do not have a fixed reference point you do not know if you are moving, or if the object you are looking at is moving, e.g. parallel trains. Sense of balance may be able to help detect movement.
6. Situations a) and b) have the same impact speed, 10 km/h; so the damage from the collisions will be similar.

   b) Could be much worse if the driver lost control and hit a stationary object.

   c) The impact speed is much higher; 130 km/h; so the consequences would be very serious.

Answers to Worksheet 1.1.5

1. a) Car A: 70 m; car B: 80 m b) Car A: 7 m/s; car B: 8 m/s

   c) Car B is 1 m/s faster. d) 55 m

   e) The additional car is 1 block ahead of car A in picture 1, and 2.5 blocks behind in picture 2.
2. a) Check for correct scales, positions and arrows. If shown travelling left to right, Alex is 200 m from the left-hand end and Georgie is 100 m from the left-hand end.

   b) 500 m from the left-hand end.

   c) The cars should be alongside each other 500 m from the left-hand end.
3. a) Asma is at the far right-hand end in the first diagram, and 200 m from the right-hand end in the second diagram.

   b) Not very likely; there is a risk of a head-on collision in just over 3 s.

   c) Overtake as fast as possible; wait for a dual carriageway; be patient; choose not to overtake, because it is unsafe.

   d) Police car is at the far left-hand end in first diagram, and at the far right-hand end in the second.

   e) They need to be able to judge speed of a car and judge risks well. They must not put the public in danger.

1.1.6 Understanding forces

Lesson overview

Learning objectives

- Recognise different examples of forces.
- List the main types of force.
- Represent forces using arrows.

Learning outcomes

- List some types of force and label diagrams to show the direction of forces. [O1]
- State the main types of force and draw force diagrams to show the size and direction of forces. [O2]
- Describe the main types of force and accurately draw force diagrams to explain the relative size and direction of applied forces and their effects. [O3]

Skills development

- Working scientifically: 2.6 Construct explanations
- Developing numeracy: resolve forces acting in different directions
- Developing literacy: extract information from diagrams (Q 3 - 6)

Resources needed pictures (e.g. of tennis player, plane or bird taking off, roller coaster, vehicle on tow); suction jumper toy; wind-up mechanical toy; ball floating in a bowl of water; pendulum of large mass; air track and glider; toy car on a ramp; Worksheet 1.1.6

Common misconceptions When an object is stationary, no forces are acting on it. When an object is moving there must be a force acting on it.

Key vocabulary force, balance, gravity, air resistance

Teaching and learning

Engage

- Identify the students' experience of forces from KS2 by displaying a range of images that show different situations in which forces are in action. Give the students two minutes to **identify** some of the forces. Collect feedback, drawing out a range of descriptions and key words. Make a note of some ideas (incorrect and incomplete as well as correct), so that they can be displayed and revisited later. [O1]

Challenge and develop

- Explain how to represent forces using arrows (see the Student Book for examples). The direction of an arrow shows the direction that the force is acting. Force arrows should be labelled so they are not confused with any arrows showing direction of movement. The length of the arrow can represent how big the force is. [O1, O2]

  High demand students may be able to draw force arrows to scale.

- Challenge the students, by examining a range of objects and equipment (see *Resources needed*), to **draw force diagrams** with arrows showing the direction, location and size of forces. [O1, O2]

- Ask the students to **consider** these three questions:
  - Are forces always present?
  - Can you have movement without forces?
  - Can forces be present even when there is no movement?

  Encourage students to present tentative ideas as well as those they are sure about. [O3]

- Students **discuss** the forces that they have identified. Encourage them to **identify** evidence and observations that support or contradict their answers to the questions. Feedback should give the opportunity to highlight where new ideas or evidence can lead to scientists modifying their views, and should ensure that all students have drawn the force arrows correctly. [O1, O2, O3]

Explain

- **Pair talk** The students produce verbal or written **explanations** in relation to the three questions in *Challenge and develop*, above. Appropriate answers include:
    - Forces are present in most/all examples; gravity is exerting a pulling force in most cases.
    - Once an object is moving it will keep going even if no forces are acting (e.g. a spacecraft in outer space).
    - When forces are in balance there is no change in movement.
- The students can then complete the first two tasks of Worksheet 1.1.6. [O1, O2, O3]

Consolidate and apply

- **Listening triads** Working in groups of three, the students revisit the images and ideas in the starter activity. Each student takes on a role – talker, questioner or recorder. The talker **explains** something; the questioner **asks for clarification**; the recorder **makes notes and gives a report** at the end of the conversation. Then the roles can be changed. [O1, O2, O3]

Extend

- Students who are able to progress further can complete the third task on Worksheet 1.1.6. [O3]

Plenary suggestions

Learning triangle Students draw a large triangle with a smaller inverted triangle inside it. In the three outer triangles they write something they have seen, something they've done and something they've discussed. Then they add to the central triangle something they have learned.

Answers to Student Book questions

1. Pulling force. 2. Gravity. 3. Pushing force from the engines; lift force from the wings.
4. The downward pulling force of gravity; air resistance causing drag against forward motion.
5. Gravity is balanced by the lift from the wings; the force from the engines is balanced by drag.
6. The increased team would produce a bigger force. The forces from each team would no longer be balanced, and there would be movement in the direction of the larger force – the stronger team would pull the weaker team forwards.
7. The forward-pushing force should be bigger than any other forces (road friction/air resistance); and should be in the direction that the car will move.
8. In each situation the students should show at least two forces – e.g. for the sailing boat they could show the pushing force of the wind and the resistance of the water.

Answers to Worksheet 1.1.6

1. a) i) Two arrows acting along the rope, pointing outwards, equal in size and opposite in direction; no movement.
    ii) Right-hand force arrow larger than left-hand force arrow; movement to the right.
    iii) Left-hand force arrow larger than right-hand force arrow; movement to the left.
    b) The first diagram is drawn as for (a) (iii). The second diagram has the left-hand force arrow unchanged, the right-hand force arrow larger, and the movement is to the right.
    c) i) There is no movement (or, if already moving, movement continues at the same speed and in the same direction).
    ii) The teams move in the direction of the larger force (or resultant force).
2. a) It will continue at the same speed and in the same direction unless another (unbalanced) force acts.
    b) Air resistance; weight/gravity c) Weight of the ball (gravity); upwards-supporting force from ground
3. The burning produces a pushing force (due to the expansion of gases) that propels the firework upwards into the air. The pushing force is larger than the weight/gravity force. Air resistance acts to slow the rocket down. When the burning stops, the force of weight/gravity pulls the rocket back to Earth.

1.1.7 Understanding gravitational fields

Lesson overview

Learning objectives

- Describe gravity as a non-contact force.
- Explore the concept of gravitational field and weight.
- Relate this concept to life on Earth.

Learning outcomes

- Describe the effect of an object being in a gravitational field. [O1]
- Explain the relationship between gravity and weight. [O2]
- Explain weight in relation to the idea of a gravitational field. [O3]

Skills development

- Working scientifically: 2.1 Analyse patterns
- Developing numeracy: use formulae to calculate answers
- Developing literacy: describe supporting evidence, compare and contrast situations and design activity (Q 3, 4, 9 & 10)

Resources needed flip chart paper; marker pens; calculators; top-pan balance; beaker of water; forcemeter; rubber bung; Worksheet 1.1.7

Common misconceptions Heavy objects fall faster than lighter objects. Gravity is linked to the Earth's rotation.

Key vocabulary non-contact force, gravitational field, gravitational field strength, field

Teaching and learning

Engage

- Identify the students' prior knowledge of different types of fields by asking them to work in groups of four to **record their ideas** on flip chart paper, which they **share** with others. Some may need prompts: different types of fields, characteristics, similarities and differences, how they can be detected or measured. [O1, O2]

- Display the students' main ideas about gravitational fields, including any vague or incorrect ones, with a view to respecting all suggestions and to accepting, modifying or rejecting them later in the lesson. [O1, O2]

  High demand students may comment on the relationship between gravity and weight.

Challenge and develop

- **Pairs to fours** The students **describe** whether or not the strength of the gravitational field of a planet is uniform, and if not how it varies. (It depends on the mass of the planet and distance from the planet.) Emphasise that the strength of a gravitational field of a planet does not depend on the presence or absence of other objects within the field. Task 1 of Worksheet 1.1.6 can support this activity. [O1, O2]

- Discuss why different objects have different weights, even though the gravitational field they experience is the same. (Weight depends on mass.) Check that the students understand what 'mass' is (a quantity of matter: number and type of particles) and that gravitational fields are a pulling force. [O1, O2, O3]

- Introduce the formula that links weight and mass (see the Student Book): weight = mass × gravitational field strength ($W = mg$). ('Weight' and 'gravitational force' are the same, which is why weight is measured in newtons (N).) [O3]

- Ask students to **calculate** gravitational field strength using an example object with a mass of 10 kg that weighs 100 N, and by substituting the values and solving the equation. (100 N = 10 × g, so g = 10). From a rearranged equation, students can **identify** the correct unit for gravitational field strength (g = weight ÷ mass, so g is measured in N/kg). [O2, O3]

Explain

- Using the formula for weight ($W = mg$) and the value for gravitational field strength (g) of 10 N/kg, the students **explain** why objects of different masses have different weights on Earth (task 2 of Worksheet 1.1.7). [O1, O2, O3]

  High demand students may be able to **explain** how differences in the weight of an object on different planets can be linked to the gravitational field strength of each planet.

Consolidate and apply

- Ask the students to use the idea of gravitational field to **explain** why, when measuring weight, it is necessary to specify where the measurement is taken (for example on the *surface* of *the Earth*). [O2, O3]

- **Pairs to fours** Ask the students to **compare** the weights of a rubber bung in air and in water (demonstration will suffice) and **suggest** how this might relate to the ideas of weight and mass. (Weight is a force that can vary; mass is fixed.) [O2, O3]

Extend

For students able to progress further:

- Explain to students that 'acceleration due to gravity' is due to the gravitational field strength and they have the same value. So at a location where the acceleration due to gravity is 10 m/s^2, the field strength is 10 N/kg. Students can now complete task 3 of Worksheet 1.1.7. [O3]

- Ask students to **suggest** what equipment and method would be needed to measure the gravitational field strength at a particular location. (They may suggest time-lapse photography or light gates to measure speeds and calculate acceleration.) [O3]

Plenary suggestions

Learning triangle Ask the students to draw a large triangle with a smaller inverted triangle that just fits inside it (so they have four triangles). In the outer three, ask them to think back over the lesson and write in the respective triangles something they've seen, something they've done and something they've discussed. Then they add something they've learned in the central triangle. [O1, O2, O3]

Review Go back to the students' statements from the *Engage* activity above and discuss how the statements might be amended in the light of new learning. [O1, O2, O3]

Answers to Student Book questions

1. Gravitational forces pull objects towards the centre of the Earth.
2. The area in which the gravity acts.
3. Pulling force of the Moon's gravitational field causes the sea (ocean) tides.
4. Gravity is a non-contact force; a tug-of-war involves a contact force. Also, gravity pulls down towards the centre of the Earth (i.e. vertically) whereas a tug of war involves exerting forces horizontally.
5. The mass of the object and the gravitational field strength at its location.
6. a) 250N b) 100kg
7. Gravitational field strength, which varies with distance and location, determines how strongly an object is pulled; its weight. The number and type of particles (mass) in the object are fixed.
8. a) diagram should show force downwards due to gravity (weight) and equal and opposite force upwards provided by the balance.
9. Acceleration due to gravity and gravitational field strength are equivalent, so have the same value. The field strength does not depend on the object; it depends on the object's position in relation to the Earth.
10. Drop two spherical objects of equal mass but different densities, so one has a larger size. If they hit the ground at different times, air resistance is an influence, because all other variables are controlled. Students might also mention measuring techniques and repeating trials.

Answers to Worksheet 1.1.7

1. a) False; weight depends on the strength of the gravitational field. b) True c) False; mass depends on the number and type of particles in an object. d) True e) False; it extends well into space, beyond the atmosphere.
2. Students should make correct reference to matter/particles, gravitational field strength, and the formula $W = mg$.
3. Students should refer to the formula $W = mg$ to show how weight depends on mass. The mouse weighs 1 N, which is the force it is pulled down by. The elephant weighs 50 000 N; both accelerate due to gravity at 10 m/s^2.

1.1.8 Understanding mass and weight

Lesson overview

Learning objective

- Explain the difference between mass and weight.

Learning outcome

- Answer questions that draw on the distinction between mass and weight. [O1]

Skills development

- Working scientifically: 2.6 Construct explanations
- Developing numeracy: comparing and contrasting physical quantities
- Developing literacy: construct descriptions and explanations (Q4 & 6)

Resources needed bag of sugar (or flour or other dry goods) – see Technician notes 1.1.8

Key vocabulary mass, weight, gravity

Teaching and learning

Engage

- Challenge students to **identify** what is the weight of a bag of sugar (or flour or similar) and what is its mass. [O1]
- Show video clips of people on the Moon, in a space station and so on, and ask students to **explain** whether the people have weight and whether they have mass. [O1]

Challenge and develop

- Ask students to **explain** the difference between mass and weight. Suggest that the former is related to the amount of material present and the latter to the effects of gravity. [O1]

Explain

- Challenge students to **explain** what causes them to have weight and what this weight depends upon. [O1]
- Ask students to **suggest** why they think that confusion exists between the concepts of mass and weight, and how they can avoid such confusion. [O1]

Consolidate and apply

- Ask students to **apply** their understanding of mass and weight to the context of space travel and how it would affect astronauts in different ways at different times. [O1]
- Ask students to **explain** why, when descending in an express lift, they might feel as if they weigh less. Draw out from comments that this is an illusion caused by the rapid descent of the lift. [O1]
- Challenge students to **suggest** situations in which altering the mass or distance affects weight. For example, a spacecraft that has used most of its fuel has less mass than one that has full tanks and will weigh less in the same gravitational field. If it is nearer to a planet the gravitational field strength will be greater and it will weigh more. [O1]

Extend

For students able to progress further:

Ask students to **suggest** how the challenge of remaining physically fit in the context of microgravity could be met. Space travellers can do exercises that help to keep their muscles in shape, such as compressing a spring. [O1]

Challenge students to **explain** how 'reduced gravity aircraft' (also known as vomit comets) can reproduce conditions of zero gravity. The aircraft flies in an arc. This means that (for a short time) it is descending as it would in free fall so the occupants 'float around' inside the aircraft. They aren't weightless but feel as if they are as they are falling at the same rate as their surroundings. [O1]

Answers to Student Book questions

1. Ideas such as: people do not understand the scientific use of the terms; we say 'weigh' sometimes when we mean 'measure its mass'; when we weigh ourselves on bathroom scales the unit is kg, but it should be N.

2. The mass would be the same on both; because the number and type of particles does not change. The weight would be bigger on the bigger planet; because the force of gravity would be greater.

3. Damage is caused by the impact between the two cars. The mass of the two cars is the same on the Moon as on the Earth. Only the weight differs and this is a force acting downwards, which is not relevant in the impact.

4. The further away you are from any planet or star, the weaker the gravity.

5. c) Gravity from the Earth would gradually weaken as the spacecraft got further away. At a point between the Earth and the Moon, the pull of gravity from each would balance – this point is closer to the Moon than the Earth. As the spacecraft travelled further from Earth, the pull of gravity towards the Moon would become bigger than the pull of the Earth.

6. Gravity from the Earth would gradually weaken as the spacecraft got further away. At a point between the Earth and the Moon, the pull of gravity from each would balance – this point is closer to the Moon than the Earth. As the spacecraft travelled further from Earth, the pull of gravity towards the Moon would become bigger than the pull of the Earth.

28   © HarperCollins*Publishers* Limited 2017

1.1.9 Understanding gravity

Lesson overview

Learning objectives

- Explain what gravity is.
- Understand how gravity varies according to where you are in the solar system.
- Apply ideas about gravity to various situations.

Learning outcomes

- Give a clear explanation of what causes gravity, with examples. [O1]
- Explain how, in various places, the different gravitational field causes the same mass to have different weights. [O2]
- Explain, given appropriate information, the effect of gravity in comparative terms. [O3]

Skills development

- Working scientifically: 2.8 Justify opinions
- Developing numeracy: understanding the relationship between variables
- Developing literacy: explain differences and compare and contrast situations (Q4 - 6)

Resources needed bag of sugar; forcemeter – see Technician notes 1.1.9

Common misconceptions

- Gravity depends on being within the Earth's atmosphere.
- Gravity acts downwards, rather towards the centre of the Earth.
- There is no gravity in space/on the International Space Station (ISS).
- Gravity depends on a planet (or satellite) spinning on its axis.

Key vocabulary force, gravity, mass

Teaching and learning

Engage

- Hold up a bag of sugar and ask students to consider what forces are acting upon it. Then ask students to consider how this would change if you were on the surface of a different planet. [O1]
- Show video clips of astronauts on the surface of the Moon and discuss how they move. Ask students to describe what it might feel like to be working in a situation where gravity is one sixth the strength of the Earth's gravitational field. [O1, O2]

Challenge and develop

- Show students Table 1.1.9 of the Student Book and discuss the row headings, then ask them to explain what this shows about weight in different places. [O1, O2]

Explain

- Ask students to work in small groups to formulate in words their ideas about what gravity is and why it varies from one place to another. [O1, O2, O3]

Consolidate and apply

- Ask students to consider the truth of the statement 'the larger the planet, the greater your weight at the surface', to research data and formulate a response. A good response will identify that it's the mass of the planet that is crucial and although larger planets tend to have more mass, this isn't necessarily the case. [O1, O2]

- Ask students to read 'A gravity puzzle' in the Student Book and then to explain why this might seem to be a puzzle. [O1]

Extend

- Ask students to suggest what they could deduce about a planet simply by being told what the bag of sugar weighed at its surface. [O1, O2, O3]

- Ask students to answer Q8 in the Student Book and then challenge them to explain which ideas they had used to develop answers. [O1, O2, O3]

- Challenge students to, using data from the student book and elsewhere, suggest whether there is a correlation between:

  - The mass of a planet and the strength of its gravitational field

  - The distance of a planet from the Sun and the strength of its gravitational field [O1, O3]

Plenary suggestions

- Ask students to identify something they have learned in this lesson that was new. [O1, O2, O3]

- Ask students to identify a challenge that gravity provides to space exploration. [O1, O2, O3]

- Ask students to consider if it were possible for the Earth's gravitational field to be halved in strength, would this would be a good thing (or not), and why. [O1]

Answers to Student Book questions

1. The Earth's gravitational field gets weaker as the distance from the Earth increases..
2. The strength of the Moon's gravitational field started to have an effect.
3. Because the mass of the Moon is less than that of the Earth.
4. On the Earth.
5. Moon, Mercury/Mars (joint), Venus, Earth
6. The gravitational fields vary significantly so the force opposing your jump would be very different.
7. a) A force pulling you towards the Earth.

   b) You would start moving towards the Earth; and would fall faster and faster.
8. a) No weight. b) Reduced weight. c) Weight a fraction of that on the Earth's surface.

1.1.10 Checking students' progress

The *Checking your progress* section in the Student Book indicates the key ideas developed in this chapter and shows how students progress to more complex levels. It is provided to support students in:

- identifying the key ideas;

- developing a sense of their current level of understanding;

- developing a sense of what the next steps in their learning are.

It is designed either to be used at the end of a chapter to support an overall view of progress, or alternatively during the teaching of the chapter. Students can self-assess or peer-assess using this as a basis.

It is helpful to encourage students to provide evidence from their understanding or their notes to support their judgements. In some cases it may be useful to explore the difference in the descriptors for a particular idea so that students can see what makes for a 'higher outcome'.

It may be useful with some descriptors to provide examples from the specific work done, such as an experiment undertaken or an explanation developed and recorded. If marking and feedback use similar ideas and phrases this will enable students to relate specific marking to a more general sense of progress.

To make good progress in understanding science students need to focus on these ideas and skills:

Students who are making modest progress will be able to:	Students who are making good progress will be able to:	Students who are making excellent progress will be able to:
Explain how to find the speed of an object.	Explain the concept of speed and how the formula for speed is derived.	Apply understanding of the speed formula to explain how speed cameras work.
Collect data about distance travelled and time taken for different journeys.	Present data collected or given as distance–time graphs.	Construct distance–time graphs for complex journeys.
Describe features of distance–time graphs.	Analyse distance–time graphs to describe an object's movement at different stages in a journey	Explain distance–time graphs for complex journeys, including where an object travels at different speeds and accelerates at different rates.
Describe a situation where objects are travelling at different speeds.	Apply the idea of relative speed to two objects involved in overtaking or collision.	Apply the concept of relative motion to several moving objects in a variety of situations.
Identify different forces acting upon an object.	Calculate the resultant of several forces acting in the same dimension.	Relate the resultant force to the motion of the object.
Identify the direction that a force is acting in.	Represent the direction of forces in a diagram.	Use a force diagram to identify a resultant
Identify gravity as a pulling force and recognise that mass and weight are not the same.	Describe what is meant by mass, explain how gravity forces affect weight, explain why weight varies from planet to planet and explain the term 'weightless'.	Explain weight as a gravitational attraction between masses which decreases with distance; explain the difference between mass and weight.
Identify gravity as a non-contact force	Explain the difference between contact and non-contact forces.	Compare gravity with other forces.
Recall the units of mass and force.	Recall the units of gravitational field strength.	Explain why gravitational field strength has those units.
Explain how mass affects weight.	Use the formula weight = mass x gravitational field strength to determine weight.	Use the formula weight = mass x gravitational field strength to determine mass.
Explain what causes an object to have weight.	Describe how gravity affects the weight of an object.	Explain the relationship between gravitational field and the weight of an object.
Describe how an object's weight can vary.	Predict how an object's weight would vary depending on its position in relation to large bodies such as planets.	Use the concept of a gravitational field to explain various phenomena, including the orbits of planets around stars.

1.1.11 Answers to Student Book end of chapter questions

This table provides answers to the Questions section at the end of Chapter 1 of the Student Book. It also shows how different questions assess attainment in terms of the focus and style of a question as well as the context. Question-level analysis can indicate a student's proficiency in approaching different aspects of scientific understanding and different types of answer.

Q	Answer	Marks available	Focus			Style			Context			
			Knowledge & understanding	Application	Evaluation of evidence	Objective test question	Short written answer	Longer written answer	Speed	Mass, weight and gravity		
1	c	1	1			1			1			
2	c	1	1			1			1			
3	B	1	1			1				1		
4	b	1	1			1				1		
5	a	1	1									
6	c	1		1		1			1			
7	• Distance–time graph with x-axis labelled 'Time' over 0–4 minutes; y-axis labelled 'Distance' over 0–500 metres	1		1			1		1			
	• For the first horse, a straight line from point (0, 0) to point (4, 500)	1		1			1		1			
	• For the second horse, initially an upward curve from point (0, 0)	1		1			1		1			
	then the line is horizontal for 1 minute, then an upward curve finishing at point (3, 500)	1		1			1		1			
8	d	1		1		1				1		
9	a	1		1		1				1		
10	b	1		1		1				1		
11	a	1			_1_	1				1		
12	Its trajectory would be a straight line, starting as a tangent to its Earth orbit	1			_1_		1			1		
13	• Objects, including stars, orbiting around the same point suggests something with a very strong gravitational field. • A dark area of space at the location of the black hole because no light can escape the strong gravitational field. • As the spaceship entered the gravitational field of the black hole, it would accelerate towards the black hole.	1			_1_			_1_		1		

1.2.0 Electromagnets: Introduction

When and how to use these pages

The Introduction in the Student Book indicates some of the ideas and skills in this topic area that students will already have met from KS2 or from previous KS3 work. It also provides an indication of what they will be studying in this chapter. *Ideas you have met before* is not intended to comprehensively summarise all of the prior ideas, but rather to point out a few of the key ones and to support the view that scientific understanding is progressive. Even though students might be meeting contexts that are new to them, they can often use existing ideas to start to make sense of them.

In this chapter you will find out indicates some of the new ideas that the chapter will introduce. Again, it isn't a detailed summary of content. Its purpose is more to act as a 'trailer' and generate some interest.

The outcomes, then, will be: recognition of prior learning that can be built on; and interest in finding out more.

There are a number of ways this introduction can be used. You might, for example:

- use *Ideas you have met before* as the basis for a revision lesson as you start the first new topic

- use ideas on the *Ideas you have met before* as the centre of spider diagrams, to which students can add examples, experiments they might have done previously, or what they found interesting

- make a note of any unfamiliar/difficult terms and return to these in the relevant lessons

- use ideas from *In this chapter you will find out* to ask students questions, such as:
  - Why is this important?
  - How could it be used?
  - What might we be doing in this topic?

Overview of the chapter

The chapter starts by exploring static electricity, the concept of charge and the idea of a field. Although students are unlikely to have studied electrostatics before, they will have met other non-contact forces (gravity and magnetism) and are, of course, very likely to have experienced the effects of static electricity.

The chapter then proceeds to link the concepts of current, voltage and resistance with the observed behaviour of circuits. Students may well have built circuits previously and met ideas around conductors and insulators, the need for a complete circuit and the effect of altering the number of components in a circuit. They are likely to have used terms such as current (as in, flow around a circuit) and voltage (as in cells) but unlikely to have used resistance or set up parallel circuits.

This chapter uses both current and voltage (or potential difference, the preferred term at GCSE) as concepts that can be used to explain how circuits work. It also introduces the concept of resistance, both as a way of describing the effect of components in a circuit and as the ratio of voltage to current. These ideas are related to both parallel and series circuits.

Obstacles to learning

Students may need extra guidance to deal with the following common misconceptions:

- **Static electricity:** students may think that static electricity is a different kind of electricity or that items are either simply 'charged' or 'not charged', as opposed to there being two types of charge.
- **Insulators and conductors:** all metals conduct electricity equally well. Students may well think that a material is either a conductor or not, and that all non-metals are insulators. They may think that solutions cannot conduct and that dire consequences await those who 'mix electricity and water'.
- **Current:** electric current is used up in a circuit. Charges are produced by a battery and flow all the way around the circuit.
- **Voltage:** voltage and current are interchangeable. The voltage is not related to the battery. Energy in the circuit is used up.
- **Series and parallel circuits:** the arrangement of components will have no effect on the voltage and current.

How the Programme of Study is covered by the Student Book

Big idea	Topic	Lesson	Programme of study reference
Electromagnats	Voltage and resistance	1.2.1 Describing electric circuits	Other processes that involve energy transfer: completing an electrical circuit Electric current, measured in amperes, in circuits
		1.2.2 Understanding energy in circuits	Other processes that involve energy transfer: completing an electrical circuit Electric current, measured in amperes, in circuits Potential difference, measured in volts, battery and bulb ratings
		1.2.3 Explaining resistance	Potential difference (p.d.), measured in volts, battery and bulb ratings Resistance, measured in ohms, as the ratio of p.d. to current
	Current	1.2.4 Describing series and parallel circuits	Series and parallel circuits, currents add where branches meet and current as flow of charge
		1.2.5 Comparing series and parallel circuits	Electric current, measured in amperes, in circuits Series and parallel circuits, currents add where branches meet and current as flow of charge Potential difference, measured in volts, battery and bulb ratings
		1.2.6 Investigating static charge	Non-contact forces: forces due to static electricity
		1.2.7 Explaining static charge	Separation of positive or negative charges when objects are rubbed together: transfer of electrons, forces between charged objects
		1.2.8 Understanding electrostatic fields	Non-contact forces: forces due to static electricity Separation of positive or negative charges when objects are rubbed together: transfer of electrons, forces between charged objects The idea of electric field, forces acting across the space between objects not in contact

How the AQA KS3 Syllabus is covered by the Student Books and Teacher Guide

Voltage and resistance

	Student Book	Teacher Guide
Know		
We can model voltage as an electrical push from the battery, or the amount of energy per unit of charge transferred through the electrical pathway.	2.2	2.2
In a series circuit, voltage is shared between each component. In a parallel circuit, voltage is the same across each loop.	2.5	2.5
Components with resistance reduce the current flowing and shift energy to the surroundings.	2.3	2.3
Skill: Calculate resistance using the formula: resistance (Ω) = potential difference (V) . current (A).	2.3	2.3
Potential difference (voltage): The amount of energy shifted from the battery to the moving charge, or from the charge to circuit components, in volts (V).	2.2, 2.3	2.2, 2.3
Resistance: A property of a component, making it difficult for charge to pass through, in ohms (Ω).	2.3	2.3
Electrical conductor: A material that allows current to flow through it easily, and has a low resistance.	2.3	2.3
Electrical insulator: A material that does not allow current to flow easily, and has a high resistance.	2.3	2.3
Apply		
Draw a circuit diagram to show how voltage can be measured in a simple circuit.	2.1	2.1
Use the idea of energy to explain how voltage and resistance affect the way components work.	(2.4)	(2.4)
Given a table of voltage against current. Use the ratio of voltage to current to determine the resistance.	2.3	2.3
Use an analogy like water in pipes to explain why part of a circuit has higher resistance.	2.2	2.2
Extend		
Predict the effect of changing the rating of a battery or a bulb on other components in a series or parallel circuit.	2.4	2.4
Justify the sizes of voltages in a circuit, using arguments based on energy.	(2.4)	2.2
Draw conclusions about safety risks, from data on voltage, resistance and current.		2.4

Current

	Student Book	Teacher Guide
Know		
Current is a movement of electrons and is the same everywhere in a series circuit. Current divides between loops in a parallel circuit, combines when loops meet, lights up bulbs and makes components work.	2.1, 2.4	2.1, 2.4
Around a charged object, the electric field affects other charged objects, causing them to be attracted or repelled. The field strength decreases with distance.	2.6, 2.7, 2.8	2.6, 2.7, 2.8
Fact: Two similarly charged objects repel, two differently charged objects attract.	2.8	2.8
Negatively charged: An object that has gained electrons as a result of the charging process.	2.7	2.7
Positively charged: An object that has lost electrons as a result of the charging process.	2.7	2.7
Electrons: Tiny particles which are part of atoms and carry a negative charge.	2.7	2.7
Charged up: When materials are rubbed together, electrons move from one surface to the other.	2.7	2.7
Electrostatic force: Non-contact force between two charged objects.	2.6	2.6
Current: Flow of electric charge, in amperes (A).	2.1	2.1
In series: If components in a circuit are on the same loop.	2.4, 2.5	2.4, 2.5
In parallel: If some components are on separate loops.	2.4, 2.5	2.4, 2.5
Field: The area where other objects feel a gravitational force.	2.6	2.6
Apply		
Describe how current changes in series and parallel circuits when components are changed.	2.4, 2.5	2.4, 2.5
Turn circuit diagrams into real series and parallel circuits, and vice versa.	(2.4)	(2.4)
Describe what happens when charged objects are placed near to each other or touching.	2.6	2.6
Use a sketch to describe how an object charged positively or negatively became charged up.	(2.7, 2.8)	(2.7, 2.8)
Extend		
Compare the advantages of series and parallel circuits for particular uses.	2.5	2.5
Evaluate a model of current as electrons moving from the negative to the positive terminal of a battery, through the circuit.	(2.3)	2.1
Suggest ways to reduce the risk of getting electrostatic shocks.	2.6	2.6

1.2.1 Describing electric circuits

Lesson overview

Learning objectives

- Describe and draw circuit diagrams.
- Explain what is meant by current.
- Explain how materials allow current to flow.

Learning outcomes

- Recognise and use symbols to represent components in a circuit; investigate electrical conductors and insulators. [O1]
- Describe what current is, using models and analogies. [O2]
- Explain how electrical conductors work, using models; explain the strengths and weaknesses of different models and analogies that describe how current works. [O3]

Skills development

- Working scientifically: 2.1 Analyse patterns
- Developing numeracy: use symbols to represent physical objects
- Developing literacy: use analogies to understand phenomena (Q 4 - 6)

Resources needed cells; connecting leads; light bulbs; crocodile clips; switch; selection of metals and non-metals to test; 2 or 3 ammeters; Worksheet 1.2.1 (final page printed onto card); Practical sheet 1.2.1; Technician's notes 1.2.1

Common misconceptions Energy in a circuit is used up because the battery runs out. Current in a circuit is used up.

Key vocabulary component, electrical conductor, electrical insulator, ammeter, ampere

Teaching and learning

Engage

- Ask the students to play 'matching pairs' using the cards cut out from Worksheet 1.2.1. They should **match up** the name of each component with the diagram representing it. [O1]
- Review the success criteria for drawing electric circuits. These criteria include: using a ruler to draw straight lines to represent the wires; using the correct circuit symbols to represent different components; and ensuring that the circuit is closed and has no gaps.

Challenge and develop

- Remind the students of the terms 'conductor' and 'insulator'. Ask them to complete task 1b of Worksheet 1.2.1, **predicting** which materials are likely to be conductors and which insulators. They can then **build** the circuit shown on Practical sheet 1.2.1 to test their predictions. [O1]
- Discuss electric current using the ideas in 'Components in electric circuits' and 'Using models to explain current' in the Student Book. Use the suggested analogies to develop ideas further. [O2]
- Discuss why conductors allow electric currents to pass but insulators do not. [O1, O2]

  Ask high demand students to **develop** their own model/analogy to show how a conductor works. [O3]

- Ask the students to draw their own representations of a simple circuit with a light bulb, with annotations, **explaining** how electric current works to transfer energy to the light bulb. Select different students to **share** their ideas. They should clearly show that current is not used up in the circuit, but enables the transfer of energy. [O1, O2]

High demand students should **discuss** the strengths and weaknesses of the shared analogies. [O3]

Explain

- Demonstrate how to use an ammeter (in a simple series circuit with a battery and a bulb). Connect ammeters at different points in the circuit and ask the students to **measure** the current in each part. Ask them to use their previous ideas to **explain** their findings. [O1, O2]

Consolidate and apply

- Ask the students to **consider** the circuits in task 2 of Worksheet 1.2.1. They should **predict** what the ammeter readings are in the given spaces – they could **build** the circuits to test their ideas. [O2]
- Ask the students to answer the Student Book questions. [O1, O2, O3]

Extend

- Students able to progress further could **explain** what is happening in the different circuits in task 3 of Worksheet 1.2.1. They should use their own models to **account for** differences in current between the circuits. [O3]

Plenary suggestions

True or false? Play a true/false quiz using questions such as those suggested here:
- Circuits will work if there is a gap in them (F)
- The current is the same all over the circuit (T)
- A voltmeter measures current (F)
- Electrical conductors will not allow current to pass through (F)
- All metals are good conductors of electricity (T)
- The current in a circuit gets used up (F)

Answers to Student Book questions

1. It is a conductor.
2. Include: correct symbols for bulbs and cells; straight lines (drawn using a ruler) for all wires; and no gaps in the circuit.
3. So there is a standard way of representing what is in a circuit; this is useful for making circuits from circuit diagrams.
4. *Water analogy*: *low current*, slow-moving stream; *high current*, fast-moving stream.
   Coal truck analogy: *low current*, few coal trucks moving; *high current*, many coal trucks moving.
5. Coal truck analogy; because it conveys the idea of something being transported around the circuit; and being dropped off; the water analogy does not do this in the same way.
6. *Water analogy*: water is flowing all the time; there is no delay; and flow is at a constant rate; so this is a strength of the analogy. Water, however, can be removed from the river or added to it – this is a limitation.
   Coal truck analogy: the trucks do not all move together or at the same rate, so this is a limitation. The number of trucks moving may differ during the circuit – this is another limitation.
7. Because current is the flow of electrons in the conducting wires; electrons are not removed or added when they are connected to a battery. While the battery is on it makes the charges flow, but they cannot escape anywhere and be lost.

Answers to Worksheet 1.2.1

1. a) A – 5; B – 7; C – 2; D – 1; E – 9; F – 3; G – 8; H – 6; I – 4
   b) *Conductors*: all the metals and carbon (graphite); *insulators*: plastic and glass.
2. a) Diagram shown with straight lines, no breaks. Explanation of how current is the flow of charge in the connecting wires; transferring energy from the battery to the components.
   b) i) Both ammeters will read 3 A. ii) Both ammeters will read 5 A c) 2 A.
3. a) A conductor has free charged particles (electrons) that can move; an insulator has very few charged particles that can move.
   b) The second circuit has more batteries; suggesting that increasing the number of batteries produces a larger current.

1.2.2 Understanding energy in circuits

Lesson overview

Learning objectives

- Describe what the voltage does in a circuit.

Learning outcomes

- Recognise the units of voltage; use different models to describe voltage. [O1]
- Relate current and voltage to different models. [O2]

Skills development

- Working scientifically: 2.2 Present data
- Developing numeracy: identify trends and patterns
- Developing literacy: use comparisons and analogies to construct explanations (Q5 & 6)

Resources needed a selection of electrical appliances (mix of battery-powered and mains-powered); 4 × 1.5 V cells; insulated connecting leads; crocodile clips; at least 4 standard circuit bulbs; at least 4 voltmeters; switches; Worksheet 1.2.2; Technician's notes 1.2.2

Common misconceptions Voltage and current are the same thing. Voltage and current get used up by the circuit.

Key vocabulary voltage, volt, voltmeter, potential difference

Teaching and learning

Engage

- Display a range of electrical appliances, including some that use batteries and others that use mains electricity. Introduce the term 'voltage' and its units. Ask the students to look at the appliances and their voltage ratings. ***Do not allow*** them to switch on the appliances. Ask them to complete task 1 of Worksheet 1.2.2, **recording** the voltage used by each appliance and the source of electricity (battery or mains). Can they **identify** any patterns? Can they **give reasons** why some appliance use batteries and others need mains electricity? [O1]

Challenge and develop

- Discuss the meaning of the term 'voltage'; use the analogies given in the Student Book. [O1]

- Demonstrate to the students a number of circuits set up with different numbers of cells and just one light bulb. First show a circuit with one cell and one bulb. Demonstrate how to connect the voltmeter in parallel with the bulb and discuss the reasons for this, using the Student Book. Then show a circuit with two cells and the same bulb – demonstrate the difference in voltage. Finally show a circuit with three cells and the same bulb. Ask the students to **predict** the voltage across the bulb. [O1]

- The students should **identify** the pattern between the number of cells and the voltage. [O1]

- Select different students to **role-play** how voltage provides a 'push' to drive a current, and also the energy that the current transfers. Discuss the different analogies presented in 'Using analogies to explain voltage' in the Student Book, and any others that you may have. [O1, O2]

- **Group work** Using a real circuit, ask the students to **consider** each of the models/analogies in turn. Ask them to **identify the strengths and weaknesses** of each when used to explain what is happening in each of the circuit diagrams in task 2 of Worksheet 1.2.2. Take feedback from the groups. [O2, O3]

Explain

- **Small groups** Ask the students to **develop** their own analogy to explain voltage and how it affects the current. They should **draw a diagram** or **role-play** their idea to explain how it works. [O2]

  High demand students should **consider the strengths and weaknesses** of their analogies. [O3]

Consolidate and apply

- Ask students to **consider** each of the statements in task 3 of Worksheet 1.2.2. They should **decide** whether or not their analogy can explain each of the statements, and **refine** their analogy if possible. [O2, O3]

- They should answer the Student Book questions. [O1, O2, O3]

Extend

- Students able to progress further should **predict** and **explain** what will happen to a circuit when more than one light bulb is added. Is there any change in the voltage or the current? They should use an analogy to **explain**, and also **consider the strengths and weaknesses** of their analogy. [O2, O3]

- Challenge students to use ideas about energy transfer, to explain the effects of increasing the voltage in a circuit [O2]

Plenary suggestions

Understanding voltage and current Ask students to **rank** the circuits in Worksheet 1.2.2 in order of which has the highest voltage, and then which is likely to have the largest current. Then return to the appliances used at the start of the lesson. Can the students now use ideas about voltage to **explain** why different appliances require a different source of electricity? [O1, O2]

Answers to Student Book questions

1. There is no 'push' to make the current flow if there is no voltage.   2. 3 V.
3. Circuit B; there is more voltage; so a bigger 'push'; which transfers more energy to the circuit.
4. It would have much more energy; and be able to run faster; if it could take the much higher voltage.
5. *Straw analogy*: the first circuit will be like blowing very hard through the straw; a high flow of air will come out of the straw; which models lots of energy being transferred to the current. The second circuit will be like blowing gently through the straw; only a small stream of air (the current) will come out. *Waterfall analogy*: first circuit is like a high waterfall resulting in a large flow of water; the second like a small waterfall; so only a trickle flow of water.
6. The air in the straw (the current) comes from the mouth (the battery). In reality the charges in a circuit come from the wires not from the battery; similarly the water in the river comes from the waterfall, which also represents the battery; so this is a limitation.

Answers to Worksheet 1.2.2

1. Table correctly completed with appliance, voltage and mains/battery power source.

   a) Appliances that use high voltages are likely to use mains electricity. b) Voltage provides the push to drive the current.

2. *Circuit 1:* Voltage from the cell provides the energy to push the current, which is transferred to the light bulb. *Circuit 2:* One extra cell means there is double the voltage, so a higher push, and more energy is transferred to the bulb; the bulb is twice as bright as the bulb in circuit 1. *Circuit 3:* Two bulbs means the energy from the battery is shared between them, so they are each half as bright as the bulb in circuit 1; the same current flows through each bulb, as in circuit 1. *Circuit 4:* Double the voltage of circuit 1 is shared between twice as many bulbs, so same brightness as circuit 1. Appropriate analogy applied to each case.

3. a) Circuit 1: 1.5 V; circuit 2: 3 V; circuit 3: 0.75 V; circuit 4: 1.5 V.

   b) Analogies correctly applied with a clear understanding of how well each is supported. The river analogy is:

   Statement 1 – water (charge) comes from the waterfall (voltage); so this analogy does not support this idea well.

   Statement 2 – water is always moving as a result of the 'push' from the waterfall; so this idea is supported well.

   Statement 3 – water can be removed from the river (evaporation) and added to (rain); so the analogy does not hold here; if the water were in a closed pipe it would work better.

   Statement 4 – if a water wheel were to be placed in the river, the energy from the water would be transferred to the wheel; without water being used up; so the analogy holds here.

1.2.3 Explaining resistance

Lesson overview

Learning objectives

- Explain what resistance is and how it affects the circuit.
- Investigate and identify the relationship between voltage and current.
- Explain some factors affecting resistance.

Learning outcomes

- Describe the term 'resistance' and recognise the units; collect reliable data from circuits. [O1]
- Describe the relationship between voltage, current and resistance; present results using appropriate graphs. [O2]
- Derive a mathematical relationship between voltage and current, and make predictions from it. [O3]

Skills development

- Working scientifically: 2.1 Analyse patterns
- Developing numeracy: use formulae to perform calculations
- Developing literacy: apply analogies to construct explanations (Q2 & 3)

Resources needed graph paper; samples of conductors and insulators; equipment for practical, per group: D.C. ammeter (up to 1 A), D.C. voltmeter (up to 5 V), 1 ohm fixed resistor, variable power supply D.C. up to 6 V, insulated connecting leads, crocodile clips (at least four), rheostat (up to 10 ohms and 1 A), switch; Worksheet 1.2.3; Practical sheet 1.2.3; Technician's notes 1.2.3

Key vocabulary resistance, free electron, ohm, conductor, insulator

Teaching and learning

Engage

- Give the students samples of conductors and insulators. Remind them of prior learning and review the terms 'conductor' and 'insulator'.

- Demonstrate a model of the atoms in a conductor and in an insulator, such as a transparent tube of fixed polystyrene balls to represent the atomic nuclei and small marbles to represent free charged particles. The conductor should have many, many more charged particles compared with the insulator. The insulator could have larger polystyrene balls, as greater obstacles to the movement of charged particles. Discuss the differences between the two. [O1]

Challenge and develop

- Use 'What is resistance?' in the Student Book to introduce the idea of resistance. Use the analogies provided. Online simulations may also help. [O1]

- Demonstrate different circuits to discuss the effect of resistance. Start with a circuit that has one battery and one light bulb. Connect the bulb in series with the battery, switch and ammeter. Close the switch and note the ammeter reading. Now connect another bulb in series. Explain that this has the effect of increasing the resistance in the circuit. Note the effect on the brightness and the ammeter reading. [O1]

- Discuss how the resistance of the circuit is changed when the bulb is added. Ask the students to **predict** what would happen, and why, if there were three light bulbs – test their predictions. [O1, O2]

- Return to just one bulb in the circuit and add a rheostat. Adjust the rheostat to show how it changes the resistance in the circuit, and the effect this has on the current. [O1, O2]

- **Group work** Ask the students to **investigate** the relationship between resistance, current and voltage, following the instructions on Practical sheet 1.2.3. Ask the groups to **present their results** graphically and **analyse** them using the questions on the practical sheet. [O2]

High demand students should **identify a mathematical link** between current, voltage and resistance. [O3]

Explain

- Ask the students to **write an explanation** of their results. They should use one analogy and show how this can be applied to their results. They could **identify strengths and weaknesses** of the analogy. [O2, O3]

Consolidate and apply

- Ask the students to complete Worksheet 1.2.3 and to answer the Student Book questions. [O1, O2, O3]

- Ask the students to consider analogies that they have previously developed to explain voltage and current. Can they now **adapt** these analogies to incorporate ideas about resistance, and **identify the strengths and weaknesses** of these? [O2]

Extend

- Students able to progress further should **develop** an analogy of voltage, current and resistance, which can incorporate the mathematical link. [O3]

Plenary suggestions

Summarising knowledge Ask the students to write a summary **explaining** the terms 'voltage', 'current' and 'resistance' and how they relate to one another. [O1, O2, O3]

Answers to Student Book questions

1. a) Circuit A. b) There is a smaller resistance in this circuit; so a higher current will flow.
2. Obstacles are the resistance in the circuit; people are the charge.
3. The bulb would shine more brightly; there is less resistance in platinum; which would allow a higher current to flow.
4. Divide the potential difference (voltage) by the current.
5. a) The six values are (to 1 d.p.): 30.0 Ω, 27.1 Ω, 31.0 Ω, 32.5 Ω, 33.3 Ω, 32.1Ω.

   b) They rise and fall a little but are broadly similar.

Answers to Worksheet 1.2.3

1. a) Resistance is a measure of the opposition to the flow of charge.

   b) *River analogy*: a conductor is like a river with lots of water and no boulders; an insulator is like a river with very little water and lots of boulders. *Coal truck analogy*: a conductor is like lots of coal trucks travelling on a motorway with no roadworks or obstructions due to breakdowns; an insulator is like a road full of road works and traffic lights with only a few coal trucks on it.

2. The resistance is fixed so there is the same constant opposition to the flow of charge; when the voltage is increased, there is a bigger push; so the current flows faster. With a fixed resistance the increase in voltage will affect the flow of charge directly.

3. a) 2 ohms. b) The current would decrease.

   c) This is true; the voltage determines how much push the current is given; the resistance determines how much opposition there is to the flow of charge; the ratio between the amount of push and the amount of opposition determines the flow; which is the current.

Answers to Practical sheet 1.2.3

2. Graph should have voltage on the *x*-axis and current on the *y*-axis.

   a) A straight line graph through the origin indicates that the current is directly proportional to the voltage.

   b) Consistent, repeat readings confirm if the results are reliable.

3. a) Voltage ÷ current should be (roughly) equal for all data.

   b) As the voltage increases, the current increases proportionally; when the resistance in the circuit is fixed. This is because the charges in the connecting wires are given a bigger push with higher voltages and increase proportionally in their flow. The resistance in this circuit does not alter with higher voltage.

4. The resistance will have altered so voltage/current will have a different value (though this will remain similar as the voltage is altered).

5. This will depend on the resistance but can be calculated from I = V/R

1.2.4 Describing series and parallel circuits

Lesson overview

Learning objectives

- Describe how the voltage, current and resistance are related in different circuits.
- Understand the differences between series and parallel circuits.

Learning outcomes

- Recognise circuits as being either series or parallel, and identify the features of each. [O1]
- Draw and interpret circuit diagrams for series and parallel circuits; predict the brightness of bulbs in these circuits. [O2]
- Explain why components behave differently in series and parallel circuits. [O3]

Skills development

- Working scientifically: 2.1 Analyse patterns
- Developing numeracy: identify patterns in data
- Developing literacy: identify advantages and disadvantages of two different solutions (Q6)

Resources needed equipment for demonstration, and per group: 3 × 1.5 V cells, 6 bulbs, insulated connecting wire, 2 switches; Worksheet 1.2.4; Technician's notes 1.2.4

Common misconceptions The arrangement of a circuit has no effect on the components.

Key vocabulary series circuit, branch, parallel circuit

Teaching and learning

Engage

- Give small groups of student's bulbs, leads and batteries. Challenge them to see if they can **find** a way to build circuits in which two bulbs are just as bright as one bulb. Give them a time limit of 2 minutes. [O1]

Challenge and develop

- Demonstrate a simple circuit using a battery, a light bulb, an ammeter and a switch connected in series. Connect another similar circuit alongside the first, but this time connect two identical light bulbs in series. Before turning on the switch, ask the students to **recall** previous learning and **predict** what will change when the second light bulb is added – ask them to **explain** their ideas. Finally, demonstrate a third circuit alongside the other two, this time connecting two bulbs in parallel. Ask the students to **compare** the series and parallel arrangements and to **describe** what differences they can see. Ask them to **predict** what will happen to the brightness of the light bulbs in the parallel configuration. Select different students to **make responses** and discuss their ideas. [O1, O2]

- Introduce the terms 'series' and 'parallel'. Ask the students to complete task 1 of Worksheet 1.2.4, **drawing** circuit diagrams for the two arrangements and **predicting** what would happen if a light bulb were to be removed from the series circuit and then from the parallel circuit. [O1, O2]

Explain

- Give small groups of students six bulbs, leads, switches and a battery. Ask them to **design** their own series and parallel circuits, each having three bulbs. They should **draw** the circuit diagrams and **predict** the brightness of the bulbs in each arrangement (task 2 of Worksheet 1.2.4). Allow them to **build** the circuits to **test** their predictions. [O1, O2, O3]

- The students can then **annotate** their circuit diagrams, or draw larger ones and **explain** what they think is happening to the current, voltage and resistance in each case (task 3 of Worksheet 1.2.4). [O3]

- Select different groups to **show** their annotated diagrams and discuss their ideas. Challenge any misconceptions they may have. [O1, O2, O3]

Consolidate and apply

- Ask the students to answer the Student Book questions. [O1, O2, O3]

- **Pairs** Ask students to work in pairs and to **draw** circuit diagrams with a motor, bulb and buzzer connected first in series and then in parallel. Ask them to **explain** how the behaviour of the components will change in the different types of circuit. [O1, O2, O3]

Extend

- Students able to progress further could **investigate** circuits that are part series and part parallel. They should **make predictions** about the brightness of bulbs in each case and **explain** what is happening to the current, voltage and resistance. [O2, O3]

- Challenge students to make suggestions, supported by evidence, about the safety implications of:

  - a circuit having a higher supply voltage.

  - A greater current flowing in a circuit [O3]

Plenary suggestions

Compare series and parallel circuits Ask the students to **write a comparison** of series circuits and parallel circuits – what are the main differences between them? [O1, O2, O3]

Answers to Student Book questions

1. Voltage = 9 V; resistance = 9 ohms.
2. a) Same. b) Brighter. c) Same.
3. All the components would stop working; the circuit is no longer closed.
4. The drawing should represent the descriptions.
   a) The voltage in the two circuits will be the same overall; because they have the same number of cells.
   b) The current in the circuit with three bulbs will be smaller than in the circuit with one bulb.
   c) The three bulbs will be less bright than the single bulb.
5. a) Check that the circuit diagram is drawn correctly and according to conventions.
   b) In the parallel circuit, each bulb would be as bright as if it were the only bulb connected to the battery; in the series circuit each bulb would be much dimmer.
6. *Advantages of series*: if there is a fault with one component the current stops flowing; which can protect the other components.
   Disadvantages of series: if bulbs are connected in series and one has a fault, none of the lights will work.
   Advantages of parallel: if one light bulb is faulty, all the others will continue to work.
   Disadvantages of parallel: the battery will not last as long as it would if the components are connected in series.

Answers to Worksheet 1.2.4

1. a) i) and ii) Check that the circuit diagrams are drawn correctly; and according to conventions.
   b) i) The other bulb will go out. ii) The other bulb will stay on.
2. a) *In series*: the three bulbs will be equally dim; and less bright than a series circuit with two bulbs.
   b) *In parallel*: the bulbs will be equally bright; and just as bright as in a circuit with just one bulb; the bulbs will also be much brighter than the bulbs in the series circuit.
3. a) *Three bulbs in a series circuit*: the resistance in the circuit has increased; the voltage remains the same; the current in the circuit is the same everywhere; but is lower than for two bulbs; due to the increased resistance. The amount of energy is now divided across the three bulbs, instead of two; so they are all less bright compared with two bulbs.
   b) *Three bulbs in a parallel circuit*: there are three branches; each behaving like an individual circuit; each branch has the same resistance as a circuit with one bulb; because there is only one bulb in each branch. The current across the branches is shared; but the voltage across each is the same; so the same energy is transferred as it would be for one bulb; all the bulbs light up equally brightly; as if there was only one bulb in the circuit.

1.2.5 Comparing series and parallel circuits

Lesson overview

Learning objectives

- Investigate and explain current and voltage in series and parallel circuits.
- Explain the circuits in our homes.

Learning outcomes

- Make measurements of current and voltage in series circuits and in parallel circuits. [O1]
- Use models to explain what is happening to the current and voltage in series and parallel circuits; calculate the current and the voltage in series and parallel circuits. [O2]
- Make predictions about current and voltage in different circuit arrangements; explain how the domestic ring main works. [O3]

Skills development

- Working scientifically: 2.6 Construct explanations
- Developing numeracy: identify trends in data
- Developing literacy: describe disadvantages with a presented solution (Q5)

Resources needed 1 rope (5 m long); 4 short ropes (1 m long); equipment per group: four bulbs, four cells (1.5 V), insulated connecting wires, D.C. ammeters (0–5 A), D.C. voltmeters (0–10 V), crocodile clips, switch; Worksheet 1.2.5; Practical sheet 1.2.5; Technician's notes 1.2.5

Common misconceptions The current in circuits is used up. The voltage is the same in all circuits.

Key vocabulary current, in series, in parallel

Teaching and learning

Engage

- **True/false** Have a class quiz using statements such as:
  - In a parallel circuit the bulbs are arranged side by side. (F)
  - There is no difference in the brightness of the bulbs if they are in series or in parallel. (F)
  - Two bulbs in parallel are brighter than the same two bulbs in series. (T)
  - The battery runs out faster if the bulbs are in parallel. (T)
  - 100 bulbs in parallel will be just as bright as if there were just one bulb in the circuit. (T)

Challenge and develop

- **Small groups** The students should **set up** three series circuits – one with two bulbs, one with three bulbs and one with four bulbs, as shown on Practical sheet 1.2.5. They should **measure** the current and the voltage across one of the bulbs in each circuit and in the main part of the circuit, as shown in the diagram on the practical sheet, and **record** their results. [O1]

- The students can then be introduced to the rope model (in which a circle of students hold a large loop of rope and the 'battery' makes it move round) to **simulate** circuits, **explaining** the effects obtained. Other models can be used. [O2]

- Next, ask them to **set up** three parallel circuits and **make measurements** of voltage and current, using the same number of bulbs as before, as described on Practical sheet 1.2.5. They should **record** the values and answer the corresponding questions. The students should then **model** each circuit using the rope model, to **explain** the values obtained. [O1, O2]

- If possible, show a video of the domestic ring main and use the 'Household circuits' section of the Student Book to help explain how it works. Discuss the advantages and disadvantages of supplying household electricity in this way. [O3]

Explain

- Select different groups to **demonstrate** their model of each type of circuit from Practical sheet 1.2.5. Students should **explain** the values of current and voltage obtained. [O1, O2]

  Ask high demand students to use the rope model to **explain** to the class how the domestic ring main works. [O3]

Consolidate and apply

- Ask the students to answer the questions from Worksheet 1.2.5 and the Student Book, **calculating** values of current and voltage where appropriate. [O1, O2, O3]

  Ask high demand students to carry out some **research** and produce a poster about the domestic ring main. [O3]

Extend

- Students able to progress further could **design** their own circuits containing part series and part parallel components. They could **make predictions** of the values of current and voltage across different components and then **set up** the circuits to **test** their predictions. [O2]

Plenary suggestions

Circuit problems Ask students to draw their own series and parallel circuit diagrams with numerical values for the voltage across the battery and the current in the main circuit, and then challenge each other to **predict** the values for current and voltage across the components.

Answers to Student Book questions

1. It will decrease; the voltage is shared between three lights instead of two.
2. Double the voltage will mean that the lights will be twice as bright; if the current in the main circuit remains at 2 A, the current in each branch will be 0.2 A.
3. You could use a series circuit because it would split the 240 V between the 20 bulbs. Alternatively, a transformer could be used to provide 12 V to a parallel circuit.
4. Parallel circuit.
5. Each appliance receives 240 V and unused sockets aren't breaks in the circuit. An additional response might be that if an appliance fails it doesn't cause everything else to stop working.

Answers to Worksheet 1.2.5

1. *Series circuit*: the current is the same; the voltage is shared between the components.

   Parallel circuit: the current is shared between each branch; the voltage is the same across each branch.

   In a parallel circuit, the total sum of current in all the branches is the same as the current in the main circuit.
2. *Circuit 1*: A = 9 ÷ 3 = 3 V; B = 3 A; *Circuit 2*: C = 9 V; D = 3 ÷ 3 = 1 A
3. a) R = 9 ÷ 3 = 3 ohms b) 1 ohm c) 4 ohms d) I = 12 ÷ 4 = 3 A e) They are the same brightness.

Answers to Practical sheet 1.2.5

1. a) The current should decrease with the number of light bulbs, but it remains equal to the current in the main part of the circuit.

   b) The voltage across a bulb should decrease with increasing numbers of bulbs.

   c) The current through any one bulb should be the same irrespective of the number of bulbs.

   d) The voltage should remain the same across all components in the circuit; irrespective of the number of bulbs.
2. a) The current in the circuit will be $^1/_5$ of the current with one bulb on its own.

   b) The voltage across one bulb will be $^1/_5$ of the battery voltage.

   c) The current through a bulb will be the same as it was with fewer bulbs in the circuit.

   d) The voltage will be the same as in the other cases.

1.2.6 Investigating static charge

Lesson overview

Learning objectives

- Recognise the effects of static charge.
- Explain how static charge can be generated.
- Use evidence to develop ideas about static charge.

Learning outcomes

- Describe how static charge can be produced and detected. [O1]
- Explain the charge mechanism at work in various contexts. [O2]
- Explain what static electricity is. [O3]

Skills development

- Working scientifically: 2.13 Estimate risks
- Developing numeracy: identify and recognise factors
- Developing literacy: identify and describe evidence (Q6 & 7)

Resources needed inflated balloon, equipment per group: 2 balloons, static electricity rods (e.g. nylon, polythene), rods of other material (e.g. metal, wood), cloths (wool, fur), scrap paper, cotton thread, sticky tape, card or paper, stand and clamp; Worksheet 1.2.6; Practical sheet 1.2.6; Technician's notes 1.2.6

Key vocabulary charge, static electricity, field, attract, repel

Teaching and learning

Engage

- Stimulate the students' **thinking** with a simple demonstration of an effect of static electricity (e.g. rubbing a balloon on a jumper and sticking it to a wall). From prior knowledge they should be able to **identify** this as static electricity and also give other examples such as charging from a carpet and discharging through a door handle. [O1]

Challenge and develop

- The students **experiment** with rubbing balloons to **collect evidence** to decide if contact or non-contact forces are involved and if attraction, repulsion or both can occur. They can use Practical sheet 1.2.6. [O1, O2, O3]
- They then **test** a variety of materials to find out which can be charged by rubbing and attempting to pick up small scraps of paper. [O1, O2]
- They **observe** that static electricity can also involve repulsion by suspending a changed nylon rod in a paper cradle/thread so that it can rotate freely and then bringing another charged nylon rod towards it. [O2, O3]
- Ask the students to **compare** different situations in which there is a static electric charge and identify what creates the charge (rubbing, friction). [O2]

  High demand students may be able to **suggest** ideas about charged particles being transferred.

Explain

- The students work in groups of three to **discuss** and **explain** the ideas they have discovered about static electricity, and then **present** them to the class, possibly as a slideshow. [O1, O2, O3]

Consolidate and apply

- Ask the students to complete tasks 1 and 2 of Worksheet 1.2.6. [O1, O2]

- Ask them to **suggest** how they could find out if surfaces (walls, screens, benches) around the room are statically charged or not. (Test if scraps of paper/dust are attracted.) [O1, O2]

- **Pair talk** Ask the students to **discuss** and **compare** the effects of static charge with magnetism in task 3 of Worksheet 1.2.6 and be prepared to **feed back** their ideas. [O3]

  High demand students may be able to **compare** and **contrast** fields due to static charge, magnetism and gravity.

Extend

- Ask students able to progress further to **suggest** or **find out** how static electricity could be removed from a charged item. [O2]

Plenary suggestions

'I think that is …because …' Ask the students to **summarise the evidence** in relation to the following statements, and to accept or reject the statements as appropriate: [O1, O2, O3]
- Static electricity exerts a non-contact force.
- Objects can be charged by rubbing.
- Some charged objects repel each other, some attract.
- When an object is charged it has a force field around it.

Answers to Student Book questions

1. Metals; carbon.
2. Still or stationary.
3. It must not be in contact with another conductor.
4. An electrostatic field; a force of attraction.
5. The force can act from a distance; for example, when scraps of paper jump to a charged comb.
6. Suspend one comb on a thread (non-conducting) and bring the other close to it.
7. If you had something that was attracted by the balloon (for example, a strip of tissue paper or a strand of hair) you could hold it different distances away and see the force of attraction change as it was deflected by different amounts.
8. Magnetism.
9. Avoid combinations of materials that produce a static charge. For example, shoes on nylon carpets often generate a charge but other carpet materials, such as wool, are less likely to.

Answers to Worksheet 1.2.6

1. a) and c) are true
2. a) The charge leaks away through the wall or air; no force of attraction remains.
   b) Static charge is more likely to be generated between shoes and carpet than between shoes and wood.
3. Students should only partially agree, they should describe the similarities and differences outlined above to justify.

Answers to Practical sheet 1.2.6

3. Non-contact force.
4. Positive and positive repel; negative and negative repel; positive and negative attract.

1.2.7 Explaining static charge

Lesson overview

Learning objectives

- Explain static charge in terms of electron transfer.
- Apply this explanation to various examples.

Learning outcomes

- Describe how electrons may be transferred from one object to another. [O1]
- Relate the concept of electron transfer to observed effects. [O2]
- Use the concept of electron transfer to explain the effectiveness of charging and discharging. [O3]

Skills development

- Working scientifically: 2.3 Draw conclusions
- Developing numeracy: use ideas about positive and negative values
- Developing literacy: construct descriptions and explanations (Q5 - 9)

Resources needed van de Graaff generator with earthing sphere and accessories (e.g. Perspex container containing polystyrene balls; bunch of Terylene threads on a single plug (fits into the top of the globe); LED; stack of aluminium foil tart cases); rubber insulating mat (for a person to stand on); Worksheet 1.2.7; Technician's notes 1.2.7

Key vocabulary electron, positively charged, negatively charged, charged up, electrostatic force

Teaching and learning

Engage

- Use a van de Graaff generator (see Technician's notes 1.2.7) to demonstrate a static electricity effect so that the students can **recall** the main points from the previous lesson. Invite them to **make suggestions** about why rubbed objects may become charged. [O1]

  High demand students may be able to use ideas about particles and electricity to **suggest** the idea of charged particles.

- Refer the students to a simple atomic model – negative electrons orbiting a nucleus containing neutrons and positive protons (for example Figure 1.2.7a in the Student Book) and ask them to **decide** if this supports their suggestions. [O1]

Challenge and develop

- Explain that electrons can transfer easily from some substances during rubbing. Ask students to answer questions 5 and 6 in the Student Book. (For question 6 they need to realise that some materials lose electrons more easily than others.) [O1, O2]

- If students did not compare the attraction or repulsion of combinations of rods in the previous lesson (see Practical sheet 1.2.6) they should do that now: nylon/nylon; nylon/polythene; polythene/polythene. Ask them to **describe** and **draw** the distribution of electrons on the rods and to **identify the rules** (like charges repel; unlike charges attract). [O1, O2]

- Students **observe** more electrostatic effects with the van de Graaff generator. For example:
  - charge the globe and discharge with the earthing sphere held a few centimetres away;
  - charge a volunteer student by asking them to stand on a rubber mat and to hold the globe when the generator is started;
  - use accessories such as a cluster of threads, a Perspex container containing polythene balls, or a stack of aluminium foil tart cases;
  - light an LED from the top of the globe.

Ask the class to **interpret the evidence** and relate it to the movement and distribution of electrons. [O1, O2, O3]

High demand students should be able to think in terms of relative numbers of electrons when **considering** the size of charge.

Explain

- **Pair work** Allocate different electrostatic effects to pairs of students. Each pair produces a poster for display to **explain** their effect. Ensure that all effects are covered across the class. [O1, O2, O3]

  High demand students should be able to use their posters to **explain** more challenging ideas in greater depth.

Consolidate and apply

- Ask the students to **compare** how noticeable the attraction is between two recently charged rods and then between ones that have been left for some time. Can they explain the difference in terms of loss of electrons to the surroundings? [O1, O2, O3]

- As reinforcement, ask the students to complete task 3 of Worksheet 1.2.7. [O1, O2, O3]

  Task 3 of the worksheet provides extra challenge for high demand students.

Extend

- Ask students able to progress further to **find out** how the theory of static electricity developed.

Plenary suggestions

The big ideas Ask the students to write down, individually, three things they have learned during the lesson. Then ask them to **share** their facts in groups and to **compile** a master list of facts, with the most important at the top. Take feedback. [O1, O2, O3]

Answers to Student Book questions

1. Protons; neutrons; electrons.
2. There are equal numbers of protons (positive charge) and electrons (negative charge) so the charge is balanced/neutralised.
3. By gaining electrons.
4. By losing electrons.
5. Electrons are transferred from the rod to the cloth; so the cloth becomes negatively charged.
6. Charging involves electrons being transferred. Some pairs of materials transfer electrons more easily than others; in some cases, electrons may be transferred from the rod to the cloth.
7. The strands start to repel each other and your head; some of them may start to rise up and stand out.
8. You could hold the comb near something such as bits of tissue paper, to show that they were attracted.
9. The electrons gradually leak away from the comb; your hair gains electrons from the comb or its surroundings.

Answers to Worksheet 1.2.7

1. a) Diagram should show the charges of the particles as well as labels for protons, electrons and neutrons.
   b) When it is rubbed, it loses electrons.
2. a) Attraction happens when positive is brought towards negative; repulsion occurs between positive and positive or negative and negative.
   b) A: one rod with + signs, one with − signs; B and C: both rods + or both rods − .
   c) Diagrams and labels should show charges and attraction/repulsion.
3. a) Atoms contain positive particles in the nucleus; which are surrounded by negative particles; some of which are free to move. When positive and negative particles no longer balance; an object is statically charged.
   b) LED being lit; electrical sparks; insulators and conductors behave differently.

1.2.8 Understanding electric fields

Lesson overview

Learning objectives

- Explain static electricity in terms of fields.
- Explain how charged objects affect each other.

Learning outcomes

- Describe the electric field around a charged object. [O1]
- Explain how we can use the idea of a field in relation to static charge. [O2]
- Use the idea of induced charge to explain field effects and compare this with magnetism. [O3]

Skills development

- Working scientifically: 2.13 Estimate risks
- Developing numeracy: use positive and negative values
- Developing literacy: construct explanations (Q7 & 8)

Resources needed nylon and polythene rods; woollen sock or cloth; gold leaf electroscope; tin can; balloon; digital coulombmeter (optional); Worksheet 1.2.8; Technician's notes 1.2.8

Key vocabulary electrostatic field

Teaching and learning

Engage

- Demonstrate the deflection of a fine stream of water by a charged rod (or refer to Figure 1.2.8a in the Student Book). Tell the students that the water has no charge and in this lesson they will try to solve the problem of how uncharged materials can be attracted or repelled. [O1, O2, O3]

- Ask the students to **devise questions** about what they need to know to **solve** the problem of water being deflected. [O1, O2, O3]

  High demand students may make links to magnets attracting some unmagnetised materials.

Challenge and develop

- Ask the students to **identify evidence** that a wall is not normally charged (dust does not stick or no reading on a coulombmeter). They then **observe** the failure of an uncharged balloon to stick to a wall and the sticking of a charged balloon. [O1, O2]

- Present the students with four possible models of charge distribution on the surface of a normal wall: no charges; even distribution of positive and negative charges; all negative charges; all positive charges. The students **use evidence** from previous lessons to choose the best model (even distribution of positive and negative charges). [O1, O2]

- Ask the students to **suggest** ideas about the effect of bringing a negatively charged balloon towards a wall. (The field from the balloon repels electrons in the wall, leaving the surface positive. Refer to Figure 1.2.8b in the Student Book.) [O1, O2, O3]

  High demand students may be able to **suggest** how their ideas could be tested (e.g. using a coulombmeter to see if the change in charge distribution can be detected).

Explain

- Demonstrate a gold leaf electroscope. Challenge the students to **explain** how the charge is distributed during the charging and discharging. Ask them to **draw diagrams**. [O1, O2]

High demand students could be challenged to **describe** this without the use of diagrams to **develop** their skills in written explanations.

Consolidate and apply

- The students **observe** how a gold leaf electroscope can be charged using a cloth and rod in a tin can, so that the leaf remains deflected because the charge is conserved. See Technician's notes 1.2.8 for more details about the procedure. [O1, O2]

- The students complete the tasks in Worksheet 1.2.8. [O1, O2]

- They **compare** the effects they have seen in the lesson to magnetic field effects. [O3]

Extend

- Students able to progress further can **observe** and **explain** the effect of the electrostatic field round a charged object as it is brought towards the electroscope. [O3]

Plenary suggestions

Revisit starter The students revisit the questions they devised at the start of the lesson and provide answers. [O1, O2, O3]

What we have learned The students **write a summary** of the main learning points on large sheets of paper. The papers are circulated so that ideas are **shared**. Different groups **clarify** any doubts or contradictions and finalise their learning points. [O1, O2, O3]

Answers to Student Book questions

1. An electrostatic field.
2. The water is attracted; even though it is not touching the rod.
3. Equal numbers of positive and negative charges; balance each other.
4. A positive field attracts negative particles; and repels positive particles; and vice versa.
5. Diagram should show an even distribution of + and – charges in unaffected water; and an uneven distribution in the affected water; showing attraction of negative particles towards the positive charges on the rod.
6. The metal is a good conductor; so the charge can flow away.
7. In damp weather the static charge can become neutralised; because electrons are transported by the water in the air.
8. a) The globe is positive so it attracts electrons from the person.

   b) Electrons flow onto the globe; so the positive charge is neutralised.
9. Avoid situations with pairs of materials rubbing against each other that can produce a charge, such as certain clothing or brush materials moved across hair.

Answers to Worksheet 1.2.8

1. a) + and – charges should be drawn evenly distributed.

   b) Both balloons are negatively charged; and repel each other.

   c) Diagram should show the balloon hanging down; at an angle; because it is attracted towards the rod.

   d) The balloon should be hanging at an angle; away from the rod; or be moving away.
2. a) A: insulator; B: copper strip; C: gold leaf.

   b) When the electroscope is charged; the gold leaf is repelled from the copper strip; because they have the same charge.

   c) There is an induced negative charge on the gold, and the lower part of the copper strip; causing repulsion.

   d) Charge a rod on a cloth, so that electrons are transferred to the rod. Bring the rod towards the cap of the electroscope so that the leaf deflects. Touch the cap so that electrons can flow away from the electroscope. Remove the rod, which leaves the electroscope positively charged.
3. a) Give an electroscope a known charge. Bring the object with unknown charge towards the electroscope. If the leaf drops, the unknown charge is the opposite to the charge on the electroscope.

   b) Compare the degree of deflection of the gold leaf, when the objects are held at a set distance from the disc.

1.2.9 Checking students' progress

The *Checking your progress* section in the Student Book indicates the key ideas developed in this chapter and shows how students progress to more complex levels. It is provided to support students in:

- identifying those ideas;

- developing a sense of their current level of understanding;

- developing a sense of what the next steps in their learning are.

It is designed to be used either at the end of a chapter to support an overall view of the progress, or alternatively during the teaching of the chapter. Students can self-assess or peer-assess using this as a basis.

It is helpful to encourage students to provide evidence from their understanding or their notes to support their judgements. In some cases it may be useful to explore the difference in the descriptors for a particular idea so that students can see what makes for a 'higher outcome'.

It may be useful with some descriptors to provide examples from the specific work done, such as an experiment undertaken or an explanation developed and recorded. If marking and feedback uses similar ideas and phrases this will enable students to relate specific marking to a more general sense of progress.

To make good progress in understanding science students need to focus on these ideas and skills:

Students who are making modest progress will be able to:	Students who are making good progress will be able to:	Students who are making excellent progress will be able to:
Explain how conductors and insulators are used in electrical safety.	Suggest and follow appropriate safety strategies when using circuits.	Suggest ways of safety management based on information about the electricity being used.
Recognise arrangements of electric circuit components in series and in parallel.	Use circuit diagrams to construct real series and parallel circuits and vice versa.	Suggest the advantages of series and parallel circuits for particular applications.
Describe what is meant by current, voltage and resistance.	Apply a range of models and analogies to describe current, voltage and resistance.	Evaluate different models and analogies for explaining current, voltage and resistance.
Know that a complete circuit is needed for current to flow.	Know that current is a movement of electrons and is therefore a flow of charge.	Know that current is divided between the loops in a parallel circuit.
Know that resistance reduces the current flowing.	Explain the idea of resistance using models such as water flow in pipes.	Understand that resistance is the ratio of voltage to current.
Understand that voltage is also called potential difference and this makes current flow around a circuit.	Understand that in a series circuit the potential difference is shared by the components.	Understand that potential difference is the amount of energy transferred from the battery to the charge or from the charge to the components.
Describe the relationship between current, voltage and resistance in a qualitative way.	Use data to identify a pattern between current, voltage and resistance.	Use data and the mathematical relationship between current, voltage and resistance to carry out calculations.
Describe the effect that a charged object has on other charged objects.	Explain what is meant by an electrostatic field.	Suggest how objects may become electrostatically charged.
Know the two types of static charge.	Explain how electron transfer can result in either type of charge.	Explain the operation of a circuit using the idea of electrons moving from the negative to the positive terminals of a power supply.
Describe how friction between objects may cause electrostatic charge through the transfer of electrons.	Explain various examples of electrostatic charge; use ideas of electron transfer to explain different effects.	Explain why some electrostatic charge mechanisms are more effective than others.

1.2.10 Answers to Student Book end of chapter questions

This table provides answers to the Questions section at the end of Chapter 2 of the Student Book. It also shows how different questions assess attainment in terms of the focus and style of a question as well as its context. Question-level analysis can indicate a student's proficiency in approaching different aspects of scientific understanding and different types of answer.

Q	Answer	Marks available	Focus			Style			Context		
			Knowledge & understanding	Application	Evaluation of evidence	Objective test question	Short written answer	Longer written answer	Circuits	Static electricity	
1	c	1	x			x			x		
2	Any two from: • series components are connected one after the other; in one continuous loop • parallel components are connected separately in their own loop; between the terminals of a cell • parallel circuits have branches	2	x				x		x		
3	c	1	x			x				x	
4	c	1		x		x			x		
5	Increased voltage would be shown by the 'boots' 'kicking harder'.	1		x			x		x		
	Increased resistance would be indicated by the pipes being narrower.	1		x			x		x		
6	Suitable response, e.g. test if one rod can pick up more small identical pieces of paper or if one rod can attract small identical pieces of paper from further away than the other rod.	2		x			x			x	
7	Graph correctly plotted, with scaled axes and labels 	4			x			x	x		
8	a)	1	X				X		X		
	b) 0.25A	1		X			X		X		
	c) Ammeter added to either side of the cells (i.e. not adjacent to either bulb)	1		x			X		X		
	d) The other will stay lit	1	x				x		x		
	Total possible	17	6	7	4	3	10	4		14	3	

1.3.0 Energy: Introduction

When and how to use these pages

The Introduction in the Student Book indicates some of the ideas and skills in this topic area that students will already have met from KS2 or from previous KS3 work. It also provides an indication of what they will be studying in this chapter. *Ideas you have met before* is not intended to comprehensively summarise all of the prior ideas, but rather to point out a few of the key ones and to support the view that scientific understanding is progressive. Even though students might be meeting contexts that are new to them, they can often use existing ideas to start to make sense of them.

In this chapter you will find out indicates some of the new ideas that the chapter will introduce. Again, it isn't a detailed summary of content. Its purpose is more to act as a 'trailer' and generate some interest.

The outcomes, then, will be: recognition of prior learning that can be built on; and interest in finding out more.

There are a number of ways this can be used. You might, for example:

- use *Ideas you have met before* as the basis for a revision lesson as you start the first new topic
- use *Ideas you have met before* as the centre of spider diagrams, to which students can add examples, experiments they might have done previously or what they found interesting
- make a note of any unfamiliar/difficult terms and return to these in the relevant lessons
- use *In this chapter you will find out* to ask students questions such as:
  - Why is this important?
  - How could it be used?
  - What might we be doing in this topic?

Overview of the chapter

For many students this will be the first time they have formally studied the concept of energy. Although they will have used the term before and will have ideas about what it means, this is nevertheless a good opportunity to explore some key features.

The chapter starts by considering food as a personal energy store and then looks at energy being transferred, and at different rates. The concept of 'stores and transfers' is then explored. The chapter uses the model adopted by the current KS3 Programme of Study (and the GCSE specifications) in which energy transfer is seen not as a cause of changes but as a result of those changes. Energy is understood as residing in stores and being transferred from one store to another if changes happen.

The idea of energy is then applied to the context of electricity supply. Electricity is useful for a number of reasons but a principal one is the ease with which energy can be transferred in a variety of different ways. Later in the chapter the concepts of kinetic energy, elastic potential energy and gravitational potential energy are introduced and used as ways of understanding transfers.

Obstacles to learning

Students may need extra guidance with the following terms and concepts:

- **Energy transfer and change:** It is often thought that the transfer of energy causes change. It does not: energy is transferred as a result of change. The quantity of energy stored before the change is the same as the quantity stored after the change, even though the form of storage has changed (conservation of energy). Students' instinct may be to use phrases such as energy 'all being used up' or something as having 'run out of energy'; these are less helpful ideas than asking where the energy has been transferred to. It is a common misconception that energy can be converted into a force, and also that it can be created. Students may also think that energy cannot be transferred from one object to another unless they are in physical contact.

- **Potential energy:** Students may perceive 'potential' energy as being different from 'real' energy. It is harder to understand that an object being squashed or raised up has energy in the same way that a moving object does.

- **Gravitational potential energy:** Students may think that gravitational potential energy (GPE) depends on the route an object took to gain height or upon its speed. They may not appreciate how it is related to mass or height.
- **Elastic potential energy:** Students may think that this energy store is linked to tension only and not to compression, or that it is unrelated to how easy it is to stretch or compress something.
- **Motion:** Students may think that 'motion energy' isn't linked to the mass of an object, or is always greater for lighter objects (because they move faster), or doesn't apply to objects that are falling.

How the Programme of Study is covered by the Student Book

Big idea	Topic	Lesson	Programme of study reference
Energy	Energy costs	1.3.1 Understanding energy transfers by fuels and food	Energy as a quantity that can be quantified and calculated; the total energy has the same value before and after a change Comparing energy values of different foods (from labels) (kJ) Other processes that involve energy transfer: metabolism of food, burning fuels
		1.3.2 Comparing rates of energy transfers	Comparing power ratings of appliances in watts (W, kW) Comparing amounts of energy transferred (J, kJ, kW hour)
		1.3.3 Looking at the cost of energy use in the home	Comparing power ratings of appliances in watts (W, kW) Comparing amounts of energy transferred (J, kJ, kW hour) Domestic fuel bills: fuel use and costs
		1.3.4 Getting the electricity we need	Calculation of fuel uses and costs in the domestic context: fuels and energy resources
		1.3.5 Using electricity responsibly	Calculation of fuel uses and costs in the domestic context: comparing power ratings of appliances in watts (W, kW), comparing amounts of energy transferred (J, kJ, kW hour), domestic fuel bills, fuel use and costs and fuels and energy resources
	Energy transfers	1.3.6 Energy stores and transfers	Processes that involve energy transfer and changes in systems, including: energy as a quantity that can be quantified and calculated; comparing the starting with the final conditions of a system and describing increases and decreases in the amounts of energy
		1.3.7 Exploring energy transfers	Other processes that involve energy transfer: changing motion, dropping an object, completing an electrical circuit, burning fuels Energy as a quantity that can be quantified and calculated; the total energy has the same value before and after a change.
		1.3.8 Understanding potential energy and kinetic energy	Other processes that involve energy transfer: changing motion, dropping an object
		1.3.9 Understanding elastic potential energy	Other processes that involve energy transfer: stretching a spring. Work done and energy changes on deformation. Comparing the starting with the final conditions of a system and describing increases and decreases in the amounts of energy in elastic distortions

How the AQA KS3 Syllabus is covered by the Student Books and Teacher Guide

Energy costs

	Student Book	Teacher Guide
Know		
We pay for our domestic electricity usage based on the amount of energy transferred.	3.3	3.3
Electricity is generated by a combination of resources which each have advantages and disadvantages.	3.4	3.4
Calculate the cost of home energy usage, using the formula: cost = power (kW) x time (hours) x price (per kWh).	3.3	3.3

	SB	TG
Fact: Food labels list the energy content of food in kilojoules (kJ).	3.1	3.1
Power: How quickly energy is transferred by a device (watts).	3.2	3.2
Energy resource: Something with stored energy that can be released in a useful way.	(3.4)	(3.4)
Non-renewable: An energy resource that cannot be replaced and will be used up.	3.4	3.4
Renewable: An energy resource that can be replaced and will not run out. Examples are solar, wind, waves, geothermal and biomass.	3.4	3.4
Fossil fuels: Non-renewable energy resources formed from the remains of ancient plants or animals. Examples are coal, crude oil and natural gas.	3.4	3.4
Apply		
Compare the amounts of energy transferred by different foods and activities.	3.1, 3.2	3.1, 3.2
Compare the energy usage and cost of running different home devices.	3.2	3.2
Explain the advantages and disadvantages of different energy resources.	3.5	3.5
Represent the energy transfers from a renewable or non-renewable resource to an electrical device in the home.	3.4, 3.5, 3.6	3.4, 3.5, 3.6
Extend		
Evaluate the social, economic and environmental consequences of using a resource to generate electricity, from data.	3.5	3.5
Suggest actions a government or communities could take in response to rising energy demand.	3.5	3.5
Suggest ways to reduce costs, by examining data on a home energy bill.	3.3, 3.5	3.3, 3.5

Energy transfer

	Student Book	Teacher Guide
	SB	TG
Know		
We can describe how jobs get done using an energy model where energy is transferred from one store at the start to another at the end.	3.6	3.6
When energy is transferred, the total is conserved, but some energy is dissipated, reducing the useful energy.	3.7	3.7
Thermal energy store: Filled when an object is warmed up.	3.6	3.6
Chemical energy store: Emptied during chemical reactions when energy is transferred to surroundings.	3.6	3.6
Kinetic energy store: Filled when an object speeds up.	3.6	3.6
Gravitational potential energy store: Filled when an object is raised.	3.6	3.6
Elastic energy store: Filled when a material is stretched or compressed.	3.6	3.6
Dissipated: Become spread out wastefully.	3.6	3.6
Apply		
Describe how the energy of an object depends on its speed, temperature, height or whether it is stretched or compressed.	3.6	3.6
Show how energy is transferred between energy stores in a range of real-life examples.	3.6, 3.7	3.6, 3.7
Calculate the useful energy and the amount dissipated, given values of input and output energy.	3.7	3.7
Explain how energy is dissipated in a range of situations.	3.7	3.7
Extend		
Compare the percentages of energy wasted by renewable energy sources.	(3.4, 3.6, 3.7)	3.4
Explain why processes such as swinging pendulums or bouncing balls cannot go on forever, in terms of energy.		3.6
Evaluate analogies and explanations for the transfer of energy.		3.7

1.3.1 Understanding energy transfer by fuels and food

Lesson overview

Learning objectives
- Describe the use of fuels in the home.
- Explain that foods are energy stores and that the amount stored can be measured.
- Explain that energy is not a material and can be neither created nor destroyed.

Learning outcomes
- Recall the types of fuel used in the home. [O1]
- Explain that foods store different quantities of energy that can be measured. [O2]
- Explain that when energy is transferred from fuels and food, the total amount of energy before and after remains the same; it is just stored differently. [O3]

Skills development
- Working scientifically: 2.14 Examine consequences
- Developing numeracy: extract and interpret data
- Developing literacy: extract evidence to support the construction of explanations (Q4 - 6)

Resources needed food packets or labels; various electrical appliances with their power ratings showing; Worksheet 1.3.1 (the final page copied onto card); Technician's notes 1.3.1.

Key vocabulary fuel, kilowatt-hour (kWh), joule

Teaching and learning

Engage
- Ask the students how their home is heated, how they get hot water at home and which electrical appliances are in their home. This is not a 'competition' and needs to be approached sensitively. An alternative might be for the students to ask the question of other teachers in school, but the students will need advance warning (e.g. during the previous lesson). It might also help if teachers are primed that this will happen. [O1]

Challenge and develop
- Ask the students to read the 'Fuels and energy in the home' section in the Student Book and to answer questions 1–3. [O1]
- **Pair work** When they have answered the first three Student Book questions, ask the students to complete task 1 of Worksheet 1.3.1. This might be done competitively, with students working in pairs to **solve** the puzzle. When they have finished they can hand in their answers and when all have finished, the first correct answer to have been handed in can be identified. [O1]
- Review with the students what they know about the energy content of food. If possible it would be helpful to have a variety of food packets and labels to look at. Discuss how energy is stored in the body. [O2]
- Ask them to **recall** earlier work and to state how the energy content of food is measured. [O2]

Explain
- Ask the students to answer questions 4–6 in the Student Book and then to complete task 2 of Worksheet 1.3.1. The final question in the task could be part of a whole class discussion about energy intake and expenditure. Make sure that the students **understand** the central idea of transfer, together with the concept of conservation of energy. [O2]
- Remind the students of previous lessons in which they learned about energy stores and transfers. Ask them to **give some reasons** why the rate of energy transfer is important. [O2]
- Ask the students to read the 'Transfers and stores' section in the Student Book and to answer questions 7 and 8. [O3]

Consolidate and apply

- Ask the students to complete task 3 of Worksheet 1.3.1. [O3]

Extend

- Ask students able to progress further to **think of** different ways that transferred energy is stored. Ask them to **consider** what is meant by the terms 'useful energy' and 'wasted energy'. This will re-introduce the idea that not all of the energy is transferred in a desired change – for example an electric light bulb also generates heat. Ask students to **discuss** what they think is meant by the 'efficiency' of an electrical appliance. [O3]

Plenary suggestions

Summaries Arrange the students in pairs. Ask each pair to **write a sentence** that summarises something that they have learned in the lesson. Encourage pairs to **share** their statement with the class. [O1, O2, O3]

Answers to Student Book questions

1. Gas; coal; oil; wood.
2. Electricity meter; gas meter.
3. a) Electricity can be used to power a wide range of appliances, small amounts can be stored and transported easily and it is clean at the point of use. However it can dangerous at high voltages and some of the ways of producing it are polluting.

    b) Gas can be used to transfer energy as thermal energy and controlled very easily; it is well suited to domestic applications such as cooking and heating. However it is flammable and can cause explosions. Incomplete combustion releases dangerous gases and all combustion is polluting.
4. The body makes compounds from food, which act as energy stores in the body's cells.
5. It helps people to choose healthy diets.
6. The table shows that the 100g sample contains 1347 kJ of energy.
7. Any suitably described physical or chemical change: for example, heating water in a kettle, where energy is transferred to the water, the kettle and the surroundings; or burning a candle, where energy is transferred to the products of combustion (carbon dioxide and water) and to the surroundings.
8. a) It is being transferred as thermal energy.

    b) It is being transferred from the chemical store in the wax to the thermal store of the surroundings.

Answers to Worksheet 1.3.1

1. The use of gas and electricity in homes is measured using meters.
2. a) *Very low*: 0.10 – 0.52 kJ/g; *Low*: 0.63 – 1.48 kJ/g; *Medium*: 1.6 – 3.7 kJ/g; *High*: 4.1 – 8.9 kJ/g

    b) i) 2360.4 kJ ii) 3927.0 kJ

    c) If energy intake exceeds energy expenditure, the body's food store increases, and so does body mass.
3. a) They would be the same

    b) Light

    c) If less heat is produced less energy needs to be supplied to have the same brightness so the bulb will be cheaper to run.

    d) In this case the thermal energy released is the useful output and the light is wasted.

1.3.2 Comparing rates of energy transfers

Lesson overview

Learning objectives

- Describe what is meant by 'rate of energy transfer'.
- Recall and use the correct units for rate of energy transfer.
- Calculate quantities of energy transferred when change happens.

Learning outcomes

- Recall that the rate of energy transferred is calculated as the quantity transferred divided by the time taken for it to be transferred. [O1]
- Use the watt as the unit of energy transfer in calculations. [O2]
- Calculate quantities of energy transferred using power ratings and time measurements. [O3]

Skills development

- Working scientifically: 2.3 Draw conclusions
- Developing numeracy: use formulae to calculate solutions
- Developing literacy: extract information from text to use (Q7, 8 & 9)

Resources needed sticky notes; 100 cm^3 and 400 cm^3 beakers; cotton wool (or other insulating material); thermometer; hot water; a number of electrical/electronic devices that have their power ratings shown; Worksheet 1.3.2; Technician's note 1.3.2.

Key vocabulary power, watt, kilowatt

Teaching and learning

Engage

- Ask the students to **write** on a sticky note one reason why it might be necessary to control the speed of energy transfer, **giving** an example to illustrate. Ask them, one by one, to stick their notes on a wall. As each new note is added, rearrange them into groups containing similar reasons and examples. [O1]

Challenge and develop

- It is likely that one group of sticky notes will be about keeping things warm by slowing down the rate of energy transfer. Demonstrate this by showing the difference between how quickly water cools when it is in a glass beaker compared with when the water is in a glass beaker that is placed in a larger beaker with insulating material packed in the gap between the two. [O1]
- Ask the students to read the 'Comparing rates of energy transfers' section in the Student Book and to answer questions 1–3. Some may find the everyday use of the word 'power' and its scientific meaning a little confusing. [O1]
- Ask the students to complete task 1 of Worksheet 1.3.2. [O1]
- Raise the question of what units might be used to measure the rate of energy transfer. [O2]

Explain

- Introduce the watt as the unit for measuring the quantity of energy (joules) transferred per second. Arrange a variety of electrical/electronic devices so that the students can move around the room to look at them. Ask the students to **write down** what they are and their power ratings. [O2]
- Reinforce the use of units by asking the students to answer questions 4–6 in the Student Book. [O2]
- Ask them to complete task 2 of Worksheet 1.3.2. The students could work in pairs, especially for part c). [O2]
- Follow up the work on comparing rates of energy transfer by asking the students to read the 'Quantities of energy transferred' section in the Student Book and to answer questions 7 and 8. [O3]

Consolidate and apply

- **Pairs** Ask the students to complete task 3 of Worksheet 1.3.2. [O3]
- Encourage the students to **share** with the class the benefits and disadvantages they listed for using standby modes on electronic devices and gadgets. [O3]

Extend

- Ask students able to progress further to look at the information from the Energy Saving Trust's website and from its report 'Powering the nation – household electricity-using habits revealed', which are detailed on Worksheet 1.3.2. Ask them to **explain** why turning off devices, rather than just leaving them on standby, might reduce the energy consumed by up to 16%. [O3]

Plenary suggestions

Learning triangle Ask the students to draw a learning triangle (a large triangle with a smaller inverted triangle that just fits inside it, so there are four triangles in total). Ask them to think about the lesson and to write in the outer three triangles something that they've seen, something that they've done and something that they've discussed. Then ask them to add in the central triangle something that they've learned. [O1, O2, O3]

Answers to Student Book questions

1. 2000 W.
2. a) Electric oven. b) Laptop
3. 100 J.
4. It needs to transfer energy quickly.
5. 10 W.
6. 20 J/s.
7. 216 kJ.
8. 4500 J (4.5 kJ).
9. a) 2 592 000 J (2592 kJ) b) 864 000 J (864 kJ)

Answers to Worksheet 1.3.2

1. a) Decreases; stored; conduction.

   b) All curves should start at 80 $^\circ$C and show that the rate of cooling slows down until they reach the same room temperature.

   i) The graph for the *copper can* should have the steepest initial curve, showing the fastest rate of cooling.

   ii) The graph for the *glass beaker* should be the next steepest.

   iii) The graph for the *polystyrene cup* should be the least steep.

   The difference in the steepness of the initial curve should be bigger between copper and glass, than it is between glass and polystyrene.

2. a) The rate of transfer of energy. b) 65 J.

   c) i) E has a higher power rating than A.

   ii) The power can be changed from the lowest value (defrosting) to the highest value (high).

   iii) Measure the temperature rise in a given volume of water heated for a specified length of time; calculate the energy transferred in a certain time for each appliance; a number of times.

3. a) Energy needed = 4.2 × 300 × (100 – 20) = 100 800 J (or 100.8 kJ).

   b) Time taken = 100 800 ÷ 2000 = 50.4 seconds.
   It will take a little longer because some energy is transferred to the kettle itself and to the surroundings. The faster the kettle boils, the lower this unwanted energy transfer will be.

   c) The summary needs to highlight the convenience of the standby mode (e.g. easy to pick up the remote control and turn the TV on), but contrast this with the extra energy consumed and paid for while devices are in standby mode.

1.3.3 Looking at the cost of energy use in the home

Lesson overview

Learning objectives
- Describe the information a typical fuel bill provides.
- Explain and use the units used on a fuel bill.
- Explain how the cost of energy used can be calculated.

Learning outcomes
- Recall the type of information given on a fuel bill. [O1]
- Explain units of energy and how they are converted from one to another. [O2]
- Calculate the cost of energy from information about power and time. [O3]

Skills development
- Working scientifically: 2.4 Present data
- Developing numeracy: extract and use data to perform calculations
- Developing literacy: identify and suggest various solutions (Q7)

Resources needed Worksheet 1.3.3

Common misconceptions Energy is consumed in homes, which implies that it is being used up.

Key vocabulary kilowatt-hour (kWh)

Teaching and learning

Engage
- Ask the students to **think about** previous lessons and to **write down** the units used for the quantity of energy and the rate of energy transfer (power). [O1, O2]

Challenge and develop
- Ask the students to look at Figure 1.3.3a in the Student Book. Read the 'Fuel bills' section of the Student Book as a class and then ask the students to work in pairs to answer questions 1–3. [O1, O2]
- **Pair work** Next, ask the students to work in pairs and read through the two sections 'Calculating the energy used by domestic appliances' and 'Calculating the cost of energy used' in the Student Book. They should then answer Student Book questions 4–7. [O2, O3]

Explain
- To reinforce their answers to Student Book questions 1–3, ask the students to complete task 1 of Worksheet 1.3.3. [O1, O2]
- Similarly, to reinforce their learning and their answers to Student Book questions 4–7, ask the students to complete task 2 of Worksheet 1.3.3. [O2, O3]

Consolidate and apply
- **Pair work** The lesson has focused on energy calculations. To draw many of the ideas together, ask the students to work in pairs to complete task 3 of Worksheet 1.3.3. [O2, O3]

Extend
- Ask students able to progress further to **think about** the relative costs of electricity and gas, and to **explain** why electricity is more expensive than gas. [O3]

Plenary suggestions

Highlighting uncertainties Ask the students to **write down** one thing about energy (quantities, rates of transfer and use in the home) that they are sure of, one thing that they are unsure of and one thing that they need to know more about – they should be specific. Then, working in groups of five or six, ask the students to **share** and **discuss** what they have written. This discussion may lead to some students gaining a better understanding of previous uncertainties, and it may also lead to new uncertainties emerging. After the discussion ask each group to **share** what they is confident about, what they are less sure about and what they need to know more about. Draw these responses together to identify revision topics. [O1, O2, O3]

Answers to Student Book questions

1. One joule is a very small amount of energy; the numbers would be too large to write on a bill.
2. a) £17.36 b) £19.24
3. A standing charge pays for fixed costs (e.g. keeping the home connected to the network, meter reading, maintenance, emergency gas supplies, and government initiatives such as carbon-reduction commitments and supporting vulnerable households). [Note: Students do not need to know all of these, just that the energy costs to a consumer are more than the fuel itself.]
4. a) 3600 kJ

   b) 360 kJ

   c) 108 kJ
5. *Energy* is a quantity stored in different ways. *Power* is a measure of how quickly energy is transferred during a change.
6. a) 1.08p

   b) 4.00p

   c) Gas is a cheaper fuel looking at the cost per unit of energy. Running the gas oven costs more because the oven has to be run for much longer.
7. Various ways of reducing energy consumption, e.g.turning off appliances not being used, such as light bulbs, ensuring insulation is effective, such as hot water tanks and house insulation, ensuring devices are efficient, such as replacing filament bulbs with low energy light bulbs,ensuring thermostats are not set too high.

Answers to Worksheet 1.3.3

1. a) Meter 1 is for electricity (units kWh); meter 2 is for gas (units m^3/h).

   b) Meter 1: 6543 kWh; meter 2: 8634 m^3.

   c) An energy company has fixed costs that are the same no matter how much energy is used (e.g. maintenance work, billing costs). These costs are covered by the standing charge. The other cost is for the fuel consumed, which varies from home to home and from month to month.
2. a) 6.5p

   b) 3.2p
3. Students are not expected to give a detailed method. Equal volumes of water must be used, and the temperature rise must be the same in each case. Suitable suggestions should be made for measuring the quantity of energy transferred by electric current and by burning gas (the volume of gas used would need to be measured). There should be a considered safety assessment. Repeat data should be obtained to check reliability.

1.3.4 Getting the electricity we need

Lesson overview

Learning objectives

- Describe ways of generating electricity.
- Explain advantages and disadvantages of different methods.
- Evaluate the consequences of using various generating method.

Learning outcomes

- Identify several different ways of producing electricity on a large scale. [O1]
- For each of these, identify advantages and disadvantages. [O2]
- Produce a balanced view of the contribution a particular method could make. [O3]

Skills development

- Working scientifically: 2.13 Estimate risks
- Developing numeracy: extract and use data from tables
- Developing literacy: explain differences and compare and contrast situations (Q6 - 10)

Resources needed a hand-crank dynamo (or device such as a hand-crank torch or radio); a domestic appliance (e.g. lamp, hairdryer, food whisk); images of power-generation methods (conventional, nuclear and renewable); a hand-held water wheel or windmill; an electric kettle; Worksheet 1.3.4

Common misconceptions Students may not understand that any electricity generation system is simply transferring energy from one store to another and that the quantities can be tracked. They may think that some processes can increase the amount of energy available.

Key vocabulary renewable, fossil fuel, environment, photovoltaic

Teaching and learning

Engage

- Show students a hand-crank device and ask them to explain in terms of energy transfer what is happening. [O1]
- Demonstrate an appliance such as a lamp, hairdryer or food whisk. Ask students to suggest where the energy came from, if it could ever run out and whether it is having any negative environmental impact. [O1, O2]
- Show students images of various power-generation methods and ask them to suggest what they are, how they work and what the implications of such installations are. [O1, O2]

Challenge and develop

- Show students a diagram similar to Fig 1.3.4a and explain briefly how generating electricity works. Explain various stages by use of a kettle, windmill or water wheel (similar to turbine), and a hand-cranked device. Ask students to explain the energy transfers that are taking place. [O1]
- Show students an image of nuclear power station and explain that it is the first stage that is different to the fossil fuel power station. [O1]
- Show images of various renewable electricity systems and challenge students to identify what they are, how they work and the pros and cons of each. [O1, O2]

Explain

- Ask students to suggest for each of the three main fuel types (fossil, nuclear and renewable) how they might compare in terms of the factors listed under 'Making decisions about which generating methods to use' in the Student Book. [O2]
- Ask students to look at the table of typical costs (Table 1.3.4) and suggest why there is a range of costs. Ask students to suggest why the costs vary and to identify factors that might push the cost up or down. [O2]

Consolidate and apply

- Ask students to select a particular type of generation technology and summarise key characteristics of it. If students do this in groups, each taking a different one, findings can be compared. Then ask students to complete Worksheet 1.3.4. [O2, O3]
- Ask students to consult Table 1.3.4 and consider whether this would affect their judgment as to which technology to use to supply power to a particular area. Alternatively, give students a setting (an island works well) and ask them to suggest a means (or, better still, a combination of ways) to keep the area supplied with power. [O1, O2, O3]

Extend

- The 'supplying the island with power' activity can be extended by getting teams of students to compete for the contract to supply the island with power, pitching on the basis of operating cost (take median values from Table 1.3.4), environmental impact and reliability of supply. [O1, O2, O3]
- Ask students to suggest how geothermal energy might compare with the technologies listed in Table 1.3.4, in terms of environmental impact and reliability. [O1, O2, O3]
- Ask students to suggest why a combination of supply technologies might be a good idea. [O3]
- Challenge students who are capable of making further progress to research data on wasteful energy transfers by various renewable energy sources and use this to inform views about the value of these sources [O2, O3]

Plenary suggestions

- Divide the class into two and display a picture of a particular means of generating electricity. One team has to offer as many advantages and the other team as many disadvantages as they can.
- Set up a continuum line across the classroom whereby one end is labelled 'love it' and the other 'hate it'. As each kind of technology is called out, students stand at the point on the line they feel reflects their attitude. They can be challenged to explain why.

Answers to Student Book questions

1. Oil and gas (also peat).
2. a) Pollution; decreasing supply of fuel; b) Nuclear waste and contamination; decreasing supply of resource.
3. Release of gases such as carbon dioxide (greenhouse gas), sulphur dioxide or nitrous oxides (causing acid rain). Coal produces ash and soot.
4. If there is a leak the surrounding area could be contaminated with radioactive material. The used fuel rods from nuclear power stations stay dangerous for thousands of years and have to be contained.
5. There isn't a continuous supply either of sunshine or of wind so the energy would either need to be stored in some way or supplemented by some other source.
6. They may have an effect on the environment such as the appearance of landscapes (e.g. wind farms or solar cells) or affect wildlife (e.g. tidal barrages or hydro electric power)
7. The system would be entirely dependent on the price and supply of gas.
8. To reduce the emission of greenhouse gases and effect on climate change.
9. Susceptible to wave damage, less accessible so maintenance costs high, harder to bring power onto land.
10. The problem with coal isn't that it is inefficient but rather that it causes pollution and that coal supples are becomng exhausted.

Answers to Worksheet 1.3.4

1. It will put the land to good use, generating electricity which can be used or sold.
2. The exposed location means plenty of daylight, which is good, and the poor soil won't matter.
3. They won't need to pay for electricity to run the milking parlour and they can make a profit by selling spare electricity.
4. Heating water to turn it into steam.
5. Oil, gas, peat – anything that will burn and has a reasonably high energy content.
6. The pollution caused includes carbon dioxide (greenhouse gas), sulphur dioxide (acid rain), ash and soot.
7. Cold water will condense steam into water, so a good supply is useful.
8. Having the photovoltaic panels will reduce the pollution but they can't be relied on because they are dependent on daylight; so a fossil-fuelled station is needed as back up.

1.3.5 Using electricity responsibly

Lesson overview

Learning objectives

- Apply the concept of energy transfers to a device such as a hand-crank torch.
- Critique claims made for the running costs of fluorescent light bulbs.
- Evaluate actions that could be taken in response to rising energy demand.

Learning outcomes

- Develop an explanation about how energy has been transferred in a device. [O1]
- Comment on the arguments made for low-energy light bulbs. [O2]
- Propose and critically evaluate ideas to respond to rising energy demand. [O3]

Skills development

- Working scientifically: 2.14 Examine consequences
- Developing numeracy: extract and use data to perform calculations
- Developing literacy: justify ideas and suggest how ideas can be presented persuasively (Q8, 9 & 10)

Resources needed a hand-crank dynamo or device (e.g. a hand-crank torch or radio); filament and low-energy light bulbs (preferably with a similar light output), ideally both fluorescent and LED; mains supply energy meter; Worksheet 1.3.5; Technician's notes 1.3.5

Common misconceptions Students may imagine that all bulbs emitting similar amounts of light are using similar amounts of electrical energy.

Key vocabulary dissipated, fluorescent, filament

Teaching and learning

Engage

- Show students a hand-crank torch or radio and demonstrate how it is charged up and discharged. Ask students to suggest the relationship between the cranking and the amount of light. [O1]
- Explain that a similar situation exists in a car which has a large rechargeable battery, charged up by the engine and storing energy to be used in the starter motor the next time it is used. Ask students to suggest why this arrangement tends to work well in the summer but in the winter more cars get flat batteries. [O1]
- Ask students how long the power on their mobile phone lasts between charging up times and ask for suggestions as to why the figure varies quite a lot. [O1]

Challenge and develop

- Explain to students that although energy can be used to do a variety of things, it is all still energy (i.e. there aren't different types). Energy can be stored and it can be transferred between stores. Ask students to suggest how that can be applied to a device such as a hand-crank torch. [O1]
- Demonstrate one of the mains light bulbs and ask students to suggest where energy is being transferred from and to. [O1]
- Demonstrate different types of light bulb (filament, fluorescent and LED) and ask students to comment on why they think that some are more economical than others. [O1, O2]
- Explain to students how the running costs of one type of bulb are calculated and ask them questions to emphasise key points and ensure that understanding is clear. [O1, O2]

Explain

- Provide students with the data for two types of light bulb and ask them to do the calculations to get the figures for the annual cost. [O2]
- Alternatively use data from a local shop or online shopping to obtain the data. Students can be involved in doing this research. [O2]

- Ask students to read 'Investigating claims for low-energy light bulbs' in the Student Book and answer questions 4–7. [O2, O3]

Consolidate and apply

- Ask students to complete Worksheet 1.3.5, on choosing light bulbs. [O2, O3]

Extend

- There has been some controversy about the withdrawal of filament bulbs from the market by EU directive and some newspapers have run campaigns objecting to this, sometimes referring to the 'grey light' that low-energy bulbs produce. Provide students with an example of such an article (e.g. www.dailymail.co.uk/news/article-3394807/Light-bulbs-banned-EU-make-comeback-breakthrough-means-use-energy.html or www.livescience.com/3179-light-bulb-generates-controversy.html) and ask them to comment on the key points. [O2, O3]

Plenary suggestions

- Ask students to indicate the extent to which they are convinced that low-energy light bulbs should be used universally, and why.
- Ask students to devise a one-sentence catch phrase to promote low-energy light bulbs on a radio advertisement.

Answers to Student Book questions

1. It would charge the battery up more and the bulb could be lit for longer.
2. If they were in series they would be dimmer. If they were in parallel we would get more light but the battery would run down more quickly.
3. No – energy is being transferred from the person turning the handle.
4. The fluorescent bulb is cheaper to run.
5. Yes – the savings in electricity over the life of the bulb are more than the extra cost of the bulb.
6. Because it uses much less electricity.
7. The LED bulb will use 0.03 units per day, which will cost 0.39p. Over the year this is £1.43. If the LED bulb costs £10 but lasts 20 years this is 50p/year. The total is £1.38, less than the fluorescent bulb.
8. Depends on students' responses but should include justifications such as economical, not polluting and reliable. A good response is likely to include several types so that the environmental advantages of renewables can be used without the intermittent nature of some of them becoming a problem.
9. Answers might include: by being able to buy more energy-efficient appliances; by being told how to use less energy; by living in energy-efficient homes; by understanding how to save money overall.
10. Answers might include: show people calculations of the cost of buying/using the appliance over its lifetime; tell people about the links between electricity use and global warming.

Answers to Worksheet 1.3.5

1. Answers could include: release plenty of light, cheap to buy, not use too much electricity.
2. Answers could include: use much less electricity, don't waste energy as heat, last longer.
3. Answers could include: tend to be more expensive to buy, may not produce full amount of light output straight away.
4. One year.
5. £0.99
6. 2.4p
7. £8.76
8. £9.75
9. CF: 10 years, £0.50, 0.48p, £1.75, £2.25; LED: 20 years, £0.50, 0.24p, 0.88p, £1.38
10. a) If the light is used for fewer hours it will take longer for the low-energy bulbs to pay off their higher price.
    b) If electricity goes up in price all the light bulbs will be more expensive to run but the running costs of the filament bulb will increase more.
    c) If the LED bulb comes down in price it will cost less to run for the year.

1.3.6 Energy stores and transfers

Lesson overview

Learning objectives

- Investigate a model of energy.
- Describe energy stores and transfers.
- Apply the energy model to different situations.

Learning outcomes

- State examples of energy stores. [O1]
- Identify examples of ways in which energy is transferred. [O2]
- Use the 'stores and transfers' model of energy to explain a range of simple situations. [O3]

Skills development

- Working scientifically: 2.3 Draw conclusions
- Developing numeracy: understand how models can be used to represent changing quantities
- Developing literacy: critique application of an analogy (Q11)

Resources needed a variety of devices that transfer energy (e.g. torch, clockwork mouse, book to put up on shelf, toy car and ramp, Bunsen burner, solid fuel to burn, food to eat, pendulum); Worksheet 1.3.6; Technician's notes 1.3.6

Common misconceptions Students may regard energy as capable of being 'used up' or 'produced' and may find it counter-intuitive that the quantity of energy stored before the change is the same as the quantity stored after the change, even though the form of storage has changed. It is a common misconception that energy can be converted into a force, and also that it can be created. Students may also think that energy cannot be transferred from one object to another unless they are in physical contact.

Key vocabulary thermal energy store, chemical energy store, kinetic energy store, gravitational potential energy store, elastic energy store

Teaching and learning

Engage

- Show students a variety of situations in which energy is being transferred and ask them to collaborate in pairs to draft sentences to say what is happening. [O2]
- Ask students for suggestions about ways in which energy can be stored. Draw out some examples and make a list. [O1]

Challenge and develop

- Present students with a context such as a Bunsen burner heating a beaker of water and ask students to suggest what stores there are in this and how the energy is being transferred from one to another. Repeat with another context, such as the clockwork mouse. [O1, O2, O3]
- Show images or video clips and ask students to identify stores and transfers. [O1, O2, O3]

Explain

- Use 'Examples of stores and transfer' (cooker, swing, trampoline) from the Student Book and ask students to develop explanations of these using the model of energy being transferred from one store to another. [O1, O2, O3]
- Set up examples of energy transfers (bulb, buzzer, motor, weight being raised, etc.) as a circus of experiments for students to explore and develop explanations about the way in which energy is being transferred. [O1, O2, O3]

Consolidate and apply

- Ask students to identify their own examples of situations in which energy is being transferred and annotate sketches to show what is happening. [O3]
- Set up a pendulum and ask students to explain what is happening in terms of stores and transfers. [O3]

Extend

- Suggest, with examples such as the pendulum, or the Bunsen and water, that not all the energy is being transferred from one store to another (intended) store but rather that some energy is transferred in less useful ways. Ask students to identify other situations (such as ones explored in this lesson) in which the transfers are not completely efficient. [O3]
- Challenge students to suggest why processes such as swinging pendulums or bouncing balls cannot go on forever, in terms of energy. [O3]

Plenary suggestions

- Keep one of the examples to the end (e.g. food to be eaten) and ask students to identify the stores and transfers. [O1, O2, O3]
- Ask each group of students to identify a different way in which energy can be stored. [O1, O2]

Answers to Student Book questions

1. More energy will be transferred to the boxes.
2. Energy will be transferred to each of the boxes so if there are more boxes the total amount of energy transferred will be greater.
3. The energy is spread out (dissipated) and the temperature change is very small.
4. Range of answers possible, including catapult, clock spring, bungee line.
5. Some will go into the pot, some into the nearby parts of the cooker and some into the surroundings.
6. When the child is stationary they have no kinetic energy (KE) but even at the low point in the swing they are still above the ground and therefore still have some gravitational potential energy (GPE).
7. The pendulum is transferring energy between two stores – the bob's GPE store and its KE store.
8. As the ball falls energy is transferred from its GPE store to its KE store but on hitting the ground it is transferred to the ball's elastic energy store. It is then transferred back to the KE store and then to the GPE store.
9. Energy is gradually transferred to the environment, mainly via air resistance.
10. Energy is transferred to the environment, via air resistance, heat and sound.
11. This is a good way of showing that energy can be transferred from one store to another and that all the energy should be accounted for. In real energy transfers however, the process is rarely 100% efficient; often some energy is transferred to other stores.

Answers to Worksheet 1.3.6

1. a) No
   b) Yes
   c) Yes
   d) No
   e) Yes
2. a) Energy is being transferred from the microwave generator in the oven by waves to the food, increasing its thermal energy store.
   b) Energy is transferred from the chemical energy store in the battery by the flow of current and then light and heat to the surroundings, which is a store.
   c) Thermal energy is transferred from the store in the cup and drink to the surroundings, which store it.
3. Energy is transferred to the train, increasing its gravitational potential store as it climbs. As it runs down each slope, energy is transferred from its gravitational potential store to its kinetic energy store but transferred back again as it climbs the next slope. However, some energy is transferred to the environment as heat and sound, so the train's total energy becomes less and less.

1.3.7 Exploring energy transfers

Lesson overview

Learning objectives

- Recognise what energy is and its unit.
- Describe a range of energy transfers using simple diagrams.
- Use a Sankey diagram as a model to represent simple energy changes.

Learning outcomes

- Define the unit of energy and describe some simple energy transfers. [O1]
- Interpret and draw energy transfer diagrams. [O2]
- Use Sankey diagrams to explain a range of energy changes and demonstrate that all energy is accounted for. [O3]

Skills development

- Working scientifically: 2.15 Review theories
- Developing numeracy: communicate numerical information diagrammatically
- Developing literacy: translate between written and diagrammatically presented information (Q4, 5 & 7)

Resources needed range of items for demonstrating energy transfers (e.g. a simple electrical circuit switching on a bulb or a buzzer, a kettle, a candle burning, an iPod); images of energy transfers (e.g. torch, solar calculator, hand warmer, wind chime, solar panel, hairdryer, electric heater, a log fire, wind turbine, car, cake); squared paper; Worksheet 1.3.7; Technician's notes 1.3.7

Common misconceptions Energy is used up/created. Energy is a kind of stuff. Fuels are energy.

Key vocabulary joule, energy transfer diagram, Sankey diagram

Teaching and learning

Engage

- Write the word 'ENERGY' on the board and ask the students to provide as many words as they can which they associate with it. Turn this into a mind map. [O1]

Challenge and develop

- Demonstrate a range of energy transfers. This could include a simple electrical circuit switching on a bulb or a buzzer, a kettle, a candle burning or someone running on the spot. Tell the students that all these changes involve energy. [O1]
- Explore the meaning of the term 'energy' during these demonstrations, and remind students that the unit for energy is the joule (J). Ensure that the students understand that energy is transferred in a number of ways, including by electricity, heat, movement, sound and light. You could mention the term 'kinetic energy' for energy transferred by movement. [O1]
- Discuss the energy transfers in each of the demonstration scenarios and model how to draw simple energy transfer diagrams, and also, for higher-attaining students, Sankey diagrams to represent them (see the Student Book).

  Emphasise the fact that all energy is always accounted for – it cannot be created or destroyed, only transferred by different processes. Students can attempt the tasks on Worksheet 1.3.7. [O1, O2, O3]

  Task 3 on Worksheet 1.3.7 asks high demand students to **draw Sankey diagrams** using the given values.

Explain

- Group the students in ability groups of four. Provide them with a differentiated circus of activities or images for them to **investigate**. Ask them to sketch their **predictions** using simple energy transfer diagrams or Sankey diagrams as appropriate. [O2, O3]

71

Low demand students could be given, for example, a torch, a solar calculator, a hand warmer, a wind chime.

Standard demand students could be given a hairdryer, a pictures of a log fire and an electric heater.

High demand students could be given pictures of a wind turbine, a car, a cake.

- Review the students' answers. Discuss the idea of some energy transfers being useful and some not. [O2, O3]

Consolidate and apply

- Sketch on the board some example Sankey diagrams, which include non-useful energy transfer(s). Working in ability pairs, the students **write an explanation** of what the diagrams show. Ask them to **identify** the useful and useless energy transfers. See if they can **predict** the appliance(s) transferring the energy. [O2, O3]

Extend

For students able to progress further:

- Remind students of the idea of *energy efficiency*. For Sankey diagrams they have encountered (e.g. question 6 of the Student Book), ask the students to **calculate** the efficiency of the energy transfer – (useful energy transferred/total energy transferred) × 100%. [O3]
- Ask them to **consider** what could be done to make the transfers more efficient (question 7 in the Student Book). [O3]
- Ask students to consider various ways they have met of describing and explaining energy transfers and suggest, with reasons, which they find useful. [O1, O2, O3]

Plenary suggestions

What have I learned? Return to the mind map from the beginning of the lesson and ask the students to amend their earlier ideas in light of their learning. [O1, O2, O3]

Answers to Student Book questions

1. The lit candle and the light bulb.
2. a) The candle on the left is transferring energy to the surroundings by light and heat.

   b) The right-hand candle is not lit, so it is not possible to transfer energy.
3. Energy is transferred to a bulb by electricity; then energy is transferred from the bulb by light and heat to the surroundings.
4. a) Electrical energy → energy by heat + energy by sound.

   b) Electrical energy → energy by heat + energy by light.

   c) Chemical energy → energy by heat + energy by sound + energy by light.
5. a) *Useful*: thermal; *unwanted*: sound b) *Useful*: thermal; *unwanted*: light c) *Useful*: thermal and light; *unwanted*: sound
6. 25%
7. Check the proportions on the diagrams; that the useful movement energy transferred points to the right; that the heat and sound transferred point downwards.
8. Suggestions such as reduce friction in the motor.

Answers to Worksheet 1.3.7

1. a) Torch: electrical energy → energy by light (+ energy by heat); b) Solar panel: energy by light → electrical energy; c) Wind chime: kinetic energy → energy by sound.
2. a) A: 6 J by heat; B 7 J by heat; C 65 J by heat and sound; D 5 J by sound; E 6 J by heat and sound; F 30 J by heat and sound.

   b) Check the grids are shaded correctly with the right number of squares for energy transferred usefully and energy wasted.
3. Check the proportions on the diagrams; and that the useful energy transferred points to the right and the non-useful energy transferred point downwards.

1.3.8 Understanding potential energy and kinetic energy

Lesson overview

Learning objectives

- Recognise energy transfers due to falling objects.
- Describe factors affecting energy transfers related to falling objects.
- Explain how energy is conserved when an object falls.

Learning outcomes

- Describe examples of energy transfer that include gravitational potential energy. [O1]
- Describe how changing height and gravity affect gravitational potential energy. [O2]
- Analyse different situations explaining how gravitational potential energy is transferred and how energy is conserved. [O3]

Skills development

- Working scientifically: 2.15 Review theories
- Developing numeracy: identify increasing and decreasing quantities
- Developing literacy: interpret diagrams to develop explanations (Q4 & 5)

Resources needed bouncy ball; *per student group*: three water balloons; bucket; paper towels, metre ruler; Worksheet 1.3.8; Technician's notes 1.3.8

Common misconceptions Only objects that are moving can have energy.

Key vocabulary kinetic energy, gravitational potential energy

Teaching and learning

Engage

- Refer to the Student Book. Discuss the 'teaser' photo of the vertical drop ride and what is happening in terms of energy transfer. Introduce the idea of *gravitational potential energy* (GPE) and its link to height. [O1]
- Alternatively, demonstrate a bouncy ball being dropped from different heights. Ask the students to **make observations** about the height of rebound. Question them about why the ball behaves in this way and encourage them to use ideas about GPE and energy transfer. [O1]
- Working in pairs, ask the students to **discuss** a range of different situations where GPE is involved and the energy transfers that take place. Take feedback and list their ideas on the board. [O1]

Challenge and develop

- Show a video of Olympic-standard divers in action. Discuss the energy transfers from diving boards of different heights. Question the students about the energy transfers taking place at certain points of a dive and explore the differences for different heights. [O1, O2]
- Introduce the factors that affect gravitational potential energy, using the second section in the Student Book. Discuss how GPE is dependent on the force of gravity as well as the height of the object. Discuss the transfer between GPE and kinetic energy (KE), reminding the students that the total energy after a change is the same as the total energy before – energy is 'conserved'. [O2, O3]
- Establish the link between KE and speed – the more KE there is, the faster the object moves. [O2]
- With the students working in mixed ability groups of four, provide each group with Worksheet 1.3.8, three identical water balloons, a bucket, paper towels and a metre rule. Ask them to **plan an investigation** to find the minimum height of drop to burst a water balloon. [O2]
- Select one or two groups to present their plans. Ask the class to comment on the quality of the plans and **identify any areas for improvement.**

- Ask the groups to **discuss** how to safely carry out the investigation. Take feedback from their ideas. Discuss how to record the results. [O2]
- After a discussion about acting sensibly and responsibly, allow groups to **carry out** their investigation in a suitable place and to **record their results**. Ensure that all water is mopped up afterwards. [O2]

Explain

- Ask groups to **explain their results** using ideas about energy transfer. An energy transfer diagram should accompany each explanation. [O2, O3]

  High demand students should be able to account for all the energy transferred at the point of the balloon bursting, and at other heights of the drop. They should **identify** all the useful and useless energy transfers involved.

- Students should answer questions 3–6 in the Student Book to reinforce their understanding of how height and gravity affect GPE and to **analyse** further situations using GPE. [O2, O3]

Consolidate and apply

- Introduce the principle of a hydro-electric dam. (If possible, show a video of one working.) [O1, O2, O3]
- In pairs, ask the students to **explain** how this is a useful example of transferring GPE. Ask the students to draw an energy transfer diagram to show all the changes. They should **explain** how energy is conserved. [O1, O2, O3]

Extend

For students able to progress further:

- Ask them to **carry out some research** and produce their own Sankey diagram for the Three Gorges plant identifying all the possible causes of wasted energy. [O1, O2, O3]
- They could **find out** how to improve the efficiency of hydroelectric plants. [O3]

Plenary suggestions

What do I know? Ask the students to **reflect on** one thing from the lesson they are sure about, one thing they are not sure about and one thing they need to find out more information on. Ask them to work in groups of five or six to agree on group lists, and ask each group to say what they decided. Then agree as a class about what they are confident about, what they are less sure of and what things they want to know more about. [O1, O2, O3]

Answers to Student Book questions

1. Joule, J 2. Gravity 3. 10 m high 4. Saturn 5. a) A b) C c) A d) C
6. The graph(s) should show a decreasing line for GPE and an increasing line for KE.

Answers to Worksheet 1.3.8

1. a) Height
   b) Various
   c) Balloon bursts or not
   d) Various
   e) Amount of water in the balloon; type of balloon; surface of the floor; the height from the same place
   f) Various
   g) Slipping on wet floors; people getting wet
   h) Mop up spillages; use screen to avoid splashes
2. a) If the balloon bursts at one height but not 10 cm below, carry out the investigations at intermediate heights to get an accurate value for height. Use a ruler with a millimetre scale.

   b) Repeat the investigation until three similar readings are obtained; omit anomalous results in mean value calculation.
3. a) Compare results with those of another group. b) See if repeat readings are close in value.

   c) Answers may include: use an accurate digital height-measuring device to measure the height from which the ballon is dropped.

1.3.9 Understanding elastic energy

Lesson overview

Learning objectives

- Describe different situations that use the energy stored in compressing and stretching elastic materials.
- Describe how elastic potential energy in different materials can be compared.
- Explain how elastic potential energy is transferred.

Learning outcomes

- Recognise that work is done when energy is transferred by elastic potential energy. [O1]
- Investigate how different materials transfer energy by elastic potential energy. [O2]
- Use models to account for differences between different elastic materials. [O3]

Skills development

- Working scientifically: 2.15 Review theories
- Developing numeracy: identify increasing and decreasing quantities
- Developing literacy: devise describe investigation (Q3)

Resources needed toys that use elastic potential energy (e.g. dart gun, bow and arrow, wind-up toy); lengths of wool or string; equipment for practical, per group (1 m smooth plank (preferably oiled) with two nails inserted on either side, two rulers, sticky tape, at least three different types of elastic band, a 500 g weight); Worksheet 1.3.9; Practical sheet 1.3.9; Technician's notes 1.3.9

Common misconceptions Force and energy mean the same.

Key vocabulary elastic potential energy

Teaching and learning

Engage

- Ask the students to **recap** three things they remember about elastic potential energy. They could begin to fill in a 'KWL grid' – 'what I Know; what I Want to know; what I have Learned'. [O1]
- Show a video of a bungee jump or a catapult being fired. Ask the students, in pairs, to **discuss the energy transfers** taking place. [O1]
- Review the students' ideas about the energy transfers in the video, and use the Student Book to explain the term 'elastic potential energy'. Discuss the relationship between energy transferred and work done. [O1]
- Demonstrate different toys that use elastic potential energy (e.g. a dart gun, a bow and arrow, wind-up toys). Discuss with students where the energy comes from. [O1]
- Students should draw up a list of other examples of applications of elastic potential energy. [O1]

Challenge and develop

- Provide the students with three different types of elastic band. Ask them to **follow the instructions** on Practical sheet 1.3.9 and **investigate** which materials can store and transfer the most elastic potential energy. Discuss students' findings. [O1, O2, O3].

  Ask high demand students to **suggest** possible reasons for differences between materials.
- Explore with the students why elastic materials behave in the way that they do. Referring to 'Explaining elastic potential energy' in the Student Book, then use lengths of wool or string as a model to represent the molecules in long chains, which straighten out when a force is applied to them. Apply the model to how elastic materials behave under force, and discuss how the stored elastic potential energy is released (when the elastic material returns to its original shape). [O3]

Explain

- Ask the students to complete task 1 of Worksheet 1.3.9, which asks them to **draw an energy transfer diagram** for a situation involving elastic potential energy, and to consider useless energy transfers and work done. [O1, O2]
- Ask the students to **write an explanation** of the energy transfer in different elastic materials, using diagrams to show how the materials behave and transfer energy to do work. Task 2 of Worksheet 1.3.9 asks students to consider why elastic is able to stretch more easily than a stiff spring. [O2, O3]

  High demand students should be able to **explain the behaviour** of different elastic materials using the particle model (task 3 of Worksheet 1.3.9). [O3]

Consolidate and apply

- Working in pairs, ask students to imagine they work for a bungee jump company. Ask them to prepare a sales leaflet **explaining** how a bungee jump works, and how effective it is at transferring elastic potential energy. [O2, O3]

Extend

- Ask students able to progress further to **compare** and **contrast** gravitational potential energy and elastic potential energy. They should **explain** how each is transferred, writing which is the most effective at storing and transferring energy, and give examples of their applications. [O2, O3]

Plenary suggestions

Review Return to the KWL grid, partly completed at the start of the lesson. Ask the students to complete the grid, reflecting on what they have learned. Ask them to **consider** if there are any more things they want to find out. [O1, O2, O3]

Answers to Student Book questions

1. Catapult.
2. Energy is stored in a spring when it is compressed; when the spring is released, the energy is transferred by movement; causing 'Jack' to bounce up.
3. a) They should stretch the elastic by the same distance; use an identical object to fire; carry out the investigation at the same time; under the same wind conditions.

   b) They should measure how far the object travelled; this gives a measure of how much energy is transferred.
4. Stored energy is transferred by chemical reactions in a person's muscles to energy for movement in the arm. This is transferred to energy by movement in the spring of the clock. The energy is stored as elastic potential energy in the spring until it is released. It is then transferred to energy by movement to make the clock cogs turn around. Then energy is transferred slowly over time, making the hands move.
5. No; most materials don't have a structure that allows the lengths of the molecules to be altered.
6. Find the work done by each and compare the values.

Answers to Worksheet 1.3.9

1. a) Chemical energy in muscles → elastic potential energy in bow string (useful) + heat (useless) → kinetic energy of arrow (useful) + sound energy (useless). b) Force exerted on bow string; the amount of useless energy transferred.
2. a) The type of material and how easy or hard it is to stretch. If it is harder to pull back (i.e. a bigger force is required), then more elastic potential energy can be stored.

   b) It is harder to squash or stretch a stiff spring, so a lot of energy (transferred from movement) can be stored and then slowly released when the car is moving up and down. If an elastic rope were used it would release the energy quickly because it is easy to stretch.
3. A model showing particles moving closer together when the spring is squashed; some idea that a lot of force is needed to push the particles together compared with an elastic rope where the long strands of molecules are straightened when pulled.

1.3.10 Checking students' progress

The *Checking your progress* section in the Student Book indicates the key ideas developed in this chapter and shows how students progress to more complex levels. It is provided to support students in:

- identifying those ideas;
- developing a sense of their current level of understanding;
- developing a sense of what the next steps in their learning are.

It is designed either to be used at the end of a chapter to support an overall view of progress, or alternatively during the teaching of the chapter. Students can self-assess or peer assess using this as a basis.

It is helpful to encourage students to provide evidence from their understanding or their notes to support their judgements. In some cases it may be useful to explore differences in the descriptors for a particular idea so that students can see what makes for a 'higher outcome'.

It may be useful with some descriptors to provide examples from the specific work done, such as an experiment undertaken or an explanation developed and recorded. If marking and feedback uses similar ideas and phrases, this will enable students to relate specific marking to a more general sense of progress.

To make good progress in understanding science students need to focus on these ideas and skills:

Students who are making modest progress will be able to:	Students who are making good progress will be able to:	Students who are making excellent progress will be able to:
Describe how jobs get done, using an energy model where energy is transferred from one store to another.	Explain that energy is transferred from one type of energy store to another when change happens.	Explain that all changes, physical or chemical, result in a transfer of energy.
Recall that energy is measured in joules.	Explain that it is sometimes better to measure energy in kilojoules or kilowatt hours.	Carry out calculations of quantities of stored and transferred energy.
Describe what is meant by rate of energy transfer.	Identify the rate at which electrical appliances transfer energy (their power rating), using the correct units (watts or kilowatts).	Compare rates of energy transferred when electrical appliances are used.
Use the power rating of an appliance to calculate the amount of energy transferred.	Compare the energy usage of different appliances.	Calculate the cost of energy usage: cost = power (kW) x time (hours) x cost (pence per kWh).
Recognise that energy is transferred by a range of different processes.	Interpret and draw energy transfer diagrams for a range of different energy transfers.	Use Sankey diagrams to explain a range of energy changes and demonstrate that all energy is always accounted for.
Identify simple energy transfers that involve gravitational potential, elastic, kinetic, thermal and chemical energy.	Explain how energy is transferred using elastic, chemical and gravitational potential energy.	Analyse changes in gravitational potential energy in different situations.
Recognise that electricity is generated in a variety of ways.	Describe advantages and disadvantages of various ways of generating electricity.	Use data to evaluate social, economic and environmental consequences of a particular way of generating electricity.
Give examples of renewable and non-renewable energy resources.	Explain the advantages and disadvantages of renewable and non-renewable energy resources.	Explain the challenges involved in moving towards a more renewable energy supply system.
Identify how appliances that transfer energy result in some energy being dissipated, reducing the useful energy.	Suggest ways in which energy dissipation in a process could be reduced.	Suggest ways in which a home energy bill could be reduced.
Understand that food is a fuel.	Explain that food labels provide information about the different amounts of energy in various foods.	Explain that energy is transferred from the chemical energy store when we perform physical activities.

1.3.11 Answers to Student Book end of chapter questions

This table provides answers to the Questions section at the end of Chapter 3 of the Student Book. It also shows how different questions assess attainment in terms of the focus and style of a question as well as the context. Question-level analysis can indicate a student's proficiency in approaching different aspects of scientific understanding and different types of answer.

Q	Answer	Marks available	Focus			Style			Context	
			Knowledge & understanding	Application	Evaluation of evidence	Objective test question	Short written answer	Longer written answer	Energy costs	Energy transfer
1	b	1	x			x			x	
2	d	1	x			x				x
3	Reasonable example, such as: • battery • lamp	1 1	x x				x x			x x
4	Energy stored as gravitational potential energy is transferred by movement.	1 1	x x				x x			x x
5	• As the archer pulls back and stretches the string, energy is transferred from stores in the body to the stretched string. • When released, the arrow shoots forward. Energy stored elastically in the string is transferred to the moving arrow, where it is stored kinetically.	1 1		x x			x x			x x
6	• energy is transferred from the chemical energy store of the gas to the kinetic energy store of the turbine generator; • energy is transferred from the kinetic energy store of the turbine generator by electricity to the appliances being powered.	2		x			x			x
7	Any two from: • for equal quantities of the types of milk, the total energy stored decreases from whole (full cream) to skimmed milk; • milk contains three types of substance: protein, carbohydrate and fat; • the masses of protein and carbohydrate per 100 cm^3 are similar for all three types of milk; • the differences in energy stored are due to the quantities of fat in milk.	2			x			x	x	
8	c	1		x		x			x	
9	An electric kettle needs to transfer energy more rapidly.	1		x			x		x	
10	Hydrogen; with two reasons from: • high value of energy per gram; • no carbon dioxide emissions; carbon dioxide is a greenhouse gas that contributes to global warming; • availability compared with fossil fuels.	2			x		x		x	
	Total possible	**16**								

1.4.0 Waves: Introduction

When and how to use these pages

The Introduction in the Student Book indicates some of the ideas and skills in this topic area that students will already have met from KS2 or from previous KS3 work. It also provides an indication of what they will be studying in this chapter. *Ideas you have met before* is not intended to be a comprehensive summary of all the prior ideas, but rather to point out a few of the key ones and to support the view that scientific understanding is progressive. Even though we might be meeting contexts that are new to us, we can often use existing ideas to start to make sense of them.

In this chapter you will find out indicates some of the new ideas that the chapter will introduce. Again, it isn't a detailed summary of content. Its purpose is more to act as a 'trailer' and generate some interest.

The outcomes, then, will be recognition of prior learning that can be built on and interest in finding out more. There are a number of ways this can be used. You might, for example:

- use *Ideas you have met before* as the basis for a revision lesson as you start the first new topic
- use *Ideas you have met before* as the centre of spider diagrams to which students can add examples, experiments they might have done previously or what they found interesting
- make a note of any unfamiliar/difficult terms and return to these in the relevant lessons
- use *In this chapter you will find out* to ask students questions such as:
  - Why is this important?
  - How could it be used?
  - What might we be doing in this topic?

Overview of the chapter

This chapter is about waves, and specifically about light and sound. There is a strong focus on wave properties and wave characteristics; this lays foundations for a more theoretical understanding of the nature of waves. However, it also develops a more detailed understanding of the nature of light and sound and the way in which these are used.

There are links with biological topics: sight and hearing are explored, as is the way that colour is perceived. The range of technical terminology is extended, with several key terms being introduced which may be new to students but which will be used repeatedly in secondary science. There is also a use of models to explain phenomena such as refraction.

Obstacles to learning

Students may need extra guidance with the following common misconceptions:

- **Sound:** students may think that: sounds are only made or only exist in the air; you don't need materials to make sounds; pitch and loudness are the same; sounds waves travel instantaneously; sounds can be heard in space; the ear only consists of the part we can see; loud sounds cannot harm the ear; ultrasounds are very loud sounds.
- **Reflection and absorption:** some students may think that an object either absorbs or reflects light, and that it cannot do both; they may not appreciate that all objects absorb and reflect light to different degrees.
- **Ray model of light:** students may not find it easy to reconcile a representation of light as beams or rays with one of wave fronts; this is a challenge because both of these are models and students may not accept that models are used as and when useful, as opposed to being given a definitive view.

How the Programme of Study is covered by the Student Book

Big idea	Topic	Lesson	Programme of study reference
Waves	Sound	1.4.1 Exploring sound	Sound produced by vibrations of objects; sound waves are longitudinal
		1.4.2 Describing sound	Sound produced by vibrations of objects, in loudspeakers; detected by their effect on microphone diaphragm and the ear drum Frequencies of sound waves, measured in hertz (Hz)
		1.4.3 Hearing sounds	Sound produced by vibrations of objects, detected by their effects on microphone diaphragm and the ear drum Waves transferring information for conversion to electrical signals by microphone
		1.4.4 Understanding how sound travels through materials	sound needs a medium to travel, the speed of sound in air, in water, in solids
		1.4.5 Learning about the reflection and absorption of sound	Echoes, reflection and absorption of sound
	Light	1.4.6 Exploring properties of light	The transmission of light through materials: absorption, diffuse scattering and specular reflection at a surface
		1.4.7 Exploring reflection	Use of the ray model to explain imaging in mirrors, the pinhole camera, the refraction of light and action of convex lens in focusing (qualitative); the human eye
		1.4.8 Exploring refraction	
		1.4.9 Seeing clearly	Colour and the different frequencies of light, white light and prisms (qualitative only); differential colour effects in absorption and diffuse reflection
		1.4.10 Exploring coloured light	colours and the different frequencies of light, white light and prisms (qualitative only); differential colour effects in absorption and diffuse reflection.

How the AQA KS3 Syllabus is covered by the Student Books and Teacher Guide

Sound

	Student Book	Teacher Guide
Know		
Sound consists of vibrations which travel as a longitudinal wave through substances. The denser the medium, the faster sound travels.	4.1, 4.4	4.1, 4.4
The greater the amplitude of the waveform, the louder the sound. The greater the frequency (and therefore the shorter the wavelength), the higher the pitch.	4.2	4.2
Facts		
Sound does not travel through a vacuum.	4.4	4.4
The speed of sound in air is 330 m/s, a million times slower than light.	4.1	4.1
Keywords		
Vibration: A back and forth motion that repeats.	4.1	4.1
Longitudinal wave: Where the direction of vibration is the same as that of the wave.	4.1	4.1
Volume: How loud or quiet a sound is, in decibels (dB).	4.1	4.1
Pitch: How low or high a sound is. A low (high) pitch sound has a low (high) frequency.	4.2	4.2
Amplitude: The maximum amount of vibration, measured from the middle position of the wave, in metres.	4.2	4.2
Wavelength: Distance between two corresponding points on a wave, in metres.	4.2	4.2
Frequency: The number of waves produced in one second, in hertz.	4.2	4.2
Vacuum: A space with no particles of matter in it.	4.4	4.4
Oscilloscope: Device able to view patterns of sound waves that have been turned into electrical signals.	4.2	4.2
Absorption: When energy is transferred from sound to a material.	4.5	4.5
Auditory range: The lowest and highest frequencies that a type of animal can hear.	4.3	4.3
Echo: Reflection of sound waves from a surface back to the listener.	4.5	4.5

Apply		
Explain observations where sound is reflected, transmitted or absorbed by different media.	4.5	4.5
Explain observations of how sound travels using the idea of a longitudinal wave.	4.1	4.1
Describe the amplitude and frequency of a wave from a diagram or oscilloscope picture.	4.2	4.2
Use drawings of waves to describe how sound waves change with volume or pitch.	4.2	4.2
Extend		
Suggest the effects of particular ear problems on a person's hearing.	4.3	4.3
Evaluate the data behind a claim for a sound creation or blocking device, using the properties of sound waves.		4.4
Use diagrams to compare the waveforms a musical instrument makes when playing different pitches or volumes.		4.2

Light

	Student Book	Teacher Guide
Know		
When a light ray meets a different medium, some of it is absorbed and some reflected. For a mirror, the angle of incidence equals the angle of reflection. The ray model can describe the formation of an image in a mirror and how objects appear different colours.	4.7	4.7
When light enters a denser medium it bends towards the normal; when it enters a less dense medium it bends away from the normal.	4.8	4.8
Refraction through lenses and prisms can be described using a ray diagram as a model.	4.8	4.8
Skill: Construct ray diagrams to show how light reflects off mirrors, forms images and refracts.	4.7, 4.8	4.7, 4.8
Fact: Light travels at 300 million metres per second in a vacuum.	4.10	4.10
Fact: Different colours of light have different frequencies.	4.10	4.10
Incident ray: The incoming ray.	4.7	4.7
Reflected ray: The outgoing ray.	4.7	4.7
Normal line: From which angles are measured, at right angles to the surface.	4.7	4.7
Angle of reflection: Between the normal and reflected ray.	4.7	4.7
Angle of incidence: Between the normal and incident ray.	4.7	4.7
Refraction: Change in the direction of light going from one material into another.	4.8	4.8
Absorption: When energy is transferred from light to a material.	(4.7)	(4.7)
Scattering: When light bounces off an object in all directions.	4.7	4.7
Transparent: A material that allows all light to pass through it.	4.6	4.6
Translucent: A material that allows some light to pass through it.	4.6	4.6
Opaque: A material that allows no light to pass through it.	4.6	4.6
Convex lens: A lens that is thicker in the middle which bends light rays towards each other.	4.8	4.8
Concave lens: A lens that is thinner in the middle which spreads out light rays.	4.8	4.8
Retina: Layer at the back of the eye with light detecting cells and where image is formed.	4.9	4.9
Apply		
Use ray diagrams of eclipses to describe what is seen by observers in different places.	4.6	4.6
Explain observations where coloured lights are mixed or objects are viewed in different lights.	4.10	4.10
Use ray diagrams to describe how light passes through lenses and transparent materials.	4.8	4.8
Describe how lenses may be used to correct vision.	4.9	4.9
Extend		
Use a ray diagram to predict how an image will change in different situations.	(4.8, 4.9)	4.8
Predict whether light will reflect, refract or scatter when it hits the surface of a given material.	4.7	4.7
Use ray diagrams to explain how a device with multiple mirrors works.	4.7	4.7

1.4.1 Exploring sound

Lesson overview

Learning objectives

- Identify how sounds are made.
- Describe how sound waves transfer energy.
- Explain how loud and quiet sounds are made.

Learning outcomes

- Recognise the need for vibrations to make sound waves. [O1]
- Describe the features of a longitudinal sound wave. [O2]
- Use the slinky model to make connections between loudness and amplitude. [O3]

Skills development

- Working scientifically: 2.6 Construct explanations
- Developing numeracy: extract data and compare quantities
- Developing literacy: draw on information and ideas to develop explanations (Q4 & 6)

Resources needed range of musical instruments (including string, wind and percussion) signal generator; loudspeaker with the cover off; rice; sound-producing items for an activity circus (e.g. triangle, whistle, bell, guitar, wind chimes); decibel meter; slinky spring; Worksheet 1.4.1; Practical sheet 1.4.1; Technician's notes 1.4.1

Common misconceptions Material objects are not needed to make sounds.

Key vocabulary vibrate, longitudinal wave, decibel (dB), volume, amplitude

Teaching and learning

Engage

- Show the students video clips of inspiring sounds. Explore how we make sounds and why there are so many different sounds. [O1]
- Ask the students to make a sound and touch their voice box. What do they notice? Discuss what happens when they change the tone and loudness of their voice. [O1]
- Play some different musical instruments and ask the students to **observe** and **discuss** in pairs how different sounds are made. Question them about the need for vibrations. [O1]

  For example:

  • Where do the vibrations come from?

  • What do you think happens to the vibrations when the sound is loud, or when it is quiet?

  • How do you think the vibrations change with higher- and lower-pitched sounds?

Challenge and develop

- Demonstrate a loudspeaker with the cover off, so the students can see the 'drum'. Put some rice grains on its surface and turn on the sound using a signal generator. If the frequency is low enough and the volume high enough, the students can observe the rice grains jumping. Ask them to **make observations** of what happens when the sound is made louder. Link this with the amount of energy transferred. You could introduce the decibel as the unit of loudness. [O1]
- Set up an activity circus with different sound-producing items. Ask the students to **investigate** how each item makes a sound, how a loud sound is made and how a quiet sound is made. They should **record** how the sound is produced and how it can be altered in loudness (Worksheet 1.4.1). If a decibel meter is available, students can **record** the values of the sounds made when they are hit/plucked with a similar energy. They can use Practical sheet 1.4.1. [O1]

- Demonstrate a slinky spring, to show how sound waves are produced and how longitudinal vibrations make the wave transfer energy. [O1, O2]
- Challenge pairs of students to use the slinky to **model** how to make a sound louder and softer, explaining what they are doing and why. Ensure that they understand the relationship between the energy of the vibration and the loudness. [O1, O2]
- Ask them to **identify** how the longitudinal slinky wave changes with greater energy input ('louder sound'). They should notice there is greater compression (coils more squashed together) and rarefaction (coils pulled further apart). Introduce the term *amplitude*, for the 'size' of the vibration. [O1, O2, O3]

Explain

- Relate the movement of the coils of the slinky spring to the movement of air particles as a sound wave progresses. [O1, O2]
- Ask the students to **describe** a particular sound and to **explain** how it is sent from the object to reach our ears. [O1, O2]

High demand students could **consider** how sound travels in the sea.

Consolidate and apply

- Play three sounds of different volume. Ask the students to draw and label a longitudinal wave to represent them. Ask them to **explain** what has changed in the wave in each case. [O2]
- Ask the students to answer the questions on Worksheet 1.4.1. [O1, O2, O3]

Extend

- Students able to progress further can **research** how different animals on land and in the sea produce vibrations to make their sounds. They could present a one-minute talk. [O1]

Plenary suggestions

Definitions Ask the students to write or draw definitions to **explain** the meaning of 'vibration', 'longitudinal wave' and 'amplitude'. [O1]

Answers to Student Book questions

1. When the metal bell is hit by the clanger, it vibrates and passes the vibrations to the air particles.
2. The vibrations of the instruments/voices cause nearby air particles to vibrate. These air particles bump into others, transferring the vibrations through the air; until they reach the ears in the audience.
3. The particles vibrate to and fro about their rest position; resulting in some being squashed together and some being pulled apart.
4. It passes on from one 'layer' of particles to the next; away from the source of sound.
5. 1d; 2a; 3b; 4c.
6. It decreases with distance from the source of sound; the energy has spread out.

Answers to Worksheet 1.4.1

1. b) *Drum*: drumskin is hit; causing the skin to vibrate; and pass the energy to the air particles; *recorder*: column of air in the recorder tube vibrates; and as it passes through the holes the vibrations are passed through the surounding air; *guitar*: strings are plucked; causing vibration of the strings; that transfers to the air particles.
2. Vibrates; strings; air; invisible; energy; waves; energy; amplitude.
3. The following ideas should be included: how the vibration is made; the vibration causing air particles to be squashed together and others to move apart; the energy of the wave is passed on from layer to layer of air particles in a longitudinal wave; loud sounds transfer more energy than quiet sounds; because the amplitude of the longitudinal wave is greater.

1.4.2 Describing sound

Lesson overview

Learning objectives

- Explain what is meant by pitch.
- Understand frequency, wavelength and amplitude.
- Relate sounds to displayed waveforms.

Learning outcomes

- State what is meant by the term 'frequency' and how it relates to the pitch of sound. [O1]
- Relate the terms 'frequency', 'wavelength' and 'amplitude' to different waves. [O2]
- Draw and interpret wave diagrams that represent different sounds. [O3]

Skills development

- Working scientifically: 2.1 Analyse patterns
- Developing numeracy: relate quantities to graphical representations
- Developing literacy: interpret diagrams to develop explanations (Q3 - 6)

Resources needed mini-whiteboards (optional); graph paper; equipment for the demonstration (oscilloscope, loudspeaker, signal generator, slinky spring, microphone); pieces of coloured wool or ribbon; drinking glasses with different amounts of water in them; instrument such as a recorder; Worksheet 1.4.2; Technician's notes 1.4.2

Common misconceptions Pitch and loudness mean the same.

Key vocabulary pitch, waveform, wavelength, amplitude, oscilloscope

Teaching and learning

Engage

- Recap ideas from the previous lesson. Hand out mini-whiteboards or paper. Play one note on an instrument such as a recorder. Play the note at four or five different levels of loudness. Ask the students to listen and draw one vertical line each time you play a note – the louder the note, the longer the line. Relate these lines to the amplitude of the note. [O2]

- Now play some different notes on the instrument. Ask the students to describe the differences between them. Introduce the term *pitch*. Ask the students to draw a horizontal line for each note – the lower the pitch, the longer the line. [O1]

Challenge and develop

- Set up a static sinusoidal trace on an oscilloscope connected to a signal generator (or use software); also connect a loudspeaker. Explain that the trace represents features of the sound wave. Use the Student Book diagrams to relate loudness and pitch to different parts of the wave. Make the sound louder and quieter so the students can **observe** what happens to the waveform (**L**oud note = **L**arge amplitude). Now change the pitch so they can see the change in wavelength (**L**ow note = **L**ong wavelength and **L**ow frequency). Avoid sustained loud, low frequencies and high frequencies because both can cause some individuals to experience unpleasant sensations. [O1, O2, O3]

- Use the slinky model in conjunction with the oscilloscope. Ask the students to **compare** the two waveforms, **identifying** different parts of the wave in each. Ask them to **predict** how to change the slinky model to represent differently pitched notes. If necessary, attach different pieces of coloured wool or ribbon to the slinky to help the students to see different parts of the wave more clearly. [O1, O2, O3]

85

- Now connect a microphone to the oscilloscope, in place of the signal generator. Ask some students to play notes or sing into the microphone. The students should see that a real sound is not a pure note (not a single wave form), but more complex, combined waves that give the characteristic sound quality. [O3]

- Ask the students to answer questions 1 to 6 in the Student Book. [O1, O2, O3]

Explain

- Demonstrate making sounds by running a finger over the rim of the glass. Use glasses holding different amounts of water (or show a video of this). Ask the students to work in pairs and **think of an explanation** for the change in pitch they can hear. [O1, O2, O3]

- Ask them to **explain the differences** between the amplitude, frequency and wavelength, the pitch and the loudness of the sound waves produced, using words and wave diagrams in their explanations. [O1, O2, O3]

Consolidate and apply

- **Group work** Ask the students to make up a short 'tune' by drawing different wave diagrams in succession. They should alter the pitch and the loudness of the sounds. They should then give these to another group and ask the group to either play or sing the notes. [O3]

  High demand students might be expected to think up a greater variety of/ more complex notes.

- Ask the students to **complete** the tasks on Worksheet 1.4.2. Task 1 provides the students with an opportunity to **describe** and **demonstrate** an understanding of how technology can enable us to 'see' sounds. [O1, O2, O3]

Extend

- Ask students able to progress further to do question 7 in the Student Book and then to **find out about** other applications of waveforms. [O3]

Plenary suggestions

Definitions Ask the students to add to their list of definitions from the previous lesson, including the terms frequency, pitch, wavelength, oscilloscope, signal generator, loudspeaker, microphone.

Answers to Student Book questions

1. Any sensible answers.
2. How high or low (pitched) the note is.
3. It is easier to see and measure the amplitude and wavelength.
4. a) Increases in height (amplitude). b) Decreases in wavelength.
5. a) A and/or B b) D   c) B; it has the biggest amplitude; and a higher frequency than A; so it transfers more energy per second.
6. *Loud high-pitched*: large amplitude; high frequency (short wavelength); *quiet low pitched*: small amplitude, low frequency (long wavelength).
7. Initially a very large amplitude and quite high frequency; then it decreases in amplitude significantly; and decreases slightly in frequency.

Answers to Worksheet 1.4.2

1. Answers should include the use of the signal generator to generate different sounds and the oscilloscope to provide a visual representation.
2. *High frequency*: waveforms should be produced with small wavelengths and many waves.
   Low frequency: only a few waves in the box; same amplitude as the first diagram; but longer wavelength.
3. a)–c) Check diagrams. d) Sound gets quieter. e) Sound gets lower pitched.
   f) The person whispering would generate a waveform of smaller amplitude than the person speaking.

1.4.3 Hearing sounds

Lesson overview

Learning objectives
- Explain what is meant by audible range.
- Understand how the ear detects sounds.
- Apply ideas about sound to explaining defects in hearing.

Learning outcomes
- Understand the structure of the ear. [O1]
- Explain that the ear can detect certain frequencies and not others. [O2]
- State ways in which hearing may be impaired [O3]

Skills development
- Working scientifically: 2.14 Examine consequences
- Developing numeracy: use prefixes for units when handling large numbers
- Developing literacy: extract information from diagrams (Q5)

Resources needed mini-whiteboards; model ear; equipment for practical, per group (a balloon, a cardboard tube, a sheet of flexible card, sticky tape); signal generator, loudspeaker, CRO; Worksheet 1.4.3; Practical sheet 1.4.3; Technician's notes 1.4.3

Common misconceptions The ear is simply the part outside our head that we can see. We can hear allsounds if we listen carefully enough.

Key vocabulary hearing range, sound waves, microphone

Teaching and learning

Engage

- Ask for silence. When it is quiet, ask the students to **identify** any noises they can hear, and if possible the direction from which the sound is coming, and write these on a mini-whiteboard. This should demonstrate how sensitive their hearing is, and that we are surrounded by background noise all the time. Point out that two ears used together allow us to identify the direction from which a sound is coming. [O1]

Challenge and develop

- Show the students a model of the ear. Point out how the outer ear (the visible part) is linked to the middle ear by the ear canal and the ear drum, and how the middle ear connects to the inner ear. Discuss the different parts of the ear and their functions. [O1]

  Give extra support if needed, using an online animation of how the ear works.

- Ask the students to complete task 1 of Worksheet 1.4.3. [O1]

- Use a signal generator and loudspeaker to play notes of various frequencies and demonstrate that there is an upper limit to the audible range of humans. If notes are played in the range of 15kHz to 24kHz most people will hear some but not all. Playing them other than in ascending order negates the possibility of some students imaging they can hear everything. If a CRO is linked to the signal generator, it shows that notes are still being produced, even if they can't be heard. [O2]

- Hand out Practical sheet 1.4.3, which asks students to **make a model** of the ear. This lends itself to small group work. Provide each group with a balloon, a sheet of card, a cardboard tube and some sticky tape. The practical sheet also has some questions. [O1]

- Select different students to show their ear models. Ask those who have compared the ear with the microphone to **present their ideas** and take questions. [O1]

  High demand students can attempt task 3 of Worksheet 1.4.3, which gives a diagram of a microphone and asks them to **compare** and **contrast** the ear and the microphone. Ask them to produce a presentation to **explain** and **compare** the two systems of receiving and processing sound. [O1]

Explain

- Ask the students to **imagine** they are a sound wave. Ask them to write a story to **explain** what happens to them as they pass through each part of the ear. They can refer to the flow chart in Figure 1.4.3a in the Student Book to help them. [O1]

- Ask students to either use their model or a diagram and to explain how hearing can become impaired. [O3]

Consolidate and apply

- Ask the students to think about which parts of the ear can be affected when people become deaf, and about possible causes of deafness. They can **discuss** this in pairs. [O1, O3]

- Ask students to research and report back on the audible range of other animals. [O2]

- **Pairs to fours** Ask the pairs to share their ideas with each other. Then take feedback. [O1, O3]

Extend

- Ask students able to progress further to **research** how an animal without an outer ear, such as an insect or a fish, detects sound and to **compare** their hearing system with ours. [O2, O3]

Plenary suggestions

What am I? Think of a part of the ear. Prompt students to ask questions that can only be answered by 'Yes' or 'No', to try to guess which part of the ear it is. [O1]

Answers to Student Book questions

1. 1000.
2. Humans cannot hear sounds of those frequencies.
3. As human hearing goes up to 20 kHz and dogs' hearing up to 45kHz, a dog whistle needs to be in the range of 20 – 45kHz.
4. Some sound vibrations are very small; energy will be lost in travelling through the ear.
5. a) Auditory nerve b) Ossicles c) Ear drum
6. There is no way to replace damaged nerve cells or hair cells in the cochlea.
7. Elderly people and those who have been exposed to loud noise or have suffered ear infections.

Answers to Worksheet 1.4.3

1. a): Ear canal; b) Ossicles; c) Semicircular canals.
2. a) *Outer ear.* Its shape gathers energy from sound waves and guides them down the canal. Ear drum: very tight but slightly elastic; so it can move according to the vibrations given; the tighter it is the more sensitive it will be to fine vibrations.

   b) *Middle ear.* Ossicles: these three bones are connected but able to move; the movement of one bone affects the others. They have a much smaller surface area compared to the ear drum, enabling the sound waves to be amplified.

   c) *Inner ear* Cochlea: filled with fluid which moves with vibrations of the sound waves. Tiny hairs on the surface send electrical signals to the auditory nerve.
3. a) *Ear*: sound waves are funnelled into the ear canal.

   Microphone: sound waves are incident on the diaphragm.

   b) *Ear*: vibrations of the ear drum are passed on to the ossicles.

   Microphone: sound waves are converted into an electrical signal; and passed on to an electronic amplifying unit.

   c) *Ear*: vibrations of the ossicles are passed to the cochlea; where special cells convert the vibrations to an electric signal; for transmitting to the brain via the auditory nerve.

   Microphone: vibrations of the diaphragm cause a coil of wire to vibrate in the field of a magnet; which produces an electrical signal for transmission onwards.

Answers to Practical sheet 1.4.3

1. a) tube   b) cone
2. it vibrates

1.4.4 Understanding how sound travels through materials

Lesson overview

Learning objectives

- Recognise how the speed of sound changes in different substances.
- Use the particle model to explain why there are differences when sound travels through solids, liquids and gases.

Learning outcomes

- Understand that sound needs a medium in order to travel. [O1]
- Understand that sound travels at different speeds through different media. [O2]
- Use the particle model to explain why sound is carried faster through some materials than others. [O3]

Skills development

- Working scientifically: 2.1 Analyse patterns
- Developing numeracy: interpret data in tables
- Developing literacy: interpret diagrams to develop explanations (Q4 - 6)

Resources needed Worksheet 1.4.4; Practical sheet 1.4.4; Technician's notes 1.4.4. String can telephone. Dominoes.

Common misconceptions Sound travels at the same speed, irrespective of medium, sound doesn't need a medium, sound travels faster through air, sound can't travel through solids or liquids

Key vocabulary particle, vacuum, hypothesis

Teaching and learning

Engage

- Ask students if they've heard the statement "In space, no-one can hear you scream." Ask if they think it's true, why it is or isn't and how it could be tested. [O1]
- Ask students if they've heard stories about native Americans putting their ear to railway lines to hear if a train was coming, and whether they think this might work. [O1, O2]

Challenge and develop

- Ask students to put their ear to the table top and to tap on the table, gently, some distance away. Ask them to judge whether they can hear the sound better through the table or by raising their head and listening to it travel through the air. [O1, O2]
- Provide students with a model of sound travelling, such as a line of railway wagons being pushed at one end, a line of students being pushed (carefully) at one end, a line of up-ended dominoes being pushed at one end and ask how the energy is being transferred and what the wagons/students/dominoes represent. Draw out from the discussion that these show the necessity of a medium. [O1]

Explain

- Provide students with a diagram showing particles (such as Fig 1.4.4b) as arranged in different states and ask students to consider how this might affect the ability of the material to carry sound. [O1, O2, O3]
- Ask students to look at the table showing the speed of sound in different materials (Table 1.4.4) and relate this to the state of matter of each of those materials. Ask students to write a sentence or two drawing a conclusion from this data suggesting the link between the state of matter and how fast sound travels through it. [O1, O2, O3]

Consolidate and apply

- Ask students to answer questions 1-3, thinking about what enables sound to travel. [O1, O2, O3]

- Demonstrate a string can telephone (using two cans, connected by string) and ask students to suggest how it works and why the string has to be taut for it to work. [O1, O2]

- Ask students to suggest how they could demonstrate that sound won't travel through a vacuum. [O1]

Extend

- Ask students to answer questions 4-6. [O1, O2, O3]

Plenary suggestions

- Ask students to write a sentence about why sound travels faster through a solid, to share it with a learning partner and then to jointly produce a better sentence drawing on the two first attempts. Invite a few students to share their sentences by reading them out loud.

Answers to Student Book questions

1. It needs a medium to carry the energy.
2. Because the energy from the sound causes the particles to vibrate; this energy is then carried along the solid as the particles vibrate against each other.
3. a) diamond, b) carbon dioxide, c) solids.
4. Ice: as a solid the arrangement of the particles will be better at carrying vibrations and transmitting energy.
5. Because the arrangement of the particles in some solids is more effective at transmitting energy than the arrangement in others.
6. (For example): if a material is heated it will expand and the particles will move further apart. This means they won't be so good at transmitting vibrations and sound will travel through it more slowly.

Answers to Worksheet 1.4.4

1. a) Sound can't travel through a vacuum
   b) Sound can travel through the air inside the space suits and through the solid material of the helmet.
   c) Radio waves can travel through a vacuum.
2. a) Sound travels well through water.
   b) Sound travels well through the solid table top.
   c) Sound travels well through metal pipes
   d) Sound travels better (and faster) through metal rails than through the air.
3. Diagram showing particles vibrating and colliding.

1.4.5 Learning about the reflection and absorption of sound

Lesson overview

Learning objectives

- Recognise which materials affect the quality of sound.
- Analyse the effect of different materials on sound waves.
- Use ideas about energy transfer to explain how soundproofing works.

Learning outcomes

- Name materials that reflect and absorb sound. [O1]
- Design an investigation and collect evidence about the ability of different materials to reflect and absorb sound. [O2]
- Explain why some materials are good at reflecting and absorbing sound. [O3]

Skills development

- Working scientifically: 2.3 Draw conclusions
- Developing numeracy: interpret diagrams using various shapes
- Developing literacy: use information to construct proposal (Q6)

Resources needed decibel meter; images of concert halls, auditoriums and interiors of cars; two cardboard tubes at least 30 cm long; modelling clay to keep the tubes in place; a ticking clock; decibel meter if available; a selection of different materials such as stiff cardboard; plastic; aluminium foil; ceramic tiles; cork; egg cartons; scissors; Worksheet 1.4.5; Practical sheet 1.4.5; Technician's notes 1.4.5

Common misconceptions All materials reflect sound equally.

Key vocabulary reflection, absorption, soundproofing

Teaching and learning

Engage

- Ask the students to imagine being in a room where there is a party going on. Ask:
  - Why is the sound we hear much quieter if we go into the room next door?
  - Where has the energy been transferred to?

  Establish that much of the sound in the party room is absorbed by the items in the room, and that some is reflected from the walls – only the remainder is transmitted through the wall to the room next door. [O1]

- Then ask 'What would the sound be like in the corridor if the door were open?', 'How does sound get round corners?'. Bring out ideas that sound travels in all directions, and some materials are good at reflecting the path of the sound waves. [O1]

Challenge and develop

- Group the students in fours and provide them with Practical sheet 1.4.5 and the materials outlined in Technician's notes 1.4.5. Ask them to **design an investigation** to find out how well different surfaces absorb or reflect sound. If possible supply each group with a decibel meter. [O2]

- Ask the groups to share their ideas about how they intend to control key variables, and what they will measure. Discuss any points arising, and establish how to collect accurate, valid and reliable evidence. [O2]

- Allow the groups to **carry out** their investigation and collect results. [O2]

- Ask the students, in their groups, to **develop their own hypothesis** about why some materials absorb sound and others reflect it. [O1, O2, O3]

- The students **share** and **discuss** results and hypotheses. Use the Student Book to explain how materials behave when sound is incident on them and why some materials are better at absorbing sound than others. Ask them to answer questions 1–3 in the Student Book. [O1, O2, O3]

Explain

- Ask the students to answer the questions on Worksheet 1.4.5. Task 2 asks them to draw an annotated diagram of a material that is effective at reflecting sound and one that is effective at absorbing sound. Ask pairs of students to **compare** and **contrast** the diagrams they have drawn, **explaining** the features of the materials that make them effective in what they do. [O2, O3]

High demand students should use the particle model in their explanation of energy absorption (task 3 of Worksheet 1.4.4). [O3]

Consolidate and apply

- **Pair talk** Ask the students to read the second and third sections of the Student Book. Show some images of concert halls, auditoriums and interiors of cars. Ask them to **discuss** in pairs all the surface features, **describing** the different types of materials and surface shapes they see, and **explaining** how they are used to good effect. [O1, O2, O3]

Extend

- Ask students able to progress further to **evaluate** three different car interiors, **explaining** how effective each is at reducing sound and what improvements could be made. [O3]

Plenary suggestions

Learning triangle Ask the students to draw a large triangle with a smaller inverted triangle that just fits inside it (so they have four triangles). Ask them to **reflect on their learning** from the lesson and write in the outer three triangles: something they've seen, something they've done, something they've discussed. Then ask them to add in the central triangle something they've learned.

Alternatively, ask the students to tell a partner three things they have learned today, two things they have found hard and one thing they can put into practice from today's lesson.

Answers to Student Book questions

1. Sound waves do not travel through or bounce back off the material; energy from the waves is transferred to the material.
2. a) There would be an echo nearly as loud as the original sound.

   b) You would probably hear no echo; only the original sound.
3. For example: to stop too many echoes in buildings such as concert halls; to reduce engine noise in cars and planes; to reduce traffic noise in houses and buildings.
4. a) A reflected sound quieter than the source sound. b) Hardly any reflected sound.
5. It is transferred to air particles and particles in the absorbing material as heat.
6. Any suitable design with different types of sound-absorbing materials.

Answers to Worksheet 1.4.5

1. *Good absorbers*: cloth, egg boxes, foam, bubble wrap. *Good reflectors*: concrete, metal, wood, glass, ceramic tiles.
2. a) Hard, flat materials are good at reflecting sound.

   b) Materials with lots of air pockets are good at absorbing sound; the energy from the sound waves is trapped in the air pockets.

   Annotations could indicate features such as smooth or rough surfaces and properties such as state of matter and density.
3. The idea of the energy of sound transferring to heat as sound waves bounce around the air pockets; causing the particles of air to move around randomly, colliding with one another.

1.4.6 Exploring properties of light

Lesson overview

Learning objectives

- Describe how light passes through different materials.
- Explain the difference between opaque and translucent materials.
- Explain how shadows are formed in eclipses

Learning outcomes

- Recall that light passes through transparent materials. [O1]
- Explain how light is absorbed by opaque materials and how this causes effects such as shadows and eclipses. [O2]
- Compare diffuse scattering and specular reflection. [O3]

Skills development

- Working scientifically: 2.1 Analyse patterns
- Developing numeracy: interpret diagrams that represent three dimensional arrangements
- Developing literacy: interpret diagrams to develop explanations (Q4 - 7)

Resources needed samples of transparent, translucent and opaque materials, including frosted glass; blank cards for the loop game; equipment for the practical, per group (3 plastic cups, torch, pen or pencil, coloured water); Worksheet 1.4.6; Practical sheet 1.4.6; Technician's notes 1.4.6

Common misconceptions Light can only be reflected from shiny surfaces (such as a mirror). An object either absorbs or reflects light, and cannot do both.

Key vocabulary transparent, opaque, translucent, absorption, scattering, reflection

Teaching and learning

Engage

- Review the idea of waves by asking the students to complete task 1 of Worksheet 1.4.6. Introduce the idea that light travels much faster than sound. Raise the question 'Does light travel at the same speed through all materials?' [O1]
- Ask students if they have ever seen an eclipse and if they know what an eclipse is. Canvas ideas about how they occur. [O2]

Challenge and develop

- Show the students samples of materials that are transparent, translucent and opaque – but don't mention the terms at this stage. Organise the students into pairs or small groups and ask them to **sort** the materials into groups and to **explain** their reasons for the groupings they choose. Ask them to answer questions 1 and 2 in the Student Book. [O1]
- Ask the students, in their pairs, to **carry out an investigation** into transparent, translucent and opaque plastic materials, following the instructions on Practical sheet 1.4.6. Remind them that they should **make notes** of their observations. [O2]

Explain

- When the students have completed the practical investigations, ask them to **share** their results. [O2]
- Through discussion, introduce the idea of light passing through transparent materials and being reflected by opaque materials. Introduce the term 'specular reflection' to describe reflection at smooth, shiny surfaces. Explain that this is why they can see reflections of themselves when they look in, for example, a mirror or a highly polished car. [O3]

- Ask the students to **suggest** what happens when light strikes a translucent material. Introduce the idea of 'diffuse reflection'. Ask them to look at Figure 1.4.6c in the Student Book to understand how diffuse reflection happens. [O3]
- Ask the students to answer questions 4–6 in the Student Book and to complete task 2 of Worksheet 1.4.6. [O3]
- Ask students to explain how eclipses occur, why a total eclipse is only seen on one part of the Earth at any time, and which properties of light cause eclipses to occur. [O2]

Consolidate and apply

- **Pairs/small groups** Give the students some transparent plastic cups (from Practical sheet 1.4.6). Ask them to breathe on the cups and to note what happens – the surface of the cup becomes fogged up. Invite them to **explain** what is happening. Guide them to the idea that the 'fog' is water from their breath that has condensed on the cup. It consists of tiny droplets – these produce diffuse reflection. [O2, O3]
- If available, get a piece of frosted glass. Ask whether it is transparent, translucent or opaque, and then what happens when light strikes it. Now stick a piece of clear sticky tape to the surface. Ask the students what has happened and why. The area with the tape becomes transparent – this is because the tape has a smooth, flat surface that produces specular reflection. [O2, O3]
- Ask students to study Figure 1.4.5g on solar eclipses and then to draw a diagram to explain what happens during a lunar eclipse. [O2]

Extend

Ask students able to progress further: to **explain** why polishing things makes them shine [O3]; to read the 'Understanding eclipses' section of the Student Book, answer questions 7 and 8, and then to complete task 3 of Worksheet 1.4.5 [O2, O3]; to suggest, with the assistance of diagrams, why although the Moon is much smaller than the Sun, it usually completely blanks it out in a total eclipse. [O2]

Plenary suggestions

- **Loop game:** Ask each student to **write a question** on a piece of card about how light is absorbed by different materials, and then to write (on a different-coloured piece of card) the answer. Collect, shuffle and redistribute the cards so that each student has one question and one answer. The first student reads out the question they have and the student with the correct answer answers. This second student then reads out what is written on their question card. Continue the game until all the questions have been answered.

Answers to Student Book questions

1. For example: water; glass; clear polythene; air.
2. Shadows from opaque objects are darker than those from translucent objects.
3. It blocks all the light from passing through.
4. You would see the Moon travel across part of the Sun, but not totally obscure it.
5. As the Moon is orbiting the Earth (and the Earth is orbiting the Sun) the three bodies are only aligned for a few minutes.
6. A lunar eclipse is only visible from the side of the earth facing the Moon.
7. Diagram for total lunar eclipse would look like Figure 1.4.6f; that for a partial lunar eclipse would have the Moon partly in the Earth's shadow. i.e the three bodies are not in perfect alignment.

Answers to Worksheet 1.4.6

1. a) a) glass b) wood c) frosted glass

   b) annotated diagrams should show a) some light being reflected, some absorbed, none passing through, b) some light passing straight through and some being reflected, c) some light passing through but in varying directions, and some being reflected
2. a) Diagram should show Earth with a circular shadow of the Moon on it (significantly smaller than the Earth).
   b) Diagram should show a paler shadow around the dark shadow.
3. Suggestions about surprise, panic, awe and supernatural explanations being offered.

Answers to Practical sheet 1.4.6

Results: A is transparent; B is translucent; C is opaque.

Analysis: The observations suggest that light waves strike transparent materials and pass straight through. When light waves strike translucent materials, some light passes straight through, while some is reflected. When light waves strike opaque materials no light passes through; it is all reflected.

1.4.7 Exploring reflection

Lesson overview

Learning objectives

- Describe how a mirror reflects light.
- Explain the difference between specular and diffuse reflection.
- Apply the law of reflection.

Learning outcomes

- Recall that the ray model is a way of showing the direction of light and where it changes. [O1]
- Describe what happens when light is reflected. [O2]
- Explain the difference between specular and diffuse reflection. [O3]
- Apply the law of reflection. [O4]

Skill development

- Working scientifically: 2.9 Collect data
- Developing numeracy: measuring and recording angles; spotting trends in data
- Developing literacy: use evidence to support explanations (Q 3 - 7)

Resources needed Ray box lamps with slot set to produce a single ray of light, white paper, plane mirrors, plasticine or other way of supporting the mirror so it stands vertically, protractors, pencils; Worksheet 1.4.7; Practical sheet 1.4.7; Technician's notes 1.4.7

Common misconceptions Light goes around things, not just in straight lines.

Key vocabulary incident ray, reflected ray, normal line, angle of reflection, angle of incidence, ray model.

Teaching and learning

Engage

- **Small groups** Hand out a plane mirror to each group of students, and possibly a torch (in which case darken the room) – but warn students not to look directly at the beam or its reflection if the torches are bright. Ask the students to experiment with the mirror and to use their observations to **draw conclusions** about the way light travels and how it is reflected. [O1, O2]

Challenge and develop

- As a whole class exercise, encourage the students to **discuss** what they have learned from experimenting with plane mirrors. [O1, O2]
- Ask students to suggest if light hits a mirror and bounces off it what link there might be between the angle the light approaches the mirror and the angle it bounces off at. [O4]
- Ask the students to look at Fig 1.4.7b and suggest what the solid lines show. Emphasise the importance of using conventions such as continuous solid lines to represent light rays and ask them to answer questions 1– 2 in the Student Book. Explain that broken lines show where rays appear to come from. [O1, O2]
- Show students examples of reflectors – one specular (e.g. mirror) and one diffuse (e.g. white board). Challenge students to suggest how they vary in terms of the way they reflect light. Then refer to Fig 1.4.7d and ask how that diagram can be used to support a better explanation. [O3]

Explain

- Invite some students to **show** their completed diagrams from task 1 of Worksheet 1.4.7 to the class and to **explain** how they decided what to draw. [O2]
- Ask students to answer Q 3-5. [O3]
- Ask the students to complete task 2 of Worksheet 1.4.7. [O2]

- Ask the students to read 'Angles of reflection' section in the Student Book and to answer questions 6-8. It would be helpful for students to carry out a practical investigation, as described in the worksheet. [O4]

Consolidate and apply

- Summarise the main features of the ray model of light. Ask the students to look at Figure 1.4.7b in the Student Book, discuss the angle of reflection and the conventions used in such diagrams, and then ask them to work individually to complete task 3 of Worksheet 1.4.7. [O1, O2, O4]

Extend

- Ask students able to progress further to answer question 9. [O2]

Plenary suggestions

Answers to Student Book questions

1. Light rays from the object are reflected by the mirror into a person's eye. The object appears to be behind the mirror.
2. a) Longer lines are needed if the object is further away; the image appears further back in the mirror.

   b) The opposite is true when objects are closer to the mirror.
3. Specular reflection results in light rays that have approached at the same angle to the surface being reflected at the same angle. This means, for example, that an image of an object can be formed. Diffuse reflection means that rays approaching from the same angle are reflected in diferent directions. The light is still reflected but no image is formed. (Note that the law of reflection still applies but because of the undulating surface it results in reflection in different directions.)
4. Different parts of the surface are at different angles so the light rays are reflected in different directions.
5. If the surface of the water is choppy it will reflect rays in different directions, so no clear image is formed.
6. $20°$. Note that both angles are measured from the normal.
7. The angle between the incident ray and the normal would then be $30°$, so it would be reflected at $30°$ (or at $60°$ to the surface of the mirror).
8. Yes, but the image would be distorted.
9. Diagram should show one mirror at $45°$ across the top left corner of the diagram and another at $45°$ across the top right corner. A light ray should be drawn from B to the second mirror, to the first and then to A. The line should be solid, continuous and be from B to A.

Answers to Worksheet 1.4.7

1. Completed diagrams showing real and virtual rays.
2.

   a) Specular; So the rays form an image

   b) Diffuse; So the rays are reflected in all directions

   c) It might reflect a lot of light in one direction; for example, a car headlamp beam all reflected straight back could dazzle the driver of the car.

3. Correct ray diagrams, similar to Figure 1.4.6b in the Student Book; angles of incidence and reflection should be equal; extended dashed lines behind the mirror should meet at the image position; image should be same distance behind mirror as object is in front.

1.4.8 Exploring refraction

Lesson overview

Learning objectives
• Describe how light is refracted when it enters a different medium.
• Explain how this can cause it to change direction.
• Apply ideas about refraction to understanding lenses.

Learning outcomes
• Identify the key features of convex and concave lenses. [O1]
• Explain how a convex lens affects light rays and produces an image. [O2]
• Explain what happens when light is reflected and when it is refracted. [O3]

Skills development
• Working scientifically: 2.6 Construct explanations
• Developing numeracy: use and interpret diagrammatical representations
• Developing literacy: use evidence to develop explanations (Q7)

Resources needed concave and convex lenses of various strengths; white screens (e.g. A4 card); ray box lamps and ray box lamp prisms (to represent lenses); triangular and rectangular prisms; Worksheet 1.4.8 large straight-sided glass jar of water, metre ruler;

Key vocabulary convex, concave, refraction, focus, prism

Teaching and learning

Engage
• Provide students with a selection of convex and concave lenses of different focal lengths and ask them to identify ways in which the lenses are similar and how they vary. [O1]
• Provide students with convex lenses and white screens. Turn out the lights in the room and ask the students to project an image of the window (or, if possible, the view beyond it) onto the screen. Ask them to identify key features of the image. [O2]

Challenge and develop
• Ask students to set up, working in groups, a ray box lamp producing several parallel rays. Then ask them to put in a lens shape so that the rays pass through it and see what effect it has. Ask students to draw conclusions about convex and concave lenses following the instructions on Practical sheet 1.4.8. [O1, O2]
• Use a diagram such as Fig 1.4.8b to explain that light waves can be thought of and represented as a series of wave crests. Use this to explain how light bends when it reaches a denser medium. [O3]

Explain
• Ask students to explore how a single light ray is affected in the direction it travels by a triangular prism and then by a rectangular prism. Demonstrate, or ask students to set up apparatus to show the effect of arranging two triangular and one rectangular prisms as in Figure 1.4.8d. Ask them to predict what will happen and then ask them to suggest how this explains how a convex lens makes ray converge. [O2, O3]

Consolidate and apply
• Challenge students to suggest how Fig 1.4.8d can be modified to show the effects of a convex lens being thinner or fatter. [O3]
• Ask students to construct an explanation of the way in which a concave lens works by modifying Fig 1.4.8d and answer Q5. [O3]

Extend

- Explain to students that although we draw light rays as straight lines, in fact light can also be thought of as a series of waves. Explain that using this model helps explain certain behaviours such as refraction. Use Fig 1.4.8b to support the explanation. This can be enhanced by using activities such as students marching in rows and slowing down when they reach the boundary to a denser medium. [O3]

- Use the example of an optical fibre to show how light can be trapped in a medium, repeatedly reflected and guided from one end to the other. [O3]

Plenary suggestions

- Ask students to draw diagrams showing refraction of three parallel rays by a) convex and b) concave lens and then to add two more rays (parallel to and in between the existing three). [O1, O2]

Answers to Student Book questions

1. They slow down.
2. It would be reflected.
3. Diagram showing the rays crossing over and continuing.
4. The lens will be less powerful; it will still make the rays close in but they'll meet further away from the lens.
5. A concave lens will make the rays spread out.
6. A hand lens is a convex lens. It gathers light rays and makes them converge. Some of these rays enter the eye and are focused into an image by the eye.
7. a) It makes light rays spreading out or parallel close in.

   b) It makes light rays spreading out or parallel spread out, travelling away from each other.

Answers to Worksheet 1.4.8

1.
   a) Capturing still or moving image.   Film or light sensor.
   b) Enlarging view of distant object.   On eye.
   c) Enlarging view of near object.   On eye.
   d) Projecting large image.   Screen or wall.

2. Light travels through transparent materials, such as glass an air.

3.
   a)

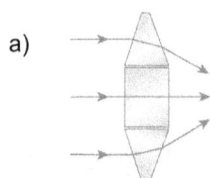

   b) Top and bottom prisms are inverted and central block is narrower. The rays diverge, like this:

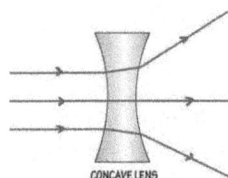

CONCAVE LENS

1.4.9 Seeing clearly

Lesson overview

Learning objectives
- Describing how the human eye works.
- Explaining how the eye focuses on objects different distances away.
- Applying ideas about lenses to the correction of vision.

Learning outcomes
- Explain how an image is formed by the eye. [O1]
- Describe how the eye produces a clear image of objects different distances away. [O2]
- How vision may be defective and can be rectified by lenses. [O3]

Skills development
- Working scientifically: 2.14 Examine consequences
- Developing numeracy: interpret graphical representations
- Developing literacy: interpret diagrams to develop explanations (Q1 - 4)

Resources needed model of eye to show effects of lenses; Worksheet 1.4.7

Key vocabulary lens, cornea, retina, optic nerve, convex, concave, refraction, focus, nearsightedness, farsightedness.

Teaching and learning

Engage
- Ask students to work in pairs and suggest an initial explanation of how the eye works. Take feedback and draw out key points such as 'light entering through the front of the eye' and 'there's a lens'. [O1]
- Ask students to recall ideas from the previous lesson about how lenses affect the direction that light rays travel in and ask them to suggest why this might be useful in both understanding how the eye works and also how spectacles and contact lenses work. [O2]

Challenge and develop
- Show students a diagram of the eye (e.g. Fig 1.4.9b) and explain what happens to light entering the eye. [O1]
- Use pinhole cameras (or demonstrate with one) that replacing the pinhole with a convex lens produces an image on the back of the camera. As with the eye, it is reduced in size and inverted. Indicate that this is a model of the way the eye forms an image. [O1]
- Point out, however, with the model used, that the image is only focused if the object is a certain distance away. With care, it can be shown that altering the position of the lens rectifies this; students should be able to suggest why this isn't the way the eye works. [O1, O2]

Explain
- If possible, acquire a cow's eye (or similar) and dissect it to remove the lens. Show that the lens is not only transparent but is flexible so that its shape can be changed. Challenge students to explain how this makes focusing on objects different distances away possible. [O1, O2]
- Ask students to use Fig 1.4.9c to explain to each other how the lens focuses on objects different distances away. [O1, O2]
- Ask students to study Fig 1.4.9d and identify which of those diagrams shows a situation in which a person's vision would be blurred and how lenses have been used to correct this. [O1, O2, O3]

Consolidate and apply

- By means of a model or diagram, explain to students how the lens in the eye focuses rays onto the retina. Then ask students to work out what would happen if the lens in the eye was a) too powerful b) not powerful enough and represent their ideas diagrammatically. [O1, O2, O3]
- Ask students to make notes to record their understanding of how convex and concave lenses can rectify the defects of longsightedness and shortsightedness. [O3]
- Explain that actually some of the refraction of light rays takes place at the cornea. Ask students to produce a modified diagram, showing how light is refracted both at the cornea and at the lens to make rays meet at the retina. [O2]

Extend

- Ask students to develop an explanation as to why a) some people can see distant objects clearly but need spectacles for close work; b) other people need spectacles only for distance vision. [O1, 2, O3]
- Ask students to suggest how the lens in the eye alters in strength, given that it is flexible and supported around its edge by tiny muscles. [O1, O2]

Plenary suggestions

- Draw an outline of the eye and show where rays from a viewed object meet (or would meet). Ask students to complete the diagram showing what the lens in the eye is doing. In the case of them not meeting at the retina, ask students to draw a second diagram showing how the vision can be corrected.

Answers to Student Book questions

1. Lens (students may also, correctly, suggest cornea).
2. It needs to make the rays close in (converge) and meet on the retina.
3. The image is inverted because rays coming from different parts of the image have crossed over in the eye.
4. It needs to make the light rays converge (close in).
5. Spectacle lenses are rigid whereas the lens in the eye is flexible.
6. The nearer the object is, the more the rays need to be refracted and so the more powerful the lens needs to be. It does this by being fatter and there's a limit as to how fat it can get.
7. Diagram should be like the second part of Fig 1.4.9c, showing how the rays are being bent at a larger angle by a more powerful lens.

Answers to Worksheet 1.4.9

1. Any suitable quiz question, based on section 'The human eye' of the Student Book.
2. Focusing images on the card from different distances away involves changing the distance between the lens and the card. However, the eye performs the same function by changing the shape of the lens.
3. a) They are meeting too soon – in front of the retina.
   b) Concave.
   c) The diagram should look like the third one on the series on Fig 1.4.9d.

1.4.10 Exploring coloured light

Lesson overview

Learning objectives
- Describe how a spectrum can be produced from white light.
- Compare the properties of light at different frequencies.
- Explain how light of different wavelengths can be split and recombined.

Learning outcomes
- Recall ways that a spectrum can be made, including using a prism. [O1]
- Explain that the colour of light in a spectrum depends on its frequency. [O2]
- Explain that the higher the frequency, the shorter the wavelength and the more light is refracted. [O3]

Skills development
- Working scientifically: 2.1 Analyse patterns
- Developing numeracy: interpret graphical representations
- Developing literacy: interpret diagrams to develop explanations (Q3 - 7)

Resources needed equipment for the demonstration (prism(s), diffraction grating(s), water spray bottle that produces a fine spray); for the practical per group (small mirror, white card, water, shallow plastic or glass trough, transparent plastic sheets of different colours, protractor); Worksheet 1.4.10 (printed in colour); Practical sheet 1.4.10; Technician's notes 1.4.10

Common misconceptions White light is made up of discrete colours. Colour is a property of objects rather than of reflected light.

Key vocabulary wavelength, spectrum, frequency

Teaching and learning

Engage
- **Small groups** Arrange the students in groups of three and ask them to **carry out** the practical work described in Practical sheet 1.4.10. This involves investigating what happens when white light passes through different-coloured pieces of transparent plastic. This is best done either outside or close to a window on a sunny day. Artificial light sources, such as torches, do not produce good spectra. Groups of three work well – one student holding the mirror, one the white card and the other the transparent plastic sheets. [O1]

Challenge and develop
- Ask the students to **describe** ways that spectra can be produced, other than by the method investigated in the practical. If possible, demonstrate prisms, diffraction gratings and a fine water spray. [O1]
- Ask the students to **think about** what happens when the coloured transparent sheets are used, prompting them, if necessary, by mentioning absorption and transmitted light. [O1]

Explain
- Talk about the visible spectrum, emphasising that the spectrum is continuous (has no sharp boundaries). Ask the students to complete task 1 of Worksheet 1.4.10 and to answer questions 1 and 2 in the Student Book. [O1]
- Ask the students to read the 'Different wavelengths' section in the Student Book, and to answer questions 4–7. They may do this individually or in small groups, or through a whole class discussion. It may be necessary to spend a little time ensuring that the students have grasped the idea that the extent of diffraction depends on the wavelength of the light wave. [O2, O3]
- Ask the students to work individually to complete task 2 of Worksheet 1.4.10. When they have made their measurements, suggest that they work in small groups to **discuss** the 'scale model' explanation. The

diagram of three light waves on Worksheet 1.4.10 is drawn so that the wavelengths are in a similar ratio to those of 'typical' waves in the red, green and blue regions of the visible spectrum. [O2, O3]

Some students are likely to need guidance and prompting.

Consolidate and apply

- Ask the students to **recall** what they know about the ray model of light. Check that they remember drawing diagrams to show how light rays are reflected and refracted. [O3]
- **Pair talk** Ask the students to work individually to complete task 3 of Worksheet 1.4.10. Then give them some time to **compare** their own completed diagrams with those of a partner. If there are differences, encourage **discussion** about what they have drawn in their pairs and, if it helps, with another pair. [O2, O3]

Extend

- Ask students able to progress further to **look again** at the way a spectrum was produced using a mirror and water. From their understanding of using a prism to make a spectrum, and the idea of diffraction being dependent on wavelength, ask them to **draw ray diagrams** to **explain** the spectrum that is produced using a mirror and water. [O2, O3]

Plenary suggestions

Loop game Arrange the students in groups of five. Each student **writes a question** on a card about the visible spectrum and the wavelengths of light of different colours. They write the answer to their question on a different-coloured card. Collect and redistrubute the cards so that each student has one question and one answer. Now, ask one student to read out the question they are holding – and the student with the correct answer card has to identify themselves and read out the answer. This student then reads the question on the card they were given, and so on. [O1, O2, O3]

Answers to Student Book questions

1. It is a continuous spectrum of colours that changes smoothly from red to violet.
2. Red; violet.
3. The shorter the wavelength, the higher the frequency.
4. White light consists of waves with differing wavelengths. The shorter its wavelength, the more a light wave is refracted.
5. Yellow.
6. The solution absorbs light of other wavelengths but does not absorb red light; the red light is transmitted, so the solution is transparent (at least at some wavelengths).
7. Green in all cases. It absorbs light from the red and violet ends of the spectrum, and reflects the light that is not absorbed (green).

Answers to Worksheet 1.4.10

1. Waves; wavelengths; human eye; spectrum.
2. a) A = 3.9 cm; B = 3.0 cm; C = 2.7 cm.

   b) If students calculate the ratios of 'typical' (mid-range) red, green and blue light waves, they will see that the ratios are very similar to those calculated from the drawings.
3. a) Diagram should show red and blue rays absorbed, and only the green ray transmitted.

   b) Diagram should show green and blue rays absorbed, and the red ray reflected.

Answers to Practical sheet 1.4.10

6. a) A continuous spectrum is seen, with the red end opposite the edge of the mirror resting on the bottom of the trough.

   b) The angle should be about 30°.
7. Results: the red sheet lets only light in the red region of the spectrum through; green, the green region; blue, the blue region; similar results for other coloured plastic sheets.

1.4.11 Checking students' progress

The *Checking your progress* section in the Student Book indicates the key ideas developed in this chapter and shows how students progress to more complex levels. It is provided to support students in:

- identifying those ideas;

- developing a sense of their current level of understanding;

- developing a sense what the next steps in their learning are.

It is designed either to be used at the end of a chapter to support an overall view of the progress, or alternatively during the teaching of the chapter. Students can self assess or peer assess using this as a basis.

It is helpful to encourage students to provide evidence from their understanding or their notes to support their judgements. In some cases it may be useful to explore the difference in the descriptors for a particular idea so that students can see what makes for a 'higher outcome'.

It may be useful with some descriptors to provide examples from the specific work done, such as an experiment undertaken or an explanation developed and recorded. If marking and feedback uses similar ideas and phrases this will enable students to relate specific marking to a more general sense of progress.

To make good progress in understanding science students need to focus on these ideas and skills:

Students who are making modest progress will be able to:	Students who are making good progress will be able to:	Students who are making excellent progress will be able to:
Recognise that sound energy is transferred by waves and describe how sound waves are made in different situations.	Explain how longitudinal waves carry sound. Relate the terms frequency, wavelength and amplitude to sounds.	Interpret and devise wave diagrams to represent different sounds of different frequency and amplitude.
Know that sound consists of vibrations in a medium.	Know that sound travels faster in some media than others.	Understand that the denser the medium, the faster the sound travels.
Recognise an echo as a reflection of sound.	Recognise that some materials are good at reflecting sound and others can absorb it.	Explain what is meant by reflection and absorption of sound.
Know that sound can be represented by a waveform.	Explain how the waveform represents the amplitude and wavelength of the sound.	Interpret waveforms for different sounds.
Understand that we hear sound because of vibrations travelling through a medium.	Explain that we can hear a certain range of frequencies.	Suggest how various ear problems might affect a person's hearing.
Recognise that light can be reflected by some materials and absorbed by others.	Explain the differences between transparent, translucent and opaque materials.	Use diagrams to explain the difference between specular reflection and scattering.
Describe the ray model of light, using the idea that light travels in straight lines.	Explain the difference between reflection and refraction, and describe what happens when light waves are refracted.	Use ray diagrams to explain reflection and refraction.
Use the conventions of a ray diagram correctly.	Use a ray diagram to show what happens when light is reflected.	Use a ray diagram to show what happens when light is refracted.
Recognise convex and concave lenses.	Explain how convex and concave lenses affect light.	Explain how lenses can be used to correct defects of vision.
Describe the formation of a spectrum from white light.	Explain how white light can be split into a continuous spectrum of colours, called the visible spectrum.	Use the concepts of reflection and absorption of light to explain why some materials (transparent, translucent and opaque) are coloured.
Explain how shadows are formed.	Explain how solar and lunar eclipses occur.	Explain why eclipses may be total or partial.
Describe how light of different colours varies in terms of frequency.	Explain how various colours can be obtained by using the three primary colours.	Explain how the colour of an object is affected by the colour of light it is illuminated with.

1.4.12 Answers to Student Book end of chapter questions

This table provides answers to the *Questions* section at the end of Chapter 4 of the Student Book. It also shows how different questions assess attainment in terms of the focus and style of a question as well as the context. Question level analysis can indicate students' proficiency in approaching different aspects of scientific understanding and different types of answer.

Q	Answer	Marks available	Focus			Style			Context		
			Knowledge & understanding	Application	Evaluation of evidence	Objective test question	Short written answer	Longer written answer	Sound	Light	
1	b	1	x			x			x		
2	Long wavelength – low pitch. Large amplitude – loud.	2	x				x		x		
3	a	1	x			x				x	
4	d	1	x			x				x	
5	b	1		x		x				x	
6	d	1		x		x				x	
7	The different-coloured pieces of glass are absorbing and reflecting light from different parts of the visible spectrum.	1		x			x			x	

#	Answer	Marks									
8	Convex lens – rays are refracted (or bent) so that they converge (close in) Concave lens – rays are refracted (or bent) so that they diverge (spread out)'	1		x				x		x		
9	Faster …	1		x				x		x		
	…because the particles are more closely packed and good at transferring energy from vibrations.	1										
10	The sound has travelled 165m in 0.5s …	1			x			x	x			
	… which is out and back, so the prey is 82.5m away.	1										
11	Suitably completed diagram that traces the refracted ray back to where the eye perceives the object's origin to be (the eye doesn't allow for refraction and assumes the light will have travelled in a straight line).	1			x		x			x		
12		2			x					x		
	The rays cross over twice.	1			x		x					
	Total possible:	1 8										

1.5.0 Matter: Introduction

When and how to use these pages

The Introduction in the Student Book indicates some of the ideas and skills in this topic area that students will already have met from KS2 or from previous KS3 work. It also provides an indication of what they will be studying in this chapter. *Ideas you have met before* is not intended to comprehensively summarise all of the prior ideas, but rather to point out a few of the key ones and to support the view that scientific understanding is progressive. Even though students might be meeting contexts that are new to them, they can often use existing ideas to start to make sense of them.

In this chapter you will find out indicates some of the new ideas that the chapter will introduce. Again, it isn't a detailed summary of content. Its purpose is more to act as a 'trailer' and generate some interest.

The outcomes, then, will be recognition of prior learning that can be built on, and interest in finding out more.

There are a number of ways this can be used. You might, for example:

- use *Ideas you have met before* as the basis for a revision lesson as you start the first new topic

- use *Ideas you have met before* as the centre of spider diagrams, to which students can add examples, experiments they might have done previously or what they found interesting

- make a note of any unfamiliar/difficult terms and return to these in the relevant lessons

- use ideas from *In this chapter you will find out* to ask students questions such as:
  - Why is this important?
  - How could it be used?
  - What might we be doing in this topic?

Overview of the chapter

In this chapter, students will develop what they learned about states of matter in Key Stage 2 to explain the properties of solids, liquids and gases using the particle model. They will learn to apply the standard model to explain particular phenomena, such as changes of state, thermal expansion, diffusion, density, concentration and pressure. Students develop use of scientific terminology to explain processes such as changes of state and diffusion.

Students will extend and further develop their ideas on separation from KS2, for example, revisiting the use of sieving and developing this to include filtration. New separation techniques (chromatography and distillation) are introduced. Students investigate dissolving and there is a focus on developing and extending the students' use of technical language to describe processes, for example solvent, solute, solution. Students describe the uses of different separation techniques and explain the differences between the substances that allow each method to be used successfully.

This chapter offers the opportunity for students to apply a model of particles to a range of processes and phenomena. It also offers students a range of opportunities to develop practical skills and problem-solving skills through the context of separating mixtures. Students should identify and select appropriate apparatus.

Obstacles to learning

Students may need extra guidance with the following terms and concepts:

- **Particle model:** Students should be clear about accurate representation of particles in solids, liquids and gases. When representing a substance, its particles should all be the same shape and size. In a solid, there should be no gaps between the particles and the arrangement should show clear uniformity. In liquids, all particles should be touching another liquid particle.

- **Gases:** Students often think there is air in between gas particles: there is nothing between gas particles.

- **Density:** This depends on the mass and the volume. Not all big objects sink (e.g. timber) and not all small object float (e.g. stone). Gases have different densities: some, such as carbon dioxide, will sink in air.

- **Changing state:** There is no temperature change at the melting point and boiling point. Latent heat energy goes into changing the particle arrangement and internal energy from one state into another. Evaporation and boiling are not the same thing: evaporation takes place at all temperatures between the melting point and the boiling point; only part of the liquid changes into a gas. Boiling only occurs at the boiling point, when all the liquid changes into a gas.

- **Dissolving:** Misconceptions include that dissolving is a chemical reaction. There is also potential for confusing very similar terms such as solute, solvent and solution. When making up solutions, the volumes do not simply add up. The solute particles fit into the spaces between the solvent particles, resulting in a lower total volume compared with the sum of the individual volumes.

- **Solubility:** Solubility of gases decreases with temperature because the particles gain in energy, overcoming the solute-solvent forces and coming out of solution.

How the Programme of Study is covered by the Student Book

Big idea	Topic	Lesson	Programme of study reference
Matter	Particle model	1.5.1 Using particles to explain matter	The properties of different states of matter (solid, liquid and gas) in terms of the particle model, including gas pressure
		1.5.2 Understanding solids	
		1.5.3 Understanding liquids and gases	
		1.5.4 Exploring diffusion	Diffusion in liquids and gases driven by differences in concentration. Diffusion in terms of the particle model
		1.5.5 Explaining changes of state	Changes of state in terms of the particle model
	Separating mixtures	1.5.6 Separating mixtures	Mixtures, including dissolving. Simple techniques for separating mixtures: filtration
		1.5.7 Exploring solutions	Mixtures, including dissolving
		1.5.8 Understanding distillation	Simple techniques for separating mixtures: distillation
		1.5.9 Exploring chromatography	Simple techniques for separating mixtures: chromatography. The identification of pure substances

How the AQA KS3 Syllabus is covered by the Student Books and Teacher Guide

Particle model

	Student Book	Teacher Guide
Know		
Properties of solids, liquids and gases can be described in terms of particles in motion but with differences in the arrangement and movement of these same particles: closely spaced and vibrating (solid), in random motion but in contact (liquid), or in random motion and widely spaced (gas).	5.1	5.1
Observations where substances change temperature or state can be described in terms of particles gaining or losing energy.	5.1	5.1
Fact		
A substance is a solid below its melting point, a liquid above it, and a gas above its boiling point.	5.5	5.5
Keywords		
Particle: A very tiny object such as an atom or molecule, too small to be seen with a microscope.	5.1	5.1
Particle model: A way to think about how substances behave in terms of small, moving particles.	5.1	5.1
Diffusion: The process by which particles in liquids or gases spread out through random movement from a region where there are many particles to one where there are fewer.	5.4	5.4
Gas pressure: Caused by collisions of particles with the walls of a container.	5.3	5.3
Density: How much matter there is in a particular volume, or how close the particles are.	(5.1)	(5.1)
Evaporate: Change from liquid to gas at the surface of a liquid, at any temperature.	5.5	5.5
Boil: Change from liquid to a gas of all the liquid when the temperature reaches boiling point.	5.5	5.5
Condense: Change of state from gas to liquid when the temperature drops to the boiling point.	5.5	5.5

	Student Book	Teacher Guide
Melt: Change from solid to liquid when the temperature rises to the melting point.	5.5	5.5
Freeze: Change from liquid to a solid when the temperature drops to the melting point.	5.5	5.5
Sublime: Change from a solid directly into a gas.	5.5	5.5
Apply		
Explain unfamiliar observations about gas pressure in terms of particles.	5.3, 5.4	5.3, 5.4
Explain the properties of solids, liquids and gases based on the arrangement and movement of their particles.	5.5	5.5
Explain changes in states in terms of changes to the energy of particles.	5.5	5.5
Draw before and after diagrams of particles to explain observations about changes of state, gas pressure and diffusion.	5.1	5.1
Extend		
Argue for how to classify substances which behave unusually as solids, liquids or gases.		
Evaluate observations that provide evidence for the existence of particles.		
Make predictions about what will happen during unfamiliar physical processes, in terms of particles and their energy.		

Separating mixtures

	Student Book	Teacher Guide
Know		
A pure substance consists of only one type of element or compound and has a fixed melting and boiling point. Mixtures may be separated due to differences in their physical properties.	5.6	5.6
The method chosen to separate a mixture depends on which physical properties of the individual substances are different.	5.6	5.6
Skill: Use techniques to separate mixtures.	5.6	5.6
Fact: Air, fruit juice, sea water and milk are mixtures.	5.6	5.6
Fact: Liquids have different boiling points.	5.8	5.8
Solvent: A substance, normally a liquid, that dissolves another substance.	5.7	5.7
Solute: A substance that can dissolve in a liquid.	5.7	5.7
Dissolve: When a solute mixes completely with a solvent.	5.7	5.7
Solution: Mixture formed when a solvent dissolves a solute.	5.7	5.7
Soluble (insoluble): Property of a substance that will (will not) dissolve in a liquid.	5.7	5.7
Solubility: Maximum mass of solute that dissolves in a certain volume of solvent.	5.7	5.7
Pure substance: Single type of material with nothing mixed in.	5.6	5.6
Mixture: Two or more pure substances mixed together, whose properties are different to the individual substances.	5.6	5.6
Filtration: Separating substances using a filter to produce a filtrate (solution) and residue.	5.6	5.6
Distillation: Separating substances by boiling and condensing liquids.	5.8	5.8
Evaporation: A way to separate a solid dissolved in a liquid by the liquid turning into a gas.	5.5	5.5
Chromatography: Used to separate different coloured substances.	5.9	5.9
Apply		
Explain how substances dissolve using the particle model.	5.7	5.7
Use the solubility curve of a solute to explain observations about solutions.	5.7	5.7
Use evidence from chromatography to identify unknown substances in mixtures.	5.9	5.9
Choose the most suitable technique to separate out a mixture of substances.	5.6	5.6
Extend		
Analyse and interpret solubility curves.	5.7	5.7
Suggest a combination of methods to separate a complex mixture and justify the choices.		
Evaluate the evidence for identifying a unknown substance using separating techniques.		

1.5.1 Using particles to explain matter

Lesson overview

Learning objectives

- Recognise differences between solids, liquids and gases.
- Describe solids, liquids and gases in terms of the particle model.

Learning outcomes

- Use accurate observations to draw inferences about the properties of solids, liquids and gases. [O1]
- Draw circle diagrams and other models to demonstrate the differences between the arrangement of particles in solids, liquids and gases. [O2]
- Use particle diagrams to explain the differences in energy and the forces on the particles in different states of matter. [O3]

Skills development

- Working scientifically: 2.15 Review theories
- Developing numeracy: interpret diagrams of three dimensional phenomena
- Developing literacy: apply models to develop explanations (Q 5 - 8)

Resources needed sticky labels; equipment for demonstration (beaker of ice cubes, 2 beakers of water, Bunsen burner, tripod, gauze) and for practical 'circus' (see Technician's notes sheet 1.5.1); Worksheet 1.5.1; Practical sheet 1.5.1 (the last page copied onto card); Technician's notes 1.5.1

Common misconceptions Particles in a solid do not move. Particles in a liquid do not touch. In particle diagrams, the particles do not have to be the same size/shape. There is air between the particles of a gas.

Key vocabulary particle, particle model, energy, intermolecular forces, density

Teaching and learning

Engage

- Review the idea that all matter is made up of particles. Ask the students what they understand by the term 'model' and how models might be important in science.
- Demonstrate the three states of matter in water, using a beaker of ice, a beaker of water and a beaker of boiling water. Ask the students to **devise questions** about their observations and to write these on a sticky label in 30 seconds. Collate these into common areas and review and answer them at the end of the lesson. [O1]
- Ask the students to **infer** one common thing all the states have and one thing that is different about them. [O1]

Challenge and develop

- **Group activity** Each group member should have a role – a chairperson, two recorders of observations and two organisers of equipment and materials. Ask them to follow the instructions on Practical sheet 1.5.1 – they are going to **investigate** and **record** observations about solids, liquids and gases. [O1]

  Low demand students can use the cards from page 3 of Practical sheet 1.5.1 to help them with their explanations.

- Ask the groups to answer the questions on Practical sheet 1.5.1 and **think about** how the particles are behaving to account for their observations and to summarise their inferences. Each group should **develop** its own particle model for the three states. Each chairperson should **present** their group's model. [O1, O2]

  High demand students could **think about** what other observations they would need to carry out to **confirm** their ideas.

Explain

- Show the students the accepted version of the particle model in the Student Book and/or use a simulation. Ask them to **identify** any differences between their models and the accepted model. Ask the students how the accepted particle model is different from theirs. What could account for the differences? What further investigations are needed to prove the accepted model? [O2, O3]

Consolidate and apply

- Working in groups of eight, the students **role-play** being particles in solids, in liquids and in gases, **explaining** their actions. [O2, O3]

  Alternatively, for high demand students, provide pairs of students with polystyrene balls, cocktail sticks and a large sheet of paper. Ask them to **make models** of solids, liquids and gases showing the energy and the forces between the particles.

- Ask all the students to **draw** their own particle diagrams for a solid, a liquid and a gas on a poster with annotations to **explain** their arrangement, energy and forces. They should **link** one piece of evidence from their practical work to each state. They should attempt all the tasks of Worksheet 1.5.1 and answer the questions in the Student Book. [O2]

Extend

- Ask students able to progress further to **explain** how the particle model might change for a solid at −50 °C compared with one at 20 °C, and why at 20 °C metals are solids, water is a liquid and oxygen is a gas. [O3]

Plenary suggestions

Scientists Ask the students to **reflect** in pairs on how they have worked as real scientists. What skills have they shown? Why was it important to develop a model from their observations? Why did they need to compare their model with the accepted model?

Question time Read out at least five of the questions devised at the start of the lesson on sticky labels. Select different students to provide answers. Save any questions that cannot be answered for the appropriate lesson.

Answers to Student Book questions

1. Any three solids (e.g. metal, plastic and wood); any three liquids (e.g. oil, water and petrol); any three gases (e.g. air, oxygen, carbon dioxide).
2. The particles in *solids* are very close together in a regular arrangement; in *liquids* they are still touching but have no regular arrangement; in *gases* they are very far apart in a random order.
3. Any suitable cartoon that correctly reflects the energy of the particles in different states.
4. Steam.
5. The particles in *air* are not held together strongly; so your hand can easily pass through the air; very little resistance. The particles in a *solid* are close together; with very strong forces; preventing your hand from going between the wood particles.
6. It is easier to pull jelly apart; the forces between jelly particles must be weaker than between metal particles.
7. Jelly is less dense than a solid metal because the forces between the jelly particles are weaker. In a metal, the particles are held together more tightly by a stronger force.
8. Larger intermolecular forces are needed to hold particles with high energy together than particles of lower energy.

Answers to Worksheet 1.5.1

1. *Solid* – all the particles should be the same size; and touching each other; in a regular arrangement.

   Liquid – all the particles should be the same size; and touching each other; there is no regular arrangement.

   Gas – all the particles should be the same size; not touching; with no regular arrangement.
2. a) The particles can vibrate; but they cannot move about. b) The particles can move around; but they are still in contact with each other. c) The particles move quickly; in all directions.
3. a) i) Particles have the least energy; and move slowly. ii) Particles have more energy; and move slowly.

   iii) Particles have the most energy; and move very quickly; in a random motion.

   b) i) Very strong intermolecular forces; holding the particles in position.

   ii) Less strong than in solids; forces hold the particles together; but they are not strong enough to stop them moving from their positions. iii) Very weak intermolecular forces.

   c) *Solid* – strong forces; so a hand cannot push through; *liquid* – forces are not strong enough; to stop a hand; *gas* – weak forces; so a hand passes through easily.

1.5.2 Understanding solids

Lesson overview

Learning objectives

- Describe the properties of solids.
- Relate the properties and behaviour of solids to the particle model.

Learning outcomes

- Describe how the properties of solids vary. [O1]
- Explain some properties of solids using the particle model. [O2]
- Adapt the particle model to explain differences in the properties of different solids. [O3]

Skills development

- Working scientifically: 2.6 Construct explanations
- Developing numeracy: understand and apply numerical scales
- Developing literacy: develop explanations using ideas and evidence (Q3 - 6)

Resources needed mini-whiteboards; sticky notes; A3 paper; equipment for demonstration (candle, block of metal, sodium metal, glass trough of water, safety screen, scalpel, tile, 2 red 4 mm leads, heatproof mat, light bulb, battery, 2 crocodile clips, 12 V A.C. supply with earthing point, goggles, safety gloves) and for practical 'circus', per group (see Technician's notes 1.5.2); card sort; Worksheet 1.5.2; Practical sheet 1.5.2 (second page copied onto card); Technician's notes 1.5.2

Common misconceptions Particles in all solids are the same.

Key vocabulary malleable, strength, hardness, soluble, conduct, alloy

Teaching and learning

Engage

- **Show and tell** Provide the students with mini-whiteboards. Ask them to **draw** the particle model for a solid and **show** their drawings. Identify and challenge any mistakes (for example particles of different sizes and incorrect structure).
- Show the students a candle and a block of metal. Ask them to feel them and to **describe** as many differences in their properties they can think of. Make a list and come back to this at the end of the lesson. [O1]

Challenge and develop

- **Group work** Working in groups of three, the students work through Practical sheet 1.5.2. Ensure that they wear safety goggles throughout, if they are using metal filings. Ask the students to **investigate** the different properties of solids and to **record** their observations. [O1, O2]
- Using the Student Book to help, ask students to answer the questions on Practical sheet 1.5.2, and to **make predictions** about what the particle models for the different solids must be like. They can sort the cards from page 2 of the Practical sheet to help them further. Ask them to work in their groups to **draw annotated** particle posters for at least three of the solids they have investigated. [O1, O2, O3]
- Ask each group to display their posters around the room. Provide each group with sticky notes and ask them to **peer review** each poster, saying two positive things and one area where they could be improved. Allow time for groups to address any comments and make necessary improvements. [O2, O3]

Explain

- Demonstrate the properties of sodium. Show how sodium can be easily cut with a scalpel, how it floats on water, how it reacts with water and how it can conduct electricity. [O1, O2]

- Ask the students to **plan** and **carry out** a role-play, modelling the particles in sodium, where possible, to explain all the properties they can identify through this demonstration. [O1, O2, O3]

  Low demand students should **identify** all the properties.

  Standard demand students should **draw/act out** a particle model for sodium, **explaining** how the model accounts for the properties

  High demand students should **produce/act out** different particle models, accounting for each property shown.

Consolidate and apply

- Ask the students to attempt the tasks of Worksheet 1.5.2 and answer the Student Book questions. [O1, O2, O3]

- **Pair work** Provide the students with the descriptions of different solids with the particle models to match up from the card sort. Ask them to **match** the cards and **suggest** an example of the solid described. [O1, O2]

Extend

- Ask students able to progress further to carry out some **research** into less familiar solids (e.g. titanium, potassium and brass). They should **produce** their own card sort game, which matches cards showing the particle models with cards showing their properties and uses. [O3]

Plenary suggestions

Properties Return to the list of properties compiled at the start of the lesson. Ask the students to add to the list. [O1]

'Top Trumps' The students could **produce** their own 'top trump' cards of the different solids they investigated using the results from their investigation. [O1]

What we have learned Ask the students to **reflect on** three things they have learned about solids and the particle model. [O1, O2, O3]

Answers to Student Book questions

1. Ductility.
2. Diamond is the hardest material; and will be able to drill through any material.
3. The particle model should show that most of the particles are small; with only a few much larger particles.
4. The arrangement of the particles in an alloy does not allow for smooth layers; this makes it much harder to pull the metal into thin wires.
5. Use thicker springs; to show strong intermolecular forces; and thinner ones for weaker forces.
6. Copper is very hard and strong; wax can break easily and is soft. The particle model should show that copper has much stronger intermolecular forces than wax; copper is ductile.

Answers to Worksheet 1.5.2

1. Hardness; strength; ductility; solubility; conduction of heat; and electricity.
2. a) Sodium and iron are metals; both will conduct heat; and electricity.

   b) Sodium is soft but iron is hard; sodium reacts with water very quickly but iron reacts very slowly; iron is ductile but sodium is not very ductile.
3. a) The particle model should show that copper is hard, with strong intermolecular forces.

   b) The particle model should show that copper conducts electricity – e.g. Figure 1.5.2c in the Student Book.

Answers to Practical sheet 1.5.2

A–3
B–1
C–2

1.5.3 Understanding liquids and gases

Lesson overview

Learning objectives

- Describe the properties of liquids and gases.
- Relate the properties and behaviour of liquids and gases to the particle model.

Learning outcomes

- Describe some properties of liquids and gases. [O1]
- Design and carry out an investigation to compare the viscosity of different liquids. [O2]
- Use the particle model to explain experimental data and applications of liquids and gases. [O3]

Skills development

- Working scientifically: 2.1 Analyse patterns
- Developing numeracy: interpret diagrams of three dimensional phenomena
- Developing literacy: develop explanations using ideas and evidence (Q3 - 6)

Resources needed images or examples of liquids and gases in different applications; equipment for demonstrations (large lit candle, 2 large beakers, sodium bicarbonate, vinegar, gas syringe full of air, balloon full of air, bottle of fizzy drink) and for practical, per group (see Technician's notes 1.5.3a and 1.5.3b); Worksheet 1.5.3; Practical sheet 1.5.3; Technician's notes 1.5.3a, Technician's notes 1.5.3b

Common misconceptions All liquids behave in the same way. Gases don't dissolve in water, they just make bubbles.

Key vocabulary gas pressure, kilopascal, viscosity, compression

Teaching and learning

Engage

- Show some images or examples of liquids and gases in different applications. Ask the students to **identify** the properties which are helpful in each application. [O1]

Challenge and develop

- Ask the students to **summarise** all the properties of liquids and gases and write them on the board. Question them about the evidence for these properties. They may struggle with evidence for the properties of gases.

  a) Demonstrate the ability of carbon dioxide to flow (see the instructions in Technician's notes 1.5.3a). Ask the students to **explain** their observations.

  b) Demonstrate the compression of gases using a gas syringe and a balloon. Ask the students to **explain** why liquids cannot be compressed but gases can.

  c) Show the bubbles in a fizzy drink. Ask questions about what this shows about the solubility of carbon dioxide. Ask 'How could we prove that some of the carbon dioxide dissolves in the water?'. [O1]

- Arrange the students in mixed ability groups. Ask them to **design an investigation**, using Practical sheet 1.5.3 for guidance, of the effect of temperature on the flow of liquids. They should **plan** to collect valid and reliable evidence. Recap the meanings of the terms 'valid' and 'reliable' and discuss how these apply to their design. Check through each group's plans and then ask them to **carry out** their investigation and **record** their observations. A suggested procedure is:

  - Place a beaker of oil in water baths at five different temperatures, e.g. 5, 20, 25, 30 and 40 °C.
  - Check with a thermometer that the oil has reached the required temperature.
  - Place the viscometer in the clamp stand and position a small beaker under the viscometer.

- Fill the viscometer with oil and time how long it takes to empty.
- Repeat this three times at each temperature and calculate averages. [O1, O2]
- The students should produce graphs of their results. [O1, O2]
- Using the Student Book to help, the students should **write an explanation** of their findings. Select different groups to **share** their results and analysis. [O3]

Explain

- Demonstrate the collapsing can experiment, using the instructions in Technician's notes 1.5.3b. Ask the students to work in pairs to **draw** particle diagrams, **explaining** what they have observed. [O3]

Consolidate and apply

- Ask the students to work in pairs to produce two annotated posters about liquids and gases. They should **explain** all the properties they have come across, using adapted versions of the particle model. [O1, O3]
- Ask the students to attempt the tasks of Worksheet 1.5.3 and answer the questions in the Student Book. [O1, O2, O3]

Extend

- Present students with some unusual substances such as cornflour and water, jelly, bubbles of foam, sponge and ask students to classify each and to present an argument for the classification of each. [O1]
- Tell students able to progress further that gases increase in viscosity with increasing temperature, but that the viscosity of liquids is reduced as their temperature increases. Ask them to **develop** their own hypothesis and attempt to develop the particle model to explain this. [O3]

Plenary suggestions

Evidence Return to the list of properties of liquids and gases compiled earlier. Ask the students to add any further evidence from their learning this lesson.

Venn diagram Ask the students to **draw** a Venn diagram to summarise the properties of liquids and gases, putting common properties in the centre.

Answers to Student Book questions

1. For example flushing toilets; putting liquids in moulds; 'dry ice' on stage.
2. a) The temperature; the amount of liquid used; the time to allow the liquids to flow.
   b) A temperature below 10 °C; about 20 cm^3 of oil; about 5 minutes.
3. Oxygen is a gas and gases have space between the particles and so can be pushed closer together. In water (liquid) and ice (solid) the particles cannot be pushed closer together.
4. a) Liquid nitrogen: closer particles than nitrogen gas.
   b) ice, closer particles than water; water, closer particles than steam.
   c) Liquid deodorant particles closer than as sprayed from the can.
5. There are fewer particles so there is less pressure.
6. Three diagrams each showing particles as in a gas and so not touching but with particles further apart at low pressure, closest together at high pressure and in between at medium pressure.

Answers to Worksheet 1.5.3

1. a) Ability to flow. b) Ability to flow and take the shape of the container. c) Ability to flow and be compressed.
   d) Ability to take the shape of the container and be compressed. e) Ability to take the shape of the container and be compressed. f) Ability to take the shape of the container and be compressed.
2. a) Use the same amount of liquid; allow the liquids to flow in the same type of tube; use the same temperature.
   b) 20 seconds c) i) A bar graph. ii) Data for independent variable is discrete.
   iii) The scale of the graph would be awkward because it needs to have a range from 1 to 10 000.
3. Diagrams should show the honey–honey particles having much stronger forces than the water–water particles; the honey particles are likely to be much larger than the water particles.

1.5.4 Exploring diffusion

Lesson overview

Learning objectives

- Use the particle model to explain observations involving diffusion.

Learning outcomes

- Describe how diffusion occurs in liquids and gases. [O1]
- Explain observations relating to diffusion in terms of particles. [O2]
- Make predictions, using ideas about particles, relating to factors affecting the rate of diffusion. [O3]

Skills development

- Working scientifically: 2.11 Plan variables
- Developing numeracy: understand and apply concepts such as 'concentration gradient'
- Developing literacy: develop explanations using ideas and evidence (Q3 - 7)

Resources needed equipment for demonstration (3 × 250 ml beakers with different concentrations of cordial) and practical 'circus', per activity (see Technician's notes); Worksheet 1.5.4; Practical sheet 1.5.4; Technician's notes 1.5.4

Common misconceptions Diffusion occurs in solids.

Key vocabulary diffusion, equilibrium, concentration gradient

Teaching and learning

Engage

- **Pair talk** The students should **discuss** and **write down** three things they can remember about diffusion. Use the Student Book to recap ideas about diffusion. [O1, O2]
- Show the students three containers each with a different concentration of cordial. Ask them to **predict** what would happen if the solution with the highest concentration was put into the container with the lowest concentration, so the solutions could mix. [O2, O3]

Challenge and develop

- Set up a circus of three different investigations for students to **make observations**. Ask the students to **follow the procedures** given on Practical sheet 1.5.4 and to **record** their observations. In Experiment 2, only allow the students to add the chemicals to the Petri dish if you have given them specific permission: lead nitrate is TOXIC and may only be used by students Year 9 and above. If you have any doubts at all about the students using this themselves, add the chemicals to the Petri dishes yourself. See Technician's notes 1.5.4. When the students have completed one investigation, they should move on to the next. [O1, O2]
- Ask selected students from different groups to **role-play** what is happening to the particles in each of the investigations. [O1, O2]
- Discuss different ways in which the rate of diffusion could be increased in each case. [O2, O3].

Explain

- **Pair work** Ask the students to **draw** annotated particle diagrams to **explain** the observations in each investigation. Task 2 of Worksheet 1.5.4 may be used for support here. [O1, O2, O3]

Consolidate and apply

- Use the 'Explaining diffusion' section in the Student Book to discuss the reaction between concentrated ammonia and hydrochloric acid in a long glass tube. Explore the way the reaction occurs and the part that diffusion has to play. Discuss why the product is not formed in the centre of the tube. [O1, O2, O3]

- **Pair talk** Ask the students to **consider** all the different factors affecting the rate of diffusion – task 3 of Worksheet 1.5.4 will help. Ask them to **develop an explanation**, using particle diagrams, for why one particular factor is likely to have the greatest impact on the rate of diffusion. They should explain why the other factors are likely to have less effect. [O2, O3]

Extend

- Tell students able to progress further that chromatography is an example of diffusion. Show them the chromatogram from their practical investigation. Ask them to **draw a particle model** of the chromatogram to **explain** how diffusion makes this process possible. They can **carry out some research** to help them. Ask students to reflect on how what they have seen and learned provides evidence for the existence of particles. [O3]

Plenary suggestions

Diffusion speeds Ask the students to consider all the investigations and demonstrations they have seen in the lesson. Ask them to **rank** the investigations/demonstrations in order of where diffusion occurred fastest to where it occurred slowest. [O2, O3]

Answers to Student Book questions

1. Making a drink using cordial; the particles diffuse throughout the water; stirring just helps this process.
2. There are fewer particles the further away you are from the source; they have spread out.
3. The one with the ink in pure water; because it has biggest concentration gradient.
4. a) placing a spoonful of cordial in 50 cm^3 of hot water
   b) adding a spoonful of coffee to 50 cm^3 of cold water.
5. Diffusion would occur much more slowly.
6. Heat the tube: the particles will gain energy; and move more quickly.
7. Ammonia particles are smaller; and will move faster than the hydrochloric acid particles; so they will meet the hydrochloric acid particles closer to where the latter have diffused from.

Answers to Worksheet 1.5.4

1. a) The red food colouring in the hot water diffuses further and faster; than the blue colouring in the cold water.
   b) A yellow solid would form in the water between the two crystals.
2. a) The particles in the hot water move faster; and will carry the dissolved food colouring faster; so the red food colouring will spread further and faster.
   b) The crystals dissolve in the water; and diffuse away from the source; because these areas are at a high concentration. They form closer to the lead nitrate crystal; because its particles are heavier; and will not diffuse as fast as the potassium iodide particles.
3. a) An increase in temperature increases the rate of diffusion; the particles have more energy and so can be carried further and faster.
   b) The bigger the particles, the harder it is to diffuse; because the particles will not be carried as far. (For example, lead nitrate particles and hydrogen chloride particles, see above, are the heavier particles; so the initial reactions occurred nearer to them; because they did not diffuse as far.)
   c) The steeper the concentration gradient, the faster the rate of diffusion. (For example, a dilute solution of cordial will not diffuse as quickly as a concentrated solution when put in a beaker of water.)

1.5.5 Explaining changes of state

Lesson overview

Learning objectives

- Recognise changes of state as being reversible changes.
- Use scientific terminology to describe changes of state.
- Explain changes of state using the particle model and ideas about energy transfer.

Learning outcomes

- Describe and recognise changes of state, using correct terminology and the particle model. [O1]
- Interpret and explain data relating to melting and boiling points. [O2]
- Describe the processes occurring in evaporation and boiling using the particle model. [O2].

Skills development

- Working scientifically: 2.6 Construct explanations
- Developing numeracy: relate numerical scales to ideas such as melting and boiling points
- Developing literacy: develop explanations using ideas and evidence (Q3 - 6)

Resources needed poster paper; graph paper; paper glue; equipment for demonstrations and for practical, per group (see Technician's notes 1.5.5); Worksheet 1.5.5; Practical sheet 1.5.5; Technician's notes 1.5.5

Common misconceptions Temperature increases during changes of state. All solids have the same melting point.

Key vocabulary evaporate, boil, condense, melt, freeze, sublime

Teaching and learning

Engage

- Recap ideas about changes of state using ideas from the Student Book. Ask the students to complete the activity in task 1 of Worksheet 1.5.5. [O1]

Challenge and develop

- Demonstrate the melting of salol (phenyl salicylate) and the boiling of water. While doing so, select a group of eight students to **model** being the salol particles as the solid is heated. Alternatively, or additionally, show a simulation of a solid being melted and a liquid being heated to boiling. Ask the students to **record** all the changes they **observe** as the solid and liquid change state. Introduce and define the terms 'melting point' and 'boiling point' and apply these to the role-play. Challenge any misconceptions during this. [O1, O2]

- Demonstrate, or show a video of, carbon dioxide (dry ice) or iodine subliming (see Technician's notes 1.5.5). Ask the students to **compare** the melting of wax to the heating of carbon dioxide or iodine. They should notice there is no liquid phase for carbon dioxide or iodine. Introduce the term 'sublimation'. [O1]

- Ask the students to **follow the instructions** on Practical sheet 1.5.5 and **record** the temperature as the stearic acid is heated – if time allows they should do the same for ice. They should **collect** reliable data and **work out** mean temperatures. Ask them to draw graphs of their findings. [O1, O2]

- Discuss their graphs. Encourage the students to **explain** what is happening at each part of their graph, and ask them to **compare** these for the two substances investigated. Use the Student Book to support this. [O1, 2].

Explain

- Working in pairs, ask the students to **make posters** of their graphs, including annotations to explain what is happening to the particles at each step. [O1 & 2]

Low demand students should be able to **identify** the parts where changes of state are taking place. They should also be able to **describe** how the arrangement and movement of the particles are changing, and how these might be different for the two substances.

Standard demand students should be able to **describe** how the energy and forces between the particles are changing. They should **identify** the melting and boiling points.

High demand students should be able to **explain** why the temperature does not change during the changes of state. They should be able to **explain** differences between the two substances.

Consolidate and apply

- Ask the students, working in their pairs, to do task 2 of Worksheet 1.5.5. They should use the cards to position the melting points and boiling points on the thermometer scale as appropriate, and then answer the questions, and also question a) of task 3. [O2]

Extend

- Ask students to **make a list of applications** in which evaporation might be needed to take place quickly, and situations where evaporation must be prevented. [O2]

- Ask students able to progress further to **research** and use the particle model to **explain** the strategies that two different animals and two different plants use to reduce unwanted evaporation. [O3]

Plenary suggestions

What I have learned Ask each student to **share** with their partner all the new ideas learned in the lesson.

Answers to Student Book questions

1. Freeze some water to make ice; then heat the ice to make water.
2. a) Changing a solid to a liquid. b) Changing a gas to a liquid. c) Changing a liquid to a gas.
   d) Changing a liquid to a solid. e) Changing a solid to a gas.
3. The intermolecular forces between copper particles are much higher; than those between aluminium particles.
4. Hydrogen has weaker intermolecular forces than mercury; the strongest intermolecular forces are in ice.
5. It is more likely to take place near the boiling point. The temperature is higher; so there is more heat transferred to the liquid particles; so more will evaporate.
6. *Boiling* is where the whole of the liquid changes to a gas at a fixed temperature. *Evaporation* is where some of the particles escape to become a gas; at temperatures between the melting point and the boiling point.

Answers to Worksheet 1.5.5

1. Close together; vibrate; kinetic energy; intermolecular forces; melting; liquid; quickly; intermolecular forces; boiling; gas.
2. Check that the cards are correctly placed on the thermometer.
   a) i) Gas ii) Liquid; b) i) Liquid ii) Gas
3. In *boiling* the whole liquid changes into a gas; bubbles can be seen throughout the liquid; this happens at a fixed temperature. In *evaporation* only the surface of the liquid changes into a gas; this happens at any temperature between the melting point and boiling point.

1.5.6 Separating mixtures

Lesson overview

Learning objectives

- Recognise the differences between substances and use these to separate them.

Learning outcomes

- Describe how to separate simple mixtures. [O1]
- Choose and explain appropriate separation techniques. [O2]
- Clearly explain the choice and method of separation using the correct terms. [O3]

Skills development

- Working scientifically: 2.14 Examine consequences
- Developing numeracy: n/a
- Developing literacy: create key or flow diagram (Q9)

Resources needed picture of fruit salad; filter paper; salt solution; sand; cordial; water; oil; separating funnel; sawdust; flour; gravel; iron; aluminium pins; vinegar; Worksheet 1.5.6 (the second page copied onto card); Technician's notes 1.5.6

Common misconceptions All liquids are soluble. Liquids are soluble. All metals are magnetic.

Key vocabulary filter, mixture, filtration, insoluble, immiscible, pure substance

Teaching and learning

Engage

- Revise the difference between a pure substance and a mixture, drawing a diagram to illustrate the idea.
- Show the students a picture of a fruit salad, and ask questions such as 'How do we know this is a mixture?', 'How can the components be separated?' The introduction to Lesson 1.5.6 in the Student Book answers this question.
- Extend the discussion by asking further questions to link the discussion such as 'Can we separate salt and water in the same way?', 'Why not?'. [O1, O2]

Challenge and develop

- Ask the students to **describe** and **explain** to a partner how a mixture of rock and sand could be separated. Focus on clear language – ensure that students know the difference between 'describe' and 'explain' (this is because ...). [O1, O2]
- **Pairs to fours** Pairs of students explore an issue briefly, and then double up to fours to share and **identify** the best answer from their group to feedback to the class.
- Share the rules for mixtures with the students (Table 1.5.6 in the Student Book). Explain that separations by physical methods do not involve chemical reactions because they exploit the differences in *physical* properties (e.g. magnetic) of the substances in the mixture. [O1]
- Ask the students to **consider** iron filings and sand, asking questions such as 'What properties do they have in common?', 'What is the difference between them?', 'How can they be separated?'. [O1, O2]

  High demand students could **consider** the differences between iron and sulfur and iron sulfide, if appropriate.

- Ask the students to play the pairs card game on Worksheet 1.5.6 (task 1) to consolidate their thinking about the different methods that can be used to separate mixtures of substances. [O1, O2, O3]

Explain

- Through **discussion** with a partner, students should **suggest** a method for the separation of salt and sand by **identifying the differences** between them. [O1, O2, O3]

- Demonstrate folding a filter paper and explain that the soluble substance (filtrate) passes through while the insoluble substance (residue) remains. This is shown in Figure 1.5.6c of the Student Book. [O2, O3]

- The students should separate salt solution from sand by filtration. Follow the experiment with a class discussion, asking students to **suggest** how the salt could be separated from the water (by boiling the water to leave a residue). [O1, O2, O3]

Consolidate and apply

- Show mixtures of cordial/water and oil/water. Explain the difference between 'miscible' and 'immiscible'. Ask students to **consider** different mixtures of liquids. Ask questions such as 'Do liquids dissolve liquids?'. Students need to appreciate the difference between dissolving solids (soluble/insoluble) and mixing liquids (miscible/immiscible). [O1, O2]

- **Discuss** how immiscible liquids can be separated. Demonstrate and explain the use of a separating funnel. Figure 1.5.6d can be used to support the demonstration. [O2, O3]

Extend

- Ask students able to progress further to **explain the difference** between insoluble and immiscible; physical properties and chemical properties; mixtures and compounds. [O2, O3]

Plenary suggestions

Separating substances Give the students a range of substances and ask them to **identify** and **explain** a suitable separation technique (e.g. sawdust and water; flour and gravel; iron and aluminium pins; vinegar and olive oil). [O1, O2, O3]

Answers to Student Book questions

1. Sieves have visible holes/larger holes; filters have very small holes/holes that are not visible; filters are often made of paper that is folded; sieves can be used to separate solids of different-sized particles; filters can separate soluble and insoluble substances.
2. Separate the tea leaves/ground or solid coffee from the liquid you drink; remove the solid tea/coffee from the drink.
3. Sieving.
4. No; just the iron filings.
5. No; nickel chloride is a compound and is not magnetic (pure nickel is magnetic); lead is not magnetic.
6. Physical methods of separation use differences in physical properties, which are unaffected when things are mixed together.
7. Vinegar and oil are immiscible/do not mix/separate out.
8. Sugar is soluble and will pass through the filter paper with the water.
9. Diagram showing these separation choices: both substances are solids of different-sized particles – sieving; one is magnetic – magnet; one is an insoluble solid, the other is a liquid – filtration; a soluble substance – evaporation; both substances are liquids: if immiscible – separating funnel (if miscible – distillation, covered in Lesson 1.5.8).

Answers to Worksheet 1.5.6

1. Students may need some discussion time to match the cards on the first run through, so they may benefit from additional plays of the game. The cards should pair up as follows: *magnet* – iron powder and talcum powder; *evaporation* – sugar and water; *sieve* – stones and sand; *shake and leave to settle* – carbon dioxide from a fizzy drink; *filter paper* – water and sand; *separating funnel* – olive oil and water.
2. a) Neither metal is magnetic; so neither is attracted.

   b) They are miscible; a separating funnel works for liquids where one floats on top of the other.

   c) The sand and ink will both pass through the sieve; if the grains of sand are small enough.

   d) The water in both types of milk would evaporate; and leave the other components behind.
3. a) Oil floats on water so even if it is vigorously mixed it will float back to the top.

   b) Contain and concentrate the oil using a floating boom. Use buckets or pumps to remove the oil. If water is still present use a separating funnel.

1.5.7 Exploring solutions

Lesson overview

Learning objectives

- Explain the terms solvent, solution, solute and soluble.
- Separate a soluble substance from water.
- Analyse patterns and present data to explain solubility.

Learning outcomes

- Describe the effect of temperature on dissolving. [O1]
- Use the correct terms to describe dissolving. [O2]
- Use data to draw conclusions about solubility. [O3]

Skills development

- Working scientifically: 2.15 Review theories
- Developing numeracy: interpret graphs
- Developing literacy: explain how models can be adapted to fit new situations (Q8 & 9)

Resources needed copper sulfate (or alum); water; beakers; spatulas/spoons; see Technician's notes 1.5.7; Worksheet 1.5.7; Practical sheet 1.5.7; Technician's notes 1.5.7

Common misconceptions All crystals are the same shape. Crystals do not contain any water.

Key vocabulary solvent, solute, dissolve, solution, soluble/insoluble, solubility

Teaching and learning

Engage

- **Quiz** Ask the students to **recall**, **define** and exemplify the key words – soluble, solute, solution, solvent, mixture, dissolve. [O2]
- Explore the students' understanding of the terms by giving more abstract clues (e.g. not soluble, not a liquid, not a mixture). [O2]

Challenge and develop

- **Pair talk** Show the students the data on temperature and sugar solubility in Table 1.5.7 of the Student Book. Ask them, working in pairs, to compile a list of things that can be **inferred** from the table. [O1, O2]
- **Snowball activity** Ask the pairs to form larger groups to **discuss** and list their responses. Turn this into a class discussion, so that groups can **compare** lists, ticking off or adding points they did not pick up. [O1, O2, O3]
- Review and highlight the quality of the students' responses in terms of descriptions, explanations and analysis/conclusions. [O1, O2, O3]
- Draw up and share with the students a progressive list of criteria for marking the quality of responses later in the lesson. [O1, O2, O3]

Explain

- Ask the students to **consider** whether the sugar would continue to dissolve if even more were added. What would they see? Explain the idea of saturated solutions and that crystals start to re-form at this point. [O3]
- Students make a saturated solution of copper sulfate or alum (or work with a ready-prepared solution) and produce crystals at room temperature. They then observe a demonstration of making crystals by heating

saturated copper sulfate solution and **compare** the crystal formation both by evaporation at room temperature and by heating. (Technician Notes 1.5.7, Practical Sheet 1.5.7) [O2, O3]

Consolidate and apply

- Ask the students to **recall** and **explain** what happens to crystals during dissolving. Reinforce the concept of 'dissolving', explaining that crystal formation is the reverse. [O2]

- Discuss what happens when water evaporates from a solution. Model evaporation using students /counters/ animation (i.e. the solute particles get closer together and there are fewer water particles in the solution as it evaporates). [O2, O3]

  High demand students could be challenged to **suggest** what will happen if the water is evaporated more quickly or more slowly.

Extend

- Ask students able to progress further to **interpret the solubility graphs** in Figure 1.5.7c in the Student Book and then answer questions 7–9. To carry out their analysis they should use the criteria identified in *Challenge and develop* above as a checklist or mark scheme for their analysis. [O3]

Plenary suggestions

Creating crystals Show the students pictures of natural crystals (e.g. amethyst geodes or the Naica giant crystals in Mexico, Student Book Figure 1.5.7b). Ask the students to write down an explanation of how they were formed. The students should then use the criteria identified earlier in the lesson (*Challenge and develop*) to peer mark their work (e.g. description, explanation, analysis/conclusions). [O1, O2, O3]

Answers to Student Book questions

1. A mixture of a solute (solid) and a solvent (liquid).
2. More sucrose dissolves at higher temperatures.
3. As a (line) graph.
4. 420 g.
5. Sodium nitrate.
6. Yes, because from the graph in Figure 1.5c up to about 80 g will dissolve at 20 °C.
7. As the temperature of the solvent increases, solvent particles have more energy and move more quickly. This allows the solvent molecules to separate the solute molecules more quickly, dissolving them.
8. There are stronger solute–solute forces between less soluble solutes; and stronger solute–solvent forces for more soluble solutes.
9. Particles move around more at higher temperatures so there are more spaces; so more solute particles can fill the spaces. *Strengths* – shows why more solute can be dissolved; at a higher temperature. *Limitations* – does not show that the particles have more energy at a higher temperature.

Answers to Worksheet 1.5.7

1. Dissolving is involved in the household activities a), c), d), e) and g).
2. a) For example:

Temperature (°C)	0	20	40	60	80
Mass of potassium nitrate dissolved (g)	13	47	77	103	125
Mass of sodium nitrate dissolved (g)	73	88	102	122	148

Ensure that a ruler is used, and that quantities and units are labelled.

b) Check that students have already done this style of graph in Maths. The activity may need to be modified or adapted by providing scaffolding and concentrating on one particular aspect of graph drawing.

3. a) Both compounds increase in solubility as temperature increases; sodium nitrate ($NaNO_3$) is more soluble at all temperatures; the solubility of potassium nitrate (KNO_3) increases faster as temperature rises.

b) It is a material made from a combination of chemical substances.

c) Plants absorb water and dissolved substances through their roots; they have no ability to 'eat' solids.

d) They could all be 'washed' away and wasted when it rains heavily; thus could pollute rivers and lakes.

1.5.8 Understanding distillation

Lesson overview

Learning objectives
- Use distillation to separate substances.
- Explain why distillation can purify substances.

Learning outcomes
- Describe distillation. [O1]
- Explain the physical processes involved in distillation. [O2]
- Suggest ways to separate mixtures and explain reasoning. [O3]

Skills development
- Working scientifically: 2.1 Analyse patterns
- Developing numeracy: relate numerical scales to ideas such as boiling points
- Developing literacy: develop explanations using ideas and evidence (Q7)

Resources needed evaporating basin; watch glass/tile; materials and equipment as detailed in the Technician's notes; boiling water; boiling tubes; delivery tubes; salt solution; condenser; ink; Worksheet 1.5.8a, Worksheet 1.5.8b copied onto card; Practical sheet 1.5.8, Technician's notes 1.5.8

Common misconceptions Boiling and evaporation are the same. The water in the condenser mixes with the substances being separated.

Key vocabulary distillation, vapour, condense, purify, evaporation

Teaching and learning

Engage
- Ask the students to **recall** and **demonstrate** their understanding of the three states of matter and changes of state by working in pairs to produce/complete a simple flow diagram (e.g. solid → liquid → gas → liquid → solid) and labelling appropriate stages (i.e. freeze, boil, condense, melt). [O2]
- Review the results and explore the students' understanding of melting and boiling points being the temperatures at which the changes of state occur, and link these to freezing and condensing points (i.e. same point/temperature in reverse). [O2]

Challenge and develop
- Demonstrate the evaporation of a salt solution in an evaporating basin. Ask the students to **explain** the processes using questions such as 'Why does separation work?', 'Where does the water go?', 'How could the water be captured?'. [O2]
- Demonstrate the condensation of steam from the evaporating basin by holding a watch glass/tile above the basin. Highlight the fact that steam is the name we give to water vapour and that it is a gas. Ask the students to **identify** the disadvantages and safety implications of the process (e.g. hot steam, spitting salt). [O2]

Explain
- Ask the students to perform a simple distillation using boiling tubes and a delivery tube to separate salt and water – they can use Practical sheet 1.5.8. During the process students should **consider** what happens and also how the method differs from the evaporating basin method. [O1, O2]
- Ask the students to **feed back** their observations (e.g. salt does not spit/dry out as quickly/can collect the water in distillation but cannot in evaporation basin method/may appear to be quicker to complete).

- Support the students in drawing accurate line diagrams to model and demonstrate the processes (i.e. heating, boiling, cooling, condensing; label solution, liquid, solid, gas/water vapour/steam etc.). [O1, O2]

Consolidate and apply

- Demonstrate the use of distillation to separate two liquids (e.g. ink and water) using a condenser, or have groups of students **observe** the process from a number of sets of apparatus set up around the room. [O1, O2]

- Ask the students to label the equipment on Worksheet 1.5.8a and **explain** the benefits and uses of distillation (e.g. identify liquids as boil/condense, keep flammable liquids away from naked flame) (sections 1 and 2 of Worksheet 1.5.8a). [O1, O2]

- Ask students to apply what they have learned about separation techniques to solve problems of separating specific mixtures. Ask students to read 'The challenge of separating' in the Student Book and devise ways of separating four mixtures. They should be encouraged to explain their reasoning. This could be completed as an extended writing or group talk task focused on developing explanations. Allow students to test hypotheses if time allows. [O3]

Extend

- Provide students with scenarios of mixtures made of several substances and ask them to suggest how each mixture would be separated, justifying their choices. [O3]

- Ask students able to progress further to **develop a model**, cartoon or 'drama' to explain the processes that take place during distillation. Use counters or circles to show differences in the distribution and movement of solute and solvent particles in the starting flask, the vapour, the condenser and collecting vessel. [O2]

Plenary suggestions

Distillation cards Give the students the set of cards from Worksheet 1.5.8b to sequence the processes that occur during distillation. [O1, O2]

Answers to Student Book questions

1. The window is colder than the steam/water vapour; so the gas condenses/turns back to liquid/water.
2. A double glass tube that carries hot vapour from the boiling liquid through the inner tube, while cold water runs through the outer tube.
3. The cold water condenses the vapour so it can be collected as a liquid.
4. Perfume; petrol; vodka; (essential oils, fuels, alcoholic drinks).
5. The thermometer gives the temperature of the vapour/boiling point; so you know which substance is being separated (i.e. which is a gas (in the condenser) and which is still liquid (in the flask)).
6. They have different boiling points/ethanol has a lower boiling point/turns to vapour/gas first; and can be condensed and collected before the water boils.
7.

Mixture	Separation technique	Explanation
Ink and water	Distillation	Ink and water are liquids with different boiling points
Icing sugar and sugar cubes	Sieving	Both solid, but different sizes
Saltwater and sand	Filtration	Saltwater has salt dissolved in it and so will pass through a filter, but sand has bigger particles and won't
Iron filings and copper turnings	With a magnet	Iron is magnetic, but copper isn't

Answers to Worksheet 1.5.8a

1. a), b) A, seawater, solution or mixture that is to be separated

   B, thermometer; to check the boiling point of the vapour

   C, condenser; to cool the water to make it condense back into a liquid

   D, cold water; cools the condenser

   E, beaker; collects the product – the solvent from the original mixture

   F, distilled water; one of the products

   G, heat; speeds up evaporation of the water/solvent

2. Distillation prevents the liquids coming into contact with the naked flame and as alcohol is flammable, this is safer than other methods. Using a thermometer allows identification of the liquid being separated by its boiling point.

3. Any sensible, scientifically correct ideas.

Answers to Worksheet 1.5.8b

The correct sequence is B, E, D, C, A, F.

1.5.9 Exploring chromatography

Lesson overview

Learning objectives

- Use chromatography to separate dyes.
- Use evidence from chromatography to identify unknown substances in a mixture.

Learning outcomes

- Identify mixtures using chromatography. [O1]
- Describe how to separate a mixture using chromatography. [O2]
- Use evidence from chromatography to explain the composition of mixtures. [O3]

Skills development

- Working scientifically: 2.9 Collect data
- Developing numeracy: relate features on a chromatogram to relative solubility
- Developing literacy: incorporate features such as comparisons and risks in written accounts (Q7 - 9)

Resources needed sugar-coated sweets/felt-tip pens/food colouring; water; pipette dropper; filter paper; beaker; pencil; Worksheet 1.5.9; Technician's notes 1.5.9

Common misconceptions Paper chromatography is the only type of chromatography. Substances have to be coloured to be separated.

Key vocabulary chromatography, chromatogram

Teaching and learning

Engage

- Give the students some sweets with sugar-coated coloured shells, felt-tip pens or food colouring and ask them to put the sweet or a dot of colour on a piece of filter paper. The students should then slowly drop water onto the sample using a pipette. Ask questions such as 'What has happened?', 'Why do you think that is?' and encourage them to **explain** their answers and use the correct terms (e.g. dissolve, soluble). The 'Separating colours' section in the Student Book supports this exercise. [O1, O2]

  Tips for carrying out successful chromatography:

  - Use water-soluble dyes/pens.
  - Making several applications of the pen/dye, allowing each to dry before the next is applied, gives a more intense colour.
  - Allow each drop of water to spread fully before the next is applied.

Challenge and develop

- Explain to the students that they need to be able to reproduce what you do exactly; therefore, as they observe the demonstration they need to make notes/diagrams etc. using the correct terms.
- Demonstrate two methods of paper chromatography: dropping; and using a wick standing in water as shown in Student's Book 1.5.9. Emphasise the terms and processes. [O2]

Explain

- Students should **investigate the composition** of coloured inks and dyes using the two methods. [O1, O2, O3]
- They will need to **produce evidence** that they have listened to you and followed instructions carefully by producing good-quality chromatograms. You might want to initiate a competition. [O1, O2, O3]

Consolidate and apply

- **Pairs to fours** Student pairs **present** their chromatograms and explanations to each other. [O1, O2, O3]

- **Peer assess** The students should **discuss** who has provided the best evidence and say why. Give feedback for areas of improvement (e.g. smaller dot of ink, put dots further apart, have less water in the beaker, put the dot further up the filter paper away from water line, find a better method of keeping the filter paper straight; do not leave in the water too long).

- Identify and summarise the key things to remember when performing paper chromatography (e.g. pencil line, ink dots as small as possible, ink dots above the water line etc). [O2]

- The students should answer the questions on Worksheet 1.5.9 to help consolidate their learning, and understand how mistakes and carelessness will affect the results. [O2]

Extend

- Present students with evidence of how certain substances were separated. Ask students to evaluate how evidence could be used to identify unknown substances using separation techniques. [O3]

- Ask students able to progress further to **interpret chromatograms** and **draw conclusions** from them, for example:

  - whether the same/different inks/dyes were used;

  - why different inks spread different distances up the filter paper. [O3]

Plenary suggestions

Chromatography quiz Ask the students to **justify** why: pencil lines are used; the water level must be below the ink spot; chromatography would not work for a permanent marker pen/oil-based paint; same dye in a different pen would always be in the same place on the same type of filter paper. [O1, O2, O3]

Answers to Student Book questions

1. It can be separated into different colours.
2. It dissolves and spreads with the water.
3. It is a way of separating mixtures/a separation method.
4. Chromatogram.
5. The pencil line will not dissolve in water.
6. Salt is white/will not show up/is a solid.
7. It separates/identifies components of a mixture; produces a pattern; identical components travel the same distance under the same conditions.
8. Chromatography uses a liquid/solvent/solubility; electrophoresis uses a gel and electric current to separate components.
9. Any reasonable answer to illustrate they should avoid contamination; such as: gloves, masks, overalls, sealed containers/bags.

Answers to Worksheet 1.5.9

1. a) The colours in the starting line would move up the paper with the dyes being analysed (if the ink used is water soluble).

   b) The permanent marker does not move because it is not soluble in water.

   c) The water, ink/dye might not soak up the paper, or might do so very slowly.

   d) The dyes could all travel to the top of the paper.

   e) The dye is washed across the paper, rather than its components separating gradually.

2. Look for clear communication, correct terminology, avoidance of mistakes such as in Q1. The students should describe or illustrate clearly how the results would show identical or non-identical food colourings.

3. a) The red dye was soluble in the water/soap and could transfer from the towel into the shirt.

   b) The red dye of the towel was probably made of a mixture of several different dyes that had different solubilities.

   c) Some of the dye may be bonded to the cloth and not wash off, or it may not be water/soap soluble.

   d) During manufacture a lot of dye is used so some will wash off. In an old towel, unbonded, water-soluble dye has already been washed away in previous washes.

   e) It depends on whether or not the dye has bonded to the material of the shirt.

1.5.10 Checking students' progress

The *Checking your progress* section in the Student Book indicates the key ideas developed in this chapter and shows how students' progress to more complex levels. It is provided to support students in:

- identifying those ideas;

- developing a sense of their current level of understanding;

- developing a sense of what the next steps in their learning are.

It is designed to be used either at the end of a chapter to support an overall view of the progress, or alternatively during the teaching of the chapter. Students can self-assess or peer assess using this as a basis.

It is helpful to encourage students to provide evidence from their understanding or their notes to support their judgements. In some cases it may be useful to explore the difference in the descriptors for a particular idea so that students can see what makes for a 'higher outcome'.

It may be useful with some descriptors to provide examples from the specific work done, such as an experiment undertaken or an explanation developed and recorded. If marking and feedback use similar ideas and phrases this will enable students to relate specific marking to a more general sense of progress.

To make good progress in understanding science students need to focus on these ideas and skills:

Students who are making modest progress will be able to:	Students who are making good progress will be able to:	Students who are making excellent progress will be able to:
Compare the properties of solids, liquids and gases.	Draw particle diagrams to demonstrate the differences between the arrangement of particles in solids, liquids and gases, and describe their different properties.	Use particle diagrams to explain the differences in energy and forces between the particles in different states of matter, accounting for differences in their properties.
Use correct terminology and the particle model to describe changes of state, including evaporation.	Interpret data relating to melting and boiling points.	Explain data relating to melting and boiling points in terms of intermolecular forces.
Describe what is meant by the terms 'concentration' and 'pressure'.	Describe the effects of changing concentration and pressure in terms of particles.	Explain the effects of changing concentration and pressure in terms of particles, and apply to processes such as diffusion and gas compression.
Describe some methods to separate mixtures.	Select and explain appropriate separation techniques.	Explain the choice and method of separation using correct terms.
Define solvent, solute, solution and soluble.	Interpret solubility graphs to compare solubility of different solutes and describe the effect of temperature on solubility.	Explain solubility and the effect of temperature in terms of particles and intermolecular forces.
Describe the process of distillation.	Explain the physical processes involved in distillation.	Identify the uses and advantages of distillation.
Identify mixtures using chromatography.	Explain how to separate a mixture using chromatography.	Use chromatograms to explain the composition of mixtures; compare chromatography and DNA analysis.

1.5.11 Answers to Student Book end of chapter questions

This table provides answers to the Questions section at the end of Chapter 5 of the Student Book. It also shows how different questions assess attainment in terms of the focus and style of a question as well as the context. Question level analysis can indicate a student's proficiency in approaching different aspects of scientific understanding and different types of answer.

Q	Answer	Marks available	Focus			Style			Context			
			Knowledge & understanding	Application	Evaluation of evidence	Objective test question	Short written answer	Longer written answer	Particle model- Solids, liquids gases and	Properties of solids, liquids and gases	Separation techniques	Solubility
1	b	1	x			x				x		
2	c	1	x			x				x		
3	Particles gain kinetic energy and move further apart	1	x				x		x			
	Viscosity decreases because the particles have more energy to overcome forces	1	x				x					
4	Condensation	1	x				x		x			
	Particles move closer together/particles all touch/description of particles in a liquid	1										
5	a	1	x			x						x
6	d	2	x			x					x	
7	Heat the saltwater until the water boils and becomes a gas.	1	x			x						x
	Collect the steam as it evaporates.											
	Cool the steam so that it returns to liquid/ condense the steam/description of condenser.	1										
	Recover the dried salt from the original dish/container.	1										
8	d	1		x		x				x		
9	c	1		x		x					x	
10	(i)	1		x		x					x	
11	Aerosols are liquids or solids suspended in a gas	1		x				x	x			
	When heated, the gas expands and the particles move further apart with more energy	1		x				x				
	The expansion means there is more	1		x				x				

		Marks									
	pressure from the gas on the sides of the container Eventually the aerosol will heat enough to blow the can apart	1		x				x				
12	a or e	1		x		x					x	
13	a) 'Delightful is the least soluble and Kyle & Tate the most' [award 1 mark]; the order of solubility from least to most being Delightful, Spoonful, Finegrade, Kyle & Tait [award 2 marks]	2		x			x					x
		2		x			x					
	b) 'Keep other factors the same (such as temperature)' [award 1 mark]. Realising that even though the masses and volumes are different, the ratio (even if not explained using that term) is the same [award the second mark]											
14	Any two from: • Butane is easier to change into a liquid • Butane has a higher boiling point, so it will change with less pressure • Less energy needs to be transferred from the butane to change it into a liquid Accept converse statements relating to hydrogen	2			x		x			x		
15	Relevant points include: • horse C had drug Y • none of the horses had drug X • horses A, B and D had neither drug	4			x			x			x	
	Total possible	31										

1.6.0 Reactions: Introduction

When and how to use these pages

The Introduction in the Student Book indicates some of the ideas and skills in this topic area that students will already have met from KS2 or from previous KS3 work. It also provides an indication of what they will be studying in this chapter. *Ideas you have met before* is not intended to comprehensively summarise all of the prior ideas, but rather to point out a few of the key ones and to support the view that scientific understanding is progressive. Even though students might be meeting contexts that are new to them, they can often use existing ideas to start to make sense of them.

In this chapter you will find out indicates some of the new ideas that the chapter will introduce. Again, it isn't a detailed summary of content. Its purpose is more to act as a 'trailer' and generate some interest.

The outcomes, then, will be: recognition of prior learning that can be built on; and interest in finding out more.

There are a number of ways this can be used. You might, for example:

- use *Ideas you have met before* as the basis for a revision lesson as you start the first new topic

- use *Ideas you have met before* as the centre of spider diagrams, to which students can add examples, experiments they might have done previously or what they found interesting

- make a note of any unfamiliar/difficult terms and return to these in the relevant lessons

- use *In this chapter you will find out* to ask students questions such as:
  - Why is this important?
  - How could it be used?
  - What might we be doing in this topic?

Overview of the chapter

In this chapter, students will develop what they learned about the properties of materials at KS2 to explore the physical and chemical properties of metals and non-metals. They will apply these properties to uses of specific metals and non-metals. Students will learn about the characteristics of chemical change. They will explore some specific types of chemical reaction such as reactions of acids with some metals, oxidation and displacement reactions, and will consider the products formed during each reaction. They will practise describing and explaining these reactions using particle diagrams and word equations. Students will learn how reactions can be used to determine a reactivity series, for example by comparing reactions of different metals with an acid, and by displacement reactions.

The students study reactions in the context of acids and alkalis, considering the reactions the two together as well as the reactions of acids with metals and carbonates. The relevance of acids and alkalis to our everyday lives is considered, as are the applications of neutralisation reactions. The students learn about the pH scale and compare the uses of different indicators.

This chapter offers a number of opportunities for students to investigate chemical changes at first hand. They study reactions to identify evidence for a chemical change and then explain the changes using equations. The students have the opportunity to use models to explore how the atoms are rearranged during reactions to make new products and to work collaboratively. Students analyse patterns in data and use these to suggest a reactivity series of various metals. They also have the opportunity to plan an investigation to compare the effectiveness of indigestion remedies and practice analysing data and suggesting improvements to a method.

Obstacles to learning

Students may need extra guidance with the following concepts:

- **Acids and alkalis:** Not all acids are dangerous – we use, and even consume, many acids. However, many acids in a laboratory need to be handled with care. Conversely, not all alkalis are safe.

- **Salts:** There are many salts, not only table salt (sodium chloride).

- **Displacement:** Students may think that all metals react in the same way, and some may have difficulty with the idea that some metals are more reactive than others. The use of models and role-play will help to clarify these ideas.

- **Reactions:** Reactions can create new products, but these depend on the atoms present in the reactants – new substances do not just 'appear', and reactants do not 'disappear'. Students may have the misconception that when carbonates react with acids, carbon dioxide is released from the carbonate. Another misconception is that all neutralisation reactions result in a solution of pH 7.

- **Combustion:** Heating and burning are not the same, and things do not 'disappear' when they burn.

How the Programme of Study is covered by the Student Book

Big idea	Topic	Lesson	Programme of study reference
Reactions	Metals & non-metals	1.6.1 Using metals and non-metals	The varying physical and chemical properties of different elements. The properties of metals and non-metals
		1.6.2 Exploring the reactions of metals with acids	Reactions of acids with metals to produce a salt plus hydrogen
		1.6.3 Understanding displacement reactions	The order of metals and carbon in the reactivity series; representing chemical reactions using formulas and using equations; displacement reactions; conservation of mass, changes of state and chemical reactions
		1.6.4 Understanding oxidation reactions	Combustion, thermal decomposition, oxidation and displacement reactions
	Acids & alkalis	1.6.5 Exploring acids	Defining acids and alkalis
		1.6.6 Exploring alkalis	Defining acids and alkalis
		1.6.7 Using indicators	The pH scale for measuring acidity/alkalinity; and indicators
		1.6.8 Exploring neutralisation	Defining acids and alkalis in terms of neutralisation reactions. The pH scale for measuring acidity/alkalinity; and indicators
		1.6.9 Investigating neutralisation	Reactions of acids with alkalis to produce a salt plus water

How the AQA KS3 Syllabus is covered by the Student Books and Teacher Guide

Metals & non-metals

	Student Book	Teacher Guide
Know		
Metals and non-metals react with oxygen to form oxides which are either bases or acids.	6.2, 6.4	6.2, 6.4
Metals can be arranged as a reactivity series in order of how readily they react with other substances.	6.3	6.3
Some metals react with acids to produce salts and hydrogen.	6.2	6.2
Fact: Iron, nickel and cobalt are magnetic elements.	6.1	6.1
Fact: Mercury is a metal that is liquid at room temperature.	(6.1)	(6.1)
Fact: Bromine is a non-metal that is liquid at room temperature.	6.1	6.1
Metals: Shiny, good conductors of electricity and heat, malleable and ductile, and usually solid at room temperature.	6.1	6.1
Non-metals: Dull, poor conductors of electricity and heat, brittle and usually solid or gaseous at room temperature.	6.1	6.1
Displacement: Reaction where a more reactive metal takes the place of a less reactive metal in a compound.	6.3	6.3
Oxidation: Reaction in which a substance combines with oxygen.	6.4	6.4
Reactivity: The tendency of a substance to undergo a chemical reaction.	6.2	6.2
Apply		
Describe an oxidation, displacement, or metalacid reaction with a word equation.	6.4	6.4
Use particle diagrams to represent oxidation, displacement and metal-acid reactions.	6.2, 6.3, 6.4	6.2, 6.3, 6.4

Identify an unknown element from its physical and chemical properties.	6.3	6.3
Place an unfamiliar metal into the reactivity series based on information about its reactions.	6.3	6.3
Extend		
Deduce the physical or chemical changes a metal has undergone from its appearance.		
Justify the use of specific metals and non-metals for different applications, using data provided.	(6.1)	(6.1)
Deduce a rule from data about which reactions will occur or not, based on the reactivity series.	6.3	6.3

Acids & alkalis

	Student Book	Teacher Guide
Know		
The pH of a solution depends on the strength of the acid: strong acids have lower pH values than weak acids.	6.7	6.7
Mixing an acid and alkali produces a chemical reaction, neutralisation, forming a chemical called a salt and water.	6.8	6.8
Fact: Acids have a pH below 7, neutral solutions have a pH of 7, alkalis have a pH above 7.	6.7	6.7
Fact: Acids and alkalis can be corrosive or irritant and require safe handling.	6.7	6.7
Fact: Hydrochloric, sulfuric and nitric acid are strong acids.	6.7	6.7
Fact: Acetic and citric acid are weak acids.	6.7	6.7
pH: Scale of acidity and alkalinity from 0 to 14.	6.7	6.7
Indicators: Substances used to identify whether unknown solutions are acidic or alkaline.	6.7	6.7
Base: A substance that neutralises an acid –those that dissolve in water are called alkalis.	(6.7)	(6.7)
Concentration: A measure of the number of particles in a given volume.		
Apply		
Identify the best indicator to distinguish between solutions of different pH, using data provided.	6.7	6.7
Use data and observations to determine the pH of a solution and explain what this shows.	6.7	6.7
Explain how neutralisation reactions are used in a range of situations.	6.8	6.8
Describe a method for how to make a neutral solution from an acid and alkali.	6.8, 6.9	6.8, 6.9
Extend		
Given the names of an acid and an alkali, work out the name of the salt produced when they react.	6.8	6.8
Deduce the hazards of different alkalis and acids using data about their concentration and pH.	6.5, 6.6, 6.7	6.5, 6.6, 6.7
Estimate the pH of an acid based on information from reactions.		

1.6.1 Using metals and non-metals

Lesson overview

Learning objectives

- Recognise the properties and uses of metals and non-metals.
- Explain the uses of metals and non-metals based on their properties.

Learning outcomes

- Identify some common properties of metals and non-metals and their uses. [O1]
- Identify similarities and differences between metals and how these relate to their uses. [O2]
- Compare and contrast the properties of metals and non-metals. [O3]

Skills development

- Working scientifically: 2.3 Draw conclusions
- Developing numeracy: n/a
- Developing literacy: incorporate key information in descriptions and explanations (Q5 - 8)

Resources needed equipment for the demonstration (four same-sized metal rods: copper, iron, brass and aluminium, each with a drawing pin stuck at one end using melted candle wax, (optional) non-metal rods for comparison, kettle, trough for water) and for the practical, per group (see Technician's notes 1.6.1); Worksheet 1.6.1; Practical sheet 1.6.1; Technician's notes 1.6.1

Common misconceptions All metals are silver-coloured, magnetic and strong. Non-metals are all solids. Gases have no mass. Air and water are elements. All gases are poisonous.

Key vocabulary ductile, malleable, sonorous, conductor, metals, non-metals

Teaching and learning

Engage

- Ask the students 'What do we use metals for?'. Working in pairs, ask students to take turns listing answers and **identifying** as many uses of metals as they can. [O1]
- Ask the students to **recall** properties of metals and then **predict** those of non-metals. [O1]
- **Group work** Encourage the students to look around the room and think about what they have done today that may involve a metal or a non-metal. In groups, they should present their thoughts as a list of ideas. [O1]

Challenge and develop

- Ask 'Why do we use metals?'. Students should use their prior knowledge and awareness of why we use metals and the properties of metals to propose answers. [O1]
- Demonstrate the thermal conductivity of metals (see Technician's notes 1.6.1), possibly contrasting with non-metals. [O1]
- Ask the students to work in pairs to **investigate** the conduction of electricity by different metals, and possibly non-metals for comparison (see Practical sheet 1.6.1 and Technician's notes 1.6.1). [O1, O2]
- **Group work** Introduce the various properties of metals, to provide appropriate terminology. The students can then **justify** each of the uses in their lists from the starter activity, **identifying** the main reasons for the use of each metal (the properties) – such as strong, shiny, high melting point. [O1, O2]

Explain

- **Envoys** Students collaborate to produce a spider diagram **recording the properties** of metals with examples for each. Using envoys, they should then **compare their findings** with other groups and give feedback (e.g. as two stars and a wish). [O1, O2]

- The students should **observe** the appearance of sulfur, iodine and carbon and **compare** them to each other and to gases and metals, answering the questions on Practical sheet 1.6.1. [O1, O3]

- The students can then **research** (using books and the internet) the properties of non-metals, and **identify** the common properties, highlighting any odd ones out. [O3]

- Emphasise that carbon is a special element, with properties of both metals and non-metals. [O1, O2, O3]

Consolidate and apply

- Demonstrate the differences between sodium and iron (e.g. shiny/dull, hard/soft, scratchability, magnetic or not, density, reactivity in water). Explain that not all metals are the same, even though they have common properties such as density and magnetism, and that the sheen on a metal lasts if it doesn't react with air (rusting). Point out that the properties dictate the uses (e.g. we couldn't use sodium instead of iron for making a car). [O1, O2]

- **Group work** Ask the students to select the best material to use for a given purpose, **justifying their choices** using the correct terms. They should then **peer assess responses** with another group. [O2, O3]

- Ask the students to **consider** if it is just the properties of a substance that dictate what we use it for. [O2, O3]

- Ask students to **collaborate** to record all the properties on cards and organise them into lists of metals and non-metals plus any that are common to both. [O1, O2, O3]

- They should individually construct a Venn diagram to show the properties of metals and non-metals with carbon in the middle with 'bits of both'. [O1, O3]

  High demand students may be able to **consider** the cost of the metals and perhaps link to the need to extract them from compounds.

  It may make it easier for low demand students to **consider** individual elements in order to construct their Venn diagram (e.g. iron, sulfur and carbon).

  High demand students could increase the complexity of their diagram by creating additional sections (e.g. solid/liquid/gas, magnetic); then **identify elements** that fit the categories. Alternatively they could create a key to identify an element.

- Ask the students to **compare** and **contrast** sodium, chlorine and sodium chloride (see Technician's notes 1.6.1). They can answer the questions in sections 1 and 2 of Worksheet 1.6.1. Point out the fact that the elements sodium and chlorine are not very useful and are dangerous in their element form, but as a salt/compound, sodium chloride is one of the safest and most useful chemicals we have. [O1, O3]

Extend

For students able to progress further:

- Ask students to **compare the uses** of the original metals and of their alloy for a particular application – iron *v* steel (rusting, strength); copper *v* brass (discolouration, strength); aluminium *v* duralumin (light, unreactive, strong) for the construction of cars, aeroplanes, buildings. You could demonstrate a smart alloy returning to its original shape to illustrate an application such as 'bendy' spectacle frames. [O1, O2, O3]

- Students able to progress further could **research** the uses of non-metal elements and of their compounds with metals. Introduce the idea that non-metals change their names when in a compound, e.g. sulfur – sulfide, oxygen – oxide etc. The students can do task 3 on Worksheet 1.6.1. [O2, O3]

Plenary suggestions

Which property is most important? Show the students a metal object (examples include kettles, bath taps, a concert stage, necklaces, a barbecue) for them to **identify the property** most relevant to its use. Ask them to **justify their choices**;. [O1, O2, O3]

What am I? Read out the properties of a substance and challenge the students to **predict** what it could be. [O1]

Answers to Student Book questions

1. Malleable; conducts heat well; conducts electricity well; shiny (when freshly cut); strong; ductile.
2. a) Conducts heat; high melting point; non-toxic; unreactive. b) Doesn't corrode with water; non-toxic. c) Light; non-toxic;doesn't corrode with water.

3. Examples may include: copper for wires because it conducts electricity, water pipes because it is ductile, is not toxic; iron for buildings because it is strong; nickel in door catch/toys/ credit cards because it is magnetic.

4. Copper is not reactive, sodium reacts with the air/water and is soft.

5. An alloy is a mixture of metals that has different properties from the metals it is made from (e.g. may be stronger).

6. Metals are good conductors of heat and electricity whereas non-metals are poor conductors; non-metals are often unreactive gases; metals are usually solids at room temperature; [other sensible comparisons].

7. Liquid at room temperature, kills bacteria.

8. Density less than air.

Answers to Worksheet 1.6.1

1. a) All the atoms in it are identical.

   b) Melt two (or more) metals together; mix them and let the mixture solidify.

   c) Elements: iron, aluminium, gold, silver, zinc, copper; alloys: steel, brass, bronze.

2. Iron gate: strong, cheap; steel bridge: strong; aluminium foil: can be made very thin, won't react with food easily, high melting point; brass clock: strong, attractive, won't oxidise; gold ring: attractive, won't oxidise or tarnish; silver necklace: attractive, won't oxidise or tarnish; zinc coating on bucket: strong, won't oxidise; bronze sword: strong, won't oxidise; copper base on saucepan: good conductor of heat.

3. a) zinc coated: strong; won't corrode   b) brass or stainless steel: strong; won't corrode

   c) zinc coated: strong; won't corrode   d) copper: very good conductor of electricity; cheap

   e) aluminium: light; bends; won't corrode   f) silver or brass: attractive; malleable; won't corrode

   g) copper, gold or silver: attractive; malleable; won't corrode   h) steel or aluminium: strong; won't corrode

1.6.2 Exploring the reactions of acids with metals

Lesson overview

Learning objectives

- Describe the reaction between acids and metals using word equations and particle diagrams.
- Explain the reaction between acids and metals.
- Compare the reactivities of different metals.

Learning outcomes

- Describe the observations made when acids react with metals. [O1]
- Explain the reaction between acids and metals. [O2]
- Compare the reactivities of different metals. [O3]

Skills development

- Working scientifically: 2.6 Construct explanations
- Developing numeracy: relate word equations to rearrangement of particles in reactions
- Developing literacy: express reactions as word equations (Q3 - 6)

Resources needed equipment for practical, per pair (dilute hydrochloric acid, dilute nitric acid, magnesium ribbon, zinc metal granules, iron filings, copper turnings, 6 test tubes in test tube rack, splints, Bunsen burner, eye protection); Worksheet 1.6.2; Practical sheet 1.6.2; Technician's notes 1.6.2

Common misconceptions When a metal reacts with an acid, it vanishes.

Key vocabulary salt, hydrogen, reactivity

Teaching and learning

Engage

- Show a web-based video of a reaction between calcium and an acid. [O1]
- Ask the students to **suggest** how they can tell that a chemical reaction has taken place. [O1, O2]
- Ask them to **explain** what the bubbles in the reaction show (a gas is produced). Tell them as well that the reaction causes an increase in temperature. [O1, O2]
- Ask the students to work in pairs to **list** some clues that a chemical reaction is taking place. Ask them to **share** their ideas as a class and to **construct** a list. If necessary, refer students to the 'Reacting acids with metals' section in the Student Book. [O1]

Challenge and develop

- Ask the students to **recap** what new products are made during the reactions; you could display this in equation form. Ask them to **suggest** how the reaction of acids with metals is different from the reaction between acids and alkalis (you can see a gas formed in a metal/acid reaction). [O2]

Explain

- **Pair work** Pairs **carry out** a practical to explore the reactions of acids with metals (using Practical sheet 1.6.2). [O1]
- The students **record** their observations. [O1]
- If time allows, ask them to **observe** reactions of other metals for evidence of hydrogen gas.
- The students could attempt tasks 1 and 2 of Worksheet 1.6.2. [O1]

- If time allows, demonstrate the reaction of copper with concentrated nitric acid. You could ask the students to **predict** the outcome before you carry out the demonstration. [O1]

Consolidate and apply

- Ask the students to **share** their findings across the class. [O1, O2]

- Share the general equation for the reaction of acids with metals with students. Ask students to work individually to answer the questions on Practical sheet 1.6.2. [O1, O2, O3]

Extend

- Ask students able to progress further to **plan** an investigation into a factor that could affect the rate of the reaction between acids and metals. Ask them to **consider** the variables that they will change, measure and control – they could also make a prediction. Section 3 of Worksheet 1.6.2 could also be used here.

Plenary suggestions

Describing and applying ideas Show a web-based video of sodium reacting with hydrochloric acid. Ask the students to **describe** what they see. Then ask them to **suggest** what products are made. Students should be able to **describe** the equation. Point out that the solution turns cloudy as sodium chloride forms. [O1, O2]

Then show a video of potassium reacting with hydrochloric acid. Ask the students to **rank** sodium and potassium in order of reactivity. [O3]

Answers to Student Book questions

1. Bubbles of gas; change of temperature; colour change; change in mass.
2. Bubbles of gas; change of temperature (increase).
3. A gas is produced.
4. Hydrochloric acid + magnesium → magnesium chloride + hydrogen.
5. The particle diagram shows that hydrogen within the nitric acid separates from the rest of the acid molecule, releasing hydrogen gas.
6. Hydrogen burns in air; a large amount of hydrogen gas could cause a big explosion.
7. Magnesium; zinc; iron; copper.
8. A lot of bubbling; steam.
9. Hydrochloric acid + magnesium → magnesium chloride + hydrogen,
   Hydrochloric acid + zinc → zinc chloride + hydrogen,
   Hydrochloric acid + iron → iron chloride + hydrogen,
   Hydrochloric acid + copper → no reaction.

Answers to Worksheet 1.6.2

1. Bubbles of gas; colour change; tube feels warmer.
2. a) From most to least reactive – magnesium; iron; copper.
   b) More bubbles; more vigorous reaction (could see a flame).
   c) Between magnesium and iron.
3. a) More bubbles; faster reaction because more acid molecules in concentrated acid.
   b) Fewer bubbles, slower reaction; reaction will stop sooner because there is less magnesium to react.
   c) More bubbles; faster reaction because the magnesium powder has a bigger surface area.

1.6.3 Understanding displacement reactions

Lesson overview

Learning objectives

- Represent and explain displacement reactions using equations and particle diagrams.
- Make inferences about reactivity from displacement reactions.

Learning outcomes

- Write word equations to represent displacement reactions; give some uses for displacement reactions. [O1]
- Use particle models to explain displacement and relate it to the reactivity series. [O2]
- Write symbol equations for displacement reactions. [O3]

Skills development

- Working scientifically: 2.4 Present data
- Developing numeracy: construct and interpret grids tabulating reactions between various combinations of reactants
- Developing literacy: draw conclusions from experimental evidence (Q3 - 6)

Resources needed a previously prepared iron nail that has been in a solution of copper sulfate overnight; iron nail and freshly prepared copper sulfate solution; equipment for practical, per group (1 cm strips of magnesium, copper, zinc, lead, iron, solutions of copper sulfate, zinc sulfate, lead nitrate, magnesium chloride, iron sulfate, 4 test tubes in a test-tube rack, 10 ml measuring cylinder, 4 thermometers, timer, safety glasses); Worksheet 1.6.3 (page 2 copied onto cards); Practical sheet 1.6.3; Technician's notes 1.6.3

Common misconceptions All metals react in the same way with the same degree of reactivity.

Key vocabulary displacement, reactivity

Teaching and learning

Engage

- Demonstrate putting an iron nail into a solution of copper sulfate – show a previously prepared sample of an iron nail in copper sulfate that has been left overnight. Ask the students to **make observations**. Write down the reactants and ask the students to predict what the products might be. Alternatively, use the images in the Student Book. [O1]

- Tell the students that you will repeat the reaction using a strip of magnesium instead of iron. Ask them to **recap** what they learned from last lesson and to **predict** how this reaction will be different from that of the iron, **giving reasons**. Ask them to **write word equations** to predict the products. [O1]

Challenge and develop

- Select three students to **demonstrate a role-play** of displacement reactions, using word cards of the reactants as given on Worksheet 1.6.3. Ask them to role-play the reaction between iron and copper sulfate. Emphasise that, because iron is more reactive than copper, it will 'snatch away' the sulfate, which is bonded to the copper. Use the students to demonstrate how this works, with the student holding the iron card 'snatching away' the student holding the sulfate card. [O1, O2]

- Introduce and define the term 'displacement reaction'. Use the 'Using displacement reactions' section of the Student Book to discuss the importance of displacement reactions and how they can be useful. [O1]

- **Group work** In small groups, students should **follow the instructions** on Practical sheet 1.6.3. They should **work out** the order of reactivity of the different metals by reacting them with solutions of different metals. [O1]

Explain

- Provide students (in groups of four) with the word cards from Worksheet 1.6.3 and the reactivity series shown in Figure1.6.3e in the Student Book. Ask them to use role-play to **explain** what will happen in the reactions they have just investigated. Select different students to **demonstrate** the reactions. [O1, O2]

  High demand students should **write balanced symbol equations** for all equations. [O3]

Consolidate and apply

- Ask the students to use the list of reactivity of metals from the Student Book and the cards from Worksheet 1.6.3 to **devise** five reactions of their own to show the idea of displacement. [O1, O2, O3]

- Students should complete tasks 1 and 2 of Worksheet 1.6.3, **writing word equations**, using the card sort first to work out what is happening. [O1, O2, O3]

- The students should answer all the appropriate questions in the Student Book. [O1, O2, O3]

Extend

- Ask students able to progress further to carry out some **research** and **make a slideshow** about three important displacement reactions, giving word and balanced symbol equations for all reactions they identify. [O3]

Plenary suggestions

Make a poster The students could **prepare a poster** for another class, to **explain** what displacement reactions are and how they are useful. Word and balanced symbol equations should be included. [O1, O2, O3]

Other models The students could think of other models/analogies to explain the displacement process. [O2]

Answers to Student Book questions

1. May see bubbles, colour change, temperature change.
2. Magnesium.
3. Zinc.
4. Zinc + iron sulfate → zinc sulfate + iron
5. Magnesium, zinc, iron, copper.
6. a) Tick.
   b) Cross.
7. Copper is less reactive and will not displace hydrogen.
8. An element higher in the reactivity series will displace an element lower in the reactivity series from its compound.

Answers to Worksheet 1.6.3

1. a) The product magnesium chloride is wrong; it should be iron sulfate + magnesium → magnesium sulfate + iron.
   b) This implies no reaction, which is wrong because iron is more reactive than lead; it should be lead nitrate + iron → iron nitrate + lead.
   c) This shows that a reaction has taken place, which is wrong; in fact no displacement occurs and the reactants remain unchanged; (however, if the potassium chloride were dissolved in water, the sodium would react vigorously, making hydrogen).
   d) The product iron is wrong; it should be copper sulfate + aluminium → aluminium sulfate + copper.
2. Correct word equations with the same elements in the reactants as in the products; in the products, the more reactive metal should be combined with the radical of the less reactive metal.
3 i) Tin will not react with iron sulfate. ii) Tin will react with lead sulfate to make lead and tin sulfate.

1.6.4 Understanding oxidation reactions

Lesson overview

Learning objectives

- Recall examples of oxidation reactions.
- Describe oxidation using word equations and particle diagrams.
- Investigate changes caused by oxidation.

Learning outcomes

- Describe evidence of oxidation reactions. [O1]
- Explain why oxidation is a chemical reaction. [O2]
- Use a simple model/word equation to explain changes during oxidation reactions. [O3]

Skills development

- Working scientifically: 2.1 Analyse patterns
- Developing numeracy: record and process data relating to mass change
- Developing literacy: summarise key ideas about reactions (Q4 - 8)

Resources needed photos of visible effects of oxidation; materials and equipment for the demonstration (three stands, bosses and clamps, two 100 cm^3 gas syringes, silica glass tubing, heat-resistant mat, Bunsen burner, thick rubber tubing for the connections, mineral wool, copper turnings, damp cloth, splint, safety screen) and for the practical, per group (see Technician's notes 1.6.4); Worksheet 1.6.4; Practical sheet 1.6.4a; Practical sheet 1.6.4b; Technician's notes 1.6.4

Common misconceptions Oxidation only happens when things burn. Burning always causes loss of mass.

Key vocabulary oxidation

Teaching and learning

Engage

- Show the students a series of photos demonstrating visible effects of oxidation (e.g. rusting gate/bridge, browning apple, tarnished silver, burning wood) and ask them to find the link between them. If the students are having difficulty, give them a clue by telling them that they all involve the same substance/reaction with the same substance (oxygen). Ask 'Which reaction might be the odd one out?'. (Fire is a fast reaction.) [O1]

Challenge and develop

- Introduce oxidation as a chemical reaction. It is not reversible and a new substance is formed. [O1, O2]
- The students should carry out an experiment to heat a folded piece of copper metal (Practical sheet 1.6.4a). Encourage them to **explain precautions** that should be taken to reduce risks when heating the metal (e.g. using tongs to hold the copper, wearing eye protection to prevent hot materials getting into the eyes). On cooling, they should open out the copper and **make observations** (the outside of the heated metal goes black and the inside remains shiny). [O1, O2]
- Ask the students to **compare** the heating of copper with the heating of magnesium they may have done in an earlier lesson: copper remains the same size, it just changes colour (may get green colouration in flame); magnesium reacts much more quickly/violently, burning with a bright white flame and leaving a white powder/ash. [O1, O2]
- Discuss how the results provide evidence of a chemical change: there are permanent changes of colour and texture/properties; a new substance is formed; you cannot get the copper back (note that some students may think the black colour is soot and that the copper remains unchanged). [O1, O2]

Explain

- Demonstrate the oxidation of copper in gas syringes (see Technician's notes 1.6.4) in order to show the removal of something (oxygen) from the air during the reaction. [O1]

- **Pair talk** The students should **observe** the reaction closely and **record their observations** following the prompts on Practical sheet 1.6.4b. They should **discuss** in pairs questions such as 'What changed?', 'Why do you think these changes have occurred?'. [O2]

- Ask the students to answer the questions on Practical sheet 1.6.4b. [O1, O2, O3]

  High demand students should be encouraged to calculate the volume of air before and after the experiment (100 cm^3 to 80 cm^3) and **justify** the volume difference (this is the volume of oxygen in 100 cm^3 of air).

Consolidate and apply

- The students should **complete** tasks 1 and 2 on Worksheet 1.6.4. [O1, O2, O3]

- Ask the students to **analyse the evidence** in Table 1.6.4 in the Student Book of the burning of magnesium, to write a word equation and to draw a circle diagram to explain the data (questions 7 and 8). [O3]

Extend

- Ask students able to progress further to complete task 3 of Worksheet 1.6.4. This asks them to write symbol equations. Note that balancing equations is not required at this stage. The worksheet task also asks students to represent other reactions as circle models, enabling them to demonstrate a clear understanding of 'atom'/'element' and 'compound'. [O3]

  High demand students may be capable of balancing symbol equations.

Plenary suggestions

Equation quiz Ask the students to **complete** or write word equations for a series of oxidation reactions (e.g. carbon to carbon dioxide; sulfur + oxygen → sulfur dioxide; making lead oxide etc.) Mini-whiteboards could be used. [O2, O3]

Answers to Student Book questions

1. It is the name given to a reaction when oxygen is added to/reacts with a substance.
2. Burning a fuel; browning an apple; rusting of iron.
3. The copper goes black/changes colour.
4. Iron + oxygen → iron oxide.
5. Change of colour in the new product during rusting; formation of new products such as ash, smoke and heat generation.
6. The silver-coloured metal changes to white ash; the magnesium metal reacted with oxygen to form white magnesium oxide.
7. Magnesium + oxygen → magnesium oxide.
8. *Start*: two unjoined same-colour circles for two Mg atoms; two touching same colour circles (different from Mg colour) for an oxygen molecule O_2. *End*: two separate pairs of joined different-colour paired circles for MgO.

Answers to Worksheet 1.6.4

1. a) There will be at least one of: permanent colour change; change in texture; generates light/heat; new substance formed; cannot get the original substance back. b) Oxides.
2. a) Check circle diagrams. b) i) Copper + oxygen (reactants) → copper oxide (product).
   ii) Magnesium + oxygen (reactants) → magnesium oxide (product).
3. a) i) Cu + O_2 → CuO ii) Mg + O_2 → MgO [balancing not required] b) Check circle diagrams.
   c) i) Zn + O_2 → ZnO ii) Ca + O_2 → CaO [balancing not required]
   d) Magnesium is a **solid** and oxygen is a **gas**. Magnesium reacts with the oxygen to form a **compound** called magnesium oxide. During the reaction the **atoms** (particles) of magnesium and oxygen combine together. Magnesium oxide is a solid. Because the oxygen has combined with the magnesium, it is heavier than magnesium on its own.

Answers to Practical sheet 1.6.4b

1. To prevent the copper turnings entering the syringe.
2. Gases expand when heated; allowing the apparatus to cool to the original temperature gives a valid reading.
3. To ensure that all the oxygen has reacted with the copper.
4. Copper + oxygen (reactants) → copper oxide (product). 5. Difference between start and end volumes.
6. Volume of gas in syringe decreases as part of it is used up in the reaction (oxygen).

1.6.5 Exploring acids

Lesson overview

Learning objectives

- Understand what an acid is.

- Identify the hazards that acids pose.

Learning outcomes

- Identify everyday substances that contain acids. [O1]

- Evaluate the hazards posed by a number of acids and how they may be reduced. [O2]

- Explain the similarities between all acids. [O3]

Skills development

- Working scientifically: 2.13 Estimate risks

- Developing numeracy: relate terms such as dilute and concentrated to proportions of particles

- Developing literacy: develop explanations using ideas and evidence (Q3 - 7)

Resources needed lemon juice; vinegar; black tea; small disposable cups; disposable spoons; drinking water; images or packaging of common acids (e.g. sulfuric, hydrochloric, nitric, ethanoic, citric) *or* packaging or objects linked to acid use (e.g. pickled foods, fruit juices, cordials, tea, paint, explosives, fertilisers, car batteries, ink); pieces of coloured card (two different colours); Worksheet 1.6.5; Technician's notes 1.6.5

Common misconceptions All acids are harmful.

Key vocabulary acid, corrosive, irritant, hydrogen

Teaching and learning

Engage

- Ask the students to taste a small amount of lemon juice, vinegar and black tea. They should use disposable spoons for each liquid and water should be provided to rinse the mouth after each sample. Ask students, in pairs, to **describe** the taste of the liquids. [O1, O2]

- Lead a class discussion to share descriptions. Establish that these liquids taste sour because they all contain an acid. [O1, O2]

Challenge and develop

- Show images or packaging of common acids. You should include sulfuric acid, hydrochloric acid and nitric acid used in the laboratory, and some of those from the 'engage' activity, such as ethanoic acid (vinegar), citric acid (lemon juice). Ask the students to **record** the name of each acid but do not explain other uses for acids at this stage. [O1]

- Show images of uses of common acids. Ask the students to work in pairs to **suggest** what each image is showing. Then reveal the name of each acid involved. Alternatively, show packaging or objects linked to each use of acids – pickled foods (in vinegar which contains ethanoic acid), fruit juices (citric acid), cordials (citric acid), tea (tartaric acid), paint (nitric acid), explosives (nitric acid), fertilisers (nitric acid or sulfuric acid), car batteries (sulfuric acid), ink (tannic acid). [O1]

Explain

- Ask the students to **read** the 'What do acids have in common?' section in the Student Book as a class. [O2]

- The students work individually to answer the questions in the Student Book. [O2]

- The students then work in pairs to **compare** and **agree** on answers. They should then **amend** their work as appropriate. [O2]

- Ask each student to **design** another question about what acids are and what they have in common. They then join with their partner and try to answer each other's question. [O2]

- Ask pairs to **share** some questions across the class. [O2]

Consolidate and apply

- Ask the students to look at the images or packaging of common acids again. Ask them to **find** and **draw** any hazard symbols. [O3]

- Lead a class discussion asking the students to **explain** what each symbol means. [O3]

- Ask the students to **rank** each of the acids and products that they have seen in terms of how dangerous they are. Ask the pairs to form fours to **compare** and **agree** the rank order. Worksheet 1.6.5 could be attempted here. [O3]

Extend

- Ask students able to progress further to evaluate each of the products and a danger associated with working with it. Students should **develop** a list of precautions to take when handling any of the products. [O3]

Plenary suggestions

Loop card game Arrange the students in groups of about eight. Each student writes an example of an acid on a piece of coloured card and writes a use on a piece of different-coloured card. The cards are mixed up and then each student chooses one 'acid' card and one 'use' card. The students then play a loop card game, with one student reading out an acid and the student who has the correct use identifying themselves. This student then reads out their acid and so on. [O1, O2]

Answers to Student Book questions

1. Lemons, oranges, vinegar, fizzy drinks, tea, etc.
2. Sulfuric acid and nitric acid.
3. Universal language; the user doesn't need to be able to read.
4. Wear gloves; wear eye protection; take care not to spill.
5. They are corrosive (destroy skin, attack metals).
6. Hydrogen; nitrogen; oxygen.
7. It is likely to be an acid because it tastes sour and contains hydrogen.

Answers to Worksheet 1.6.5

1. a) Nitric b) Ethanoic c) Citric d) Sulfuric e) Lactic
2. *Sulfuric* – fertilisers and car batteries; *nitric* – fertilisers, paints and explosives; *ethanoic* – vinegar; *citric* – citrus fruits and preservatives; *tartaric* – tea.
3. a), b) A: irritant/caution – care not to spill on skin, use eye protection; B: corrosive – great care, wear gloves and eye protection.

1.6.6 Exploring alkalis

Lesson overview

Learning objectives

- Understand what an alkali is.
- Identify the hazards that alkalis pose.

Learning outcomes

- Identify everyday substances that contain alkalis. [O1]
- Evaluate the hazards posed by a number of alkalis and how they may be reduced. [O2]
- Recognise what alkalis have in common and the hazards associated with some. [O3]

Skills development

- Working scientifically: 2.13 Estimate risks
- Developing numeracy: relate numerical scales to ideas such as pH
- Developing literacy: identifying and summarizing common features (Q7)

Resources needed bars of soap; water; paper towels; packaging from everyday alkalis (e.g. bleach, washing powder, washing-up liquid, shampoo, toothpaste, indigestion remedy, lime for soil, hair bleach, oven cleaner, disinfectant, baking powder); concentrated ammonium hydroxide (caustic soda) (optional); large sheets of paper; pens; Periodic Table; Worksheet 1.6.6; Technician's notes 1.6.6

Common misconceptions Alkalis are not dangerous.

Key vocabulary alkali, hydroxide

Teaching and learning

Engage

- Ask the students to wet their hands slightly and apply some soap. They should not wash the soap off straight away. Ask them to rub their hands together and to **describe** what they see and feel. Take some feedback and write some of the descriptive words on the whiteboard. [O1, O2]
- Explain that soap is an example of a substance that contains an alkali. Explain that other alkalis also feel soapy, although some are too harmful to be felt in this way. [O2]

Challenge and develop

- Ask the students to look at packaging from everyday alkalis. [O1]
- **Pairs to fours** Ask the students to work in pairs to **sort** these products into those that they think are harmful and those that they think are not harmful. [O1, O2]

  You could support low demand students by providing simple pictures on cards, rather than packaging, to be sorted.

- The pairs merge to form fours to **compare** their sorting. Encourage the students to look at packaging and to **ask questions** if they cannot **agree** on any product. [O1, O2]
- Discuss how harmful some of these substances can be, using caustic soda as an example. [O2]

Explain

- Ask the students to **recall** the meanings of the hazard symbols on the packaging. In pairs, the students **discuss** the precautions that should be taken with both an irritant and a corrosive alkali. [O2, O3]
- Ask some pairs to **share** their ideas about the precautions to take. Ask other students to **comment** on the ideas, **suggesting** any changes. Tasks 1 and 2 of Worksheet 1.6.6 could be used here. [O2, O3]

Consolidate and apply

- As a class, read the 'Useful alkalis' section in the Student Book. Answer the questions verbally as a class. [O1, O2, O3]

- Ask pairs of students to **consider** what life would be like without alkalis. [O1]

- The pairs **plan** and **produce** a poster highlighting the importance of alkalis and the consequences of not having alkalis. [O1, O2, O3]

- Merge the pairs to form fours and each group **peer assesses** the two posters, **recording** feedback as 'two stars and a wish'. As the students work, you could share some good examples of feedback from groups to model the process for others. [O1, O2, O3]

Extend

- Show students able to progress further some chemical formulas for other alkalis. Ask them to **suggest** which elements each alkali contains. Then ask them to **locate** the elements on the Periodic Table and **suggest** what their position tells us. Task 3 of Worksheet 1.6.6 can be used here.

Plenary suggestions

What have I learned? Ask the students to work in pairs to **suggest** three things that they have learned today. Pairs then form fours and each group **agrees** a list of three things. [O1, O2, O3]

Sharing knowledge Ask, one at a time, groups to **share** something that they learned. Work around the class asking groups to **share** a new suggestion until there are no new ideas. [O1, O2, O3]

Answers to Student Book questions

1. Bleach; oven cleaner; soap; disinfectant; washing powder.
2. *Safe* – toothpaste and baking powder; *not safe* – bleach and oven cleaner.
3. Sensible suggestions such as unable to wash; clean our teeth; clean our houses as we do now.
4. To allow blind people to know that the bottle contains a dangerous chemical.
5.

6. Caustic soda is a strong alkali and is corrosive; bleach is a weaker alkali and is an irritant.
7. They contain hydroxide 'particles'.
8. a) Calcium, hydrogen, oxygen b) sodium, hydrogen, oxygen.
9. B is stronger, A is most likely to be used in indigestion remedies.

Answers to Worksheet 1.6.6

1. Washing up liquid; soap; toothpaste.
2. a) Toothpaste; soap; shampoo.
   b) i) Caution ii) Corrosive iii) Corrosive iv) Caution
3. a) i) Sodium, oxygen, hydrogen ii) calcium, oxygen, hydrogen iii) magnesium, oxygen, hydrogen
   b) A sentence stating that alkalis contain hydroxide 'particles'.

1.6.7 Using indicators

Lesson overview

Learning objectives

- Use indicators to identify acids and alkalis.
- Analyse data from different indicators.
- Compare the effectiveness of different indicators.
- Describe what a pH scale measures.

Learning outcomes

- Give an example of an indicator and describe why indicators are useful. [O1]
- Analyse the data generated to make suggestions about the strength of an acid or alkali. [O2]
- Interpret measurements of pH made using universal indicator. [O3]

Skills development

- Working scientifically: 2.4 Present data
- Developing numeracy: relate numerical scales to pH
- Developing literacy: make comparisons and identify advantages (Q8)

Resources needed equipment for the demonstration (litmus indicator, sodium hydroxide, ethanoic acid, small beaker); resources as on Technician's notes for demonstration of universal indicator and the practical, per group (see Technician's notes 1.6.7); Worksheet 1.6.7; Practical sheet 1.6.7; Technician's notes 1.6.7

Common misconceptions Indicators turn only red or blue.

Key vocabulary indicator, litmus, neutral, strong/weak acid, strong/weak alkali, pH

Teaching and learning

Engage

- Ask the students to observe as you perform a 'magic trick'. Pour some acid into a beaker (for example 0.05 M ethanoic acid) with tiny amount of litmus solution previously wiped around bottom (so that the beaker appears empty), without explaining what the liquid is. Ask the students to **describe** their observations. [O1]

- Next pour in some alkali (for example sodium hydroxide), without explaining what the liquid is. Ask the students to **describe** their observations. [O1]

- Ask the students to **share** any ideas to **explain** the colour changes. [O1]

- Define an indicator as a substance that has different colours in acids and alkalis. Ask the students to try to **explain** the colour changes using the extra information. Take some feedback. [O1, O2]

- Ask the students to **describe** what an indicator is in their own words to a partner. They could **write** this definition down. [O1]

Challenge and develop

- Explain that some acids are stronger than others. Ask the students to suggest which is stronger – sulfuric acid or ethanoic acid. You could refer back to hazard labels and to the fact that vinegar contains ethanoic acid if the students need more information. [O2]

- Arrange the students in pairs. Ask them to **explore** and **record** the colour changes of universal indicator when it is added to a strong alkali (sodium hydroxide) and when added to a weak alkali (sodium hydrogencarbonate (baking powder)) solution, using steps 1–6 of Practical sheet 1.6.7. [O2, O3]

- Ask the students to **share** their observations across the class about the differences between strong and weak alkalis.

Explain

- Ask the students to look at Figure 1.6.7b, the pH colour chart, in the Student Book. Ask them to **describe** the position of each of the chemicals observed so far on the scale. [O2, O3]

- Ask them to **suggest** what else the pH scale shows, apart from whether a substance is an acid or an alkali. [O2, O3]

- The students work in pairs to **test** a range of substances with universal indicator using step 7 of Practical sheet 1.6.7. They should **record** their observations in a table they have **designed** themselves. [O3]

- Ask the students to **analyse** their observations and **record** the pH of each substance and whether it is a strong acid, a weak acid, neutral, a weak alkali or a strong alkali. Encourage them to reflect on the way that they recorded the results – could this be improved? Worksheet 1.6.7 could be used here. [O2, O3]

Consolidate and apply

- **Pairs to fours** Ask the students to work in pairs to **discuss** the advantages of universal indicator over other indicators used in a previous lesson. The pairs merge to form fours to **share** ideas. [O2 & 3]

- They then work individually to **produce** a creative piece of writing. They should **imagine** that they work for a company selling universal indicator. They should **write** the text for a poster to advertise universal indicator, **highlighting** its advantages over other indicators. [O2 & 3]

Extend

- Provide students able to progress further with a coloured liquid, such as cola, and ask them why it would be difficult to test this liquid with universal indicator. Ask them how they could **test** this liquid. They should then **explain** their solution to the problem using the words 'concentrated' and 'dilute'.

- Provide information about the reactions of an acid. Ask students to estimate the pH of an acid based on information from the reactions. [O2]

Plenary suggestions

Learning triangle The students work individually to **construct** a learning triangle. They should draw a large triangle with a smaller inverted triangle that just fits inside (so that they have four triangles). In the outer triangles, the students write: something they've seen; something they've done; something they've discussed.

Then in the central triangle, they write something that they've learned. [O1, O2, O3]

Answers to Student Book questions

1. An indicator is a substance that has different colours when in an acid and in an alkali.
2. Red in acid; blue in alkali.
3. A table showing a) *red litmus paper*: red in acid; blue in alkali; red in neutral.
   b) *Blue litmus paper*: red in acid; blue in alkali; blue in neutral.
4. pH 5.
5. Increases.
6. Increases.
7. a) Red. b) Red.
8. Universal indicator gives a full range of colours; so it can tell us about the strength of an acid or alkali.

Answers to Worksheet 1.6.7

1. a) Correctly coloured pH chart.
   b) Labels: A strong acids (pH 1–4); B weak acids (pH 5 and 6); C neutral (pH 7); D weak alkali (pH 8 and 9); E strong alkali (pH 10–14).
2. a) A: pH in range 11–14, strong alkali; B: pH in range 1–2, strong acid; C: pH 6, weak acid.
   b) Green (pH 7).
3. The paragraph should include the idea that universal indicator has a range of colours; linked to the strength of the acid or alkali; litmus does not indicate the strength.

1.6.8 Exploring neutralisation

Lesson overview

Learning objectives

- Recall and use the neutralisation equation.
- Use indicators to identify chemical reactions.
- Explain colour changes in terms of pH and neutralisation.

Learning outcomes

- Predict the reactants and salts made in different neutralisation reactions. [O1]
- Describe the changes to indicators when acids and alkalis are mixed. [O2]
- Explain the changes to an indicator when acids and alkalis are mixed. [O3]

Skills development

- Working scientifically: 2.10 Devise questions
- Developing numeracy: relate word equations to rearrangements of particles in a reaction
- Developing literacy: summarise key features of an experiment in writing (Q3 - 5)

Resources needed equipment for demonstration (burette, burette stand, white tile, 100 cm^3 conical flask, universal indicator solution, pH meter or pH probe and data logging equipment, eye protection, sodium hydroxide solution (0.1 M), dilute hydrochloric acid (0.1 M)) and for practical, per group (see Technician's notes); Worksheet 1.6.8; Practical sheet 1.6.8; Technician's notes 1.6.8

Common misconceptions Mixing an acid and an alkali always results in a neutral solution.

Key vocabulary neutralisation, titration

Teaching and learning

Engage

- If possible show a video clip, without sound, of real-life examples of neutralisation. Alternatively, show some images of examples of neutralisation without an explanation. [O2]
- The students should note down what they observe. [O2]
- Ask them to **suggest** links between what they have seen and take feedback. Tasks 1 and 2 of Worksheet 1.6.8 could be attempted here. [O2]

Challenge and develop

- Arrange the students in pairs. Ask them to add some universal indicator to hydrochloric acid in a conical flask. They should **record** their observations. Next, ask them to add sodium hydroxide using a dropping pipette. Again, they should record their observations. Do not give too much guidance at this point. [O2]
- Ask the students to **describe** their observations. Ask them to **explain** the pH of the various solutions they produced during this activity. [O2]
- Use the feedback to show that different groups made different observations and elicit that this depended on the amount of alkali added. [O2, O3]

Explain

- Set the groups the challenge of producing a neutral solution. The students follow the instructions on Practical sheet 1.6.8 and then answer the questions. Stress that they should work carefully to **produce** a solution of pH 7. [O2, O3]

- Demonstrate a titration (see Technician's notes 1.6.8) and ask the students to **observe** the end point of the neutralisation. [O2]

- Ask them to **discuss** the two methods of neutralisation and to **compare** the accuracy. Take feedback. [O2, O3]

- Ask the students to **note** the volumes of acid and alkali used. Take **comments** about the relationship between the two volumes, stressing that the acid and alkali are of equal concentration. [O3]

Consolidate and apply

- Ask the students to **read** the 'The neutralisation equation' section in the Student Book. [O1]

- Give some examples of acids and alkalis and ask the students to **suggest** the name of the salt produced. [O1]

- Give the names of some other salts, such as magnesium chloride, iron sulfate and calcium sulfate, and ask them to **predict** the names of the acid and alkali that would produce them. [O1]

Extend

- Ask students able to progress further to **comment** on the volumes of acid and alkali used in the titration. Stress that the acid and alkali had equal concentration. Ask them to suggest how the volume of each used would change with given changes in concentration. [O3]

Plenary suggestions

Freeze frame The students work in pairs to **display** a freeze frame of an example of neutralisation. Other members of the class **guess** what is being represented. [O1]

Answers to Student Book questions

1. Neutralisation is the reaction between acids and alkalis; in which acids and alkalis cancel each other out.
2. The pH increases; because the solution becomes less acidic.
3. Purple; to blue; to green.
4. The solution could change from green to yellow, then orange or red. This is because the solution is becoming more acidic.
5. The acid can be added more gradually/more precisely; it is easier to reach the end point.
6. Acid + alkali → salt + water
7. a) Water. b) The salt.
8. a) hydrochloric acid + sodium hydroxide = water + sodium chloride. b) sodium chloride and water

Answers to Worksheet 1.6.8

1.

When alkali is added to an acid…	…the solution becomes less acidic.
As acid is added to an alkali…	…the pH of the alkali decreases.
When a solution is neutral…	…it is pH 7
One way that acids and alkalis can be mixed carefully…	…is by titration

2. a) Alkali toothpaste; neutralises acid; from bacteria in the mouth.
   b) Antacids neutralise stomach acid.
   c) Acidic bee sting neutralised by alkaline bicarbonate.
   d) Acidic nettle sting neutralised by alkaline substance from dock leaf.
3. a) Magnesium chloride b) Sodium chloride c) Calcium sulfate d) Sodium sulfate e) Calcium nitrate

1.6.9 Investigating neutralisation

Lesson overview

Learning objectives

• Design an investigation to compare the effectiveness of indigestion remedies.

• Analyse data to identify a suitable indigestion remedy and suggest improvements.

Learning outcomes

• Describe indigestion remedies and the way that they work. [O1]

• Design a suitable investigation to compare indigestion remedies fairly. [O2]

• Analyse data to make a justified decision about the best remedy. [O3]

Skills development

• Working scientifically: 2.10 Devise questions

• Developing numeracy: evaluate quality of data using concepts such as repeatability

• Developing literacy: critically evaluate a procedure (Q7 - 9)

Resources needed equipment and materials as detailed in the Technician's notes; Worksheet 1.6.9; Practical sheet 1.6.9; Technician's notes 1.6.9

Common misconceptions Antacids neutralise stomach acid to form a neutral solution (pH 7).

Key vocabulary indigestion, heartburn, antacid, base, neutralisation

Teaching and learning

Engage

• Show some adverts for indigestion remedies and, if possible, video clips. [O1]

• Ask the students to work in pairs to **discuss** and **write down** anything that they know about indigestion or its remedies. [O1]

• If necessary, remind them that we always have acid in our stomach (approximately pH 1–2). If the sphincter at the top of the stomach opens, this acid can move up towards the throat. This causes heartburn or indigestion. Ask the students to **suggest** what indigestion remedies are. Ask them to **suggest** what the reaction between the stomach acid and the remedy is. [O1]

Challenge and develop

• **Group work** Ask the students to work in groups of four to **brainstorm** how they could **investigate** which is the most effective remedy. Encourage students to be as creative as possible at this stage and to **generate** as many ideas as possible. Allow them access to packaging during this activity (or to copies of ingredient and dosage information). [O1, O2]

• Ask the groups to **share** some of their ideas across the class. [O1, O2]

Explain

• Ask groups of four to split into pairs. The new pairs should **plan** an investigation to find the most effective remedy for indigestion. Encourage students to use the information and **discussion** from the previous activity to help them. Practical sheet 1.6.9 can be used to support planning. [O2]

• Check each group's plan for suitability and safety before allowing them to **carry out** the investigation. You will need to be flexible in terms of equipment needed. It will be useful to set up some beakers of distilled water with universal indicator added, to remind the students what neutral pH looks like. [O2]

• If the students need support, give them some ideas about how to carry out the investigation. For example:

- Use the recommended dose of remedy and, if it is in tablet form, crush it in a pestle and mortar.

- Set up two beakers of hydrochloric acid and add universal indicator to each. Keep one for comparison and add the remedy to the other.

- Observe the colour change of the indicator and record this along with any other observations.

- Repeat with at least one more remedy for comparison.

You could ask high demand students to use a pH meter to generate data about changes in pH over time.

Consolidate and apply

- Ask students to **analyse** their data to decide which indigestion remedy is the most effective (Practical sheet 1.6.9 supports this analysis). [O3]

- Encourage those students without a full set of results to **collaborate** with another group carrying out the investigation in a similar way. Worksheet 1.6.9 could be used to give practice in interpreting data. [O3]

Extend

- Ask students able to progress further to **evaluate** the investigation, **suggesting** improvements and the next steps.

Plenary suggestions

Adverts The students create an advert to promote the remedy that they have found to be the most effective. Encourage them to **consider** the adverts that were seen at the start of the lesson. Remind them of the need to educate as well as entertain an audience. [O1, O2, O3]

Answers to Student Book questions

1. Heartburn is a burning sensation in the chest and throat; caused by stomach acid moving up the oesophagus.
2. An alkali (or base) neutralises the stomach acid; making the solution less acidic.
3. Increases the pH.
4. *Independent* variable: type of indigestion remedy/antacid; *dependent* variable: time taken.
5. Starting pH, volume of acid solution, temperature of acid solution/ room.
6. How does the type of indigestion remedy affect the time taken for acid to be neutralised? (Or similar answers.)
7. The experiment is repeatable because you can take repeat readings close together.
8. 374 s, 183 s, 550 s. Acid-ease is the most effective because it increases pH from 1 to 6 in the smallest time, with an explanation of significance of increasing pH.
9. Use more accurate measuring equipment (e.g. measuring to one/two decimal points); repeat and calculate the mean.

Answers to Worksheet 1.6.9

1. C; B; A; D
2. a) Saliva is alkaline; it helps to neutralise any acid that leaves the stomach.
   b) Limestone contains calcium carbonate; which neutralises acid.
   c) Bicarbonate of soda is alkali; so it neutralises acid.
   d) This prevents acid from moving up the oesophagus easily.
3. a) A pH 3; B pH 5; C pH 4.
   b) B; it neutralises the acid to a pH nearest to neutral.
   c) C takes longer; but neutralises the acid to pH 7; so this would be better.
   d) Look for sensible suggestions such as cost, availability and taste.

1.6.10 Checking students' progress

The *Checking your progress* section in the Student Book indicates the key ideas developed in this chapter and shows how students progress to more complex levels. It is provided to support students in:

- identifying those ideas;

- developing a sense of their current level of understanding;

- developing a sense what the next steps in their learning are.

It is designed to be used either at the end of a chapter to support an overall view of the progress, or alternatively during the teaching of the chapter. Students can self-assess or peer assess using this as a basis.

It is helpful to encourage students to provide evidence from their understanding or their notes to support their judgements. In some cases it may be useful to explore the difference in the descriptors for a particular idea so that students can see what makes for a 'higher outcome'.

It may be useful with some descriptors to provide examples from the specific work done, such as an experiment undertaken or an explanation developed and recorded. If marking and feedback use similar ideas and phrases this will enable students to relate specific marking to a more general sense of progress.

To make good progress in understanding science students need to focus on these ideas and skills:

Students who are making modest progress will be able to:	Students who are making good progress will be able to:	Students who are making excellent progress will be able to:
Identify some common properties of metal elements and non-metal elements and their uses.	Classify metals and non-metals using their properties.	Identify similarities and differences between metals and how these relate to their uses; compare and contrast properties of metals and non-metals.
Identify oxidation reactions.	Explain why oxidation is a reaction.	Use models and word equations to explain changes during oxidation reactions.
Give uses of displacement reactions.	Use models to explain displacement and relate it to the reactivity series.	Write word equations to represent displacement reactions.
Identify some everyday substances that contain acids and alkalis.	Explain what all acids have in common and what all alkalis have in common.	Evaluate the hazards posed by some acids and alkalis and know how these risks may be reduced.
Give an example of an indicator and state why indicators are useful.	Explain what an indicator is and analyse results when using an indicator.	Compare the effectiveness of different indicators.
Describe some examples of neutralisation.	Describe the changes to indicators when acids and alkalis are mixed.	Explain the changes to indicators in terms of pH when acids and alkalis are mixed.
Recognise that water is one product of neutralisation.	Explain the formation of salt and water during neutralisation, giving some examples of common salts.	Predict the reactants or products of different neutralisation reactions.
Describe what indigestion remedies are and explain how they work.	Design an investigation to compare the effectiveness of indigestion remedies.	Analyse data about indigestion remedies to decide which remedy is the most effective.

1.6.11 Answers to Student Book end of chapter questions

This table provides answers to the Questions section at the end of Chapter 6 of the Student Book. It also shows how different questions assess attainment in terms of the focus and style of a question as well as its context. Question-level analysis can indicate a student's proficiency in approaching different aspects of scientific understanding and different types of answer.

Q	Answer	Marks available	Knowledge & understanding	Application	Evaluation of evidence	Objective test question	Short written answer	Longer written answer	Metals and non-metals	Acids and alkalis
			Focus			Style			Context	
1	c	1	x			x			x	
2	Zinc + hydrochloric acid → zinc chloride (1) + hydrogen (1)	2	x x				x x		x x	
3	Any two from: • shiny v dull • strong v not as strong • ductile v non-ductile • malleable v non-malleable • sonorous v non-sonorous • conductor of heat v insulator • conductor of electricity v insulator	2	x x				x x		x x	
4	Chemical (1) because a new product made/ magnesium oxide formed (1)	2	x x				x x		x x	
5	a	1	x			x				x
6	c	1	x			x				x
7	a	1	x			x				x
8	acid + alkali → salt + water	2	x x				x x			x x
9	Heartburn is caused by (stomach) acid (moving up from the stomach) The alkali neutralises the acid	2	x x				x x			x x
10	d	1		x		x			x	
11	d	1		x		x			x	

Q	Answer	Marks available	Knowledge & understanding	Application	Evaluation of evidence	Objective test question	Short written answer	Longer written answer	Metals and non-metals	Acids and alkalis
			Focus			Style			Context	
12	d	1		x		x				x
13	Alkali	2		x			x			x
	It has a pH higher than 7 / many alkalis feel soapy			x			x			x
14	Concentrated acid contains more acid particles; dilute acid contains fewer acid particles (dilute contains more water) so more acid particles to react	2		x			x			x
										x
				x			x			
15	The unknown metal is more reactive than zinc but less reactive than calcium.	2			x		x		x	
									x	
	The reaction is more vigorous than with zinc but less vigorous than with calcium.				x		x			
16	• good conductor	4			x			x	x	
	• sonorous				x			x	x	
	• low melting point				x			x	x	
	• shiny – doesn't easily react with oxygen/air				x			x	x	
17	B, A, C									x
	B has different colours in acid, alkali and neutral	3			x			x		x
										x
	A is different in acid and alkali, but not alkali and neutral				x			x		
	C is the same in all so can't distinguish acids and alkalis				x			x		
	Total possible:	30								

1.7.0 Earth: Introduction

When and how to use these pages

The Introduction in the Student Book indicates some of the ideas and skills in this topic area that students will already have met from KS2 or from previous KS3 work. It also provides an indication of what they will be studying in this chapter. *Ideas you have met before* is not intended to comprehensively summarise all of the prior ideas, but rather to point out a few of the key ones and to support the view that scientific understanding is progressive. Even though students might be meeting contexts that are new to them, they can often use existing ideas to start to make sense of them.

In this chapter you will find out indicates some of the new ideas that the chapter will introduce. Again, it isn't a detailed summary of content. Its purpose is more to act as a 'trailer' and generate some interest.

The outcomes, then, will be recognition of prior learning that can be built on, and interest in finding out more.

There are a number of ways this can be used. You might, for example:

- use *Ideas you have met before* as the basis for a revision lesson as you start the first new topic

- use *Ideas you have met before* as the centre of spider diagrams, to which students can add examples, experiments they might have done previously or what they found interesting

- make a note of any unfamiliar/difficult terms and return to these in the relevant lessons

- use *In this chapter you will find out* to ask students questions such as:
  - Why is this important?
  - How could it be used?
  - What might we be doing in this topic?

Overview of the chapter

This chapter covers the science of 'what's beneath us' and 'what's above us'. The first part of the chapter offers a taxonomy of types of rocks and a process that links them, in the form of the rock cycle. It offers a good opportunity to observe characteristics of rocks and reconcile them with the narrative of a process that often (but not always) happens incredibly slowly.

The second part of the chapter is about the Earth in Space. Again, this relates to observations and making sense of them by using a model to develop explanations. This also involves starting to appreciate extremely long timescales but also huge distances as well. The chapter finishes with a look at the way that models are used in science.

Obstacles to learning

Students may need extra guidance with the following:

- **Seasons:** On Earth, the seasons are sometimes thought to be caused by the Earth being further away from the Sun at certain points during its elliptical orbit. In fact, the tilt of the Earth on its axis is the biggest factor.

- **Stars:** Some students think that stars are balls of burning gas because they may not be familiar with nuclear fusion, so will not appreciate the difference between this and burning. Planets and stars may appear fundamentally the same to some students because both glow in the night sky.

- **Galaxies:** Interstellar distances are difficult to envisage and are many orders of magnitude greater than distances within the solar system. The unit of distance – the light year – is sometimes thought of as a measure of time.

- **The Earth:** The following misconceptions are common: the Earth is indestructible; natural resources are unlimited. Students may not accept that wind, plant roots and water are agents of weathering or that wind and water can carry material significant distances. They may find the timescale of many geological processes hard to grasp. They may find it hard to accept that loose material was once part of a solid layer, that landforms change through entirely natural processes, or that wind and water are agents of these processes.

Alternatively, they may accept that these do have an effect but see it as a minor and relatively insignificant effect as opposed to one accumulating in huge changes.

How the Programme of Study is covered by the Student Book

Big idea	Topic	Lesson	Programme of study reference
Earth	Earth structure	1.7.1 Understanding the structure of the Earth	The composition of the Earth The structure of the Earth
		1.7.2 Exploring igneous rocks	The rock cycle and the formation of igneous, sedimentary and metamorphic rocks
		1.7.3 Exploring sedimentary rocks	
		1.7.4 Exploring metamorphic rocks	
		1.7.5 Understanding the rock cycle	
	Universe	1.7.6 Describing stars and galaxies	Our Sun as a star, other stars in our galaxy, other galaxies
		1.7.7 Explaining the effects of the Earth's motion	The seasons and the Earth's tilt, day length at different times of year, in different hemispheres
		1.7.8 Exploring our neighbours in the Universe	The light year as a unit of astronomical distance
		1.7.9 Using models in science	Understanding that scientific methods and theories develop as earlier explanations are modified to take account of new evidence and ideas

How the AQA KS3 Syllabus is covered by the Student Books and Teacher Guide

Earth structure

	Student Book	Teacher Guide
Know		
Sedimentary, igneous and metamorphic rocks can be inter converted over millions of years through weathering and erosion, heat and pressure, and melting and cooling.	7.5	7.5
Fact: The three rock layers inside Earth are the crust, the mantle and the core.	7.1	7.1
Rock cycle: Sequence of processes where rocks change from one type to another.	7.5	7.5
Weathering: The wearing down of rock by physical, chemical or biological processes.	7.3	7.3
Erosion: Movement of rock by water, ice or wind (transportation).	7.3	7.3
Minerals: Chemicals that rocks are made from.	(7.3)	(7.3)
Sedimentary rocks: Formed from layers of sediment, and which can contain fossils. Examples are limestone, chalk and sandstone.	7.3	7.3
Igneous rocks: Formed from cooled magma, with minerals arranged in crystals. Examples are granite, basalt and obsidian.	7.2	7.2
Metamorphic rocks: Formed from existing rocks exposed to heat and pressure over a long time. Examples are marble, slate and schist.	7.4	7.4
Strata: Layers of sedimentary rock.	7.3	7.3
Apply		
Explain why a rock has a particular property based on how it was formed.	7.2, 7.3, 7.4	7.2, 7.3, 7.4
Identify the causes of weathering and erosion and describe how they occur.	7.3	7.3
Construct a labelled diagram to identify the processes of the rock cycle.	7.5	7.5
Extend		
Identify circumstances that indicate fast processes of change on Earth and those that indicate slower processes.		7.5
Predict planetary conditions from descriptions of rocks on other planets.		7.5
Describe similarities and differences between the rock cycle and everyday physical and chemical processes.	7.9	7.9
Suggest how ceramics might be similar to some types of rock.		7.4

Universe

	Student Book	Teacher Guide
Know		
The solar system can be modelled as planets rotating on tilted axes while orbiting the Sun, moons orbiting planets and sunlight spreading out and being reflected. This explains day and year length, seasons and the visibility of objects from Earth.	7.7, 7.9	7.7, 7.9
Our solar system is a tiny part of a galaxy, one of many billions in the Universe. Light takes minutes to reach Earth from the Sun, four years from our nearest star and billions of years from other galaxies.	7.6, 7.8	7.6, 7.8
Galaxy: Collection of stars held together by gravity. Our galaxy is called the Milky Way.	7.6	7.6
Light year: The distance light travels in a year (over 9 million, million kilometres).	7.8	7.8
Stars: Bodies which give out light, and which may have a solar system of planets.	7.6	7.6
Orbit: Path taken by a satellite, planet or star moving around a larger body. Earth completes one orbit of the Sun every year.	7.7, 7.9	7.7, 7.9
Exoplanet: Planet that orbits a star outside our solar system.	7.6	7.6
Apply		
Describe the appearance of planets or moons from diagrams showing their position in relation to the Earth and Sun.	7.8, 7.9	7.8, 7.9
Explain why places on the Earth experience different daylight hours and amounts of sunlight during the year.	7.7, 7.9	7.7, 7.9
Describe how space exploration and observations of stars are affected by the scale of the universe.	7.6, 7.8	7.6, 7.8
Explain the choice of particular units for measuring distance.	7.6, 7.8	7.6, 7.8
Extend		
Predict patterns in day length, the Sun's intensity or an object's shadow at different latitudes.		7.7
Make deductions from observation data of planets, stars and galaxies.		7.6
Compare explanations from different periods in history about the motion of objects and structure of the Universe.		7.9

1.7.1 Understanding the structure of the Earth

Lesson overview

Learning objectives

- Describe the layers of the Earth.
- Describe the characteristics of the different layers.
- Explain how volcanoes change the Earth.

Learning outcomes

- Describe the structure of the Earth and recall that the Earth's surface is constantly changing. [O1]
- Describe the characteristics of each layer of the Earth. [O2]
- Explain how the movement of tectonic plates and volcanoes changes the Earth's surface. [O3]

Skills development

- Working scientifically: 2.6 Construct explanations
- Developing numeracy: understand diagrammatical representations of three dimensional phenomena
- Developing literacy: interpret diagrams to develop explanations (Q1 - 6)

Resources needed boiled eggs or Cadbury *Creme Eggs*; peaches; *Maltesers*; modelling clay (various colours); Worksheet 1.7.1a; Worksheet 1.7.1b (copied onto card); Technician's notes 1.7.1

Key vocabulary mantle, crust, lithosphere, tectonic plate, magma, lava

Teaching and learning

Engage

- **Ideas hothouse** Organise students into pairs and ask them to **discuss** and **list** what they know about the structure of the Earth. Ask the pairs to form fours and then eights to **discuss further** and come up with an **agreed** list. One student in each group of eight **reports back** to the rest of the class. [O1, O2, O3]

Challenge and develop

- The students read the 'The Earth's layers' section in the Student Book and **discuss** the answers to questions 1 and 2. Take feedback. Ensure that they understand that in order to float, the plates must be less dense than the mantle. [O1]
- **Pair work** Ask the students, in their pairs, to complete task 1 of Worksheet 1.7.1a. [O1]
- Place two copies of the information cards from Worksheet 1.7.1b around the room. Continuing in their pairs, one student plays the role of a researcher and the other a scribe. They must **assimilate** the information and **record** it in a suitable format (e.g. bullet points or a table). [O1, O2]

Explain

- The students read the 'Features of the layers' section in the Student Book and answer questions 3 and 4. [O2]
- **Group work** Ask students to **construct a model** of the Earth using different colours of modelling clay. They then **evaluate** a range of other models of the Earth's structure (e.g. a boiled egg, a peach and a *Malteser*) using task 2 of Worksheet 1.7.1a. Explain that each of the items is like a model of the layers of the Earth. Take feedback from the class and discuss. [O1, O2]
- Show a suitable video of a volcanic eruption, and/or use recent news articles. The students then read the 'Changing the Earth's surface' section of the Student Book and answer questions 5 and 6. [O3]

Consolidate and apply

- **Group work** Ask the students to complete task 3 of Worksheet 1.7.1a. They will **write** a two-minute bulletin for a main news programme on a TV channel, **explaining** how tectonic plate movements and volcanic eruptions change the Earth's surface. They should then **present** their bulletins, which can be **peer assessed** using 'three stars and a wish'. [O3]

Extend

- Ask students able to progress further to **research** the work of Alfred Wegener and **summarise** his ideas in no more than 30 words. [O1, O3]

Plenary suggestions

Spider diagram The students can draw a spider diagram to connect all the information they have learned in the lesson. [O1, O2, O3]

Answers to Student Book questions

1. Peach.
2. To study the waves made by earthquakes and explosions.
3. *Oceanic crust*: thinner; denser rock, e.g. basalt; found under the ocean floor; *continental crust*: thicker; less dense rock, e.g. granite; found under land masses.
4. The crust is made up of plates that float on the mantle and can move very slowly, away from or towards each other.
5. Magma rises and breaks through weak areas in the crust.
6. *Magma* is molten rock under the Earth's surface; *lava* is molten rock above the Earth's surface.

Answers to Worksheet 1.7.1a

1. A – atmosphere; B – inner core; C – outer core; D – crust; E – mantle
2. For example:

Model	How is this model similar to the Earth's structure?	How is this model different from the Earth's structure?
Malteser	*Crust*: (chocolate coating) it is the thinnest layer; it is on the outside *Mantle*: central area *Outer core*: not present *Inner core*: not present	*Crust*: it is soft; not made of rock; smaller; does not crack *Mantle*: solid with air bubbles *Outer core*: not present *Inner core*: not present
Boiled egg	*Crust*: (shell) it is the thinnest layer; it is on the outside; it is rigid or hard; it cracks when pressed *Mantle*: (egg white) mostly solid; flexible *Outer core*: (yolk) it is in the centre; solid *Inner core*: not present	*Crust*: it is not made of rock; it is smaller than the real thing *Mantle*: it is white; it is the largest layer *Outer core*: yolk is not divided into two layers; not the largest layer; it is yellow *Inner core*: not present
Peach	*Crust*: (skin) it is the thinnest layer; it is on the outside *Mantle*: mostly solid, flexible *Outer core*: the layer is present *Inner core*: the seed inside the stone is solid	*Crust*: it is not made of rock; it is smaller than the real thing *Mantle*: largest layer *Outer core*: solid layer *Inner core*: not made from metal
Modelling-clay model	This will depend on the students' models	This will depend on the students' models

1.7.2 Exploring igneous rocks

Lesson overview

Learning objectives

- Describe how igneous rocks are formed.
- Explain how the pH of the magma affects the formation of rocks.
- Investigate the effect of cooling rate on the formation of crystals.

Learning outcomes

- Describe how igneous rocks are formed from molten magma and lava, and give examples. [O1]
- Explain the relationship between volcano shape, magma pH/viscosity and rock formation. [O2]
- Explain that slow cooling causes large crystals and fast cooling causes small crystals. [O3]

Skills development

- Working scientifically: 2.1 Analyse patterns
- Developing numeracy: understand relationships between variables
- Developing literacy: make and describe comparisons (Q5 & 6)

Resources needed (demonstration): wax crayons; metal crucible, clay triangle, Bunsen burner, tripod, gauze, heatproof mat, large beaker or bowl, eye protection, (practicals): cutting board, clamp and stand, 250 cm^3 beaker, thick-set honey solutions (in water) of 0%, 20%, 40%, 60% and 80% in small beakers, 10 cm^3 measuring cylinder, 3 glass slides with cover slips, 5 test tubes, test-tube rack, boiling tube containing salol, microscope, samples of basalt and granite, stopwatch, teat pipette, graph paper; large sheets of paper and coloured pens; Worksheet 1.7.2; Practical sheet 1.7.2a; Practical sheet 1.7.2b; Technician's notes 1.7.2

Common misconceptions Intrusive rocks all cooled more slowly than extrusive rocks.

Key vocabulary: igneous rock, extrusive, intrusive, viscous, fissure

Teaching and learning

Engage

- **Groups** Ask the students, in small groups, to **brainstorm** what they already know about (igneous) rocks. [O1]

Challenge and develop

- **Think, pair, share** Ask the students why the oldest rocks on the planet are igneous rocks (refer back to Lesson 1.7.1). Take feedback from the class and discuss. [O1]

- **Pair talk** The students read the 'What are igneous rocks?' section in the Student Book and **discuss** the answers to questions 1 and 2. Take feedback from the class and agree on answers. [O1]

- Melt some wax crayons into liquid 'magma' (see Technician's notes 1.7.2) and let the wax cool to form an 'igneous rock'. Model cooling at different rates by letting some wax cool at room temperature and dropping some into water to speed up cooling. The students must wear safety glasses while **observing** this demonstration. Relate the odd shapes of the water-cooled wax to the bubbles in extrusive volcanic rocks. Ask the students to **evaluate** the model. Take feedback and discuss their ideas. [O1, O3]

Explain

- **Pair work** Working in pairs, the students complete task 1 of Worksheet 1.7.2. [O1]

- Still in their pairs, the students work on the practical activity to **model** and **investigate** magma flow, following the instructions on Practical sheet 1.7.2a. Relate the rate of flow of the hot magma to the rate of cooling and crystal size (e.g. high-viscosity lava flows slowly, cools slowly and will have larger crystals than low-viscosity lava). [O2]

- Ask the students to read the 'Looking at magma' section in the Student Book and **discuss** the answers to questions 3 and 4 in pairs. Take feedback and agree on answers. [O2]

High demand students could work in pairs to complete a second practical activity, **investigating** how the rate of cooling affects crystal size, using Practical sheet 1.7.2b. [O3]

- Ask the students to read the 'Crystal size' section of the Student Book and answer questions 5 and 6. [O3]

Consolidate and apply

- Ask the students to complete task 2 of Worksheet 1.7.2. They can then **peer assess** one another's posters. [O2]

- **Pair talk/Pairs to fours** The student pairs **devise questions** (along with answers) on the topic that start with 'What', 'Why', 'When', 'Where' and 'How'. Each pair asks another pair their questions. Take feedback from the class. What did they find easy? What did they find difficult? [O1, O2, O3]

- Ask the students to complete task 3 of Worksheet 1.7.2. If they struggle with part b, give them a clue – 'friction'. [O2, O3]

Extend

- Ask students able to progress further to **research** igneous intrusions and **design** an information leaflet or web page. [O1, O2, O3]

Plenary suggestions

Five key facts Ask the students to come up with five key facts that they have learned in this lesson. Take feedback and discuss. [O1, O2, O3]

Answers to Student Book questions

1. For example: pumice; obsidian; basalt; granite; pegmatite; gabbro.
2. They have no layers; usually contain crystals; rarely react with acid; do not contain fossils.
3. Acidic magma is viscous, so does not travel far; alkaline magma is thin, runny and can travel long distances.
4. Viscous magma tends to produce steep, conical volcanoes. Non-viscous magma tends to give shallow, sloping-sided volcanoes.
5. The faster the cooling, the smaller the crystal size.
6. Intrusive rocks generally cool more slowly than extrusive rocks. However, magma in fissures can cool quickly to form rocks with small crystals; deep lava can cool very slowly to form extrusive rocks with large crystals.

Answers to Worksheet 1.7.2

1. a) Molten rock cools and hardens. b) *Intrusive* igneous rocks formed below the ground; *extrusive* igneous rocks formed above the ground.
2. a) *Acidic* magma is viscous and so does not travel far; it will cool more slowly and have larger crystals; *alkaline* magma is thin and runny; it can travel long distances; it will cool more quickly and have smaller crystals. Therefore magma with a lower pH does *not* flow as easily.
3. a) i) In trench A cooling is slower and forms larger crystals than in trench B, because less of the lava is exposed to the air. Lava at W will cool faster and form smaller crystals than lava at X, because it is closer to the surface. Lava at Y will cool faster and form smaller crystals than lava at Z, because it is closer to the surface. ii) Lava in deep trenches cools more slowly and forms bigger crystals than lava in wide trenches. Lava at the surface cools faster and forms smaller crystals than lava at the centre (or bottom) of the trench. iii) Larger crystals in rocks formed from lava at X; it will cool more slowly

   b) Basaltic lava will flow fastest; thicker liquids have more friction and so flow more slowly than thinner liquids; lava that contains less silica is less viscous and so flows faster; also, its temperature is higher; the hotter the lava is, the more quickly it will flow

Answers to Practical sheet 1.7.2a

1. (Students' own graphs.)
2. Viscosity 0% < 20% < 40% < 60% < 80% 3. Low-viscosity materials flow more quickly. 4. Repeat each concentration, (e.g. 3 times). 5. Put a small coloured circle (e.g. from a punched hole) on the liquid to act as a marker.

Answers to Practical sheet 1.7.2b

1. The quicker the rate of cooling, the smaller the crystal size.
2. Granite cooled more slowly than basalt; granite has the larger crystals.
3. Repeat the experiment a number of times and measure the crystal size.

1.7.3 Exploring sedimentary rocks

Lesson overview

Learning objectives

- Describe how sedimentary rocks are formed.
- Explain how fossils give clues about the past.
- Explain the properties of sedimentary rocks.

Learning outcomes

- Describe sedimentation in layers; name and describe three examples of sedimentary rocks. [O1]
- Describe what a fossil is and explain why these are found in sedimentary rocks. [O2]
- Explain how rocks turn into sediments. [O3]

Skills development

- Working scientifically: 2.6 Construct explanations
- Developing numeracy: n/a
- Developing literacy: accurate use of key terminology (Q6)

Resources needed smooth rounded pebbles or close-up pictures; samples of limestone, sandstone and mudstone; equipment for outdoor demonstration (2 m length of plastic gutter, plastic tank, bowl or bottle, sand and stones of various sizes, water source with spray head e.g. watering can) and for practical, per group (see Technician's notes); Worksheet 1.7.3; Practical sheet 1.7.3a; Practical sheet 1.7.3b; Technician's notes 1.7.3

Key vocabulary: weathering, deposition, sedimentary rocks, fossil, freeze–thaw, strata

Teaching and learning

Engage

- **Brainstorm in groups** Ask the students what they know about fossils. Take feedback, discuss their ideas and write them on the board for later. [O2]
- Show the students some rounded pebbles. Ask them to **suggest** three ways that the pebbles could have been made so smooth. Take feedback, discuss their ideas and write them on the board for later. [O3]

Challenge and develop

- **Group work** Ask the students to work in groups to **carry out** a practical activity to **model** making limestone using Practical sheet 1.7.3a. They should see a precipitate of calcium carbonate, which should settle. When the clay suspension is added, a layer of clay sediment should form on top of the 'limestone'. The students should then answer the questions on the Practical sheet. [O1]
- Give the students samples of limestone, sandstone and mudstone – allow the students to **examine** them using a hand lens. Ask them to **describe** what the lumps of rock consist of. Use questioning to help them to **deduce** that they are made of particles stuck together. [O1]
- Students read the 'Rocks in layers' section and **discuss** and answer questions 1 and 2. Take feedback. [O1]

Explain

- Set up a demonstration of sedimentation (see Technician's notes 1.7.3). This needs to be done outside. Ask the students to **watch** as you switch on the water at the top end, using a spray head such as is on a watering can. Ask the students to answer the questions on Practical sheet 1.7.3b. Establish that the smallest particles are transported most easily and are the last to be deposited. Relate this to deposition of sediments as rivers enter seas: pebbles are deposited first and finer sediments last. Ask the students why different layers of sediment may form. [O1, O3]

- **Pair work** Ask the students to complete task 1 of Worksheet 1.7.3 in pairs. They **sequence** the stages of sedimentary rock formation and **describe** how limestone and sandstone are made. [O1]

- **Twos to fours** In pairs, the students read the 'Looking at fossils' section in the Student Book and answer questions 3 and 4. They can then **devise** 'What', 'Why', 'Where', 'When' and 'How' questions about fossils, along with answers, and ask another pair their questions. [O2]

Consolidate and apply

- Ask the students, individually, to **describe** what a fossil is and **explain** why they are found in sedimentary rocks. They should then **peer assess** the work of a partner using task 2 of Worksheet 1.7.3. [O2]

- The students read the 'Breaking rocks' section in the Student Book and answer questions 5 and 6. [O3]

Extend

- Ask students able to progress further to work in pairs to **research** information and **produce a leaflet** on limestone and quarrying in Yorkshire. [O1, O3]

Plenary suggestions

Cartoon strip Ask the students to work in pairs and draw a cartoon strip **explaining** one of the processes learned about in the lesson (sedimentation, the formation of fossils or the weathering of rock) using task 3 of Worksheet 1.7.3). [O1, O2, O3]

Answers to Student Book questions

1. Tiny rock pieces are broken off by wind or water (also by freeze–thaw weathering, tree roots, etc.) and are deposited as sediments in water.
2. Any three from: *sandstone* is made from sand particles; *limestone* is made from the remains of tiny shells and micro-skeletons of marine organisms deposited on the seabed; *shale/mudstone* is made from small silt and clay-sized particles; *conglomerates* are made from rounded pebbles cemented together.
3. In the sea; contains shells and skeletons of sea creatures.
4. Animals or plants die, become covered in sediments, and the sediments turn to rock; some organisms are preserved in amber, glaciers, etc.
5. They bump into each other on the riverbed/seabed as they are carried in water; the sharp edges are knocked off.
6. *Deposition*: rocks and pebbles fall out of slow-moving water to the riverbed/seabed. *Compaction*: water is squeezed from lower layers by the mass and pressure from upper layers. *Cementation*: water seeps through the sediments and minerals in it can crystallise between the rock particles and cement them together.

Answers to Worksheet 1.7.3

1. a) B; A; H; G; F; C; E; D
   b) i) Limestone is made from remains of tiny shells and micro-skeletons of marine organisms deposited on the seabed. ii) Sandstone is made from sand particles.
2. a) A fossil is the remains of a dead plant or animal, preserved in rock.
   b) Fossils are found in sedimentary rock because they become covered/trapped in layers of sediments which, over time, become sedimentary rock.
3. Idea and descriptions of physical, chemical and biological weathering, causing rock pieces to be washed into rivers etc.; then rounding off of pebbles that get smaller and smaller to form sediments.

Answers to Practical sheet 1.7.3a

1. Calcium carbonate.
2. To build their shells.
3. They sink into the sediment and form fossils in the rock.
4. The clay/sand is deposited at the bottom of the sea.
5. It must be weathered and eroded.

Answers to Practical sheet 1.7.3b

1. Smaller particles will tend to be carried more easily, especially if less dense. Larger denser materials or ones that don't have a smooth shape won't be transported as easily.
2. Smaller, less dense particles move with less energy and larger or denser materials will need more.
3 & 4. Depends on material used but there is likely to be layering with lighter material deposited first.

1.7.4 Exploring metamorphic rocks

Lesson overview

Learning objectives

- Describe how metamorphic rocks are formed.
- Explain the properties of metamorphic rocks.

Learning outcomes

- Describe how metamorphic rocks are formed and give examples. [O1]
- Describe the properties of metamorphic rocks and link this to the way that they are formed. [O2]
- Explain why the properties of some metamorphic rocks make them suitable for different uses. [O3]

Skills development

- Working scientifically: 2.6 Construct explanations
- Developing numeracy: n/a
- Developing literacy: use ideas and evidence to develop explanations (Q3 - 7)

Resources needed modelling clay, equipment for the demonstrations (shallow transparent dish, e.g. large Petri dish, 100 cm^3 beaker, Bunsen burner, tripod and gauze, 2–3 spatulas of sodium chloride, heatproof mat, spatula, cloth, 1 raw egg white, a box of used matches or short lengths of spaghetti, 2 × 30 cm rulers) and for the practical, per group (see Technician's notes); Worksheet 1.7.4; Practical sheet 1.7.4; Technician's notes 1.7.4

Common misconceptions Each type of rock can only be metamorphosed into one particular type of metamorphic rock. A metamorphic rock cannot be metamorphosed. All fossils are always destroyed during metamorphosis of rocks.

Key vocabulary metamorphose, crystallise

Teaching and learning

Engage

- **Brainstorm** Explain that existing rocks can be changed into metamorphic rocks. Ask the students 'What could cause metamorphic rocks to form?'. Discuss ideas from the class. [O1]

- **Think, pair, share** Give the students some modelling clay to represent some rock. They make a ball – ask them 'What causes the modelling clay to change shape?' Elicit that pressure (from their muscles) and heat (from hands and friction) softens/reshapes the modelling clay. Ask the students 'Where do heat and pressure come from in the Earth?' Stress that with enough pressure and heat, rock such as clay can form a new type of rock called 'metamorphic rock'. Sometimes molten rock forces itself into cracks in other types of rock. The very hot magma (700–1400 °C) metamorphoses the surrounding rock. [O1]

Challenge and develop

- The students **observe** a demonstration that models metamorphosis. Put an egg white in a transparent dish. Then add 50 cm^3 of water to a beaker, add two or three spatulas of sodium chloride (to increase the boiling point) and heat to boiling over a Bunsen burner. Move the beaker from the tripod to the centre of the egg white; leave it for 10 minutes. Ask the students to **observe** the egg white. Ask 'What has happened?', 'Can the change be reversed by cooling it again?'. Discuss how this models the metamorphosis of rocks. (Raw egg white is like molten magma: it changes when exposed to heat, and the change cannot be reversed.) [O1]

- Demonstrate a simulation of the formation of slate sheets. (Slate is formed when pressure is exerted on mudstone or shale.) Pour some used matches or short pieces of spaghetti randomly over the bench, so that they lie in all directions. These represent the microscopic clay minerals in mudstone or shale. Take two 30 cm rulers and put them on either side of the matchsticks/ spaghetti. Push the rulers together forcing the 'clay minerals' to line up parallel to the moving rulers. This models clay minerals being forced to line up at right angles to the direction of applied forces (e.g. forces from two approaching plates). [O1]

- **Think, pair, share** The students read the 'Making metamorphic rocks' section in the Student Book. They **discuss** and **agree on** answers to questions 1 and 2. [O1]

Explain

- Ask students to **discuss in pairs** task 1 of Worksheet 1.7.4 and **agree on** the correct sequence. They will **draw annotated diagrams** to illustrate each stage of the process and **peer assess** another pair's work. [O1]

- Read and discuss the 'Metamorphic changes' section in the Student Book as a class. Ensure that the students understand that rocks recrystallise without melting, that the changes are permanent and that different levels of heat and pressure result in different types of minerals. [O2]

- **Group work** Ask the students to **examine** labelled samples of sandstone, limestone, mudstone, quartzite, marble and slate using a hand lens, **classify** these as sedimentary or metamorphic rocks and **explain** how they are different (Q3 in the Student Book). Take feedback from groups and agree on the answers. [O2]

Consolidate and apply

- **Pair work** Ask the students to complete task 2 of Worksheet 1.7.4. They need to **explain** what information scientists can deduce from crystals in rocks, and **identify** the pressure acting on trilobite fossils. [O2]

- Continuing in their pairs, the students **follow the instructions** on Practical sheet 1.7.4 to **investigate** the effect of pressure on fossils in rocks. Squeezing top to bottom causes small, fat fossils; squeezing side to side causes tall, thin fossils; squeezing one side up and one down causes tall, twisted fossils. Link this to scientists using fossils to deduce movements of the Earth's crust. [O1, O2]

- **Pair talk/Pairs to fours** The students read the 'Metamorphic rocks in detail' section in the Student Book, **discussing** and **agreeing on** answers to questions 5 and 6. [O3]

Extend

- Ask students able to progress further to complete task 3 of Worksheet 1.7.4. Each student **researches** a metamorphic rock. In pairs or groups, they **combine** the information they have each collected and **present** it to other students, who should **peer assess** the work. Students can answer question 7 in Student Book. [O3]

- Challenge students to examine examples of ceramics, learn how they have been formed and suggest parallels with metamorphic rocks. [O1, O2, O3]

Plenary suggestions

The big ideas The students write down three ideas they learned during the lesson. They **share** their facts in groups and **compile** a prioritised master list of facts. Take feedback and find out whether groups agreed or not. [O1, O2, O3]

Answers to Student Book questions

1. By heat and/or pressure acting on existing rocks. 2. Sedimentary.
3. Metamorphic rocks are harder; some are shiny; original features (e.g. layers and fossils) are destroyed or altered.
4. The heat melts them and the pressure squashes or destroys them.
5. Different metamorphic rocks can be formed from the same rock, depending on the heat and pressure applied.
6. In metamorphic rocks, the layers of sedimentary rocks, fossils, and the clues they give us to the origin of the rock have usually been destroyed.
7. a) They are similar in that they are non-metallic crystalline solids formed through the action of heat (modern definitions of ceramics are broader) which has changed the properties of the raw material. However, ceramics are man-made, with both the raw material (clay and other materials) and the shape selected for a purpose.
   b) Igneous rocks have formed by cooling from a molten state, unlike ceramics and sedimentary rocks, which are formed from layers of sediment. Again, this is unlike the metamorphic process.

Answers to Worksheet 1.7.4

1. a) C; D; B; A
2. a) Different minerals form at different temperatures and pressures. The new minerals can be used to estimate the temperature, depth and pressure at which the original rock was metamorphosed.
   b) They might have been destroyed. c) Horizontally squeezed by 50%. d) Vertically squeezed by 66%.
   e) It suggests that the rocks also underwent the same percentage distortion.
3. *Quartzite*, *marble* and *slate*: see the Student Book; all formed at high temperature and pressure; *schist*: from slate exposed to further heat and pressure; used as decorative rock in gardens; *gneiss*: from slate; extreme heat and pressure; used in building; *serpentine*: from dunite/peridotite; in mountains and near seabed; by slightly raised temperature; used as a carving stone and in building

1.7.5 Understanding the rock cycle

Lesson overview

Learning objectives
- Describe the rock cycle.
- Explain how rocks can change from one type to another.

Learning outcomes
- Describe simply how rocks can be changed from one type to another. [O1]
- Explain the processes involved in the rock cycle using scientific language. [O2]
- Explain how the properties of each rock type link to the processes in the rock cycle. [O3]

Skills development
- Working scientifically: 2.1 Analyse patterns
- Developing numeracy: understanding graphical representations
- Developing literacy: use ideas and evidence to develop explanations (Q3 - 6)

Resources needed rock samples (sedimentary e.g. sandstone; igneous e.g. granite; metamorphic e.g. slate); hand lens; equipment for practical, per group (see Technician's notes); large sheets of paper; Worksheet 1.7.5a; Worksheet 1.7.5b; Practical sheet 1.7.5; Technician's notes 1.7.5

Common misconceptions Mountains are unchanging.

Key vocabulary rock cycle, erosion, uplift, upfold, anticline, syncline

Teaching and learning

Engage
- **Think, pair, share** Challenge the students to **link** the different rock types together in a mind map and name the processes involved. [O1]
- **Pairs to fours** Alternatively, student pairs could **list** points they already know about the rock cycle. Fours then **discuss** it further and come up with a list of points. One student **reports** back – start to develop the rock cycle on the board as the students report back. [O1]

  High demand students may be able to attempt this independently.

Challenge and develop
- **Pair talk** Students read the 'The rock cycle' section in the Student Book and **study** Figure 1.7.5a. They then **discuss** the answers to questions 1 and 2. Take feedback and **agree on** answers. [O1]
- Arrange the class for a **team memory game** about the rock cycle. The students' instructions are given on page 1 of Worksheet 1.7.5a. The diagram of the rock cycle, to be shown to students for only brief periods, is given on page 2 of the worksheet. Encourage the students to **ask questions** in their teams, to clarify their understanding. [O1]
- The students can then work on their own to complete task 1 of Worksheet 1.7.5b. [O1]

Explain
- **Pair work** Students work in pairs to complete Practical activity 1.7.5 to **model** how rocks fold and fault. Most will probably need to be shown how to make reasonably even horizontal layers.

  Some groups of students may find the care and time needed is too much, in which case you can demonstrate the activity.
- Ask the students to **evaluate** the model from the practical activity. They should think about the spatial scale, the time scale and the lack of heat. [O2]
- The students read the 'Folding rocks' section in the Student Book and **discuss** the answers to questions 3 and 4 in their pairs. Take feedback from the class and **agree on** answers. [O2]

- **Group work** Ask the students to **look carefully** at samples of sedimentary rock, igneous rock and metamorphic rock and **compare and contrast** their appearance and structure. The students should think about colour, whether the rocks have crystals or not, whether they are shiny or not, whether they have observable particles or not, and how the particles are arranged. Ask the students to **draw** each rock in detail and **label** their drawings fully. [O1, O2, O3]
- Ask the students to read the 'Rocks on the move' section in the Student Book and answer questions 6 and 7. [O3]

Consolidate and apply

- The students carry out task 2 of Worksheet 1.7.5b to **explain** how jagged, weathered pieces of rock become smooth round pebbles. Take feedback. [O2]

  Low demand students may need a hint here: wind and water.

- Ask the students to **imagine** that they are particles in molten magma – what happens to them? The students can complete a piece of **extended creative writing** to tell the story. [O1, O2, O3]

Extend

- Ask the students to complete task 3 of Worksheet 1.7.5b, **linking** the properties of the different types of rocks to the processes that formed them. [O3]
- Challenge students to identify situations, including examples, in which geological changes may happen relatively quickly and also ones that happen relatively slowly. [O1, O2, O3]
- Challenge students to look at images and descriptions of rock samples from the Moon and suggest what this evidence shows about conditions on the Moon. Then ask students to look at descriptions of conditions on the Inner planets in the Solar System and suggest what rock samples might show. [O1, O2, O3]

Plenary suggestions

Mind map The students revisit their mind map from the *Engage* activity and add to it to show their learning about the structure of the Earth, different types of rocks and the rock cycle. [O1, O2, O3]

Answers to Student Book questions

1. Sedimentary, metamorphic and igneous rocks can be changed to sedimentary rocks by weathering, erosion and sedimentation. Sedimentary rocks can be changed to metamorphic rocks by heat and pressure. Sedimentary and metamorphic rocks can be changed to igneous rocks by heat (melting and then cooling to form the new rock).
2. *Weathering* means cracking rocks and breaking pieces off; *erosion* means breaking down rocks further into particles, which are then transported, e.g. to the sea.
3. a) Wind and water break up larger rock pieces into much smaller rock pieces; this allows them to be transported, again by wind and water.

   b) Small rock particles are deposited on a riverbed/seabed as sediments when the water (current) slows down. They are buried by new sediments forming on top of them; the new sediments compact the lower layers and squeeze the water out to form sedimentary rock.

   c) Sedimentary and other types of rock metamorphose with heat and pressure to form new metamorphic rock. Heat can also melt rocks under the crust to form magma; magma cools to form igneous rocks below and above the Earth's surface. Pressure can also cause rock folding.
4. *Anticlines*: strata are pushed up in a dome shape; *synclines*: strata are forced down in a bowl shape.
5. By uplift, which can occur due to the constant movement of the Earth's crust (e.g. during an earthquake).
6. *Quickly*: volcanic eruption; faulting; uplift; folding; (though last two can be slower) *slowly*: weathering; erosion; sedimentation; metamorphosis, melting.

Answers to Worksheet 1.7.5b

1. a) 1 with F; 2 with G; 3 with D; 4 with E; 5 with C; 6 with A; 7 with B. b) See Figure 1.7.5a in the Student Book.
2. Answers should include the ideas that: weathered pieces of rock knock against each other and are further weathered; protruding edges are knocked off; some pieces of rock fall into streams and are eroded further as they travel in the water, and as they knock into each other they gradually become smooth.
3. *Sedimentary*: softer, layered rocks because the particles are just compacted and cemented together; this makes them rough; the spaces between compacted particles make the rocks porous; fossils are usually found in sedimentary rocks, because there is no heat/pressure involved in the rocks' formation; *igneous*: interlocking crystals that formed as they solidified; they are hard with no layers; many have no gaps and are not porous; their properties depend on their composition and the temperature and pressure; *metamorphic*: hard because the minerals are lined up or arranged in uneven layers; their properties depend on the heat and pressure the rocks have been subjected to; any fossils found are often distorted.

1.7.6 Describing stars and galaxies

Lesson overview

Learning objectives

- Describe the characteristics of a star.
- Relate our Sun to other stars.
- Explain the concept of galaxies and the position of our galaxy compared to others.

Learning outcomes

- Describe the differences between the Sun, other stars and galaxies. [O1]
- Describe the relationship between the Sun, other stars and galaxies. [O2]
- Relate ideas about the Sun, stars and galaxies to evidence visible from the Earth. [O3]

Skills development

- Working scientifically: 2.15 Review theories
- Developing numeracy: using large numbers
- Developing literacy: use ideas and evidence to develop explanations (Q6 - 8)

Resources needed laptops or access to a computer suite; Worksheet 1.7.6

Common misconceptions Our solar system is at the centre of the Universe.

Key vocabulary star, nuclear fusion, red giant, neutron star, galaxy, exoplanet

Teaching and learning

Engage

- Identify the students' prior knowledge by asking them to work in small groups to **compile a fact file** about the Sun. Possible prompts to provide them with are: shape, size, energy source, origin, composition, differences from planets. [O1]

- Discuss the students' fact files and address any misunderstandings. Provide additional information such as diameter (1.3 million km) and composition (75% hydrogen plus helium and other elements). [O1]

- The students **ask questions** about things that they would like to find out about the Sun, stars and galaxies. (They will research the answers to these later in the lesson.) [O1, O2, O3]

Challenge and develop

- The students read the first two sections of the Student Book and **deduce** why stars have a finite lifespan. [O1, O3]

- If possible, show the video 'The Life Cycle of Stars' (7 minutes) from the Institute of Physics website – go to www.iop.org and search for 'Teaching astronomy and space videos', then click on the first link in the list of results. The students **make comparisons** between the different types of stars in terms of size, energy source and appearance. [O1, O3]

- They **produce a summary report** on star or galaxy observations from the National Schools' Observatory website. To do this go to www.schoolsobservatory.org.uk and click on 'Register your School'. [O1, O2, O3]

  High demand students may be able to **undertake a longer-term project** using the National Schools' Observatory.

- Students **compare and contrast** stars they have researched. [O1, O2, O3]

- They **research** some of the methods of gathering information about stars and galaxies – telescopes, measuring different types of light/radiation, measuring rates of expansion of galaxies. [O3]

Explain

- The students **describe** the similarities and differences between the Sun and other stars and then **explain** the reasons for these. [O1, O2]

- They **explain** how the Solar System would be different if the Sun were a much bigger star. [O1, O2]

  High demand students may be able to **speculate** on the likelihood of us detecting life elsewhere in the Universe.

Consolidate and apply

- The students **explain** why the age, type and distance of the nearest star are critical factors for life to exist on a planet. [O1, O2]

- They **research** answers to the questions they identified earlier in the lesson. [O1, O2, O3]

- They then complete the tasks of Worksheet 1.7.6. [O1, O2, O3]

Extend

- Ask students able to progress further to, if possible, watch the video 'The Sun' from the Institute of Physics website (see link above). Then ask the students to **explain** how fluctuations in the Sun's activity are monitored and why they are important to us. [O3]

- Challenge students to research examples of conclusions drawn by astronomers from observations made of planets, stars and galaxies. [O1, O3]

Plenary suggestions

Glossary The students **compile** a glossary of key words relating to the Sun and other stars. [O1, O2, O3]

Answers to Student Book questions

1. Hydrogen (H) and helium (He).
2. Nuclear fusion of hydrogen atoms to make helium.
3. A star such as the Sun releases energy from internal processes, and this radiates out through space (e.g. as light). Planets don't produce their own light – we see them because of reflected light.
4. It would be very strong, because of its huge mass, and the radius is small.
5. The energy source of hydrogen for nuclear fusion runs out. Fusion can continue, using helium and some other elements, but they too eventually run out.
6. For convenience, when the numbers are extremely large (or small).
7. Planets are the smallest and orbit stars. Several billion stars exist in a group called a galaxy. Many galaxies make up the Universe. The Universe includes all matter.
8. Ideas such as: peer review; making and testing predictions; collecting further data; and comparing it to the original data.

Answers to Worksheet 1.7.6

1. a) Nuclear fusion; atoms being forced together to form new atoms and release energy.

   b) Star; huge mass of hydrogen and other elements, releasing huge quantities of energy by nuclear fusion.

   c) Red giant; star that has run out of hydrogen and is fusing helium atoms to release energy, and has expanded.

2. a) Visible images from telescopes; X-rays; cosmic microwaves.

   b) The moment when the Universe formed in a massive explosion from a highly concentrated starting state.

   c) It has been continually expanding.

   d) Models help us to picture or understand objects or events that are very large, small or complex. Models can be compared and tested against reality; and then accepted, improved or rejected.

3. a) Hubble's view is not spoiled by light, dust, water vapour, other matter, or interference in the Earth's atmosphere.

   b) Hubble can see further than was possible before, allowing us to see very dim light from distant ancient galaxies. Spots of light that were thought to be single stars or clouds of gas have now been shown to be whole galaxies of stars. Light from the most distant galaxies has been travelling since shortly after the Universe formed in the Big Bang; it has given a view almost as far back as then.

   c) Hubble's mirror was fractionally the wrong shape, leading to images that were blurred. Astronauts have now fitted equipment to correct the fault, just as spectacles correct faulty vision.

1.7.7 Explaining the effects of the Earth's motion

Lesson overview

Learning objectives

- Describe variation in length of day, apparent position of the Sun and seasonal variations.
- Compare these with changes in the opposite hemisphere.
- Explain these changes with reference to the motion of the Earth.

Learning outcomes

- Describe the implications of the Earth being tilted on its axis. [O1]
- Explain changes to days and seasons in different hemispheres. [O2]
- Explain what would happen if the Earth's axis tilted by a different amount. [O3]

Skills development

- Working scientifically: 2.14 Examine consequences
- Developing numeracy: interpret graphs and understand diagrams representing three dimensional phenomena
- Developing literacy: use ideas and evidence to develop explanations (Q4 - 9)

Resources needed A room with movable furniture and closable curtains or blinds. Projector or bright lamp, globe on a stand or football, to represent the Earth, sticky label or Plasticine, larger ball, e.g. basketball or exercise ball, to represent the Sun, torch or bendy lamp and a cardboard tube, to make a parallel beam of light, sheet of flip chart paper mounted on a piece of cardboard; Worksheet 1.7.7; Practical sheet 1.7.7; Technician's notes 1.7.7

Common misconceptions Seasonal changes are due to the varying distance of the Earth from the Sun.

Key vocabulary axis of rotation, season

Teaching and learning

Engage

- The students answer a starter quiz to establish prior knowledge (task 1 of Worksheet 1.7.7). Make a mental note of the responses that indicate gaps in their knowledge. [O1, O2]

  You could ask some students to **review** their own 'starting points' by completing the first two sections of a 'KWL' grid – things I **K**now, things I **W**ant to know, things I have **L**earned.

Challenge and develop

- As the class or in groups, the students **carry out investigations** to model the effects of the Earth's motion using Practical sheet 1.7.7. In a darkened room, first work with the students using a globe or football and a bright lamp or projector exploring or demonstrating the effect of the rotation of the Earth (activity 1 on the practical sheet). Ask them to **deduce** the time for one rotation (24 hours).

- They then **model** the Earth orbiting the Sun in four stages, improving the model each time (activity 2): [O1, O2]

  - circular orbit with the Earth aligned vertically N to S with no rotation;
  - elliptical orbit with the Earth aligned vertically N to S with no rotation;
  - elliptical orbit with the Earth tilted with no rotation;
  - elliptical orbit with the Earth tilted and rotating on its axis.

  Ask the students to **deduce** the time for one orbit (1 year), the number of rotations per orbit (365) and the tilt of the Earth in relation to the Sun at opposite sides of its orbit (North Pole pointed away/towards). [O2]

- Using a globe on a stand and focusing on the section of the orbit where the northern hemisphere is tilted away from the Sun (the bright lamp or projector), stick a label on the UK. The students **observe** the effect of the Earth's tilt on day length (shorter). Repeat the demonstration with the northern hemisphere tilted towards the Sun to show longer day length. Then contrast with the southern hemisphere. [O1, O2]

- The students then **model** the effect of the Earth's tilt on the intensity of sunlight (energy) reaching the Earth (activity 3 on Practical sheet 1.7.7). [O1, O2]
- Discuss as a class the questions on Practical sheet 1.7.7. [O1, O2, O3]
- If possible, show the video 'The Seasons demo 1' (1 min 46 sec) from the Institute of Physics website – it illustrates why temperatures are lower in the winter. Go to www.iop.org and search for 'Teaching astronomy and space videos', then click on the first link in the list of results and scroll down to 'Classroom demonstrations'. [O1, O2, O3]

Explain

- The students use Worksheet 1.7.7 or their own diagrams and annotations to **explain** how changes in day length can be accounted for by the tilt of the Earth's axis. [O1, O2]

  High demand students may be able to **produce explanations** without prompts.

Consolidate and apply

- **Pairs** Working in pairs, ask the students to **discuss** and **explain** how it is possible for polar regions to have 24-hour days in the summer and the opposite in the winter. [O1, O2]
- They **discuss** and **explain** how days and seasons would be affected if the Earth's axis tilted at 45° (compared with the current 23°) or tilted at 90° (45°: exaggerated variations; 90°: little variation). [O3]

Extend

- Ask students able to progress further to use the Internet to **compare** average temperatures in the southern and northern hemispheres. (The southern hemisphere is colder because of the large area of ice and water, despite being closer to the Sun than the northern hemisphere is during the Earth's elliptical orbit.) [O2, O3]
- Challenge students to suggest, with reasons, how day length, the Sun's intensity or an object's shadow vary at different latitudes. [O1]

Plenary suggestions

Review Revisit the starter quiz, focusing on areas that students were not originally confident with. [O1, O2, O3]

KWL grid If students started a KWL grid at the beginning of the lesson, they can now complete the 'L' section (things they have learned). [O1, O2, O3]

Answers to Student Book questions

1. a) The Arctic Circle has no day; northern France has 7.5 hours. b) The Arctic Circle has a 24-hour day; northern France has 16.5 hours.
2. Day length equals night length (12 hours) in both locations. 3. The peak in day length happens on 21 Dec.
4. In the summer, the Earth is tilted towards the Sun.
5. Twice a year, around the spring and autumn equinoxes; because the tilt of the poles is not towards or away from the Sun.
6. In places on the equator the Sun never shines at an oblique angle, so seasonal changes are small. Day length also varies less than in places closer to the poles.
7. In the summer, the areas around the poles are always in sunlight, due to the tilt of the Earth on its axis.
8. Shorter days and sunlight at an oblique angle mean less energy for photosynthesis. Some may mention lower temperature, also reducing photosynthesis/growth.
9. The daily period is the same. There are more extreme differences in day and night than on Earth, because Mars is more tilted. Other seasonal variations are also more extreme due to the bigger tilt and more elliptical orbit (its distance from the Sun varies more). A year is twice as long on Mars as on Earth.

Answers to Worksheet 1.7.7

1. a) 24 hours. b) No. c) Spherical. d) The Earth is tilted away from the Sun. e) 12 hours each, with small variations.
2. a) Wide arc; but not going overhead. b) Shallower, narrower arc. c) Arc would pass overhead.

   Note: it is hard to represent the arc in two dimensions; this could be discussed with students.
3. a) At A: total daylight; at B: constant dim light; at C: total darkness; at D: constant dim light.

   b) At A and C: constant dim light; at B and D: even-length days and nights.

   c) The poles would suffer cold winters of total darkness, and hot summers of total daylight. The equator would have winter at A and C, and summer at positions B and D, because the planet is nearer the Sun at positions B and D.

1.7.8 Exploring our neighbours in the Universe

Lesson overview

Learning objectives
- Recall that the light year is used to measure astronomical distances.
- Explain the limitation of units such as kilometres in describing astronomical distances.
- Explain what causes the appearance of the Moon to change.

Learning outcomes
- Explain the need for a large unit of astronomical distance. [O1]
- Describe how light years can be used to measure distance. [O2]
- Explain why the Moon changes in appearance from the Earth. [O3]

Skills development
- Working scientifically: 2.16 Interrogate sources
- Developing numeracy: using large numbers
- Developing literacy: apply ideas and evidence to develop explanations (Q7 - 10)

Resources needed mini-whiteboards; marker pens; A4 sheets of paper; pens; metre rulers; 5 m long strip of paper; graph paper; rulers; Worksheet 1.7.8; Practical sheet 1.7.8; Technician's sheet 1.7.8

Common misconceptions The light year is a measurement of time.

Key vocabulary light year (ly)

Teaching and learning

Engage

- **Mini-whiteboard activity** The students **estimate** the approximate distance from the Earth to the Sun (149 600 000 km or nearly 150 million km). They then try to **write out** the approximate distance to the next nearest star, Sirius – approximately 5 million times further away. [O2]

  High demand students can be introduced to scientific notation for writing extremely large numbers (e.g. 1 million = 1×10^6, 1 billion = 1×10^9).

Challenge and develop

- Ask the students to **list** other units and ideas they have encountered for measuring distances on Earth and in space (task 1 of Worksheet 1.7.8). [O1]
- Discuss the need to find a measure that is based on a standard distance. Ensure that the students **realise** that light always travels at the same speed in a vacuum (300 000 km/s). Ask them to **suggest** how they would work out how far light would travel in 1 year (by multiplying by the number of seconds in a minute, hour etc). [O1, O2]

  High demand students can be asked to **convert** the speed of light into the distance travelled in longer time spans, such as an hour, day, week and year.

- Using the Student Book, introduce the light year as a measure of astronomical distance. Ask the students to **use units and nomenclature** to write the length of one light year (9 460 000 000 000 km or 9.46×10^{12} km) and also to write the figure in words (nine thousand, four hundred and sixty billion km, or nine trillion four hundred and sixty billion km). [O1, O2]
- Ask students to **compare** distances in the Universe. Ask them to read the 'Distances in the Universe' section in the Student Book and to answer questions 4, 5 and 6. [O1, O2]
- **Group work** In mixed ability groups of three, ask the students to **investigate** how parallax causes the apparent position of an object to change by different amounts at different distances, using Practical sheet 1.7.8. [O3]
- Ask the students to **explain** why we see stars as they were in the past, rather than as they are now. (The light has taken a long time to reach us on Earth.) [O3]

Explain

- The students work in pairs to produce a 30-word **explanation** of why light years are useful for measuring distances in space. They then **communicate** their explanations to the class. [O1, O2]
- They **discuss** and **explain** if and how it would be possible to travel to distant stars (task 2 of Worksheet 1.7.8). [O1, O2]

Consolidate and apply

- Using a strip of paper 5 m long stretched across the room to represent the distance between the Earth and Sirius, the students estimate where they should mark the distance between the Earth and the Sun. (On this scale it would be 0.000 001 mm or one-millionth of a millimetre). [O1, O2]
- Ask students to look at Fig 1.7.8b and work out how we get phases of the Moon. Then ask them to consider how they could explain this to a pupil in KS2. They can answer Q7 & 8. [O3]

  High demand students can complete task 3 of Worksheet 1.7.8. [O3]

Extend

- Ask students able to progress further to use the Internet to **find out about** the brightness method for measuring distances from the Earth to a star. [O1, O2]
- Apply ideas about phases of the moon to other bodies, answering Q 9 & 10. [O3]

Plenary suggestions

I think that is … because … The students suggest how feasible space travel is to distant stars. [O1, O2, O3]

Answers to Student Book questions

1. Kilometres per second 2. light years 3. The numbers are too big to be managed and compared easily.
4. Sirius is 8.6 light years away so light reaching us from that star will have set off 8.6 years ago. The actual answer therefore depends upon which year it is when the students answer the question. If it was answered in September 2017 for example, the light would have set off early in 2009.
5. The light from the more distant star has taken longer to reach us than light from the nearer star; therefore we see it further in the past.
6. As the distances are massive it takes long periods of time both for probes to reach other parts. It even takes a long time for waves to travel from those objects to us.
7. It will appear to us as a semicircle. It will either be a first quarter or a last quarter moon, depending on its stage in the cycle.
8. Through its 28-day cycle the amount of the moon we see gradually increases (to a full moon) and then gradually decreases (to a new moon). Waxing and waning are old-fashioned ways of saying growing and shrinking.
9. Yes – when you looked at the Earth you would only be able to see the part facing the Sun, so it would have phases, just as the Moon does to us (full Earth, last quarter, etc.). To a Moon dweller, the Earth would rise and set.
10. The diagram needed is simply one that shows that the orbits of Mercury and Venus are inside that of the Earth whereas the orbits of the other planets are outside that of the Earth. For a full range of phases, we need the fully illuminated face to be completely visible to us at some times and completely invisible (in other words, turned away entirely) at other times. We can do that with Mercury and Venus but the lit side of the other planets is never completely hidden to us.

Answers to Worksheet 1.7.8

1. For example, millimetre (mm); metre (m); kilometre (km); light year (ly).
2. a) Should show an appreciation of the need for the spaceship to be completely self-sustaining in all respects.

   b) They may include ideas about the impracticality with current technology, scientific understanding and cost issues. They may identify potential benefits from the project.
3. a)–d) They should draw accurate scale diagrams. Object A would appear to move by 60 mm (± 2 mm); object B would appear to move by 10 mm (±1 mm).

   e) The apparent movement is less, the further away the object is; so small errors make a big difference.

Answers to Practical sheet 1.7.8

1. It is more accurate for closer objects, because the apparent change in position of the object for a given change in observer position is greater.
2. Any suitable suggestion, e.g. the change of position of nearby objects such as trees against the background landscape when you move along in a car.

1.7.9 Using models in science

Lesson overview

Learning objectives
- Explore how we can use models to explain ideas in science.
- Construct an explanation using ideas and evidence.
- Decide if a model is good enough to be useful.

Learning outcomes
- Comment on two models and explain what they show. [O1]
- Explain why these two models are effective ways of helping us to explain certain ideas. [O2]
- State some of the reasons why scientists use models. [O3]

Skills development
- Working scientifically: 2.15 Review theories
- Developing numeracy: interpret diagrams of three dimensional phenomena
- Developing literacy: evaluate a range of models using appropriate ideas and terminology (Q4 - 8)

Resources needed For the solar system model (lamp, e.g. table lamp (but avoid trailing leads) and ball on axis, e.g. tennis ball on knitting needle); for the rock processes model (chocolate, cheese grater, aluminium foil, bun cases, evaporating basin or similar open container for hot water, foil dish); Worksheet 1.7.9; Technician's notes 1.7.9

Common misconceptions Students may think that a model is always a small-scale visual representation of something. Students may see a model only as being a way of communicating an idea to others, rather than also being a tool to help clarify ideas. Students may imagine that for a model to be valid it has to represent all aspects of something as opposed to the features relevant to the exploration.

Key vocabulary model, seasonal, sedimentary, metamorphic, igneous, represent

Teaching and learning

Engage
- Show students pictures of models such as proposed building plans, new cars, aircraft designs, etc., and ask them why these models are used. [O3]
- Say that architects now often provide clients with a computerised 'walk through' of a building design and ask students to suggest why this is often effective at identifying problems with the design. [O3]
- Show students a model that they may have met previously in science, such as one showing the structure of an atom, and ask for ideas as to its value. [O3]

Challenge and develop
- Ask students to suggest what they would need so they could show why days are shorter in winter and longer in summer. Ask them to list the equipment and suggest how it would be used. [O1]
- Add that the model also has to show why, as the day length gets shorter in the northern hemisphere, it gets longer in the southern hemisphere. Ask students to suggest why this might mean the model needs to be modified. [O1, O2]

Explain
- Either provide students with equipment or ask them to instruct you as to how the model should be used to explain varying day length at different times of year. (Task 1 of Worksheet 1.7.9 could be used.) [O1, O2]
- Ask students to comment on the extent to which this model is 'good enough' to explain what it sets out to do. [O2]

- Take students through the three models relating to geological processes, either demonstrating the models or getting students to do the activities, and ask them to explain how good the model is. (Task 2 of Worksheet 1.7.9 could be used.) [O1, O2]

Consolidate and apply

- Ask students to consider the Sun/Earth model and reflect on whether using this helped them to understand and explain how day length changes. [O1, O2]

- Ask students to consider the 'chocolate rocks' model and suggest how effective that is at getting them to understand and distinguish between those processes. [O1, O2]

Extend

- Ask students to suggest why scientists use models. (Task 3 of Worksheet 1.7.9 could be used.) [O3]

- Ask students to consider what the risks are with relying on models too heavily. [O2]

- Challenge students to research and compare explanations from different periods in history about the motion of objects and structure of the Universe. Ask them to suggest what caused the explanations to change. [O3]

Plenary suggestions

- Display an image of the Sun/Earth model and ask groups of students to suggest one thing it shows well and one thing it doesn't show as effectively. [O1, O2, O3]

- Repeat with the 'chocolate rocks' model. [O1, O2, O3]

Answers to Student Book questions

1. The part of the surface of the Earth between the equator and the North Pole.
2. When the axis at the North Pole is tilted away from the Sun, the part of the model representing the northern hemisphere spends more of each rotation without light from the lamp falling on it, whereas it is the opposite for the southern hemisphere.
3. The axis should now be tilted towards the Sun so the effect is reversed.
4. It has layers of pieces pressed together so it forms a solid layer but the pieces are still visible in the layer. The layer has been formed by pressure.
5. The material has been changed by heat.
6. It shows that when the temperature is high enough to melt the material it changes its nature.
7. a) It shows the Earth rotates, that it orbits the Sun and that its axis is tilted. Therefore it can explain seasonal variation in day length. b) It doesn't represent the right relationship between the size of the bodies and the distances between them, or the scale of the 'Sun–Earth' system.
8. It represents effectively how sedimentary processes force material together to form rocks but chocolate is naturally sticky in the way that neither sand nor lime (for example) are. It shows how heat affects the material though it doesn't show how pressure is sometimes part of the process too and it's not so good at representing the extent to which the material changes. It represents the melting and setting that is part of the igneous process but not the resulting crystalline structure.

Answers to Worksheet 1.7.9

1. a) Make the ball go round the lamp. b) Make the ball rotate on its axis. c) As the ball rotates, see that light falls on one side of it and not the other.
2. a) During one rotation the top half of the ball (the northern hemisphere) is in shadow more than light. b) The top half spends more time lit than in shade.
3. a) Student's description of chocolate. b) Small pieces pressed together hard, forming a solid.
4. a) Student's description of chocolate. b) Effect of heat softening material, changing its nature.
5. a) Student's description of chocolate. c) Effect of melting material to produce something which then sets into a different form.
6. a) Models help us to understand how something works and see what might happen if something is changed. b) They might help scientists think through their ideas and sort out what they are saying. c) There might be some features of an idea not represented in the model, so the model behaves in a different way.

1.7.10 Checking students' progress

The *Checking your progress* section in the Student Book indicates the key ideas developed in this chapter and shows how students progress to more complex levels. It is provided to support students in:

- identifying those ideas

- developing a sense of their current level of understanding

- developing a sense of what the next steps in their learning are.

It is designed to be used either at the end of a chapter to support an overall view of the progress, or alternatively during the teaching of the chapter. Students can self-assess or peer assess using this as a basis.

It is helpful to encourage students to provide evidence from their understanding or their notes to support their judgements. In some cases it may be useful to explore the difference in the descriptors for a particular idea so that students can see what makes for a 'higher outcome'.

It may be useful with some descriptors to provide examples from the specific work done, such as an experiment undertaken or an explanation developed and recorded. If marking and feedback uses similar ideas and phrases, this will enable students to relate specific marking to a more general sense of progress.

To make good progress in understanding science students need to focus on these ideas and skills:

Students who are making modest progress will be able to:	Students who are making good progress will be able to:	Students who are making excellent progress will be able to:
Name the layers that make up the Earth and recall that the Earth's surface is made of plates that move about.	Describe the characteristics of each layer of the Earth and recall that tectonic plates move very slowly.	Explain that earthquakes, volcanic eruptions and the formation of mountains can happen where tectonic plates meet; explain how volcanic activity changes the surface of the Earth.
Describe how igneous, sedimentary and metamorphic rocks are formed; give examples and describe how they can change from one type to another.	Describe the features and properties of different types of rocks, including crystals in igneous rocks, recrystallisation in metamorphic rocks and layers (burying fossils) in sedimentary rocks.	Explain the processes involved in the rock cycle and link these to how the rocks are formed.
Describe what is meant by weathering and erosion.	Identify causes of weathering and erosion.	Explain how weathering and erosion affect rocks.
Describe the relative motion of the Earth, Moon and Sun.	Explain how the motion of the Earth relative to the Sun causes day length and year length.	Explain how the relative motion of the Earth, Moon and Sun affects how we see objects from the Earth.
Explain how our current model of the Sun–Earth–Moon system is supported by evidence.	Describe how previous models varied.	Explain why previous models had been developed.
Explain how the Earth is tilted upon its axis.	Explain how the tilt of the Earth on its axis causes seasonal changes.	Explain the effects of the tilt on a planet's axis being greater or less.
Recall the time taken for light to reach Earth from the Sun and from the next nearest star.	Explain the choice of units used for measuring distances in space.	Explain how observations of stars are affected by the scale of the Universe.
Describe what a galaxy is.	Explain what has been learned from the observation of galaxies.	Explain the importance of the discovery of exoplanets.

1.7.11 Answers to Student Book end of chapter questions

This table provides answers to the Questions section at the end of Chapter 7 of the Student Book. It also shows how different questions assess attainment in terms of the focus and style of a question as well as the context. Question level analysis can indicate students' proficiency in approaching different aspects of scientific understanding and different types of answer.

Q	Answer	Marks available	Focus			Style			Context	
			Knowledge & understanding	Application	Evaluation of evidence	Objective test question	Short written answer	Longer written answer	Earth structure	Universe
1	d	1	x			x			x	
2	b	1	x			x			x	
3	b	1	x			x				x
4	c	1	x			x				x
5	d	1	x			x				x
6	c	1	x			x			x	
7	• originally it was molten	1		x				x	x	
	• then it cooled down quickly	1		x				x	x	
8	At a greater angle there would be more seasonal variation …	1		x			x			x
	… so short days would be even shorter and the climate colder/long days would be even longer and hotter.	1		x			x			x
9	• water between rock particles is gradually squeezed out	1		x			x		x	
	• by the increasing weight of new deposits on top	1		x			x		x	
10	Generally speaking, a larger mass means more moons …	1			x			x		x
	… however it doesn't follow in every case and there are several exceptions.	1			x			x		x
	Total possible:	14								

1.8.0 Organisms: Introduction

When and how to use these pages

The Introduction in the Student Book indicates some of the ideas and skills in this topic area that students will already have met from KS2 or from previous KS3 work. It also provides an indication of what they will be studying in this chapter. *Ideas you have met before* is not intended to comprehensively summarise all of the prior ideas, but rather to point out a few of the key ones and to support the view that scientific understanding is progressive. Even though students might be meeting contexts that are new to them, they can often use existing ideas to start to make sense of them.

In this chapter you will find out indicates some of the new ideas that the chapter will introduce. Again, it isn't a detailed summary of content. Its purpose is more to act as a 'trailer' and generate some interest.

The outcomes, then, will be recognition of prior learning that can be built on, and interest in finding out more.

There are a number of ways this can be used. You might, for example:

- use *Ideas you have met before* as the basis for a revision lesson as you start the first new topic

- use *Ideas you have met before* as the centre of spider diagrams, to which students can add examples, experiments they might have done previously or what they found interesting

- make a note of any unfamiliar/difficult terms and return to these in the relevant lessons

- use *In this chapter you will find out* to ask students questions such as:
  - Why is this important?
  - How could it be used?
  - What might we be doing in this topic?

Overview of the chapter

In this chapter, students will learn about the roles of the skeleton and muscles. Students will learn how movement is brought about at joints by muscles working in pairs. Different types of joints will be considered, as well as the consequences when things go wrong with the skeletal system.

Students will also learn about the structure and function of cells, including specialised plant and animal cells. They will learn about organisation in multicellular organisms and in unicellular organisms. Students will describe different types of unicellular organisms and explain adaptations of each.

This chapter offers the opportunity to make careful observations, both with the naked eye and using a microscope. Students are encouraged to describe observations using scientific vocabulary and accurate diagrams. Students will examine the consequences of developing technology to improve human movement. They will also consider how theories can change over time using the context of cell structure.

Obstacles to learning

Students may need extra guidance to deal with the following common misconceptions:

- **Movement:** All joints allow movement.

- **Muscles:** Muscles can push as well as pull.

  Nucleus: The nucleus in a cell is the same as the nucleus of an atom. The nucleus is the same as a brain in an organism – such analogies can cause confusion.

How the Programme of Study is covered by the Student Book

Big idea	Topic	Lesson	Programme of study reference
Organisms	Movement	1.8.1 Exploring the human skeleton	The structure and functions of the human skeleton, to include support, protection, movement and making of blood cells
		1.8.2 Understanding the role of joints and muscles	Biomechanics – the interaction between skeleton and muscles, including the measurement of force exerted by different muscles
		1.8.3 Examining interacting muscles	The function of muscles and examples of antagonistic muscles
		1.8.4 Exploring problems with the skeletal system	The structure and functions of the human skeleton, to include support, protection, movement and making blood cells

Biomechanics – the interaction between skeleton and muscles, including the measurement of force exerted by different muscles |
| | Cells | 1.8.5 Understanding organisation of organisms | Hierarchical organisation of multicellular organisms: from cells to tissues to organs to systems to organisms |
| | | 1.8.6 Describing animal and plant cells | Cells as the fundamental unit of living organisms, including how to observe and record cell structure using a light microscope

The functions of the cell wall, cell membrane, cytoplasm, nucleus, vacuole, mitochondria and chloroplasts

The similarities and differences between animal and plant cells |
| | | 1.8.7 Understanding adaptations of cells | The functions of the cell wall, cell membrane, cytoplasm, nucleus, vacuole, mitochondria and chloroplasts

The similarities and differences between animal and plant cells |
| | | 1.8.8 Exploring cells | Cells as the fundamental unit of living organisms, including how to observe and record cell structure using a light microscope

The similarities and differences between animal and plant cells |
| | | 1.8.9 Understanding unicellular organisms | The structural adaptations of some unicellular organisms |

How the AQA KS3 Syllabus is covered by the Student Books and Teacher Guide

Movement

	Student Book	Teacher Guide
Know		
The parts of the human skeleton work as a system for support, protection, movement and the production of new blood cells.	8.1	8.1
Antagonistic pairs of muscles create movement when one contracts and the other relaxes.	8.2	8.2
Keywords		
Joints: Places where bones meet.	8.2	8.2
Bone marrow: Tissue found inside some bones where new blood cells are made.	8.1	8.1
Ligaments: Connect bones in joints.	8.2	8.2
Tendons: Connect muscles to bones.	8.2	8.2
Cartilage: Smooth tissue found at the end of bones, which reduces friction between them.	8.2	8.2
Antagonistic muscle pair: Muscles working in unison to create movement.	8.2	8.2
Apply		
Explain how a physical property of part of the skeleton relates to its function.	8.1	8.1
Explain why some organs contain muscle tissue.	8.2	8.2
Explain how antagonistic muscles produce movement around a joint.	8.2, 8.3	8.2, 8.3
Use a diagram to predict the result of a muscle contraction or relaxation.	8.2, 8.3	8.2, 8.3
Extend		
Predict the consequences of damage to a joint, bone or muscle.	8.4	8.4
Suggest factors that affect the force exerted by different muscles.	8.3	8.3
Consider the benefits and risks of a technology for improving human movement.	8.4	8.4

Cells

	Student Book	Teacher Guide
Know		
Multicellular organisms are composed of cells which are organised into tissues, organs and systems to carry out life processes.	8.5	8.5
There are many types of cell. Each has a different structure or feature so it can do a specific job.	8.6, 8.7	8.6, 8.7
Skill: Use a light microscope to observe and draw cells.	8.8	8.8
Fact: Both plant and animal cells have a cell membrane, nucleus, cytoplasm and mitochondria.	8.6	8.6
Fact: Plant cells also have a cell wall, chloroplasts and usually a permanent vacuole.	8.6	8.6
Cell: The unit of a living organism, contains parts to carry out life processes.	8.5	8.5
Uni-cellular: Living things made up of one cell.	8.5, 8.9	8.5, 8.9
Multi-cellular: Living things made up of many types of cell.	8.5	8.5
Tissue: Group of cells of one type.	8.5	8.5
Organ: Group of different tissues working together to carry out a job.	8.5	8.5
Diffusion: One way for substances to move into and out of cells.	8.9	8.9
Structural adaptations: Special features to help a cell carry out its functions.	8.7	8.7
Cell membrane: Surrounds the cell and controls movement of substances in and out.	8.6	8.6
Nucleus: Contains genetic material (DNA) which controls the cell's activities.	8.6	8.6
Vacuole: Area in a cell that contains liquid, and can be used by plants to keep the cell rigid and store substances.	8.6	8.6
Mitochondria: Part of the cell where energy is released from food molecules.	8.6	8.6
Cell wall: Strengthens the cell. In plant cells it is made of cellulose.	8.6	8.6
Chloroplast: Absorbs light energy so the plant can make food.	8.6	8.6
Cytoplasm: Jelly-like substance where most chemical processes happen.	8.6	8.6
Immune system: Protects the body against infections.	(8.5)	(8.5)
Reproductive system: Produces sperm and eggs, and is where the foetus develops.	(8.5)	(8.5)
Digestive system: Breaks down and then absorbs food molecules.	(8.5)	(8.5)
Circulatory system: Transports substances around the body.	(8.5)	(8.5)
Respiratory system: Replaces oxygen and removes carbon dioxide from blood.	(8.5)	(8.5)
Muscular skeletal system: Muscles and bones working together to cause movement and support the body.	(8.5)	(8.5)
Apply		
Explain why multi-cellular organisms need organ systems to keep their cells alive.	8.5	8.5
Suggest what kind of tissue or organism a cell is part of, based on its features.	8.7	8.7
Explain how to use a microscope to identify and compare different types of cells.	8.8	8.8
Explain how uni-cellular organisms are adapted to carry out functions that in multi-cellular organisms are done by different types of cell.	8.9	8.9
Extend		
Make deductions about how medical treatments work based on cells, tissues, organs and systems.	(8.4)	(8.4)
Suggest how damage to, or failure of, an organ would affect other body systems.	8.5	8.5
Deduce general patterns about how the structure of different cells is related to their function.	8.7	8.7
Find out how recreational drugs might affect different body systems.		

1.8.1 Exploring the human skeleton

Lesson overview

Learning objectives

- Identify bones of the human skeleton.

- Describe the roles of the skeleton.

- Explain why we have different shapes and sizes of bones.

Learning outcomes

- Name examples of bones and identify bones of the human skeleton. [O1]

- Describe the roles of different bones. [O2]

- Work effectively in a group to learn about the structure and function of bones and make a conclusion about the effect of acid on bones. [O3]

Skills development

- Working scientifically: 2.6 Construct explanations

- Developing numeracy: n/a

- Developing literacy: develop explanations using key terminology (Q7 & 8)

Resources needed skeleton model; clean, cooked chicken bones (e.g. leg bones) plus some pre-soaked for 3–4 days in vinegar; vinegar; 500 ml glass beaker; Worksheet 1.8.1; Technician's notes 1.8.1

Common misconceptions All bones in the human skeleton have the same role.

Key vocabulary joints, bone marrow, skeleton, calcium

Teaching and learning

Engage

- Display a model of a skeleton without any discussion or explanation. Challenge the students to **estimate** the number of bones in the human body. Record some of their estimates for use later in the lesson. [O1]

Challenge and develop

- Use the skeleton model to demonstrate the different shapes and positions of the bones in the human body. [O1]

- Ask the students to choose some words to **describe** how bones vary – such as size, length and shape. [O1, O3]

- Students could name the parts of the skeleton in task 1 of Worksheet 1.8.1. [O1]. Return to the estimates of the number of bones and tell the students that there are 206 bones in the human skeleton. Ask the students to **suggest** why it is very difficult to count all the bones and explain that some tiny bones are found inside the ear. [O1]

- The students **answer** verbal questions to establish the roles of some of these bones – for example the bones in the legs for support, the bones in the arms and the backbone for movement, the bones in the skull for protection. [O2]

Explain

- Demonstrate a cut beef bone, showing the marrow in the centre (or use Figure 1.8.1b in the Student Book). Explain that marrow is where red and white blood cells are made. Ask the students to add to the list of roles of the skeleton, if necessary. Agree on the roles of the skeleton across the class. [O2, O3]

- **Group work** Ask groups of students to **find evidence** for each of the roles (using the 'Roles of the skeleton' section of the Student Book). Encourage students to **share** the task and for each to take on a specific role. [O2]

Consolidate and apply

- Show the students some clean, cooked chicken bones. Allow them to feel the bones and ask them to **describe** the bones. Put the bones in a beaker of vinegar. Ask the students to **predict** what will happen to the bones. [O1, O3]

- Leave the bones for 3–4 days before examining them or, preferably, have some bones pre-soaked in vinegar. Wash the bones and ask the students to **examine** and **describe** how the bones have changed. [O3]

- Tell the students that acids dissolve calcium. Ask them to **think** of an explanation as to why the bones became bendy and then to **discuss** this with a partner. Share ideas across the class, giving more clues if necessary. [O3]

Extend

- Ask students able to progress further to **design an investigation** linked to the effect of acids on bone. If they choose a question that can be investigated (such as how the length of the bone or the length of time affects how bendy it becomes), they could do the investigation at home. [O3]

Plenary suggestions

Sharing facts Ask the students to work individually to write down facts that they have learned in this lesson. Choose students at random to **share** one fact with the rest of the class – each must share a different fact. Encourage others to **correct** any misconceptions. [O1, O2, O3]

Answers to Student Book questions

1. a) Cranium b) Clavicle c) Scapula d) Humerus
2. Some of the bones are too small to show; others are hidden, such as bones in the ear.
3. The backbone is made up of individual bones called vertebrae.
4. Support the body; protect organs; allow movement; produce blood cells.
5. a) Lungs b) Brain
6. Knee, elbow, shoulder, etc.
7. a) Long and wide; gives strength to support the body weight.
   b) Many small bones with joints; allows the hand to bend in different directions.
   c) Curved; to protect lungs inside the chest cavity.
8. a) Not symmetrical; unlike other bones.
   b) Allows vertebrae to fit together; but still move.

Answers to Worksheet 1.8.1

1. A: Skull (cranium); B: jaw; C: collarbone (clavicle); D: shoulder blade (scapula); E: breastbone (sternum); F: ribs; G: humerus; H: backbone (vertebrae); I: radius; J: ulna; K: pelvis; L: femur; M: tibia; N: fibula
2. a) Not enough oxygen reached parts of the body
   b) Infections less likely to be fought off
   c) Much blood will be lost if injured
3. a) Without calcium, bones become bendy.
   b) Bones contain calcium; if there is not enough calcium in the blood, it is taken from the bones.

1.8.2 Understanding the role of joints and muscles

Lesson overview

Learning objectives

- Describe the roles of tendons, ligaments, joints and muscles.
- Identify muscles used in different movements.
- Compare different joints in the human skeleton.

Learning outcomes

- Describe the role of tendons, ligaments, muscles and joints. [O1]
- Describe muscles involved in different movements. [O2]
- Compare the movement allowed by different joints. [O3]

Skills development

- Working scientifically: 2.1 Analyse patterns
- Developing numeracy: n/a
- Developing literacy: summarise key ideas by tabulation (Q8)

Resources needed Skeleton model; Worksheet 1.8.2

Common misconceptions The skull is one complete bone with no joints. Joints always allow movement.

Key vocabulary tendon, ligament, cartilage

Teaching and learning

Engage

- Explain that many animals have skeletal systems similar to humans. For example, a chicken leg is similar to one of ours because it also has a femur, tibia and fibula, and a joint at the knee.
- Ask the students to **think** about where their muscles are and how they are connected with the skeletal system – they should then **share** their ideas in pairs. Encourage feedback. [O1]
- Reinforce that we have muscles all over our bodies. Ask the students to **recall** what attaches muscles to bones. Students could use task 1 of Worksheet 1.8.2. [O1]

Challenge and develop

- Carry out a simple class activity (such as writing on the whiteboard or picking up a drink) and ask the students to **describe** the muscles they are using. Encourage the students to use scientific names where possible. [O2]
- Reinforce that parts of the skeletal system work together to allow us to move.
- Ask the students to read the 'Are all joints the same?' section of the Student Book and **make notes**. Ask them to **consider** the movement that each type of joint allows. [O1, O3]
- **Pair talk** Ask the students to work with a partner to **compare** notes, **discuss** any differences and **amend** their own notes as necessary. [O1, O3]

Explain

- The students work in pairs to **match up** types of joints, the movement that they allow and give one example for each – they could use task 2 of Worksheet 1.8.2. [O1, O3]
- Ask the students to **consider** other joints in the body. A skeleton model may be useful during this activity. They should group these joints into the correct joint category. [O2, O3]

- **Pairs to fours** Student pairs can join to form fours and then **share** the examples of joints that they have grouped. [O2, O3]

Consolidate and apply

- **Charades** The students play a class game of charades: ask a volunteer to come to the front and then whisper an activity to **act out**. Alternatively, these activities could be written on cards for students to choose at random. (Examples include throwing a football, dribbling a basketball, doing press-ups, hopping on one leg, skipping, doing star jumps, kicking a football, swimming breaststroke.) [O3]

- The other students guess what the activity is and write down the answer. They then **identify** at least three bones, two muscles and two joints involved in the activity. [O1, O2, O3]

Extend

- Encourage students able to progress further to **consider** the interaction between the skeletal system and other parts of the body. For example:

  - How do the skeletal system and the muscles depend on each other?

  - How do the bones and the blood depend on each other?

  - How do the skeletal system and the breathing system depend on each other?

Plenary suggestions

Questions and answers Arrange the students in groups of four. Ask each group to **devise** a question for another group. Groups pair up and take turns to **answer** the planned questions. Ask the students to **give feedback** about any good questions that they heard. [O1, O2, O3]

You can differentiate by specifying the number of marks the question should be worth for different groups.

Answers to Student Book questions

1. *Ligaments*: attach bone to bone; *tendons*: attach muscles to bones.
2. Accelerating/decelerating quickly; changing direction quickly; landing hard/awkwardly.
3. Cardiac – heart; smooth – other body organs; skeletal – bicep.
4. Bicep, tricep, forearm.
5. a) Biceps, triceps. b) Calf muscles. c) Abdominal muscles.
6. Fixed; pivot; hinge; ball and socket.
7. a) Ball and socket. b) Hinge.
8. Table should show: ball and socket allowing forwards, backwards, circular; hinge allowing backwards and forwards movement; pivot allowing movement around a point.

Answers to Worksheet 1.8.2

1. A: jaw muscle; B: shoulder muscle; C: pectoral muscle; D: bicep; E: tricep; F: forearm muscle; G: abdominal muscles; H: quadracep; calf muscle
2. a) with iii); e.g. hip, shoulder. b) with ii); e.g. elbow, knee. c) with i); e.g. neck. d) with iv); e.g. skull.
3. a) *Tendons* attach bones to muscles; as the muscle contracts, the bone moves. We could not move without tendons.

   b) *Ligaments* attach bone to bone; joints would be loose without ligaments. Without them our movements would be less well controlled.

   c) *Cartilage* protects the ends of bones; stops them rubbing together. Without it movement would be painful and bones would wear out.

1.8.3 Examining interacting muscles

Lesson overview

Learning objectives
- Describe antagonistic muscles and give examples.
- Describe observations using scientific vocabulary.
- Explain how antagonistic muscles bring about movement.

Learning outcomes
- Describe how muscles work in pairs. [O1]
- Use observations to explain how antagonistic muscles bring about movement. [O2]
- Plan and carry out an investigation to compare muscle strength and identify muscles used in some complex movements. [O3]

Skills development
- Working scientifically: 2.6 Construct explanations
- Developing numeracy: relate position of muscle to direction of force applied
- Developing literacy: analyse and apply ideas about testing muscle strength in writing (Q7 - 9)

Resources needed equipment for demonstration (chicken leg quarter (uncooked with skin in place), scalpel, sharp scissors, plastic gloves, disinfectant, dissection board, camera) and for the practical, per group (see Technician's notes 1.8.3b); Practical sheet 1.8.3a; Practical sheet 1.8.3b; Worksheet 1.8.3b; Technician's notes 1.8.3a; Technician's notes 1.8.3b

Common misconceptions One muscle of a pair pulls, and the other pushes. Muscles that work on their own can pull and push.

Key vocabulary antagonistic muscles pair, bicep, tricep

Teaching and learning

Engage
- Ask the students to put a hand around their own bicep and tricep. Now ask them to bend and straighten their arm at the elbow. Ask the students to **describe** what they notice. [O1]
- Ask them to feel the quadricep muscle (at the front of their thigh) and the hamstring muscle (at the back of their thigh) as they bend and straighten their leg at the knee. [O1]
- Now ask them to feel the calf muscle (at the back of their lower leg) and the shin muscle (at the front of their lower leg) as they bend and flex the foot at the ankle. [O1]
- Ask the students to **discuss** what they notice about muscles with each of these movements. Collect class feedback. [O1]
- Explain that muscles that work together are called antagonistic muscles. Ask the students to **list** the antagonistic muscles from the activity they have just done. [O1]
- Ask students to work in pairs to **explore** briefly any other antagonistic muscles. Tell the students that most of our skeletal muscles work in pairs. [O1]

Challenge and develop
- Dissect a raw chicken leg (instructions provided in Technician's notes 1.8.3a). (Explain that a human leg is very much like a chicken leg in structure. Both have a femur, knee, fibula and tibia. They also both have other tissues such as ligaments, tendons, muscles and fat.) The students could take photos/videos of this. Demonstrate the presence of muscle, cartilage, tendons, ligaments and a joint. Encourage the students to **discuss** the function of each tissue during the demonstration. Students use their observations to complete an analysis using key scientific vocabulary (use Practical sheet 1.8.3a). [O1, O2] As a lead-in to the next activity, ask students to suggest what observations would indicate which chicken muscles were strongest.

Explain

- Use volunteers to demonstrate some simple fitness equipment as an introduction to **developing a plan**. For example step-ups, grip strengtheners, bicep curls using a small hand weight, calf-raises holding on to a desk for support. [O3]

- **Group talk** Arrange the students in groups of three. Ask them to **brainstorm** ideas about how they could compare the strength of different muscles. Either collect feedback across the class or visit each group in turn to listen to their ideas. Suitable ideas include: compare the strength of left and right calf muscles by counting how many calf-raises per minute on each leg are possible; compare the strength of right and left hand muscles by timing how long they can squeeze a handgrip-strengthener. [O2, O3]

- The groups then **plan** their investigation, **considering** variables and making a **prediction**. The students could use Practical sheet 1.8.3b. Assess the safety and suitability of each procedure. [O2, O3]

- The students **carry out** their investigation and **record** the results. [O3]

Consolidate and apply

- Ask the students to work individually to produce an extended piece of writing to **explain** the importance of antagonistic muscles. Provide the students with key words to include in the writing – such as 'antagonistic', 'contract', 'relax', 'joint'. [O1, O2]

  Include some new words for high demand students – ones that they need to find the definition of first, such as 'agonist', 'flexor', 'extensor'.

Extend

- Ask students able to progress further to **explore** some movements, suggesting where the antagonistic muscles that control the movement are found. Encourage them to explore tiny movements as well as more obvious larger ones. [O1, O2]

Plenary suggestions

What have we learned? Ask groups of four to **agree** and **list** three things that they have learned about muscles during this topic. Display the lists while groups **share** their feedback. Compile and display a master list using ideas from all groups. [O1, O2, O3]

Answers to Student Book questions

1. Bicep and tricep; quadriceps and hamstring; calf and shin.
2. Bicep contracts, tricep relaxes, arm bends; tricep contracts, bicep relaxes, arm straightens.
3. We need antagonistic muscles to move bones back to their original position.
4. Description of skin, fat, lots of muscle ('meat'), tendons attaching muscle to bone, cartilage around end of bones, bone marrow inside largest leg bone (femur). Description of role such as muscle in moving bones, tendons attaching muscle to bone, ligaments attaching bone to bone, marrow where red blood cells are made.
5. Hinge joint, allows movement up and down.
6. It can help us to understand structure or bones, muscles and joints, because these are similar in a chicken leg and a human leg. It helps us to understand how joints/muscles function and how to treat problems.
7. both; squeeze the handgrip strength tester as hard as possible; compare the force of each; higher force indicates stronger muscles
8. basketball player; uses arm muscles more than a footballer
9. sensible suggestion such as measuring the size of mass that can be lifted using the thighs

Answers to Worksheet 1.8.3

1. a) Antagonistic. b) Tendons; joint. c) Bicep; tricep. d) Contracts; relaxes.
2. a) a with ii); b with iii); c with i) b) front of the neck c) back of the neck
3. a) Swimming; you use arm muscles more; using these muscles strengthens them
   b) It depends on the type of training that they do; there may be a genetic factor

1.8.4 Exploring problems with the skeletal system

Lesson overview

Learning objectives

- Recall some medical problems with the skeletal system.
- Explain how some conditions affect the skeleton.
- Consider the benefits and risks of a technology for improving human movement.

Learning outcomes

- Describe some medical problems in different parts of the skeletal system. [O1]
- Research and describe treatments for problems with the skeletal system. [O2]
- Research and describe how treatments for some skeletal system problems have changed over time. [O3]

Skills development

- Working scientifically: 2.5 Communicate ideas
- Developing numeracy: n/a
- Developing literacy: use writing to construct justified suggestions (Q6 - 7)

Resources needed information/images on skeletal system problems; science (or medical) dictionaries; Worksheet 1.8.4

Key vocabulary skeletal system, fracture, osteoporosis, arthritis

Teaching and learning

Engage

- Show pictures of some skeletal problems but with no explanation. These could be shown as a rolling presentation, as web-based images or as paper images. The images could include an X-ray of a broken bone, a fractured limb in plaster, an artificial hip used for replacement, an illustration of a joint to show cartilage worn away (as in arthritis), a curved-spine X-ray of scoliosis, a photo of a muscular dystrophy sufferer in a wheelchair, bruising from a muscle tear, etc. The students try to **work out** what the lesson is about. [O1]
- Ask the students to **share** their ideas, asking others to comment on these without saying whether a guess is correct or not. [O1]
- Return to each image when the theme of the lesson has been established and ask the students to **comment** on the significance of each image. [O1]

Challenge and develop

- **Pair work** Provide pairs of students with a list of problems linked with the skeletal system (you could use the list in Worksheet 1.8.4). Ask them to **sort** the problems into 'problems related to bones', 'problems related to muscles' and 'other problems'. [O1, O2]

Explain

- **Group work** Arrange the students in groups of four. Give each member of each group a topic to **research** (e.g. fractures, arthritis, osteoporosis, muscular dystrophy). [O2]

    You could differentiate by assigning a low demand group the fracture topic.

- Provide each group with information in textbooks (such as the Student Book) or from the internet. Ask each group to **assimilate** the information and to **summarise** in notes. Remind them to **research** the cause of the problem, its treatment and how the treatment has changed over time. [O1, O2, O3]

- Approximately halfway through the research task, ask each group to **nominate** one team member to become a 'spy'. The spy visits other groups researching the same topic and looks for good practice and ideas to take back to their own team. They return and **share** what they have seen. [O1, O2, O3]

- **Envoys** At the end of the research time (approximately 10–15 minutes depending on the lesson length), each team nominates a different team member to become an 'envoy'. The envoy moves to a group researching a different topic and **teaches** that group what they have learned. [O1, O2, O3]

- The envoys return to their original group and the rest of the group **teach** the envoy what they learned from the visiting envoy. If time allows, another envoy could be selected to teach a different group. [O1, O2, O3]

Consolidate and apply

- Ask the students to work in their groups to produce an information leaflet to be displayed in a doctor's waiting room. The aim of the leaflet is to inform patients about their skeletal system disorder and also to explain the treatment possibilities. Each group should focus on their research topic. [O1, O2, O3]

Extend

- Ask students able to progress further to **create** a loop card game based on skeletal system problems. Encourage them to include questions and answers related to all the topics researched during the lesson. If time allows, test the loop card game with the class. [O1, O2, O3]

Plenary suggestions

Mind map Ask the students to work in pairs to produce a mind map/concept map linked to the skeletal system. Encourage them to **refer back** to work completed earlier in this topic for prompts about what to include.

Answers to Student Book questions

1. By (large) impacts.
2. Using plaster of Paris, fibreglass and/or pins.
3. There is a higher risk of infection.
4. The density of bones decreases; and the bones therefore become weaker.
5. Bones rub together.
6. More precise X-rays; improved surgery; increased knowledge of avoiding damage.
7. Risk of infection following surgery, risk from anaesthetic, possibility of decreased mobility following surgery. Persuasion to have replacement such as could decrease pain, increase movement or other relevant suggestions.

Answers to Worksheet 1.8.4

1. a) Osteoporosis, arthritis, fracture, scoliosis.
   b) Torn muscle, muscular dystrophy.
   c) Tendonitis, torn ligament.
2. A summary of the ideas shared during the group task, as guided by materials provided.
3. a) *Joint replacements* to replace damaged or diseased joints; *X-rays* to examine bones; *genetic screening* to estimate the possibility of inheriting or passing on a genetic condition.
   b) Ideas about how each has improved; with examples from research.
   c) All likely to improve, as science understanding and technology improve.

1.8.5 Understanding organisation in organisms

Lesson overview

Learning objectives
- Define the terms tissues, organs and organ systems.
- Body systems can be affected by certain drugs and by damage to other organs.
- Describe how some recreational drugs affect body systems.

Learning outcomes
- Explain the terms cell, tissue, organ and organ system, and the function of main organ systems in the body. [O1]
- Describe the effects of different types of drugs on the body. [O2]
- Suggest how damage to one organ can affect other body systems. [O3]

Skills development
- Working scientifically: 2.14 Examine consequences
- Developing numeracy: n/a
- Developing literacy: speculate upon consequences of a situation (Q6)

Resources Worksheet 1.8.5, with the last page copied onto card; images of different organisms

Common misconceptions Organ systems are independent of each other and do not work together. All animals contain the same organ systems. Plants do not have organ systems.

Key vocabulary tissue, organ, organ system , cell, multicellular, recreational drug

Teaching and learning

Engage

- Show the students images of a unicellular organism, a sponge, a worm, a fish and a human. Ask them to **rank** the organisms in order of complexity. [O1]
- Ask them to **identify** how the complexity differs between the organisms. [O1]

Challenge and develop

- Use the analogy of a department store to help the students understand how organisation within an organism works. Ask them to work in pairs to **make connections** between the department store organisation and the organisation of the human body. They should be able to **identify** the following: the department store is the organism; each individual department (e.g. clothing) is analogous to a body system within the organism (such as the nervous system or skeletal system); each type of clothing (e.g. shirts) in a department is analogous to an organ (e.g. brain within the body system); each type of clothing (e.g. casual or formal) is analogous to the tissue within the organ (e.g. white matter or grey matter); one particular shirt is analogous to a specialised cell within the tissue (e.g. nerve cell). [O1]

Explain

- Group the students in ability groups of four. Ask low and standard demand groups to use the cards from Worksheet 1.8.5 and correctly group together all the organ systems, their functions, organs, tissues and specialised cells (task 1 on Worksheet 1.8.5). Ask them to write an explanation of how cells 'connect' to tissues, tissues to organs etc. (task 2 on Worksheet 1.8.5). [O1]
- Introduce the idea that drugs can affect organs and, therefore, body systems. Explain to the students that there are four main types of drug – painkillers, stimulants, depressants and hallucinogens. [O2]
- Allow the students two minutes to **think about** what the characteristics of each group may be. Take feedback across the class, elucidating that painkillers stop or reduce pain, that stimulants speed up the body, that depressants slow down the body and that hallucinogens cause people to see or feel things that do not exist. [O2]
- Students **read** the 'Effects of drugs on organs and systems' section of the Student Book and **answer** the questions.

- Use verbal questioning to test understanding of which drugs affect which organ and which body system. [O2]

Consolidate and apply

- The students work individually to **produce a leaflet** to inform people about the effects of drugs. Encourage students to focus on the information included in the leaflet, rather than the layout or artwork. (If necessary, you could provide a template that students could add text to.) Remind them about the learning outcomes of the lesson and encourage them to try to demonstrate these in the leaflet. [O2]

Extend

- For students able to progress further, return to the images used at the start of the lesson. Ask them to use the 'Consequences of damage to organs' section of the Student Book to predict damage of one organ or body system. They could **discuss** which are the most vital organ systems for multicellular organisms. [O1, O3]

Plenary suggestions

Devising analogies Ask the students to devise a different analogy to **explain** the organisation in a human, and also to describe how the analogy works and where it fails. [O1, O2]

Answers to Student Book questions

1. For example: lungs – allow oxygen into the body and remove carbon dioxide; stomach – where digestion takes place; eye – enables us to see.
2. The skin is made from many different types of tissue; it has different layers; working together.
3. Nervous system.
4. Depressant; affects the nervous system and the circulatory system (may also mention breathing system).
5. a) nervous system transmits electrical signals, circulatory system sends blood around the body system, respiratory system breathes in oxygen and breathes out carbon dioxide, immune system fights infection, reproductive system fertilises eggs and protects them until birth, muscular skeletal system forms the structure and mechanics of the body, digestive system breaks down food and absorbs it; b) Muscle, bone, skin.
6. Impulses still carried around (along nerves) but the information cannot be interpreted.

Answers to Worksheet 1.8.5

1.

Skeletal	To provide support for the organism and enable movement	Muscle cell	Muscle or bone tissues	Joint
Nervous	To send messages and so control movement and behaviour	Nerve cell	Nervous tissue	Brain
Respiratory	To allow oxygen to be absorbed by the blood and carbon dioxide to be removed from the body	Ciliated epithelial cells, alveoli	Lung tissue	Lungs
Digestive	To break down food so the nutrients can be absorbed by the blood	Cells which pass acid into the stomach	Lining of the small intestine	Mouth, stomach, intestines
Excretory	To help remove waste from the body	Sweat glands	Lining of the lungs	Lungs, kidneys, bladder
Reproductive	To make new individuals	Sperm cell, egg cell	Lining of the womb	Ovary, testes
Circulatory	To move blood around the body, delivering nutrients and oxygen, and removing waste from all cells	Red blood cell, white blood cell	Capillaries	Heart

2. a) Similar cells working together are known as tissues (e.g. muscle cells work together to make muscle tissue).

   b) Similar tissues work together to make organs (e.g. the brain is made of different nervous tissues working together).

   c) Different organs make up an organ system (e.g. the mouth, stomach and intestines make up the digestive system).

3. a) Cannabis – nervous, circulatory; ecstacy – nervous, circulatory; cocaine – nervous, circulatory.

   b) Ecstasy.   c) 16–19, 20–24 and 25–29; because the use of all three drugs is the highest.

   d) Ecstasy use increases from age 16–19 to age 25–29; but then decreases. It is almost zero use at age 55–59. Credit any numerical data from graph. Cocaine use follows similar trend to ecstasy; although still some cocaine use at age 55–59. Credit any numerical data from graph.

   e) A higher proportion of 16–19 year olds use cannabis than 20–24 year olds. However, a higher proportion of 20–24 year olds use cocaine and ecstasy than 16–19 year olds. This may be because cannabis is more readily available in places where younger people go; or because cannabis is cheaper than cocaine and ecstasy, and the higher age group has more money.

1.8.6 Describing animal and plant cells

Lesson overview

Learning objectives

- Describe the structures found in animal and plant cells.
- Explain the function of some of the structures within animal and plant cells.
- Communicate ideas about cells effectively using scientific terminology.

Learning outcomes

- Label an animal cell and a plant cell. [O1]
- Compare and contrast the similarities and differences between plant cells and animal cells. [O2]
- Describe the functions of the nucleus, cell membrane, mitochondria, cytoplasm, cell wall, vacuole and chloroplast. [O3]

Skills development

- Working scientifically: 2.6 Construct explanations
- Developing numeracy: relate drawings to three dimensional phenomena
- Developing literacy: develop explanations using ideas and evidence (Q3 - 7)

Resources overhead projector; Worksheet 1.8.6a; Worksheet 1.8.6b; craft materials for making cell models (e.g. jelly or gelatine or slime, cling film, plastic bags, cardboard, elastic bands, sticky tape, coloured modelling clay, balloons, safety glasses); Technician's notes 1.8.6

Common misconceptions Cells are two-dimensional, inert objects. The nucleus of a cell and the nucleus of an atom are the same.

Key vocabulary nucleus, cytoplasm, cell membrane, mitochondria, cell wall, vacuole, chloroplast

Teaching and learning

Engage

- Show the students the illustrations of plant and animal cells in Figures 1.8.6b and c in the Student Book. Ask them to **identify** three facts about each image. [O1]

Challenge and develop

- Provide half of the students with the descriptions of different parts of an animal cell, and the other half with the descriptions of plant cells, found on Worksheet 1.8.6a. Ensure that they are clear about what the descriptions say. Provide the students with a range of different materials to select from. Ask them, in pairs, to **make a model** of their cells from the descriptions. [O1, O2]
- **Pair swap** Ask one from each pair to join with someone who made the other model. Each should **explain** their model to the other. [O1, O2]

Explain

- Select different students to show their cell models and to **explain** each part to the class. They should be able to **justify** why they chose certain materials to represent particular parts. Ask them to **identify** the features in a plant cell that are not in an animal cell. [O1, O2]

Consolidate and apply

- Provide the students with Worksheet 1.8.6b. Ask low demand students to complete task 1, **naming** each structure of the cell. Standard demand students should complete tasks 1 and 2. [O1]
- High demand students should complete all three tasks, **explaining** how the three cell parts are adapted to carry out their particular jobs. [O2, O3]

Extend

• Ask the students to **research** how cells evolved in the first place. They should **prepare** a one-minute talk to deliver to the class. [O3]

Plenary suggestions

What am I? Play 'What am I?' Think of a part of a cell, and select students to provide a question to guess the part of the cell. Only 'yes' or 'no' answers can be given.

Answers to Student Book questions

1. Under a microscope.
2. Yes.
3. Nucleus; mitichondria, other organelles.
4. Oxygen; glucose; water, carbon dioxide; urea.
5. Cell wall; vacuole.
6. Plant cell; it has more structures in it.
7. To provide them with extra strength and protection (many animals eat plants); to help with photosynthesis (chloroplasts absorb light).

Answers to Worksheet 1.8.6b

1. Refer to Figures 1.8.6b and 1.8.6c in the Student Book.
2. N = nucleus; C = chlorophyll; V = vacuole; C = cytoplasm; C = cell wall; C = cell membrane.
   Three structures in both: cell membrane; cytoplasm; nucleus.
3. a) Very thin to help small substances transfer in and out quickly.
   b) Made of cellulose to give it strength.
   c) Packed with chlorophyll, which absorbs sunlight.

1.8.7 Understanding adaptations of cells

Lesson overview

Learning objectives

- Recall the purpose of specialised cells.
- Identify examples of specialised plant and animal cells.
- Explain the structure and function of specialised cells.

Learning outcomes

- Identify different specialised animal and plant cells. [O1]
- Describe the structure of specialised cells. [O2]
- Use models to explain the function of specialised cells and how their structure enables them to do their job. [O3]

Skills development

- Working scientifically: 2.5 Communicate ideas
- Developing numeracy: n/a
- Developing literacy: develop explanations using ideas and evidence (Q5 - 7)

Resources photographs of different types of cells, selection of materials for making specialised cells (e.g. red jelly, ready-made colourless jelly, cling film, cardboard boxes, lots of elastic bands, balloons, straws, scissors, sticky tape); sets of cell cards made from page 2–4 of Worksheet 1.8.7; Worksheet 1.8.7; Technician's notes 1.8.7

Common misconceptions All plant cells contain chloroplasts. Cytoplasm is only found around the nucleus. In a nerve cell the cytoplasm extends the length of the axon.

Key vocabulary structural adaptations

Teaching and learning

Engage

- Show the students photographs or a video clip showing the wide range of different types of cell in the living world. Encourage students to **ask** questions about the variety of life on the planet. [O1]

- **'Pictionary'** Working in pairs, one student faces the board and the other has their back to the board. Display key words and ask those students facing the board to draw a picture of the word. The other student has to **guess** what it is. When one pair has guessed correctly, move on to the next word. This will help to recap ideas from the previous lesson. [O1, O2]

Challenge and develop

Group the students in ability pairs.

- Provide each pair with the cards from Worksheet 1.8.7 illustrating different specialised cells. Ask them to **sort** the cards into animal cells and plant cells. Collect feedback and discuss the features that helped them with their classification. Then provide the pairs with the description cards and ask them to **match** these to the pictures of the specialised cells. Other examples could be discussed, such as guard cells controlling whether a stoma is open or closed, as seen in the Student Book. [O1, O2]

- Then provide students with the explanation cards for each of their specialised cells. Ask them to **match** them to the correct cells. Go through the answers. [O3]

- Set up tables with suitable materials for making models of specialised cells. Ask each pair of students to select one specialised animal cell and one specialised plant cell, according to the list below, and use the descriptions and explanations, as appropriate, to **make a model** of the two cells. [O2]

    Low demand students – choose from red blood cell, egg cell, leaf cell

Standard demand students – choose from ciliated epithelial cell, sperm cell, leaf cell

High demand students – choose from muscle cell, nerve cell, root hair cell.

Explain

- **Pairs to fours** Link one pair with another, from different abilities. Then, working in groups of four, students should **explain** their models to each other, **describing** where the main structures are and how the cell is adapted to carry out its job. Select different pairs to **give explanations** about the other pairs' models. [O2, O3]

Consolidate and apply

- Using the cards from Worksheet 1.8.7 with the diagrams of specialised cells, ask pairs of students to **rank** the cells in order from the most specialised to the least specialised. Can they **suggest** why some cells have to be more specialised than others? What implications might this have in terms of replacing these cells? [O1, O2, O3]

Extend

- Provide students able to progress further with descriptions of other specialised cells, provided as 'Extension' on page 1 of Worksheet 1.8.7. Ask them to draw a labelled diagram of the cell from the description. They should **explain** how the structure helps the cell to carry out its job. This could be peer assessed. [O3]

Plenary suggestions

Model work Select a range of models made by the class. Hold up each in turn and ask the students to **identify** the name of the cell, **describe** its essential features and **explain** how it is specialised to carry out its job.

Answers to Student Book questions

1. a) In the eye b) In the ear c) In the skin.
2. In order that many different roles can be carried out, increase survival of the organism.
3. Sperm cell; nerve cell; muscle cell.
4. a) Nerve cell. b) Muscle cell. c) Sperm cell.
5. Plants carry out photosynthesis and so they need specialised cells to bring in what is needed for photosynthesis (e.g. water, carbon dioxide and sunlight).
6. Leaf cells are adapted to trap sunlight (by chloroplasts) as these are more exposed to sunlight.
7. *Leaf cell* has: many chloroplasts to capture sunlight; a thin cell membrane to allow water and carbon dioxide to enter quickly; a large vacuole to help the cell maintain its shape.

   Root hair cell has: an extended cytoplasm to enable as much water as possible to be collected; a large surface area for the extension; no chloroplasts so that maximum amount of water can be absorbed; a large vacuole to store water and sugars.

Answers to Worksheet 1.8.7

1. a) *Animal cells* A, B, C, D, G, H; *plant cells* E, F.
   b) A5; B6; C2; D1; E3; F7; G4, H8
2. A8; B5; C7; D3; E2; F1; G6; H4
3. a) Any sensible order – for example, G, C, D, A, F, H, B, E.
   b) Any sensible answer, for example: the nerve cell is more specialised than the root hair cell because it has a long extension with many more parts to it, such as the fatty insulation; the extension of the root hair is just an extension of the cytoplasm with no extra parts.

1.8.8 Exploring cells

Lesson overview

Learning objectives

- Observe cells using a microscope and record findings.
- Explain how to use a microscope to identify and compare cells.
- Explain how developments in science can change ideas.

Learning outcomes

- Use a microscope to observe animal and plant cells [O1]
- Identify the parts of a light microscope and explain the function of each [O2]
- Explain how advances have helped our understanding of cells to change over time [O3]

Skills development

- Working scientifically: 2.9 Collect data

- Developing numeracy: understanding scale and magnification

- Developing literacy: make comparisons and suggest improvements (Q6 & 7)

Resources images from light microscope; objects to use under microscope; Practical sheet 1.8.8a; Practical sheet 1.8.8b; equipment for practical, per group (see Technician's notes 1.8.8); Technician's notes 1.8.8; Worksheet 1.8.8; Practical sheet 1.8.8a; Practical sheet 1.8.8b

Common misconceptions Cells are two-dimensional, inert objects.

Key vocabulary organism, conclusion, microscope, cell, evidence, magnification

Teaching and learning

Engage

- Show microscope images observed using light microscope, for example, blood cells, bacteria, small animals (avoid showing plant cell such as onion cell or animal cell such as cheek cell). Ask students to **state** why we use a microscope.

- Demonstrate how to use a microscope. Use questioning and answering to establish the function of each part. [O2]

- Ask the students to **make observations** of a variety of different objects using the microscope – for example newspaper print, hair, a coin, a paper towel (see Technician's notes 1.8.8). Ask them to **discuss** their observations and the importance of the microscope in scientific discoveries. [O2, O3]

Challenge and develop

- Ask students to follow the instructions on Practical sheet 1.8.8a and make up a slide of a cheek cell. Ask them to draw accurate diagrams of their observations cells on their sheets. Students then follow instructions on Practical sheet 1.8.8b to make up a slide of an onion cell. Ask them to draw accurate diagrams of their observations cells on their sheets. [O1, O2]

  High demand students could be challenged to work out the actual size of the cells using the magnification calculation, magnified size + actual size × total magnification (where total magnification is objective lens magnification × eyepiece lens magnification)

Explain

- Refer the students back to the different parts of the animal cell and the plant cell from the Student Book (Lesson 1.8.6). Ask them to **relate** these to the corresponding parts of the diagrams of their slides, and to label them. If possible, link up a microscope to the overhead projector and point out the different parts from the prepared slides. Students could complete tasks 1 and 2 of Worksheet 1.8.8 and Student Book questions 1–5. [O1, O2]

Consolidate and apply

- **Pair talk.** Ask pairs to **discuss** the main steps in using a microscope to observe animal cells. Encourage students to use scientific terminology. [O1, O2]

- Ask students to **write** a guide to using a microscope to observe animal cells. The guide should include an explanation of each step and of the parts of the microscope. [O1, O2]

- **Peer assessment.** Ask students to form pairs (different from the planning pairs) to peer assess each other's guide. Success criteria could be agreed as a class prior to this, for example, numbered steps, labelled diagram(s), explanation of each step, written in the third person. [O1, O2]

Extend

- Students could **research** the electron microscope and its advantages over the light microscope (e.g. higher resolution). Ask students to **suggest** how this advance in microscope technology is useful to society. Students could attempt task 3 of Worksheet 1.8.8. [O3]

Plenary suggestions

Summarise learning Ask the students to work in pairs. Providing at least one example, one person tells their partner how they have met all the learning outcomes.

Answers to Student Book questions

1. Because cells are too small to see with the naked eye.
2. Made to look bigger than the actual object.
3. So that cells and structures can be seen (different structures take up the stain to varying degrees).
4. *Cheek cells* – separate cells, some clearly similar size and shape, almost spherical, nuclei stained darker; *onion cells* – regular, cuboid-shaped cells, wall around each cell, nuclei stained darker.
5. Comparison such as: cannot see as much detail in microscope images as drawings but can see nuclei in both, regular-shaped cells, cell wall in plant cell, similar shapes of both cells in images and drawings.
6. Electron microscope uses electrons; light microscope uses light; and electron microscope gives greater magnification than light microscopes.
7. Microscopes help scientists to understand how cells work and how cells are changed (e.g. by cancer and viruses). Better types of microscopes can help medicine to develop better treatments.

Answers to Worksheet 1.8.8b

1. a) Eyepiece lens. b) Objective lens. c) Focusing wheel. d) Light source. e) Stage.
2. a) Eyepiece lens: magnifies the image. b) Objective lens: magnifies the image. c) Focusing wheel: to focus the image. d) Light source: illuminates the specimen. e) Stage: holds the specimen and moves it further away from/closer to the objective lens.
3. a) Microscopes showed that living things do not look like the non-living things that they were thought to appear from/microscopes showed that living things have a complex structure. b) Suggestions such as: helped to diagnose illnesses such as cancers; helped scientists to understand cell structure and this helps to relate to function; allow us to carry out IVF/stem cell developments; discussion of use of electron microscopes specifically (e.g. to understand and mimic materials); to see materials/cells in greater detail; any other sensible suggestions.

1.8.9 Understanding unicellular organisms

Lesson overview

Learning objectives

- Recognise different types of unicellular organism.
- Explain how unicellular organisms are adapted to carry out functions.
- Compare and contrast features of unicellular organisms.

Learning outcomes

- Describe unicellular organisms – including yeast, bacteria, euglena, a paramecium and an amoeba – as being either prokaryotes or eukaryotes. [O1]
- Describe the functions of specialised parts of different unicellular organisms. [O2]
- Explain how different structures help organisms to survive. [O3]

Skills development

- Working scientifically: 2.3 Draw conclusions
- Developing numeracy: understand scale
- Developing literacy: summarise key ideas by tabulation (Q8)

Resources images of fossil bacteria; large poster paper and crayons; Worksheet 1.8.9

Common misconceptions All unicellular organisms are called bacteria.

Key vocabulary prokaryote, eukaryote, bacterium, unicellular, diffusion

Teaching and learning

Engage

- Show the students images of fossils of early bacteria found in rocks. Encourage them to **ask questions** about the images. Discuss evidence such as that found in rocks 3.8 million years ago, leading to the belief that life started with single-celled organisms. Introduce what is meant by a 'single-celled' organism. [O1]
- Show the students images of a simple prokaryote and a eukaryote (for example the bacterium and amoeba shown in Figures 1.8.9a and 1.8.9b in the Student Book). Ask them to **identify** similarities and differences between these two types of single-celled organism and see if they can **work out** how unicellular organisms are classified. Introduce the terms *prokaryote* and *eukaryote* and apply them accordingly to the images. Can students **identify** which is the first form of life from this classification? [O1]

Challenge and develop

- Group the students in similar ability groups of four. Give each group descriptions and diagrams of different unicellular organisms from Worksheet 1.8.9, choosing the organisms depending on each group's ability (see below). Ask each group to carry out tasks 1 and 2 from the worksheet for the organisms they have been given. [O1]
  - Low demand students should be given images and descriptions of a bacterium and an amoeba (description cards 2 and 4). Ask them to **match** the description to the diagram (task 1 on Worksheet 1.8.9). Then ask them to **complete** task 2 for these two organisms, **identifying** any interesting features in each organism that will help to classify it and features that help it to survive. [O1, O2]
  - Standard demand students should be given images and descriptions of a euglena, a bacterium and an amoeba (description cards 2, 3 and 4). Ask them to annotate the diagrams from the descriptions to **explain** different features. [O2]
  - Ask high demand students to try task 3 on Worksheet 1.8.9. Ask them to produce their own drawings (roughly drawn to scale) to show the relative sizes of the different organisms. They can use the information in the table and the descriptions given on Worksheet 1.8.9. They will need to use large poster paper. Ask

them to annotate the diagrams accordingly and to **explain** how they think each of the features helps the organism to survive. [O3]

- Ask the students to swap their diagrams with another group of the same ability to **peer assess** each other's work. They should add any missing parts and **identify** what the groups have done well and one thing they could improve on in the future. [O1, O2, O3]

Explain

- Ask the students to draw up a table, such as this one, in order to **compare** and **contrast** the organisms. [O2, O3]

Name of organism	Is it a prokaryote or eukaryote?	Does it have a cell wall?	How does it feed?	How does it move?

High demand students should be able to **explain** how the different structures enable the organisms to survive. [O3]

Consolidate and apply

- Show the students video clips of the different organisms in action, or images of them. Ask them to **identify** each of the organisms and to **describe** three distinctive features of each. [O1, O2, O3]

Extend

- **'Top trumps'.** Ask students able to progress further to devise some 'top trump' cards for each of the different organisms they have learned about in the lesson. They should rate them for: their level of specialisation; how well they can move; how big they are; how easily they can find and absorb food; whether they are a prokaryote or a eukaryote; how likely they are to survive. [O3]

Plenary suggestions

Summarising Ask the students to write a paragraph to **summarise** what they have learned about unicellular organisms. [O1, O2, O3]

What am I? Ask the students to take it in turns to think of one unicellular organism. The rest of the class **ask questions**, which can only be answered by 'yes' or 'no', to find out what the organism is. They should try and guess within fewer than ten questions. [O1, O2, O3]

Answers to Student Book questions

1. An organism made of just one cell.
2. Algae; protozoa; yeasts.
3. They may have either tails, tiny hairs and/or chloroplasts.
4. Bacterium is a prokaryote; amoeba is a eukaryote. Eukaryotes have a nucleus inside a membrane; prokaryotes do not.
5. a) They have chloroplasts. b) Absorb nutrients through a thin cell membrane.
6. Euglena contains chloroplasts to make its own food using sunlight; it has a tail to help it move towards the light.
7. Cytoplasm can flow (amoeba), cilia can beat (paramecium), flagellum/tail for swimming.
8. *Similarities*: all have a cell membrane; all have cytoplasm; all have mitochondria; all contain genetic material; all can live independently.

   Differences: some have a nuclear membrane (eukaryotes); others do not (prokaryotes); some have chloroplasts; some have cilia or a flagella, or move with flowing cytoplasm; some are very big; others are very small; some contain protective slime layers.

Answers to Worksheet 1.8.9

1. A3; B4; C5; D1; E2
2. a) *Bacterium*: has no nucleus; *yeast*: has a nucleus and fixed spherical shape; *euglena*: has cilia around the cell membrane; *paramecium*: can change its shape and has a nucleus; *amoeba*: contains chloroplasts.

   b) *Bacterium*: has a layer of slime around the outside cell wall; *yeast*: has a cell wall; *euglena*: has a flagella (tail) so it can swim; *paramecium*: cilia help it to move and find food; *amoeba*: cytoplasm flows, enabling it to move.
3. Appropriate diagrams correctly labelled and drawn to these scale sizes: bacterium 5 mm; yeast 1 cm; euglena 5 cm; paramecium 20 cm; amoeba 50 cm.

1.8.10 Checking students' progress

The Checking your progress section in the Student Book indicates the key ideas developed in this chapter and shows how students progress to more complex levels. It is provided to support students in:

- identifying those ideas;

- developing a sense of their current level of understanding;

- developing a sense of what the next steps in their learning are.

It is designed to be used either at the end of a chapter to support an overall view of the progress, or alternatively during the teaching of the chapter. Students can self-assess or peer assess using this as a basis.

It is helpful to encourage students to provide evidence from their understanding or their notes to support their judgements. In some cases it may be useful to explore the difference in the descriptors for a particular idea so that students can see what makes for a 'higher outcome'.

It may be useful with some descriptors to provide examples from the specific work done, such as an experiment undertaken or an explanation developed and recorded. If marking and feedback uses similar ideas and phrases this will enable students to relate specific marking to a more general sense of progress.

To make good progress in understanding science students need to focus on these ideas and skills:

Students who are making modest progress will be able to:	Students who are making good progress will be able to:	Students who are making excellent progress will be able to:
Identify the main bones of the skeleton.	Describe the functions of the skeleton.	Explain how different parts of the skeleton are adapted to carry out particular functions.
Describe the role of skeletal joints.	Identify some different joints and explain the role of tendons and ligaments in joints.	Compare the movement allowed at different joints and explain why different types of joints are needed.
Recall that muscles contract to move bones at joints.	Identify muscles that contract to cause specific movements.	Explain how muscles work antagonistically to bring about movement and evaluate a model.
Recognise and label basic and specialised animal cells and plant cells.	Describe the functions of the nucleus, cell membrane, mitochondria, cytoplasm, cell wall, vacuole and chloroplast.	Compare and contrast the similarities and differences between specialised animal cells and plant cells.
Describe unicellular organisms – including yeast, bacteria, euglena, paramecium and amoeba – as being either prokaryotes or eukaryotes.	Describe the function of specialised parts of different unicellular organisms.	Explain how different structures help organisms to survive.
Put the terms cell, tissue, organ and organ system in order of hierarchy, naming some common tissues, organs and organ systems in humans.	Explain the terms cell, tissue, organ and organ system and the function of some of the main organ systems in the body.	Explain the relationship between different organs of the body and predict the consequences of damage to specific organs.
Recall that a microscope magnifies an image and allows us to see objects not visible to the naked eye.	Describe and demonstrate how to observe animal and plant cells under the microscope and explain observations.	Explain the importance of the development of microscopy techniques, using examples.

1.8.11 Answers to Student Book end of chapter questions

This table provides answers to the Questions section at the end of Chapter 8 of the Student Book. It also shows how different questions assess attainment in terms of the focus and style of a question as well as the context. Question level analysis can indicate a student's proficiency in approaching different aspects of scientific understanding and different types of answer.

Q	Answer	Marks available	Knowledge & understanding	Application	Evaluation of evidence	Objective test question	Short written answer	Longer written answer	Movement	Cells
1	a	1	x			x			x	
2	c	1	x			x			x	
3	The bones are curved and form a cavity	1	x				x		x	
	in which the lungs are protected	1	x				x		x	
4	Muscles are attached to bones	1	x				x		x	
	As muscles contract, they move the bone	1	x				x		x	
5	c	1	x			x				x
6	b	1	x			x				x
7	Allows cell structures to be seen (1). For	2	x				x			x
	example, methylene blue on cheek cells/		x				x			x
	iodine on onion cells (1)									
8	b	1		x		x			x	
9	There would be a bigger range of movement/circular movement as well as backwards and forwards	1		x			x		x	
	As the elbow joint is a hinge joint it only allows forwards and backwards movement	1		x			x		x	
10	Plant cell (1) because it has a cell wall (1).	4		x				x		x
	Suggest a place other than the leaf, e.g. root			x				x		x
	(1) as has no chloroplasts (1)			x				x		x
								x		x
11	b	1		x		x				x
12	Is a eukaryote (has a nuclear membrane);	1		x			x			x
	contains chloroplasts	1		x			x			x
13	Biceps and triceps are antagonistic muscles/ a pair	1		x				x	x	
	When the bicep muscle relaxes, the tricep contracts	1		x				x	x	
		1		x				x	x	
	Each time the arm is moved downward, this works/contracts the tricep	1		x				x	x	
	Muscles won't heal while they're in use									
14	The animal cannot bend its back	1					x		x	
	Humans can bend the back because the backbone is made up of many smaller bones	1			x		x		x	
15	Figure 1.8.11b is from a light microscope and Figure 1.8.11c is from an electron microscope (1) because the latter shows more detail/higher resolution/more organelles visible (1)	2			x		x			x
					x		x			x
16	Organism B (1) because it has the largest surface area-to-volume ratio (and so diffusion is more efficient) (1)	2			x		x			x
					x		x			x
	Total possible:	**30**								

1.9.0 Ecosystems: Introduction

When and how to use these pages

The Introduction in the Student Book indicates some of the ideas and skills in this topic area that students will already have met from KS2 or from previous KS3 work. It also provides an indication of what they will be studying in this chapter. *Ideas you have met before* is not intended to comprehensively summarise all of the prior ideas, but rather to point out a few of the key ones and to support the view that scientific understanding is progressive. Even though students might be meeting contexts that are new to them, they can often use existing ideas to start to make sense of them.

In this chapter you will find out indicates some of the new ideas that the chapter will introduce. Again, it isn't a detailed summary of content. Its purpose is more to act as a 'trailer' and generate some interest.

The outcomes, then, will be a recognition of prior learning that can be built on, and interest in finding out more.

There are a number of ways this can be used. You might, for example:

- use *Ideas you have met before* as the basis for a revision lesson as you start the first new topic

- use *Ideas you have met before* as the centre of spider diagrams, to which students can add examples, experiments they might have done previously or what they found interesting

- make a note of any unfamiliar/difficult terms and return to these in the relevant lessons

- use ideas from *In this chapter you will find out* to ask students questions such as:

  - Why is this important?

  - How could it be used?

  - What might we be doing in this topic?

Overview of the chapter

In this chapter, students will learn about relationships in ecosystems. They will study the interdependence of organisms, including food webs and insect-pollinated crops and their importance to human food security. Students will learn how organisms affect, and are affected by, their environment, including the accumulation of toxic materials in food chains and the effect of predation on organism populations. Students will develop what was learned at KS2 about plant structure to further understand how flowering plants reproduce, including the role of the wind and insects in pollination. Methods of seed dispersal will be investigated with a focus on adaptations of plants for each method.

This chapter offers the opportunity to use and evaluate a model to investigate the effects of one population on another. Students will evaluate various seed dispersal methods using their own investigation plan. There is an opportunity to analyse data through an investigation into the effect of sugar concentration on pollen tubes. Students will have the opportunity to discuss global issues such as food security.

Obstacles to learning

Students may need extra guidance with the following common misconceptions:

- **Food chains and interdependence:** some students believe that arrows in food chains go from consumer to consumed. Students need to be clear that food chains show the energy flow through an ecosystem.

- **Bioaccumulation:** bioaccumulation in food chains is a commonly difficult concept.

- **Pollination and fertilisation:** these may be used interchangeably by students to mean the same process.

- **Seed dispersal:** students may think that this only occurs by wind. There may also be confusion between seeds and pollen.

How the Programme of Study is covered by the Student Book

Big idea	Topic	Lesson	Programme of study reference
Ecosystems	Interdependence	1.9.1 Understanding food webs	The interdependence of organisms in an ecosystem, including food webs
		1.9.2 Understanding the effects of toxins in the environment	How organisms affect, and are affected by, their environment, including the accumulation of toxic materials
		1.9.3 Exploring the importance of insects	The importance of plant reproduction through insect pollination in human food security
		1.9.4 Exploring ecological balance	The interdependence of organisms in an ecosystem, including insect-pollinated crops
	Plant reproduction	1.9.5 Exploring flowering plants	Reproduction in plants, including flower structure, wind and insect pollination
		1.9.6 Exploring fertilisation	Reproduction in plants, including flower structure, wind and insect pollination, fertilisation
		1.9.7 Understanding how seeds are dispersed	Reproduction in plants, including seed formation and dispersal
		1.9.8 Understanding how fruits disperse seeds	Reproduction in plants, including fruit formation and dispersal, and quantitative investigation of some dispersal mechanisms

How the AQA KS3 Syllabus is covered by the Student Books and Teacher Guide

Interdependence

	Student Book	Teacher Guide
Know		
Organisms in a food web (decomposers, producers and consumers) depend on each other for nutrients. So, a change in one population leads to changes in others.	9.1	9.1
The population of a species is affected by the number of its predators and prey, disease, pollution and competition between individuals for limited resources such as water and nutrients.	9.1	9.1
Fact: Insects are needed to pollinate food crops.	9.3	9.3
Food web: Shows how food chains in an ecosystem are linked.	9.1	9.1
Food chain: Part of a food web, starting with a producer, ending with a top predator.	9.1	9.1
Ecosystem: The living things in a given area and their non-living environment.	9.4	9.4
Environment: The surrounding air, water and soil where an organism lives.	9.4	9.4
Population: Group of the same species living in an area.	9.1	9.1
Producer: Green plant or algae that makes its own food using sunlight.	9.1	9.1
Consumer: Animal that eats other animals or plants.	9.1	9.1
Decomposer: Organism that breaks down dead plant and animal material so nutrients can be recycled back to the soil or water.	9.1	9.1
Apply		
Describe how a species' population changes as its predator or prey population changes.	9.1	9.1
Explain effects of environmental changes and toxic materials on a species' population.	9.2	9.2
Combine food chains to form a food web.	9.1	9.1
Explain issues with human food supplies in terms of insect pollinators.	9.3	9.3
Extend		
Suggest what might happen when an unfamiliar species is introduced into a food web.		
Develop an argument about how toxic substances can accumulate in human food.	9.2	9.2
Make a deduction based on data about what caused a change in the population of a species.		

Plant reproduction

	Student Book	Teacher Guide
Know		
Plants have adaptations to disperse seeds using wind, water or animals.	9.7, 9.8	9.7, 9.8

Plants reproduce sexually to produce seeds, which are formed following fertilisation in the ovary.	9.6	9.6
Fact: Flowers contain the plant's reproductive organs.	9.5	9.5
Fact: Pollen can be carried by the wind, pollinating insects or other animals.	9.5	9.5
Pollen: Contains the plant male sex cells found on the stamens.	9.5	9.5
Ovules: Female sex cells in plants found in the ovary.	9.5	9.5
Pollination: Transfer of pollen from the male part of the flower to the female part of the flower on the same or another plant.	9.5	9.5
Fertilisation: Joining of a nucleus from a male and female sex cell.	9.6	9.6
Seed: Structure that contains the embryo of a new plant.	9.6	9.6
Fruit: Structure that the ovary becomes after fertilisation, which contains seeds.	9.6	9.6
Carpel: The female part of the flower, made up of the stigma where the pollen lands, style and ovary.	9.5, 9.6	9.5, 9.6
Apply		
Describe the main steps that take place when a plant reproduces successfully.	9.5, 9.6, 9.7, 9.8	9.5, 9.6, 9.7, 9.8
Identify parts of the flower and link their structure to their function.	9.5, 9.6	9.5, 9.6
Suggest how a plant carried out seed dispersal based on the features of its fruit or seed.	9.7	9.7
Explain why seed dispersal is important to survival of the parent plant and its offspring.	9.7	9.7
Extend		
Describe similarities and differences between the structures of wind pollinated and insect pollinated plants.	9.5	9.5
Suggest how plant breeders use knowledge of pollination to carry out selective breeding.		
Develop an argument why a particular plant structure increases the likelihood of successful production of offspring.		

1.9.1 Understanding food webs

Lesson overview

Learning objectives

- Describe how food webs are made up of a number of food chains.
- Make predictions about factors affecting plant and animal populations.
- Analyse and evaluate changes in a food web.

Learning outcomes

- Describe food webs as a number of interrelated food chains. [O1]
- Predict the effects of different environmental factors on plant and animal populations (e.g. disease and drought). [O2]
- Analyse and evaluate the impact of changes in a food web. [O3]

Skills development

- Working scientifically: 2.14 Examine consequences
- Developing numeracy: understand and interpret network diagrams
- Developing literacy: develop explanations using ideas from diagrams (Q4 - 8)

Resources needed large sheets of paper; sticky labels; polystyrene packing pellets/dry leaves/ping pong balls; Worksheet 1.9.1a; Worksheet 1.9.1b copied onto card and cut up; Worksheet (teacher) 1.9.1c; Worksheet (teacher) 1.9.1d; Technician's notes 1.9.1

Common misconceptions The arrows in a food chain go from consumer to consumed.

Key vocabulary food chain, food web, producer, consumer, decomposer, trophic level

Teaching and learning

Engage

- **Pairs to fours** Identify the students' prior knowledge by asking them to work in pairs to **construct** three food chains with at least three links. The groups then merge to form fours and the new groups **select** their 'best' food chain. Take feedback from each group about their food chain and why they selected it. [O1]

  High demand students can link their food chains to make a food web.

- Ask the students to **discuss** and **explain** what the arrows mean in the food chains in their groups. Take feedback and discuss this as a class. Ensure that they understand that the arrows represent the energy flow through the food chain. [O1]

- Working in their original pairs, ask the students to read and **discuss** 'The ups and downs of food chains' section in the Student Book and answer questions 1–3. [O1]

Challenge and develop

- **Think, pair, share** The students read the 'Food webs and trophic levels' section in the Student Book individually and **think about** the answers to questions 4–6 in silence. They then pair up and **share** with their partner to agree on answers. Take feedback from the class and reach a consensus. [O1]

- Ask the students to look at the examples of food chains they noted earlier and **identify** the different trophic levels (producer, primary consumers etc.). On the whiteboard write the words 'herbivore' and 'carnivore' and ask the students what these terms mean and how they relate to the different trophic levels. [O1]

- The students work in groups to **discuss** and complete task 1 of Worksheet 1.9.1a. [O1]

Explain

- Ask the students to **discuss** in pairs the question: 'What happens to plants and animals when they die?'. Take feedback and elicit that they are broken down by decomposers. Ask 'Where will decomposers be in the food chain?', 'Why are they important?'. (They recycle nutrients.) [O1]

- Remind the students that food chains and webs show the energy flow through an ecosystem. Ask 'What happens to the energy?'. Discuss their responses. Arrange the students to **carry out** the 'Modelling energy flow' activity (see Worksheet (teacher) 1.9.1c for instructions). [O1, O2]
- The students can then complete the 'Food web' activity (task 2 of Worksheet 1.9.1a). [O1, O2]

Consolidate and apply

- The students work in groups to **construct** a food web, using the cards from Worksheet 1.9.1b, on a large sheet of paper by drawing connecting arrows. Ask 'What is the producer?', 'Which are the primary consumers?', 'Which are the decomposers?', and so on. The groups leave their web to return to later. [O2]
- They **make predictions** about the impact of different factors affecting the organisms in one food chain from their food web (e.g. if the acacia trees die; if the dingo population increases; if the rains fail). [O2]
- **Pair talk** The students read the 'Knock-on effects' section in the Student Book and **discuss** the answers to questions 7 and 8. Take feedback. [O3]

Extend

- Show an example of a different food web and ask students to suggest what might happen if an unfamiliar species is introduced into that food web. [O3]

Ask students able to progress further to: complete task 3 of Worksheet 1.9.1a, **analysing** the impact of different factors on a food web. [O3]; carry out the 'How much food is needed?' activity described on Worksheet (teacher) 1.9.1d. [O3]

Plenary suggestions

Learning triangle The students draw a large triangle with a smaller inverted triangle inside it. In the three outer triangles they write something they've seen, something they've done and something they've discussed. In the central triangle they write something they've learned. [O1, O2, O3]

Answers to Student Book questions

1. The numbers would decrease. 2. The grass biomass would increase; the fox numbers would decrease.
3. If an animal is reliant on one food source and that fails, the animal will die, so it is better to have different food sources.
4. Any animal and what it eats.
5. Break down dead plant and animal material so that nutrients are recycled back to the soil or water, worm.
6. Rabbit numbers would increase; because more grass seed becomes available.
7. Any relevant evaluation of the possible effects on the food web, for example, t   he numbers of capelin and Arctic cod would increase initially and more cod would be available for the harbour seal and polar bear. With reduction in harp seal, number of options of food would be decrease for polar bears so they would eat more cod and harbour seals. Decrease in numbers of arctic cod could result in decrease in amphipod etc.
8. The copepod photosynthesises using light to make glucose. When Arctic char eat the copepods, some energy is transferred from the copepod to the Arctic char. The capelin eat the Arctic char. Energy in the Arctic char is transferred to the capelin. Energy in the capelin is transferred to the Arctic tern when it is eaten.

Answers to Worksheet 1.9.1a

1. a) i) Phytoplankton ii) Krill iii) Arctic cod iv) Seal b) i) Arctic cod and seal ii) Krill iii) Arctic cod iv) The Sun
2. a) Any correct food chain, such as: bladderwrack → grey mullet → common seal; algae → sea urchin → herring gull; bladderwrack → winkle → crab → herring gull; algae → limpet → lobster → common seal

    b) Common seals eat more lobsters (or die) so limpets increase in number; bladderwrack seaweeds will increase.

    c) i) Increase ii) Decrease iii) Decrease
3. a) i) Shrimp, water fleas and eels all increase, so cyclops, algae and caddis fly larvae decrease; only eels are left as food for humans. ii) Algae increase dramatically; primary consumers increase etc. (Students do not know about eutrophication so this answer will suffice.) iii) Water levels reduced, so less oxygen available, and larger fish die; invertebrates decrease. iv) Young fish/shrimp decrease; more algae grow, increasing caddis fly and cyclops; shrimp and young fish then start to increase slowly. v) Fish gills block, so the fish cannot get the oxygen needed for respiration and die; less oxygen will diffuse into the water at the surface; invertebrates may survive better because they have a short life-span and reproduce quickly.

    b) It will decrease rapidly, because roach eat shrimp, carp's only food source, meaning less food is available for the carp.

1.9.2 Understanding the effects of toxins in the environment

Lesson overview

Learning objectives

- Describe how toxins pass along the food chain.
- Explain how toxins enter and accumulate in food chains.
- Evaluate the advantages and disadvantages of using pesticides.

Learning outcomes

- Describe how toxins pass along the food chain. [O1]
- Explain the process of bioaccumulation. [O2]
- Critically evaluate the use of pesticides. [O3]

Skills development

- Working scientifically: 2.14 Examine consequences
- Developing numeracy: understand concentrations and accumulation.
- Developing literacy: develop explanations using ideas and evidence (Q3 - 6)

Resources needed brightly coloured counters/coloured squares; a clear plastic bag for every student; food web predator/prey name tags (the number will depend on the number of students – in a group of 35 students have at least five levels within the food web, e.g. 12 zooplankton/shrimp/clams/worms or crab, 9 small fish, 7 large fish, 5 seals, 2 sharks; print each food web level on different coloured paper or have students colour them); Worksheet 1.9.2; Technician's notes 1.9.2

Key vocabulary fertiliser, insecticide, toxin, bioaccumulation

Teaching and learning

Engage

- Working in groups of four, the students **brainstorm** why chemicals are used in agriculture. Take feedback from the class and encourage the students to add new ideas to their list. [O1]

- Alternatively, ask the groups to **discuss** man-made pollution that affects the natural environment (e.g. acid rain, radiation poisoning and chemicals in rivers). Ask 'What causes these types of pollution?', 'What effects does it have on human and animal populations?' and 'What can be done to reduce or eliminate it?' Create a class chart outlining these points. [O1]

Challenge and develop

- Working in pairs ask the students to **read** and **discuss** the 'Why are chemicals used in agriculture?' section in the Student Book and answer questions 1–2. Take feedback from the class and encourage the students to add any new points to their list. [O1]

- **Group work** Working in groups of four, ask the students to read and **discuss** the 'Chemicals entering the food chain' section in the Student Book and answer questions 3 and 4. [O1]

- The students **discuss** and answer the following questions: 'How do poisons get into the ocean and wetlands? How do the poisons get into an animal? Do you think that the poisons stay in the body of the animal or do they leave? What do you think happens to the poisons when the small animal is eaten by a bigger animal?' (task 1 of Worksheet 1.9.2). [O1]

Explain

- The students work as a class to **model** how DDT accumulates in a marine food chain and then answer the questions in task 2 of Worksheet 1.9.2 (see note in Resources). [O1, O2]

- Working in pairs, the students read the 'Accumulation of toxins in the food chain' section in the Student Book and answer questions 5 and 6. [O1, O2]

Consolidate and apply

- Back in groups of four, the students **design a poster** using pictures, numbers, acronyms and up to 20 words to explain 'bioaccumulation'. [O1, O2]

Extend

Ask students able to progress further to:

- work with a partner to **brainstorm** ways of keeping toxins out of the waterways [O3]

- work collaboratively in groups of four to complete task 3 of Worksheet 1.9.2 and **evaluate** the advantages and disadvantages of using pesticides on crops, **giving a presentation** to the class outlining their research and conclusions. [O3]

Plenary suggestions

Question setting Working in groups of four, the students **develop questions** starting 'How, where, when, why and what' on the topic, and link these to their answers. Students **peer assess** another group's work. Take feedback. [O1, O2, O3]

Answers to Student Book questions

1. Farmers need to produce more crops in the same, or less, space and as quickly as possible; they usually specialise in either crops or livestock. If they grow crops continually, the soil is deprived of nutrients; artificial fertilisers dissolve quickly in soil water; pesticide use means more crops.
2. If farmers have no livestock; they have no manure.
3. *Primary consumer:* for example sheep, cow, bird, (named) insect, rabbits.
   Secondary consumer: for example humans, birds of prey, insect-eating birds and animals, foxes.
4. Various answers: run-off from fields; blown in wind to waterways; fall from the air; urban street run-off; pests and other insects are covered in the toxins; absorbed by plant roots; eaten by other animals.
5. Some DDT was absorbed by waterweeds; fish ate a number of waterweeds that each contained DDT; so the fish had the total DDT from each plant. Large fish ate some small fish and had the total DDT from each small fish. The otter had the total DDT from every large fish it ate; which either killed it or meant the babies were too ill to survive.
6. More large fish would survive to eat more smaller fish; then less waterweed would be eaten and it would grow more.

Answers to Worksheet 1.9.2

1. a) i) Fertilisers and/or pesticides from fields; loss of cargo from ships; ships sinking with cargo; from rivers entering oceans and wetlands. ii) From food eaten or water drunk. iii) Mostly, they stay in the body; absorbed from digestive system. iv) Poisons in small animal absorbed into bigger animal.
2. a) The shark; may survive but would be very ill, and offspring would not be healthy.
   b) The population will be destroyed.
   c) It ate lots of animals that each contained some DDT; the shark absorbed the DDT from each animal.
   d) Humans use/produce the toxins that enter the water or land on plants; the primary consumer has a small amount of toxin; the secondary consumer eats many primary consumers and absorbs the toxin from each organism; this happens all the way up the food chain until the top predator has accumulated a large amount of toxin.
3. a) *Advantages:* more food produced; diseases eradicated or controlled, e.g. malaria. *Disadvantages:* could cause colony collapse disorder in bees; accumulates in food chains; causes death.

1.9.3 Exploring the importance of insects

Lesson overview

Learning objectives

- Describe the impact of low pollination on crop production.
- Explain why artificial pollination is used for some crops.
- Evaluate the risks of monoculture on world food security.

Learning outcomes

- Describe the impact of low pollination on crop yield and how this could potentially be avoided. [O1]
- Explain why hand-pollination is cost effective for some crops. [O2]
- Analyse and evaluate the risks involved with monoculture – particularly with regard to food security in poorer countries. [O3]

Skills development

- Working scientifically: 2.15 Review theories
- Developing numeracy: n/a
- Developing literacy: summarise and evaluate key points (Q3 - 6)

Resources needed at least four types of flowers (e.g. lily, antirrhinum, hydrangea, rose); flipchart paper (or similar); Worksheet 1.9.3; Practical sheet 1.9.3

Common misconceptions Food security is guaranteed.

Key vocabulary food security, pesticide, monoculture

Teaching and learning

Engage

- Ask the students to work in groups to **discuss** what pollination is, why it is important and how animals, especially insects, help in the process of pollination. [O1]
- Alternatively, ask the students to work in pairs and **brainstorm** on a sheet of paper what they know about how plants and insects help each other to survive. [O1]

Challenge and develop

- **Think, pair, share** Ask the students to **think about** the question 'Why are some apples on the same tree small and some large?' They then **discuss** this in pairs. Take feedback. [O1]
- Ask the students to read the 'Fruit production and bees' section in the Student Book and to answer questions 1 and 2. [O1]
- The students work in pairs to complete task 1 of Worksheet 1.9.3. Ask the groups to **present** their work to the class and to **peer assess** the work of other groups using 'three stars and a wish' (the 'stars' are things they have done well, learned, understood or enjoyed, while the 'wish' is something they could improve on, need to complete or need help with). Discuss how wild bees can increase successful pollination and summarise the key points for each part of the worksheet task on the whiteboard. [O1]
- The students **examine** closely the four types of flowers provided to **identify** adaptations for pollination (bright colour, pollen guides, scent etc.) and **complete the observation record** on Practical sheet 1.9.3. (You may not want to spend long on this activity as the topic is returned to in Lesson 1.9.5 but it is a good introduction and useful here.) [O1]

Explain

- **Pairs to fours** Explain to the students that some of our foods come from plants that have both male and female flowers (e.g. cucumber) and that many farmers hand-pollinate the female flowers by collecting pollen from the male flowers and 'painting' it on female flowers. Ask the students to **discuss** with a partner why some farmers do this, and take feedback from the class. The students then form groups of four to **develop** a cartoon strip to **explain** the process of hand-pollination. [O2]

- Working in their groups, the students read the 'Ensuring pollination' section in the Student Book. They **discuss** this and answer questions 3 and 4. Take feedback from the class. Ensure that they **understand** that artificial pollination is more reliable, but that insect pollination can result in larger crops. [O2]

Consolidate and apply

- Ask the students to complete task 2 of Worksheet 1.9.3. Their task is to **assess** and **agree** the advantages and disadvantages of artificial pollination and **summarise** their ideas on flipchart paper. Display the flipcharts around the room and encourage the students to read them and to **feed back** their final ideas. [O2]

- To apply their knowledge, the students work in groups to **research** and **make a presentation** about date farming. [O2]

Extend

Ask students able to progress further to:

- work in small groups to complete task 3 of Worksheet 1.9.3 – they are to **analyse** and **evaluate** the practice of monoculture in agriculture and **explain** how farmers ensure the pollination of these crops (questions 5 and 6 in the Student Book) [O3]

- **research** robotic bees and **prepare** a slideshow to share with the class (two slides maximum). [O2]

Plenary suggestions

Achievements and goals The students **discuss** and **identify** three things they have learned in this lesson along with one thing they want to know more about and one target for future learning. [O1, O2, O3]

The big ideas The students write down the most important ideas from the lesson. They share their facts in groups and compile a prioritised master list of facts. Take feedback and find out which other group(s) agreed with the prioritised points. [O1, O2, O3]

Answers to Student Book questions

1. To ensure that there are plenty of bees to pollinate the fruit tree flowers; resulting in higher fruit yield.
2. By leaving areas of land unfarmed, and encouraging the planting of wild and cultivated flowers that bees like to feed on (e.g. clover, buddleia, lilac).
3. There are no bees to pollinate flowers, so without artificial pollination they would get no fruit from their trees.
4. *Advantage*: artificial pollination ensures that flowers are pollinated; *disadvantages*: it takes a lot of time; may not be cost effective and often reduces the size of fruits.
5. *Disadvantages* include: single crop has a short flowering period, so bees have short feeding period and then no food; flowering may not coincide with when bees are active; cash crops are grown at the expense of food crops; if the crop fails, there is no back-up. *Advantages*: can be very profitable; easy to farm very large fields and to look after just one crop.
6. Answers could include: rent bee hives to place around a crop; hand-pollinate (e.g. dates); plant strips of wild flowers that are left untended in and around the cash crop to attract bees.

Answers to Worksheet 1.9.3

1. b) i) Poster to show the importance of bees pollinating crops and wild flowers etc.

   ii) Vast areas of monoculture have destroyed hedgerows; pollen from a monoculture is restricted to a short season (and bees may not be active then); outside that short season the bees have no food.

   iii) Leave areas of land unfarmed; encourage planting of wild and cultivated flowers that bees like to feed on (e.g. clover, buddleia, lilac).

2. a) Bright colours; scent; pollen guides; nectar for them to feed on. b) To attract insects; increase chance of pollination.

   c) Simple description of at least three of: wings (e.g. sycamore); parachutes (e.g. dandelion); thick shell for water dispersal (e.g coconut, sea bean (drift seeds)); bright sugary fleshy fruits (e.g. peach); burrs or hooks (e.g. thistle); exploding (e.g. laburnum).

   d) *Advantages*: ensures pollination; can use pollen from plant with features wanted; *disadvantages*: time taken; labour-intensive; fruits often smaller.

3. See answers to Student Book questions 5 and 6. Also: cash crops grown at the expense of food crops, so while landowners can make money, the small farmers and workers often have very little food for themselves or their livestock; if the crop fails, there is no money.

1.9.4 Exploring ecological balance

Lesson overview

Learning objectives

- Describe ways in which organisms affect their environment.
- Explain why prey populations affect predator populations.
- Evaluate a model of predator–prey populations and explain the importance of predators.

Learning outcomes

- Describe some ways in which organisms affect their environment. [O1]
- Explain why prey populations affect predator populations. [O2]
- Evaluate a model of predator–prey populations and explain the importance of predators. [O3]

Skills development

- Working scientifically: 2.13 Estimate risks
- Developing numeracy: interpret graphs
- Developing literacy: describe how a model can be manipulated and what this shows (Q4 - 8)

Resources needed graph paper; lion and antelope cards for the modelling activity (at least 20 lions and 50 antelope cards per group); Worksheet 1.9.4a; Worksheet 1.9.4b

Key vocabulary ecology, environment, predator, prey, competition

Teaching and learning

Engage

- Ask the students to work in groups of four to **brainstorm** examples of organisms that affect the environment around them in a positive way or a negative way. Take feedback from the class and encourage the groups to add to their list. [O1]

Challenge and develop

- Ask the students to work in pairs to read and **discuss** the 'How organisms affect the environment' section in the Student Book and answer questions 1 and 2. Take feedback and encourage the students to add any new interactions to their list. [O1]

- Returning to the initial groups of four, students then **explore** how organisms affect their environment using task 1 of Worksheet 1.9.4a to complete fact files about animals chosen from: crown-of-thorns starfish, locusts, cane toads, decomposers, worms and kangaroos (and/or the organisms they identified during the initial brainstorm). [O1]

Explain

- Distribute Worksheet 1.9.4b and discuss scenario 1 with the class: 'What would happen to prey numbers if there were no predators?'. Explain that a population with no predators and plenty of food will increase. [O2]

- **Pairs to fours** In pairs, the students **discuss** the question 'Will it keep increasing forever?'. The pairs then merge to form fours. Take feedback – ensuring that the students understand that eventually food and space will limit the size of the population. This is the 'carrying capacity', shown in the second graph on Worksheet 1.9.4b. Watch a web-based animation to model this (e.g. from BBC Bitesize). [O1, O2]

- Move on to discuss scenario 2: 'What would happen to predator numbers if there were no prey?'. Then 'What will be the environmental impact from these two scenarios?'. The students then **study** the lynx and snowshoe hare example on Worksheet 1.9.4b. [O1, O2]

Consolidate and apply

- Working in groups of four, the students complete task 2 of Worksheet 1.9.4a, the 'Lion hunt' activity, **modelling** population growth in predator–prey populations. [O1, O2]

- Ask the students to **summarise** the relationship between the population sizes of lions and antelope. They should use the words 'if' and 'then' to show a cause-and-effect relationship. [O1, O2]

Extend

Ask students able to progress further to:

- work in pairs to **evaluate** the task 2 model of predator–prey populations (task 3 of Worksheet 1.9.4a); [O3]

- work in groups of four to **design** a poster **explaining** the importance of top predators in an environment and **explaining** how, over time, our treatment of top predators has helped to make them endangered. [O3]

  - Provide students with data showing changes in numbers in a population of a species and ask students to deduce what may have caused the changes, justifying any suggestions. [O2]

Plenary suggestions

'3–2–1' activity Ask the students to **reflect on** their learning by responding to three statements: 'Three things I learned are…'; 'Two things I found interesting were…'; 'One thing I am going to tell someone else is…'. [O1, O2, O3]

Self-assessment Alternatively they **reflect on** their own achievements and goals by completing these statements: 'Things I did well today…'; 'Things I need to remember…', 'Things I need to improve…'. [O1, O2, O3]

Answers to Student Book questions

1. Ecology is the study of interactions between organisms and their environments.
2. Examples: locust swarms decimate crops; worms aerate soil and breakdown decaying leaf litter into smaller pieces so that microbes can break it down further
3. Specialised organisms do not compete for the same resource in exactly the same place, so all can survive.
4. Correct graph drawn for primary data (preferably generations on x-axis and number of predator and prey on y-axis).
5. Prediction consistent with own data for previous generations.
6. Sensible suggestions such as: *good* – as prey increase, the predators increase; as prey decrease, predators decrease; *poor* – most animals eat more than one type of food; there was no disease; there was no hunting or poaching; the model assumes that there is plenty of water and habitats etc.
7. Disease, predators, prey, environmental conditions (e.g lack of water, low temperatures).
8. As prey numbers increase, more food for predators and number of predators increases. More prey then eaten by predators, and prey numbers decrease. Not enough food for all predators and their numbers decrease again.

Answers to Worksheet 1.9.4a

1. *Name*: crown-of-thorns starfish. *Habitat*: coral reefs. *Facts*: fertilisers and pesticides are thought to have caused a population explosion. *Interactions*: destruction of coral reefs. *Impact*: negative.

   Name: locusts. *Habitat*: Africa, Middle East and Asia. *Facts*: swarm in millions. *Interactions*: destroy vast amounts of crops. *Impact*: negative.

   Name: cane toads. *Habitat*: South America. *Facts*: successful as an invasive species in Australia, the Caribbean and the United States. *Interactions*: kill native wildlife. *Impact*: negative.

   Name: decomposers. *Habitat*: worldwide. *Facts*: they are mainly bacteria and fungi. *Interactions*: break down dead and decaying matter to release nutrients back into the soil. *Impact*: positive.

   Name: worms. *Habitat*: soil and sand. *Facts*: worm casts give a crumb-like structure to the soil. *Interactions*: create burrows to allow gas exchange in soil or sand; break up large leaves etc. into smaller pieces for bacteria and fungi to break down . *Impact*: positive.

   Name: kangaroos. *Habitat*: Australasia. *Facts*: may harass humans. *Interactions*: compete with farm animals for food and water; trample crops; eat crop roots. *Impact*: negative.

2. When lion numbers are low, the antelope can breed and increase; as lion numbers increase, the antelope population will maintain itself up to a certain point; if there are too many lions, the antelope population will decrease until it dies out; the lions will die or move elsewhere until antelope migrate to the area again and populations increase, and so on.

3. a) As prey increase, the predators increase; as prey decrease, predators decrease.

   b) Most animals eat more than one type of food; there was no disease; there was no hunting or poaching; the model assumes that there is plenty of water and habitats etc.

   c) By introducing any of the factors listed in b) into the model.

Answers to Worksheet 1.9.4b

1. Because there is an abundant supply of resources, and low interaction with predators.
2. Because of competition for food and other resources; influenced by other organisms in the environment and environmental conditions.
3. There are fewer and fewer animals competing for the remaining food.
4. Lynx usually have large populations at the same time or just after snowshoe hares do; lynx populations are always smaller than snowshoe hare populations.

1.9.5 Exploring flowering plants

Lesson overview

Learning objectives
- Identify parts of flowering plants.
- Describe the function of the parts of flowering plants and link structure and function.
- Evaluate the differences between wind-pollinated and insect-pollinated plants.

Learning outcomes
- Identify and name the male and female parts of the flowering plant. [O1]
- Explain the differences in structure and function of a range of different flowering plants including wind-pollinated and insect-pollinated ones. [O2]
- Analyse the strengths and weaknesses of wind-pollinated and insect-pollinated plants. [O3]

Skills development
- Working scientifically: 2.3 Draw conclusions
- Developing numeracy: n/a
- Developing literacy: summarise advantages and disadvantages (Q5)

Resources needed projector; two different insect-pollinated plants; examples of different wind-pollinated plants or photographs; scalpels; white tiles; hand lenses; Worksheet 1. 9.5; Practical sheet 1.9.5; Technician's notes 1.9.5

Common misconceptions All plants are either male or female – they can't have both male and female parts.

Key vocabulary carpel, anther, filament, pollen, ovary, style, stigma, pollination

Teaching and learning

Engage
- Provide the students with Worksheet 1.9.5. The first task shows a diagram of a flowering plant and all the labels. Ask them to **identify** the parts of the diagram and to **describe** the functions of as many parts as they can, from prior learning. [O1]
- Use the Student Book to discuss how plant sexual reproduction evolved from asexual processes in mosses (where plants had to touch each other in order to reproduce) to the first wind-pollinated plants. Show images or video clips of different types of flowers to explore the diversity of different ways that plants have adapted. Explore why some flowers have male and female parts on the same plant, while others have separate male and female plants. [O1, O2]

Challenge and develop
- Demonstrate how to dissect a flowering plant, using a projector if possible. Use images in conjunction with the real dissection to explain the different parts of the flowering plant and their functions. [O1, O2]
- Group the students in threes. Provide them with two different insect-pollinated plants, hand lenses, scalpels and white tiles. Students record observations using Practical Sheet 1.9.5.
- Ask the students to **dissect** one of the plants as you have shown. They can take photos or draw and label each dissection.
- Students observe wind-pollinated flowers (either flowers or images/ photographs). They should draw up their own tables to **compare** each of the different structures in the wind-pollinated and insect-pollinated plants. [O1, O2]
- Ask the students to **discuss** their findings and **review** their ideas. [O1, O2]

Explain
- Ask the students to **explain** why insect-pollinated plants are so different from wind-pollinated plants (the need to attract insects using large petals, nectar and scents). [O2]

High demand students will be able to **explain** about the position of the stamen in relation to the stigma in insect-pollinated flowers (so that pollen can be collected when insects gather nectar). They will also be able to **explain** how the structures of the anther and filament are adapted in wind-pollinated plants to enable the pollen to be effectively removed by the wind. They should be able to **identify** the advantages and disadvantages of each. [O3]

Consolidate and apply

- Task 2 on Worksheet 1.9.5 shows a range of different plants. Ask the students to **categorise** them into insect-pollinated plants and wind-pollinated plants. They should give reasons for their choices. [O2]

- Ask them to **explain** different adaptations of different insect-pollinated plants and different wind-pollinated plants. They should **identify** how different insect-pollinated plants differ from each other and suggest some reasons; and then do the same for the wind-pollinated plants (task 3 on Worksheet 1.9.5). [O2, O3]

Extend

- Students able to progress further can **research** whether insect-pollinated plants or wind-pollinated plants are more highly adapted, **describe** some adaptations and **justify** their ideas on which plants are more successful. [O3]

- Ask students to suggest how plant breeders use knowledge of pollination to carry out selective breeding (research may be required). [O3]

Plenary suggestions

What am I? One student thinks of a part of a flowering plant. The other students then have to ask questions about what the part might be. Only 'yes' or 'no' answers may be given. [O1, O2]

Spot the mistakes Show the students incorrectly labelled flowering plants and ask them to correct the errors. [O1]

Answers to Student Book questions

1. Discuss responses to this question.
2. The insect-pollinated flower has brightly coloured petals and flowers, with the stamen and stigma inside the flower. The wind-pollinated flower has very small flowers and dull, small petals; the stamen and stigma hang outside the petals.
3. Some produce perfumes or scents that will attract particular insects; others make nectar for insects to feed on; some make their flowers into structures that resemble parts of the female insect.
4. To attract as many different pollinators as possible; or to get reliability from just a few pollinators.
5. *Advantages of wind pollination*: pollen is sure to be dispersed; only small flowers needed so less energy wasted.
   Disadvantages of wind pollination: there's no guarantee that pollen will be transferred to other plants; lots of pollen needs to be made to increase the chances of successful transfer; lots of pollen wasted.
   Advantages of insect pollination: smaller amounts of pollen need to be made; there is a much higher success rate of transferring pollen to other plants.
   Disadvantages of insect pollination: elaborate mechanisms are needed to attract pollinators; if pollinators become endangered or extinct, pollination cannot occur.

Answers to Worksheet 1.9.5

1. Refer to Figure 1.9.5a in the Student Book – *petals* attract insects; *stamen* produces pollen; *stigma* receives pollen; *ovary* keeps the egg cell safe; and it is the place of fertilisation.
2. *Ragweed*: wind-pollinated – has small, insignificant flowers.
   Umbrella pine: wind-pollinated – pollen is very small and light, and can be released easily into the wind.
   Sweet pea: insect-pollinated – has a strong perfume/smell to attract insects.
   Grasses: wind-pollinated – flowers hang down in the wind; stamen is on the outside of the flower.
   Rapeseed: insect-pollinated – has brightly coloured flowers to attract insects.
   Passion flower: insect-pollinated – stigma is in a very prominent position to receive pollen from insects; brightly coloured and large petals so insects can land easily.
3. *Similarities in insect-pollinated plants*: the passion flower and the rapeseed have attractive flowers.
   Differences in insect-pollinated plants: the stigma of the passion flower protrudes very prominently above the flower, whereas with the rapeseed it is more hidden.
   Similarities in wind-pollinated plants: the grass and the ragweed have insignificant flowers.
   Differences in wind-pollinated plants: the grass has stamens that hang down from the flower so the pollen can be easily caught by the wind.

1.9.6 Exploring fertilisation

Lesson overview

Learning objectives
- Describe the processes of fertilisation in plants.
- Describe the role of pollen tubes.
- Explain how seeds are formed.

Learning outcomes
- Define pollination and describe how it happens in flowering plants. [O1]
- Describe the role of pollen tubes, and collect and analyse data linked with the growth of pollen tubes. [O2]
- Explain how fruits are formed and relate parts to the flower the fruit is formed from. [O3]

Skills development
- Working scientifically: 2.6 Construct explanations
- Developing numeracy: plot and interpret graphs
- Developing literacy: tabulate key information (Q5)

Resources needed images of different pollen grains; sticky notes; A3 paper; graph paper; equipment and materials as detailed listed in the Technician's notes; Worksheet 1.9.6; Practical sheet 1.9.6a; Practical sheet 1.9.6b; Technician's notes 1.9.6

Common misconceptions The terms 'pollination' and 'fertilisation' describe the same process.

Key vocabulary fertilisation, pollen tube, seed

Teaching and learning

Engage
- Show the students images of different types of pollen grains. Ask the students 'Can you predict whether the pollen grains are from insect-pollinated or wind-pollinated plants?'. Ask them to **summarise** the features that provide clues. [O1]
- Ask the students to **devise** five questions about pollen they want to ask and to write these on a sticky note. Come back to these questions at the end of the lesson. [O1]

Challenge and develop
- Show Figure 1.9.6b from the Student Book and ask the students to **explain** how a pollen tube is formed. Discuss how the pollen cell increases its cytoplasm once it lands on the stigma to produce a tube leading to the ovary. If possible, show the students a video clip of what happens when pollen lands on the stigma. Ask them to **identify** the structure called the pollen tube. [O1, O2]
- Discuss the differences between the processes of fertilisation and pollination. [O1]
- Group the students in fours. Tell them they are going to **investigate** the following questions:
  - How does the concentration of sugar affect the number of pollen tubes formed?
  - Does the length of the style affect the length of the pollen tube formed? (More suitable for high demand students.)
- Ask the students to **follow instructions** from either Practical sheet 1.9.6a or Practical sheet 1.9.6b (high demand students). Students investigating the concentration of sugar should count the number of pollen tubes grown from pollen from one plant. Students investigating the length of style should be shown how to measure the length of pollen tube from given plants with the correct equipment. They should draw up a table to **compare** the average length of a pollen tube with the length of style. If necessary, the pollen tubes should be grown an hour or two before the lesson so they reach a measurable length during the course of the lesson. [O2]

- Discuss what makes a good graph. Ask the students to draw graphs of their data, and to **peer assess** their graphs using criteria developed from class discussion. They should use, for example, correctly labelled axes with a sensible scale, and **decide** on a bar chart or line graph etc. [O2]

- Ask the students to **describe** and **explain** their results. [O2]

Explain

- Provide the students with Worksheet 1.9.6. The first task shows a cross-sectional diagram of a flower. You might want to copy this onto A3 paper. Ask the students to name each part and to annotate the diagram, **explaining** the process of fertilisation, in particular the roles of the stigma, style and pollen tube. They should include factors that affect the process and any adaptations to increase the chance of success of the process. [O1, O2]

- Ask the students to share their explanations. Ask them to **read** other students' work and to use sticky labels to **peer assess**, noting two good things about the explanations and one thing that needs improving.

Consolidate and apply

- Give the students some time to **make improvements** to their explanations and make any alterations.

- Ask the students to complete tasks 2 and 3 on Worksheet 1.9.6. [O2, O3]

Extend

- Ask students to **read** the 'Development of seeds', then work in pairs to **explain** what happens to the main parts of the flower following fertilisation and explain the significance.

- Ask students able to progress further to **research** the methods used by different plants to avoid self-fertilisation and to maximise cross-fertilisation. Ask them to **evaluate** at least three methods, giving strengths and weaknesses. [O3]

Plenary suggestions

What have you learned? Review the questions that the students posed at the start of the lesson. How many can they now answer as a result of their learning?

True or false? Provide the students with ten statements about pollination. Read out the statements one by one, and ask the students to stand up if a statement is true, and to stay seated if it is false.

Answers to Student Book questions

1. *Pollination* is the transfer of pollen; *fertilisation* is the nucleus of a male cell fusing with an egg cell in the ovary.
2. An accurate line graph should be plotted; with a line of best fit.
3. As the sugar concentration increases, the growth of the pollen tube increases; up to a concentration of 15%; after which any increase in sugar concentration inhibits the growth of pollen tubes.
4. Use same types of plant, same volume of solution applied, same length of time before measuring tubes.
5.

Structure	Following fertilisation
Petal	Falls off
Stamen	Falls off
Ovule	Becomes a seed
Ovary	Becomes the fruit

6. They contain both seeds and an ovary that has developed around the fruit.

Answers to Worksheet 1.9.6

1. A – ovary; B – ovule; C – carpel; D – style; E – stigma; F – pollen tube; G – anther; H – pollen grain; I – filament; J – petal. a) Stigma captures the pollen. b) Pollen tube grows down the style to the ovary.
2. Graph title: 'A graph to show how the concentration of sugar solution affects the growth of pollen tubes'; x-axis label: 'Sugar concentration (% glucose); y-axis label: 'Number of pollen tubes'.
3. a) 30%. b) No; the pollen from different flowers needs different concentrations of sugar solution. Students should have identified this in their investigation.

1.9.7 Understanding how seeds are dispersed

Lesson overview

Learning objectives

- Recognise the variety of different structures shown by different seeds.
- Describe the need for plants to disperse their seed.
- Plan an investigation into seed dispersal by wind.
- Collect data and devise questions on how plants can effectively disperse seeds.

Learning outcomes

- Describe some ways plants use to disperse their seeds and recognise dispersal methods by the structure of the seeds; [O1]
- Identify different reasons for a plant to disperse its seeds. [O2]
- Identify key variables to change, control and measure; explain how to collect accurate and reliable data in their plan. [O3]

Skills development

- Working scientifically: 2.11 Plan variables
- Developing numeracy: identify variables and select appropriate values to use; gather data.
- Developing literacy: plan investigation, draw conclusions and analyse outcomes (Q6 - 8)

Resources needed various seeds (include fruits, wind-dispersed seeds, water-dispersed seeds and prickly seeds dispersed by animals); hand lenses; Worksheet 1.9.7a; Worksheet 1.9.7b; Technician's notes 1.9.7

Common misconceptions Pollination and seed dispersal are the same thing.

Key vocabulary dispersal, germination

Teaching and learning

Engage

- Provide the students with a range of different seeds to examine using a hand lens. Ask them to draw up a table to **describe** the different characteristics of each seed and how each one might be transported. [O1]
- Ask the students to **summarise** their findings. Discuss why there are different mechanisms for transporting seeds and why it is important for seeds to germinate away from the parent plant. Include ideas relating to competition for light, water and nutrients. [O2]
- If possible, show video clips of mechanisms of seed dispersal, including exploding pods. [O1, O2]

Challenge and develop

- Show the students different seeds dispersed by the wind, or images of them. Discuss different features of the seeds and draw up a list of their strengths and weaknesses through class **discussion**. Ask the students to **make predictions** about which seeds will be transported the furthest by wind. [O1, O2]
- Group the students in fours. Provide each group with a copy of Worksheet 1.9.7a (an investigation planning template). Ask them to **plan** an investigation to answer one of these questions (split between the groups half and half):
  - How does the mass of a seed affect dispersal by the wind?
  - What is the most effective design for a seed dispersed by the wind?
- Encourage the students to **discuss** the success criteria for what makes an effective investigation plan.
- Either provide students with at least five different wind-dispersed seeds to investigate or ask them to make up their own five designs. In the latter case, make sure they are clear about aspects of their design that they

should vary – mass, wingspan or tail mechanisms – and ask them to make up sufficient 'seeds' to test, so that they can **collect** reliable evidence. [O3]

Explain

- Ask the groups to swap their plans and to **peer assess** each other's using the success criteria discussed. Ask them to **identify** all the good points relating to the plan and one target for improvement. [O3]

- Give them a few minutes of improvement time, and then select one or two groups to **describe** and **explain** different features of their plan. With low demand students, focus on the **identification** of variables; with high demand students, focus on how to **collect** reliable and accurate data. [O3]

Consolidate and apply

- Provide students with Worksheet 1.9.7b. This describes a plan for an investigation about seed dispersal, but with several mistakes. Ask the students to work through the tasks listed correcting the mistakes, **assessing the quality** of the plan and making improvements. [O3]

Extend

- Students able to progress further should broaden their plan to answer the question 'Which is the most effective means of dispersing plants – wind, water, explosion mechanisms or animals/insects?' Ask them to write a detailed account of how they would carry out this investigation and how they would collect reliable and valid evidence. [O3]

Plenary suggestions

Designing a 'super seed' Ask the students to **design** a 'super seed' that could be dispersed in many different ways. Ask them to annotate their design to **explain** its features, and give reasons why these features are effective. They should also **summarise** why it is important for plants to disperse seeds. [O1, O2, O3]

Answers to Student Book questions

1. *Dandelion* is dispersed by wind; *coconut* by water; *cucumber* by animals.
2. *Dandelion seeds* have parachute structures to help them to glide on the wind. *Coconut seeds* are large, waterproof and able to float; the plants grow near the sea so the seeds can be transported by water. The *cucumber* has seeds inside a fleshy fruit which can be eaten by animals.
3. The flowers from trees tend to be high up; which is ideal for seeds to be transported by wind; enabling them to get as far away from the parent tree as possible.
4. *Advantages*: the ground is likely to be fertile; pollinators are already in the area; there is likely to be plenty of water and nutrients because the parent tree has survived and reproduced here.

   Disadvantages: increased competition with parent plant for sunlight, water and nutrients; competition for pollinators; easy to catch a disease if the parent plant is affected.
5. It is too heavy to be carried by air; and it floats.
6. Investigation, for example changing the length of the rotors or the mass of the seed (by altering the number of paper clips or by using different material such as card). Measure the time it takes for the seed to fall or how long it stays in the air when placed in front of a fan).
7. Suitable conclusion based on own results.
8. The 'seed' which took longest to fall or travelled the furthest distance or stayed in the air for longer.

Answers to Worksheet 1.9.7b

1. a) Description and values of variables; procedure to change the height; a diagram.

   b) Headings could include 'Independent variable and values'; 'Dependent variable'; 'Control of variables and values'; 'Prediction'.

   c) No; ten different seeds have been used; this has not been controlled.
2. a) Controlling the variables – *size of seed*: use the same size; *type of seed*: use the same type; *throwing the seed*: use a hairdryer on the same setting to supply the 'wind'; *amount of real wind*: do the test indoors.

   b) No; not all the control variables have been controlled.

   c) No; repeat readings at the same heights have not been made.
3. Assess the quality of a students' revised plans according to the criteria discussed.

1.9.8 Understanding how fruits disperse seeds

Lesson overview

Learning objectives
- Describe how fruits are used in seed dispersal.
- Compare evidence about seed dispersal by wind and by fruit formation.
- Use data to evaluate different seed dispersal mechanisms.

Learning outcomes
- Collect accurate and reliable evidence to answer a scientific question about wind dispersal. [O1]
- Describe the difference between a fruit and a seed, and give many examples of fruits and their seeds. [O2]
- Explain the advantages and disadvantages of different seed dispersal mechanisms. [O3]

Skills development
- Working scientifically: 2.12 Test hypotheses
- Developing numeracy: extract data to identify patterns
- Developing literacy: account for management of variables; use ideas from table to support assertions (Q4 - 10)

Resources needed graph paper; equipment for each group of three students, resources as outlined in Technician Sheet 1.9.8; Worksheet 1.9.8

Common misconceptions Parts of the fertilised flower other than the ovary can become fruit.

Key vocabulary fruit

Teaching and learning

Engage

- Read out a mix of true and false statements about seed dispersal and ask the students to stand up whenever they hear a true statement. [O1]

  Example statements:

  - Most plants use the wind to disperse their seeds. (T)

  - Plants need to disperse seeds to improve their chance of survival. (T)

  - Seed dispersal by fruits uses the least amount of energy. (F)

- Review the terms 'reliable' and 'accurate'. Show the students explanations or provide them with statements to **discuss** as to whether they refer to accuracy or reliability. [O1]

Challenge and develop

- Ask the students to **review** their plans from Lesson 1.9.7 and identify any further amendments that need to be made. Check that plans are suitable and suggest any amendments that must be made. Ask the students to follow their (amended) plans and **carry out** their investigations into wind dispersal, **collecting** accurate and reliable evidence. [O1]

- Discuss the students' results and ask them to draw conclusions about which are the most effective seeds to be dispersed by the wind. Ask questions relating to the strength of the evidence collected. Use the terms 'reliable' and 'accurate', and distinguish between them in relation to the students' own data. [O1]

- Group students in threes. Provide each group with a range of different fruits. Explain what is meant by the term 'fruit' and describe how fruits are formed. Ask the students to **discuss** the advantages and disadvantages of producing fruits for seed dispersal. Help them to **recognise** that the plant has to use a lot of energy in making a fruit, but that this is offset by the need to produce fewer seeds. [O2, O3]

- Provide groups with the equipment to **dissect** each fruit (with appropriate safety warnings) and ask them to establish how many seeds are present in each. They should **record** their results in a table they **devise** themselves. Collect feedback and display the class results. Discuss variations between groups and reasons for these. Discuss how to produce reliable data relating to the number of seeds in each fruit. [O2]

Explain

- Show the students data in Table 1.9.8 in the Student Book on the number of seeds produced by plants that use various dispersal methods. Ask the students to write an explanation to **compare** the information in the table with their findings from the fruits they have investigated. [O2, O3]

Consolidate and apply

- Ask the students to **compare** and **contrast** wind dispersal with fruit formation. They should **explain** reasons for the success of each and **justify** their ideas about which is the more successful method. [O1, O2, O3]

- Students can then **complete** the differentiated tasks on Worksheet 1.9.8 according to their ability. [O1, O2, O3]

Extend

- Ask students able to progress further to draw up a table to **suggest** the advantages and disadvantages of all the different seed-dispersal mechanisms. [O3]

- Ask students to **produce an argument** about how particular plant structures increase the likelihood of successful production of offspring. [O3]

Plenary suggestions

Summarising Ask the students to **summarise** key points to review ideas about fruit formation.

Just a minute Select different students to speak for a minute on the topic of seed dispersal.

Answers to Student Book questions

1. The ovary of the plant after fertilisation.
2. The cauliflower.
3. The fruits are eaten by animals; and the seeds are excreted with the animal's faeces; which contains many nutrients useful for growth. So the seed lands in a medium which will help it to germinate; thereby increasing the chance of successful germination.
4. The type of seed dispersal.
5. The sample area; so that conditions of light, humidity, temperature and nutrients are likely to be similar; the time when samples are taken; so that weather and seasonal conditions are the same.
6. Using a large sample size.
7. Any sensible answer, for example: if plants become endangered, it may be important to know what the best conditions are for ensuring successful dispersal and germination.
8. Any suitable answer with a valid reason.
9. Plants that dispersed their seeds by the wind produce the most seeds; water is able to transport the seeds the furthest distance from the parent plant.
10. Graphs of 'name of plant' against 'number of seeds'; and 'name of plant' against 'average dispersal distance'.

Answers to Worksheet 1.9.8

1. *Wind dispersal* – anything resembling a dandelion, sycamore helicopter seeds, or any plant with small, light seeds on the outside that the wind can easily catch. The seeds are the small object being carried by the wind; the tissue protecting and covering the seed is the ovary.
   Fruit dispersal – diagram should show a fruit with seeds inside; the fruit labelled as the ovary; the pips as the seeds.
2. a) A suitable scale should be drawn for the graph; the x-axis should be the number of seed; the y-axis should be the mass of the fruit.
   b) i) One hypothesis would be the larger the number of seeds, the more massive the fruit. This is because the more seeds there are, the more energy they will need when they germinate; or the more seeds there are, the larger the fruit to attract more animals so the seeds can be dispersed with the minimum amount of energy. ii) The anomalous data is that for the avocado pear.
3. a) The data is not reliable; there is no sample size given for the numbers of seeds examined.
   b) A large sample of seeds needs to be examined (over 100); and a much wider variety of seeds tested.

1.9.9 Checking students' progress

The *Checking your progress* section in the Student Book indicates the key ideas developed in this chapter and shows how students progress to more complex levels. It is provided to support students in:

- identifying those ideas;

- developing a sense of their current level of understanding;

- developing a sense of what the next steps in their learning are.

It is designed to be used either at the end of a chapter to support an overall view of the progress, or alternatively during the teaching of the chapter. Students can self-assess or peer assess using this as a basis.

It is helpful to encourage students to provide evidence from their understanding or their notes to support their judgements. In some cases it may be useful to explore the difference in the descriptors for a particular idea so that students can see what makes for a 'higher outcome'.

It may be useful with some descriptors to provide examples from the specific work done, such as an experiment undertaken or an explanation developed and recorded. If marking and feedback use similar ideas and phrases this will enable students to relate specific marking to a more general sense of progress.

To make good progress in understanding science students need to focus on these ideas and skills:

Students who are making modest progress will be able to:	Students who are making good progress will be able to:	Students who are making excellent progress will be able to:
Describe an example of a simple food web.	Define producers, consumers and decomposers and give examples of each in different food webs.	Describe how changes in the population of one organism can influence other organisms in the food web.
Describe the role of insects in fruit crop production.	Explain why artificial pollination is used for some crops.	Explain what is meant by 'food security' and explain the risks posed by monoculture on food security.
Recall ways in which organisms can affect their environment.	Explain how changes in predator and prey populations affect each other.	Use data and models to predict changes to predator and prey populations based on their interdependence.
Give examples of toxins and describe how toxins pass along a food chain.	Explain how toxins accumulate in food chains.	Evaluate the advantages and disadvantages of using pesticides
Describe the roles of different parts of a flowering plant in reproduction.	Explain the differences in wind-pollinated and insect-pollinated plants.	Discuss the strengths and weaknesses of wind pollination and insect pollination.
Recognise that pollination and fertilisation are both part of plant reproduction but are two different processes.	Describe the stages of fertilisation in plants, including the role of the pollen tube.	Describe the fate of flower structures following fertilisation and the formation of seeds and fruit.
Recognise different seed-dispersal methods and relate these to the structures of the seeds.	Identify key variables that need to be controlled when investigating the effect of seed design on seed dispersal.	Explain the advantages and disadvantages of different seed-dispersal mechanisms.

1.9.10 Answers to Student Book end of chapter questions

This table provides answers to the Questions section at the end of Chapter 9 of the Student Book. It also shows how different questions assess attainment in terms of the focus and style of a question as well as the context. Question level analysis can indicate a student's proficiency in approaching different aspects of scientific understanding and different types of answer.

Q	Answer	Marks available	Knowledge & understanding	Application	Evaluation of evidence	Objective test question	Short written answer	Longer written answer	Interdependence	Plant reproduction
			Focus			**Style**			**Context**	
1	c	1	x			x			x	
2	c	1	x			x			x	
3	Decreased/destroyed habitats (1) Decreased crop/fruit yields (1) Because less pollination by bees (1)	3	x				x		x	
4	c	1	x			x				x
5	c	1	x			x				x
6	Any four from: pollen tube grows from pollen grain pollen cell nucleus travels down tube to ovary pollen cell (nucleus) reaches ovule and fertilisation takes place fertilised ovule becomes seed ovary becomes fruit.	4	x					x		x
7	Each oyster will retain some of the HAB in its body; the person will have the total amount in each oyster's body	1		x			x		x	
8	b	1		x		x			x	
9	The macaw, chimpanzee and red-eyed tree frog populations would rise uncontrollably	1		x				x	x	
	Insect populations would decrease very rapidly due to predation by the red-eyed tree frog	1		x				x		
	The orchids and banana trees would be destroyed by the large populations of herbivores	1		x				x		
	The ecosystem would collapse	1		x				x		

228

Q	Answer	Marks available	Knowledge & understanding	Application	Evaluation of evidence	Objective test question	Short written answer	Longer written answer	Interdependence	Plant reproduction
			Focus			Style			Context	
10	a and d	2		x		x				x
11	a\' Coconut (1) b Burdock seed (1)	2		x		x				x
12	The fruit is eaten by animals and it gives them energy / the fruit attracts animals because it is tasty. The energy (in the seeds) supports growth of new plants (after they pass through the animal).	2		x			x			x
13	Lynx populations go up when there are plenty of hares to eat.	2			x			x	x	
	Hare populations rise when lynx populations drop because there is less predation.				x			x		
	Peaks and troughs in lynx populations are always just behind those in hare populations. OR There are generally more hares than lynx because each lynx needs to eat a number of hares to survive.	1			x			x		
					x			x		
	Population sizes will vary, but as long as there are lynx and hares, the general pattern will be the same because lynx eat hares. OR The data covers a 75-year period so should be reliable.	1								
14	As concentration increases from 5% to 15%, the growth of pollen tubes increases (1) Between 15% and 20% as concentration increases, growth of pollen tubes decreases (1) Ignore the 200 result at 15% concentration (1)	3			x		x			x
	Total possible:	30								

1.10.0 Genes: Introduction

When and how to use these pages

The Introduction in the Student Book indicates some of the ideas and skills in this topic area that students will already have met from KS2 or from previous KS3 work. It also provides an indication of what they will be studying in this chapter. *Ideas you have met before* is not intended to comprehensively summarise all of the prior ideas, but rather to point out a few of the key ones and to support the view that scientific understanding is progressive. Even though students might be meeting contexts that are new to them, they can often use existing ideas to start to make sense of them.

In this chapter you will find out indicates some of the new ideas that the chapter will introduce. Again, it isn't a detailed summary of content. Its purpose is more to act as a 'trailer' and generate some interest.

The outcomes, then, will be: recognition of prior learning that can be built on; and interest in finding out more.

There are a number of ways this can be used. You might, for example:

- use *Ideas you have met before* as the basis for a revision lesson as you start the first new topic

- use *Ideas you have met before* as the centre of spider diagrams, to which students can add examples, experiments they might have done previously or what they found interesting

- make a note of any unfamiliar/difficult terms and return to these in the relevant lessons

- use *In this chapter you will find out* to ask students questions such as:
  - Why is this important?
  - How could it be used?
  - What might we be doing in this topic?

Overview of the chapter

In this chapter, students will learn about the variation between and within species, and the causes and types of variation. They will learn about the importance of variation within a species to prevent extinction of the species. Students will learn about human reproductive systems, including the menstrual cycle. They will study how a foetus develops, supported by the mother, and will consider the effects of various substances on a developing foetus.

Within this chapter, there are lots of opportunities for developing graph skills, including plotting and analysing both bar charts and line graphs. Students also have the opportunity to critique claims and explore what is meant by bias in sources of information using the context of the effects of smoking in pregnancy. They are encouraged to use information to form a reasoned opinion.

Obstacles to learning

Students may need extra guidance with the following terms and concepts:

- **Inheritance:** Many students think that acquired characteristics may be passed on to offspring.

- **Variation:** Some students will believe that variation must be caused by either inheritance OR the environment.

- **Puberty:** Students may think this consists of set changes at particular times.

- **Growth:** A common misconception is that cells get bigger and bigger.

How the Programme of Study is covered by the Student Book

Big idea	Topic	Lesson	Programme of study reference
Genes	Variation	1.10.1 Looking at variation	Describe what is meant by variation in a species. Explain the difference between continuous and discontinuous variation. Plot graphs to show variation.
		1.10.2 Exploring causes of variation	Identify whether a feature is inherited or determined by the environment. Understand that offspring from the same parents may show variation.
		1.10.3 Considering the importance of variation	Describe the importance of variation. Explain how variation may help a species to survive. Apply ideas about variation and survival to specific examples.
	Human reproduction	1.10.4 Understanding the female reproductive system and fertility	Describe the structure and function of different parts of the female reproductive system. Describe the process of menstruation. Describe causes of low fertility.
		1.10.5 Understanding the male reproductive system and fertilisation	Describe the structure and function of different parts of the male reproductive system. Describe fertilisation in humans.
		1.10.6 Learning how a foetus develops	Describe the role of the mother in supporting and protecting the developing foetus. Recognise the development of a foetus.
		1.10.7 Understanding factors affecting a developing foetus	Describe the effects of different factors on a developing foetus. Evaluate the strength of data. Analyse advice given to pregnant women.
		1.10.8 Communicating ideas about smoking in pregnancy	Critique claims linked with the effects of smoking in pregnancy. Identify potential bias in sources of information. Give a reasoned opinion.

How the AQA KS3 Syllabus is covered by the Student Books and Teacher Guide

Variation

	Student Book	Teacher Guide
Know		
There is variation between individuals of the same species. Some variation is inherited, some is caused by the environment and some is a combination.	10.1, 10.2	10.1, 10.2
Variation between individuals is important for the survival of a species, helping it to avoid extinction in an always changing environment.	10.3	10.3
Species: A group of living things that have more in common with each other than with other groups.	10.1	10.1
Variation: The differences within and between species.	10.1	10.1
Continuous variation: Where differences between living things can have any numerical value.	10.1	10.1
Discontinuous variation: Where differences between living things can only be grouped into categories.	10.1	10.1
Apply		
Explain whether characteristics are inherited, environmental or both.	10.2	10.2
Plot bar charts or line graphs to show discontinuous or continuous variation data.	10.1	10.1
Explain how variation helps a particular species in a changing environment.	10.3	10.3
Explain how characteristics of a species are adapted to particular environmental conditions.	10.3	10.3
Extend		
Predict implications of a change in the environment on a population.	10.3	10.3
Use the ideas of variation to explain why one species may adapt better than another to environmental change.	10.3	10.3
Critique a claim that a particular characteristic is inherited or environmental.		

Human reproduction

	Student Book	Teacher Guide
Know		
The menstrual cycle prepares the female for pregnancy and stops if the egg is fertilised by a sperm.	10.4	10.4
The developing foetus relies on the mother to provide it with oxygen and nutrients, to remove waste and protect it against harmful substances.	10.6, 10.7	10.6, 10.7
Fact: The menstrual cycle lasts approximately 28 days.	10.4	10.4
Fact: If an egg is fertilised it settles into the uterus lining.	10.5	10.5
Gamete: The male gamete (sex cell) in animals is a sperm, the female an egg.	10.5	10.5
Fertilisation: Joining of a nucleus from a male and female sex cell.	10.5	10.5
Ovary: Organ which contains eggs.	10.4	10.4
Testicle: Organ where sperm are produced.	10.5	10.5
Oviduct, or fallopian tube: Carries an egg from the ovary to the uterus and is where fertilisation occurs.	10.4	10.4
Uterus, or womb: Where a baby develops in a pregnant woman.	10.4	10.4
Ovulation: Release of an egg cell during the menstrual cycle, which may be met by a sperm.	10.4	10.4
Menstruation: Loss of the lining of the uterus during the menstrual cycle.	10.4	10.4
Reproductive system: All the male and female organs involved in reproduction.	10.4, 10.5	10.4, 10.5
Penis: Organ which carries sperm out of the male's body.	10.5	10.5
Vagina: Where the penis enters the female's body and sperm is received.	10.4	10.4
Foetus: The developing baby during pregnancy.	10.6	10.6
Gestation: Process where the baby develops during pregnancy.	10.6	10.6
Placenta: Organ that provides the foetus with oxygen and nutrients and removes waste substances.	10.6	10.6
Amniotic fluid: Liquid that surrounds and protects the foetus.	10.6	10.6
Umbilical cord: Connects the foetus to the placenta.	10.6	10.6
Apply		
Explain whether substances are passed from the mother to the foetus or not.	10.6, 10.7, 10.8	10.6, 10.7, 10.8
Use a diagram to show stages in development of a foetus from the production of sex cells to birth.	10.6	10.6
Describe causes of low fertility in male and female reproductive systems.	10.4	10.4
Identify key events on a diagram of the menstrual cycle.	10.4	10.4
Extend		
Explain why pregnancy is more or less likely at certain stages of the menstrual cycle.	10.4	10.4
Make deductions about how contraception and fertility treatments work.	(10.4)	(10.4)
Predict the effect of cigarettes, alcohol or drugs on the developing foetus.	10.7, 10.8	10.7, 10.8

1.10.1 Looking at variation

Lesson overview

Learning objectives

- Describe what is meant by variation in a species.
- Explain the difference between continuous and discontinuous variation.
- Plot graphs to show variation.

Learning outcomes

- Give examples of variation within species. [O1]
- Explain the difference between continuous variation and discontinuous variation, using examples. [O2]
- Plot graphs and use these to identify variation as continuous or discontinuous. [O3]

Skills development

- Working scientifically: 2.8 Justify opinions
- Developing numeracy: interpret information from graphs
- Developing literacy: suggest possible explanation in writing (Q6 & 7)

Resources needed at least 40 holly (or other) leaves in bags of 5, the bags labelled A, B, C etc.; tape measures; graph paper; spreadsheet software; Worksheet 1.10.1

Key vocabulary species, variation, continuous variation, discontinuous variation, correlation

Teaching and learning

Engage

- Show the students photographs of the British royal family (see task 1a of Worksheet 1.10.1). Ask them to **brainstorm** in groups: 'How are these people alike? How are they different?'. Take feedback. [O1]
- Ask the students to look at the pictures of *Cepaea nemoralis* snails in task 1c of Worksheet 1.10.1. Explain that these snails are all the same species. Ask the student pairs to **identify** how the snails vary. [O1]

Challenge and develop

- Ask the students to work in pairs to read the 'Types of variation' section in the Student Book and answer questions 3 and 4. [O2]
- **Small groups** Working in groups of three, the students **measure** one feature of members of the class. They **record** the data in a class spreadsheet, then complete parts a) and b) in task 2 of Worksheet 1.10.1. [O2, O3]
- Ask the students to **observe** and **investigate** different individuals of the same species (e.g. whether or not longer holly leaves have more prickles). The students **predict** the outcome, **decide** how to collect data and **select** a suitable sample size. Give each group one bag of leaves to investigate (see *Resources needed*). Students replace the leaves in the bag and pass to the next group. Repeat until each group has examined every bag of leaves. They **record** their data in a spreadsheet. [O1]
- The students work in pairs to **write an explanation** of the difference between variation within and across species. [O2]

Explain

- **Pair work** Still in their pairs, ask the students to read the 'Investigating variation' section in the Student Book and answer questions 6 and 7. [O2]
- The pairs then use the spreadsheets of data from both investigations (class features and leaf features) to **produce graphs**. Ideally, these should be computer-generated. [O3]

If graph-drawing software is not available, graphs with axes pre-drawn can be provided for low demand students.

- The students then **peer review** the graphs. Encourage them to **comment on** features such as labelling, use of an even scale, correct plotting, accuracy of line and size of graph. [O3]

Consolidate and apply

- Ask the students to **work independently** to complete part c) in task 2 of Worksheet 1.10.1 concerning variation in peaches. [O1, O2, O3]

- Working in groups, the students **discuss** the question in task 3 of Worksheet 1.10.1. [O3]

Extend

Ask students able to progress further:

- to work in pairs to **suggest** and **investigate** correlations using the graphs produced in this lesson (e.g. do taller students have wider arm spans?). [O3]

- to work in groups to find some leaves growing in shade and also non-shade (e.g. from a large bush), **calculate** the areas of the leaves (e.g. blackberry leaves) taken from open and shaded habitats, and to **suggest** why variations occur. [O1, O2, O3]

Plenary suggestions

Mind map Working in pairs, the students draw a mind map of what they have learned during the lesson. [O1, O2, O3]

What do I know? The students identify three things they have learned in this lesson, one thing they want to know more about and one target for future learning. [O1, O2, O3]

Answers to Student Book questions

1. A group of organisms with similar features that can produce fertile young.
2. *Humans*: e.g. eye colour (discontinuous); ear shape (continuous); hair colour (discontinuous); height (continuous); foot size (continuous); *dogs*: e.g. tail length (continuous); ear position (discontinuous); height (continuous); leg length (continuous); colour (discontinuous).
3. See answers in brackets in answers to question 2.
4. *Continuous*: the feature changes gradually over a range of values; *discontinuous*: individuals have one form of a feature or another.
5. Suitable graph for both tongue rolling and arm span. Tongue rolling: discontinuous; arm span: continuous.
6. Steps include: randomly pick a sample of 20+ leaves, from same tree; measure their lengths; count the spikes; plot a scatter graph.
7. The larger the sample size, the more accurate the investigation.

Answers to Worksheet 1.10.1

1. a) *Similar features*: all female; all have fair skin; fairly wide mouth; fairly prominent nose.

   b) Gender: count; skin colour: count; mouth size: measure; nose size: measure; for any other features identified: depends on the type of feature.

   c) Three of: colour of shell; size of shell; bands/no bands; thickness of bands; number of bands.

   d) *Colour* = count; *size* = measure; *bands/no bands* = count; *thickness of bands* = measure; *number of bands* = count.

2. a) Height; weight; eye colour; hair colour; skin colour; any suitable feature.

   b) Height and weight are continuous; eye colour, hair colour and skin colour are discontinuous.

   c) i) Line graph ii) 120–140 g iii) 146–157 g iv) Variety 1 = 130 g; variety 2 = 149.5 g v) Continuous

3. Variation gives a survival advantage to some organisms. It is important in reproduction when selecting a mate that will give offspring the best chance of survival. Weaker individuals will not survive if the environment changes.

1.10.2 Exploring causes of variation

Lesson overview

Learning objectives
- Identify whether a feature is inherited or determined by the environment.
- Understand that offspring from the same parents may show variation.

Learning outcomes
- Recognise that features such as height, eye colour, freckles, etc. are inherited, whereas scars, tooth loss, tattoos etc. are gained from the environment. [O1]
- Explain that offspring from the same parents may be very different because they have unique, random combinations of their parents' hereditary information. [O2]
- Evaluate the relative importance of genetic and environmental variation, and understand that genetic variation is essential for long-term survival whereas environmental variation can affect short-term survival. [O3]

Skills development
- Working scientifically: 2.10 Devise questions
- Developing numeracy: n/a
- Developing literacy: summarise key points using ideas and evidence (Q3 - 6)

Resources needed plant trays; oat seeds; soil and other growing mediums (e.g. vermiculite, compost, perlite); Worksheet 1.10.2; Practical sheet 1.10.2; Technician's notes 1.10.2

Common misconceptions Acquired characteristics may be passed on to offspring.

Key vocabulary inherited, genetic

Teaching and learning

Engage
- Ask the students: 'What if we were all the same? What would happen if a new disease emerged that could kill us?'. Use this discussion to reinforce why variation is so important for survival. [O3]

Challenge and develop
- **Pair work** Ask the students to work in pairs to read the 'What causes variation?' section in the Student Book and answer questions 1 and 2. Take feedback and explore with the students how some features are both inherited and caused by their environment (e.g. height). The students **discuss** and **write a list** of features that can be affected by the environment. [O1]
- The students work in their pairs to complete task 1 of Worksheet 1.10.2. [O1]
- **Pair talk/pairs to fours** Ask the question 'If you cut off a mouse's tail, will its young have no tails?'. Take feedback and stress that inherited variation passes from parents to offspring, but environmental variation is not passed on. [O1, O2]

Explain
- As a class, discuss ways in which the students think they are similar to their parents, grandparents, brothers and sisters. Then ask them to work in groups to **brainstorm** why children from the same parents look different. Take feedback and discuss the students' ideas. [O1, O2]
- Working in pairs, the students read the 'Why are offspring different?' section in the Student Book and answer questions 3 and 4. They can then complete task 2 of Worksheet 1.10.2. [O1, O2]
- **Group work** The students **begin an investigation** of what affects the height of seedlings (see Practical sheet 1.10.2). Encourage them to **make decisions** about how often they will take measurements, how many

seeds they will need in order to collect enough evidence and what their control will be. Ensure that they wash their hands after handling soil/compost. [O1]

- The students read the 'Genetic or environmental?' section in the Student Book. Ask them to work in pairs to answer question 5. Take feedback and discuss their ideas. [O2]

Consolidate and apply

- When the students have sufficient data of seedling growth (after two to three weeks), ask them to **consider** what the evidence shows. Discuss why seedling height varies (inherited and environmental factors). Ask whether the variation of seedling height in one condition is wider or less than the variation between different conditions. [O1, O2, O3]

- **Small groups** The students work in threes to **design** a poster about genetic and environmental variation, **present** their work and **peer review** the work of others. [O1, O2, O3]

- **Pairs to fours** The students answer part a) of task 3 of Worksheet 1.10.2 independently, then **share** with a partner and join with another pair to **agree on** an answer. Take feedback and discuss their ideas. [O3]

Extend

Ask students able to progress further:

- to work in groups to **brainstorm** other examples of how the environment can affect variation in plants and animals (e.g. stoats change their coat colour in response to colder temperatures) [O1, O3]

- Provide students with a claim about the cause of a specific trait (for example, a claim that freckles are an inherited trait) and ask students to critique the claim. [O1]

- to complete task 3 of Worksheet 1.10.2 to **evaluate** the importance of genetic and environmental variation in the survival of giant pandas. [O3]

Plenary suggestions

Ask me a question The students work in groups to **devise questions** starting 'How', 'Where', 'When', 'Why' or 'What' on the topic, with answers. They **answer** another group's questions and **peer assess**. [O1, O2, O3]

Answers to Student Book questions

1. *Inherited*: eye colour; shape and size of ears; etc.; *environmental* colour of nails (varnish); scars; tattoos; etc.
2. Any of: coat colour; coat pattern; length of mane; length of tail.
3. Each child gets a set of genetic information from their father and a set from the mother; the combinations are different.
4. a) Straight hair; face shape; skin colour; eyebrow shape. b) Eye colour; shape of nose; mouth shape; thickness of eyebrows; hair colour.
5. Height; weight; hair colour.
6. In the long term, genetic variation is more important than environmental, because only genetic variation is passed on to offspring. In the short term, the environmental variation may be more important if an organism is to survive (e.g. the coat colour of the stoat).

Answers to Worksheet 1.10.2

1. a) i) Variation passed on from parents. ii) Variation caused by the environment that the organism lives in.

   b) *Inherited*: female; blue eyes; shoe size; can roll tongue; *environmental*: can speak French; good at tennis; has pierced ears; has a tan; *both*: height; blonde hair. c) i) No ii) No; because environmental variations are not heritable.

2. a) i) From the parents by genetic variation. ii) Amount of water; amount of light; amounts of different minerals.

   b) They are different ages; they have inherited different combinations of information from their parents; they also have environmental differences (e.g. hair style).

3. a) There is no *inherited variation*, but the twins are affected differently by *environmental variation* – in this case ear piercing and hair cut.

   b) i) This results in less variation, which could mean that pandas will not survive long-term changes to their environment.
   ii) This increases variation, so pandas are more likely to survive changes in their environment over the long term.
   iii) Less food means that fewer pandas survive in the short term to breed and ensure the species' long-term survival.
   iv) More food means that more pandas are likely to survive in the short term, increasing long-term survival prospects.
   v) In the short term, many pandas may die; but the greater the variation between pandas, the more likely it is that enough will survive by having greater immunity to the new disease.

1.10.3 Considering the importance of variation

Lesson overview

Learning objectives

- Describe the importance of variation.

- Explain how variation may help a species to survive.

- Apply ideas about variation and survival to specific examples.

Learning outcomes

- Describe how a lack of variation can lead to extinction. [O1]

- Explain what is meant by a survival advantage and how this can benefit a species. [O2]

- Analyse data linked with an example of the advantage of variation. [O3]

Skills development

- Working scientifically: 2.14 Examine consequences

- Developing numeracy: interpret graphs

- Developing literacy: develop explanations using ideas and evidence (Q2 - 5)

Resources needed sticky notes of various colours (e.g. yellow, pink, green); images of black and white peppered moth (paper or electronic); graph paper; Worksheet 1.10.3

Key vocabulary survival advantage

Teaching and learning

Engage

- Ask each student to choose one sticky note from a choice of colours. They should leave their sticky note visible. Tell students that each sticky note represents one rabbit in a whole population.

- Students work in small groups to **discuss** what might vary between the rabbits in the population. Take feedback on suggestions. [O1]

- Students **listen** to a story about how viruses may be passed from one living thing to another. Describe a population of rabbits where some have natural resistance to a particular virus. If the virus infects a rabbit that has resistance, the rabbit survives. If the virus infects a rabbit that does not have natural resistance it dies. Tell the students that rabbits represented by pink and green sticky notes do not have resistance to the virus whereas rabbits represented by yellow sticky notes do have resistance. Ask students to **predict** what will happen to them, as a rabbit, and to others in the class. [O1, O2]

- Ask students who survived the infection to hold their sticky notes up and count how many were remaining from the total population. Tell students that this story represents the virus causing myxomatosis in rabbits. [O1, O2]

- Lead a discussion where students **predict** what would happen to the rabbit population if all had had pink or green sticky notes, and introduce the idea of extinction. [O1, O2]

Challenge and develop

- Ask students to read 'The importance of variation' in the Student Book. [O1, O2]

- **Pair talk** Ask students to **suggest** what is meant by 'survival advantage'. Pairs should suggest what the survival advantage could have been in dodos and what the survival advantage was in the rabbits that survived in the sticky note activity. [O1, O2]

Explain

- Ask students to **look** at images of peppered moths, both white and black variants. Tell students that the proportions of each variant have changed over time. [O1, O2]
- **Think, pair, share** Ask students to **suggest** reasons for the changes in proportions. Show images of each type of moth on a light and dark background as a clue when necessary. [O1, O2]
- Students complete sections 1 and 2 of Worksheet 1.10.3. [O1, O2]
- Students could then complete the questions from the Student Book. [O1, O2]

Consolidate and apply

- **Pair talk** Ask students to work in pairs to plan a piece of extended writing to explain the selective advantage of vaccinations in humans, for example, against polio or influenza.

High demand students could be asked to include a discussion about why the whole population isn't vaccinated against such illnesses.

Extend

- Students could make a game linked with selective advantages and the advantage of variation in a population.

Plenary suggestions

Big ideas Students work individually to write a list of three key learning points from the lessons on variation. Students then form small groups and compare their lists. A group list is compiled. These can be compared across the class and a class list could be compiled. [O1, O2, O3]

Answers to Student Book questions

1. Because it couldn't escape from predators/the population of other species on the island changed.
2. Colour of squirrels varies, height of giraffes varies. The red squirrel is better camouflaged in the woods and so has an advantage. The taller giraffes can reach leaves higher in the trees or may be able to spot predators more easily.
3. In unpolluted conditions, white moths are better camouflaged; in polluted conditions, dark moths are better camouflaged. The species doesn't die out because one variety is always camouflaged as conditions change.
4. Bacteria that have resistance to certain antibiotics have an advantage when that medicine is used and are more likely to survive and reproduce.
5. Because more bacteria have evolved that are resistant to methicillin.

Answers to Worksheet 1.10.3

1. Vary; survival; camouflaged; more; extinct; dodo.
2. Accurate graph drawn showing two lines plotted, suitable scale, labels.
3. a) Number of light moths decreases over time; number of dark moths increases over time, plus any further description of gradual changes.

b) Pollution in industrial areas caused changes in the bark of trees. This led to light moths being less well camouflaged and dark moths being better camouflaged. Light moths became more likely to be preyed upon by birds; dark moths were less likely to be preyed upon by birds.

c) The populations would remain more stable. This is because there is less of a decrease in light moths and less of an increase in dark moths because less pollution means tree trunk colour was less likely to change.

d) Light moths do not 'change into' dark moths or vice versa. It is more accurate to explain as 'a change in the surroundings (colour of tree bark) meant that dark moths more likely to survive/light moths less likely to survive (to reproduce to pass on their genes)'.

1.10.4 Understanding the female reproductive system and fertility

Lesson overview

Learning objectives

- Describe the structure and function of different parts of the female reproductive system.
- Describe the process of menstruation.
- Describe causes of low fertility.

Learning outcomes

- Name the main parts of the female reproductive system; describe fertilisation as being a fusion of a male nucleus and a female nucleus. [O1]
- Describe the stages of the menstrual cycle. [O2]
- Describe some factors that contribute towards low fertility in both males and females. [O3]

Skills development

- Working scientifically: 2.5 Communicate ideas
- Developing numeracy: n/a
- Developing literacy: structure writing to present solutions to problems (Q4)

Resources Worksheet 1.10.4a; Worksheet 1.10.4b

Common misconceptions Ovulation and fertilisation are the same thing.

Key vocabulary oviduct, ovary, uterus (womb), ovulation, menstruation, reproductive system, vagina, infertility

Teaching and learning

Engage

- Discuss the changes that happen during puberty. Be sensitive to how self-conscious students will be at this age. Start with peripheral changes, such as increased sweating and the need for increased personal hygiene. Ask the students to **describe** the changes that occur during puberty in boys and girls. [O1, O2]
- Introduce the term 'gametes' as the scientific word used for both male and female sex cells (sperm and egg).

Challenge and develop

- Introduce the female reproductive system using diagrams (Figure 1.10.4 in the Student Book). [O1]
- Hand out Worksheet 1.10.4b, which asks the students to **identify** the parts in a diagram of the female reproductive system and state their functions. [O1, O2]

  Give low demand students the cards from Worksheet 1.10.4b to help them match parts of the female reproductive system with their functions.

  Go through the students' responses and identify any misconceptions.

- Show the students web-based video clips of the process of ovulation and fertilisation (e.g. from the BBC Knowledge and Learning Beta). Be clear about the distinction between the two processes. Stress that without ovulation, fertilisation cannot take place. [O1, O2, O3]
- Discuss the menstrual cycle and how it works, using suitable video clips or Figure 1.10.4b in the Student Book. [O2]

Explain

- **Group work** Group the students in fours. Ask them to use the diagram in Worksheet 1.10.4a to **explore** possible reasons why fertilisation may not take place. They should compile their own table of factors, how they cause infertility and possible remedies. Ask them to check each other's answers. [O2, O3]

- Discuss with the class the overall problem of fertility and its possible consequences for individuals, families and society. You could use web resources such as NHS Choices. [O3]

- Provide key words relating either to the female reproductive system or to infertility problems. Ask the students to work in pairs, taking turns to **explain** the words to each other. [O1, O2]

Consolidate and apply

- Group the students in threes. Ask them to **role-play** being in a GP surgery. One student will be the GP and the other two will be the couple who are infertile. The role of the GP is to **explain** how ovulation and fertilisation take place, using diagrams from earlier in the lesson, and outlining the possible causes and remedies for infertility. The 'man' and the 'woman' should try to ask some difficult questions for the GP to answer. When they have completed the role-play once, if there is time, ask them to swap roles so that each person has the opportunity of role-playing the GP. [O2, O3]

  Select group(s) to show their role-play to the class.

Extend

- Referring to the third task on Worksheet 1.10.4b, ask students able to progress further to **consider** the adaptations of the female reproductive system. How is it adapted to maximise the chance of fertilisation? How successful is the system? They should **summarise** the strengths and weaknesses. [O3]

Plenary suggestions

Heads and tails Arrange students in groups of six. Ask each student to write a question about something from the topic on a coloured paper strip, and to write the answer in another colour. Within the groups, share out the strips so that each student gets a question and an answer. One student reads out their question – the student with the correct answer reads it out, followed by the question on their paper.

Answers to Student Book questions

1. In the ovary.
2. To help push the baby out.
3. Hormones cause the egg to mature and ovulation to occur.
4. External factors – don't drink alcohol, take drugs or smoke during pregnancy.
   Problems with ovulation – use hormone treatment to correct the imbalance.
   Endometriosis – surgery is needed to remove cysts.
   Blockages in the oviduct – surgery is needed to remove blockages.

Answers to Worksheet 1.10.4b

1. 1B; 2E; 3A; 4C; 5D
2. Refer to Figure 1.10.4a in the Student Book.
3. Additional annotations should include:
   - The cervix is made of strong muscle to help push the baby out.
   - The oviduct is lined with ciliated epithelial cells that help push the egg to the uterus.
   - The uterus has a good blood supply so it is ready for fertilisation to take place.

   Problems that cause female infertility: blockages can occur in the oviduct; fertilisation can occur in the oviduct, which is dangerous for the foetus; cysts can occur around the ovary, preventing the egg from being released.

1.10.5 Understanding the male reproductive system and fertilisation

Lesson overview

Learning objectives

- Describe the structure and function of different parts of the male reproductive system.
- Describe fertilisation in humans.

Learning outcomes

- Name the main parts of the male reproductive system; recognise sperm as the male sex cell. [O1]
- Describe the structure and function of the main parts of the male reproductive system; identify similarities and differences between human and plant reproductive systems. [O2]
- Describe the process of fertilisation. [O3]

Skills development

- Working scientifically: 2.6 Construct explanations
- Developing numeracy: n/a
- Developing literacy: describe features and identify crucial differences (Q4 - 6)

Resources needed images/graphs of human population and bee population (e.g. from internet search); Worksheet 1.10.5a; Worksheet 1.10.5b

Key vocabulary testicle, penis, sperm duct, semen, urethra, fertilisation, gamete

Teaching and learning

Engage

- Show the students a graph of human population over time. Ask them to **devise** five questions relating to the graph. Discuss the questions and ask the students to **suggest** possible answers. Establish all the factors that affect the population of a species.

- Now show the students a graph of bee population over time (fairly easy to find online), reminding them of earlier work on insect pollination. Ask the students to **compare** the two graphs and what effect one might have on the other, over time. Ask them to **decide** which factors they think will influence human population more strongly – reproduction or crop production? [O2]

Challenge and develop

- Recap what is meant by the terms 'cell', 'tissue', 'organ' and 'organ system'.

- **Collective memory** Group the students in mixed ability groups of four. Provide them with a blank diagram of the male reproductive system, available as Worksheet 1.10.5a. First, see if they can name any of the parts and write the labels in pencil. Tell them that each student in their group will take in it turns to look at the correct names and descriptions of each part, which are with the teacher (Figure 1.10.5a in the Student Book) for 30 seconds and then label as much of the diagram as possible from memory. The group that completes the most correct labels on the diagram will win. Ask each group to plan a strategy to help them complete the labelling on the diagram. For example, give each student one part of the diagram to focus on. Carry out the activity, allowing each student about 30 seconds to look at the teacher's diagram and about one minute to record what they remember when they return to their group. Allow each student two turns before asking the groups to swap their diagrams and mark each other's. Ask them to fill in answers for parts that are missing or incorrect. [O1, O2]

- Discuss each part of the male reproductive system in turn, using Figure 1.10.5a in the Student Book. [O1]

- Working with the cards from Worksheet 1.10.5b, pairs of students match the structures to the functions. [O1, O2]

- The second part of the worksheet provides the names of different structures and asks students to write down the function. [O2]

- Recap the structures and functions of the system and ask students to correct any mistakes. [O1, O2]

Explain

- Refer back to work in the previous lesson on the female reproductive system. Ask students to **discuss** the journey of a sperm until fertilisation of an egg. [O1, O2, O3]

- Ask the students to **consider** what could go wrong with the male reproductive system and which parts are most likely to get infected. Ask them to **think of reasons** for their answers. [O3]

    High demand students could **research** how these problems might be remedied.

Consolidate and apply

- Ask the students to look at the diagram of a flowering plant (Figure 1.9.5a in the Student Book). Ask them to **identify** corresponding parts of the plant and the human male reproductive systems. Ask them to write an explanation of how the parts are similar and how they are different. [O2, O3]

    Low demand students could write their answers in the form of a table.

    Ask high demand students to **identify** additional parts in the male reproductive system and write why these parts are needed in the human but not in the plant.

Extend

- Ask students able to progress further to **evaluate** the strengths and weaknesses of the plant's male reproductive system and the human male reproductive system. They should **compare** which is more successful at making and transferring male sex cells and the limitations of each system. [O2]

Plenary suggestions

What am I? One student thinks of one part of the male reproductive system. The other students then have to ask questions about what the part might be. Only 'yes' or 'no' answers may be given. [O1, O2]

Answers to Student Book questions

1. *Cell* = sperm; *organs* = testes, prostate gland.
2. Correctly labelled diagram; path of sperm from testes; through sperm duct; past prostate; through urethra into penis.
3. *Plants* = anther; *human* = testes.
4. Fertilisation takes place in the uterus; where the developing foetus will grow.
5. The egg cell contains nutrients essential for the early development of the foetus if the egg is fertilised.
6. *Ovulation* is the release of an egg from the ovary; *fertilisation* is a sperm cell fusing with the egg cell in the uterus.

Answers to Worksheet 1.10.5b

1. A4; B3; C1; D5; E2; F6
2. a) To carry the male genetic material and deliver it into the egg cell.
    b) To deliver the sperm to the prostate gland from the testes.
    c) To release sperm or urine out of the male.
    d) To supply vital nutrients to the sperm to enable them to survive.
    e) To make sperm cells.
3. Plants and humans have different ways of transferring the male sex cell to the female. Plants use wind or insects and are adapted for pollen to be transferred by either; humans rely on internal fertilisation.

1.10.6 Learning how a foetus develops

Lesson overview

Learning objectives

- Describe the role of the mother in supporting and protecting the developing foetus.

- Recognise the development of a foetus.

Learning outcomes

- Describe growth as reproduction of cells. [O1]
- Describe the difference between a foetus and an embryo; describe the structures and functions of different parts of a pregnant uterus. [O2]
- Choose scales to produce a line graph to show how a foetus grows during gestation; explain how a pregnant uterus is different from a normal uterus. [O3]

Skills development

- Working scientifically: 2.16 Interrogate sources
- Developing numeracy: interpret timelines
- Developing literacy: summarise key points (Q6)

Resources equipment for demonstration (Petri dish, detergent in a small amount of water, drinking straw); Worksheet 1.10.6; Technician's notes 1.10.6

Common misconceptions Growth of cells involves the enlargement of cells, not the division of cells.

Key vocabulary stem cell, foetus, gestation, placenta, amniotic fluid, umbilical cord

Teaching and learning

Engage

- Show the students a video clip showing the moment of conception and subsequent division of cells as the embryo grows. Use a model of this: demonstrate bubble formation using detergent in a Petri dish, so the students can see the bubbles multiplying to represent growth as you blow through a straw. Ask them to **discuss** the strengths and weaknesses of the model. In what way is it the same as cell growth? In what ways is it different? [O1]

Challenge and develop

- Show a video or models of a developing embryo from fertilisation to birth. Explore how the embryo starts with growing cells that are all the same (stem cells). After a few days, stem cells begin to differentiate and become specialised cells. Show an image of the embryo inside the womb after eight weeks. Ask the students to **discuss** the rate of its development and the difference between a foetus and an embryo. [O2]

- Introduce the term 'gestation' as the period of time from conception to birth. Discuss gestation, and gestation periods of different organisms as a point of interest: elephants, 2 years; cat, about 30 days; mice, about 20 days; humans, 40 weeks. [O3]

- Show the students the illustration of a pregnant uterus in Figure 1.10.6c in the Student Book. Ask them to work in pairs to **compare** this with a non-pregnant uterus and to **describe** the functions of the different parts. [O2, O3]

- Talk about birth, discussing the main steps, including the cervix relaxing and widening and the contraction of the strong muscles in the uterus to push the baby out during the birthing process.

Explain

- Show the students the diagram of the developing foetus in the Student Book (a similar diagram is in Worksheet 1.10.6, task 2). Discuss the features of the developing foetus and ask the students to **explain** how it changes over time. Students could focus on how the size of the head changes compared with the body and write down the order of the development of different organs. [O2, O3]

Consolidate and apply

- Ask students to **write** why the parts are needed in a pregnant uterus but not in a non-pregnant uterus. [O2, O3]

  Low demand students can complete the cloze exercise in the first section of the worksheet. [O1, O2]

- Show the students the data relating to development of the human embryo (task 2 of Worksheet 1.10.6). Remind them of the features of a good graph and ask them to draw a graph using the data in the worksheet. Select different students to share their graphs and answers. Ask 'What is the most surprising thing you have learned from the data?' They should then answer the questions on the worksheet. [O3]

  You may need to provide low demand students with a ready-drawn axes and scales to help them to **present** the data.

  High demand students should draw a line of best fit.

Extend

- Referring to task 3 on Worksheet 1.10.6, ask students able to progress further to **research** the gestation of non-placental animals such as birds and frogs. Can they **suggest** some advantages and disadvantages of placental and non-placental foetal development? [O3]

Plenary suggestions

True or false? Present the students with some correct and incorrect statements about foetus development and ask them to stand up if a statement is true.

Learning triangle Ask the students to draw a large triangle with a smaller inverted triangle that just fits inside it (so they have four triangles). Ask them to think back over the lesson and to write in the three outer triangles something they have seen, something they have done and something they have discussed. Then, in the central triangle, ask them to write down something they have learned.

Answers to Student Book questions

1. Growth occurs when cells divide to make new cells.
2. They have the ability to become any cell in the body.
3. Between 8 and 12 weeks. The increase for that 4 week period is 60mm whereas for other 4 week periods, the maximum increase is less.
4. The placenta transfers materials such as oxygen and glucose from the mother's blood to the baby's blood; and removes waste from the baby's blood to the mother's blood.
5. This stops the baby from bumping about in the uterus when the mother moves around.
6. The pregnant uterus contains a placenta, umbilical cord, amniotic sac and amniotic fluid. It has expanded to become up to 20 times its normal size.

Answers to Worksheet 1.10.6

1. a) See Figure 1.10.6c in the Student Book.

   b) reproducing; uterus; placenta; umbilical cord; oxygen; nutrients; amniotic fluid; protect

2. a) *Placenta* – where blood from the mother exchanges oxygen, nutrients and carbon dioxide with blood from the foetus.

   b) *Umbilical cord* – carries the foetal blood to the placenta and blood with nutrients, oxygen and glucose from the mother to the foetus.

   c) *Amniotic fluid* – a fluid surrounding the baby that protects it from damage and harm, cushioning the movements of the mother.

   d) *Uterus* – the part where the developing baby grows; the muscles are the strongest in the body to help push the baby out of the womb during birth.

   Correctly drawn graph and line of best fit. The length of the foetus increases directly with age, with a very slightly higher rate of growth at the start of development compared to the end.

3. This allows students to apply their learning in new contexts by comparing the process of development in different organisms. Suitable illustrations of the structure of a bird's egg and the development of a tadpole will be easy to find either via the internet or in older, more traditional biology textbooks.

1.10.7 Understanding factors affecting a developing foetus

Lesson overview

Learning objectives

- Describe the effects of different factors on a developing foetus.
- Evaluate the strength of data.
- Analyse advice given to pregnant women.

Learning outcomes

- Name certain substances that will affect the development of the foetus. [O1]
- Describe the effects of different substances on the development of the foetus; describe whether or not there is enough evidence to draw conclusions. [O2]
- Explain the effect of different substances on the health and development of the foetus; explain whether or not given data are reliable and valid, and suggest how to improve the quality of the data. [O3]

Skills development

- Working scientifically: 2.15 Review theories
- Developing numeracy: understand data in research summary
- Developing literacy: comment on specified features of research reports (Q5)

Resources labelled diagram (deliberately incorrect) of pregnant uterus; Worksheet 1.10.7

Key vocabulary premature, placenta, valid, reliable, sample size

Teaching and learning

Engage

- Show the students a labelled diagram of a pregnant uterus that includes some deliberate mistakes. Select students to **identify** the mistakes and to **correct** them.

Challenge and develop

- Discuss the role of the placenta in more detail, using images/diagrams. Explain that any small molecules are able to pass through the placenta – including harmful ones such as alcohol, drugs and nicotine. [O1, O2]
- Discuss the features of a good scientific survey. Include what is meant by 'sample size' and its importance in biological surveys, the terms 'validity' and 'reliability' and how they apply to scientific studies, and the need to collect unbiased evidence.
- **Group work** Working in groups of four, give the students reports of different scientific studies on the effect of alcohol drunk during pregnancy on the subsequent development of children (task 2 of Worksheet 1.10.7). Ask the students to **analyse** these, **identifying** the questions being asked, the variables being controlled, how the evidence is collected, the sample size used and what was found out. They should use these to establish how valid and reliable the studies are. Collect feedback from the different groups and discuss their ideas. [O2, O3]

Explain

- Ask the students to write a leaflet to pregnant mothers **explaining** how to ensure that their babies develop as well as they can, and what the consequences are if they take certain substances during pregnancy or if they omit essential nutrients. [O1, O2, O3]

  Standard and high demand students should use data from the case studies in Worksheet 1.10.7 to support their ideas.

Consolidate and apply

- In groups of three, ask the students to imagine they are conducting a survey to find out how exercise in pregnancy affects the growth of a developing foetus. Ask them to **devise** a plan to collect valid and reliable data. Select students to **feed back** their ideas. Ask the class to comment on the studies.

Extend

- Ask students able to progress further to **research** studies on other aspects of foetal development, such as the effects of taking nutrient supplements during pregnancy (e.g. folic acid). Ask them to **evaluate** the evidence, **describing** how valid and reliable the data are. [O3]

Plenary suggestions

- **Which is which?** Provide students with a list of substances such as alcohol, nicotine, folic acid, carbon monoxide, unhealthy drugs such as heroin, fish oils, carbon dioxide and oxygen, nutrients such as vitamins and minerals. Ask them to **identify** which substances can pass from the mother to the foetus, which can pass from the foetus to the mother and which are likely to be too big to pass. [O1, O2, O3]

Answers to Student Book questions

1. The mother takes these chemicals into her body.
2. It would die; it would not be able to obtain oxygen, glucose or nutrients.
3. If the mother drinks alcohol, smokes, takes unsuitable drugs such as marijuana or cocaine, or has a poor diet lacking in nutrients (in particular folic acid), the development of the foetus can be adversely affected.
4. The advice is given because there is evidence that following these guidelines will increase the chances of having a healthy baby. Advice should include: do not smoke, drink or use drugs during pregnancy; take folic acid.
5. a) Not very reliable; only 127 babies were investigated; the amount of alcohol was not recorded.

   b) Not very reliable; the sample size is small; twice as many smokers were sampled as non-smokers.

Answers to Worksheet 1.10.7

1. *Harm the foetus*: alcohol; nicotine; carbon monoxide; drugs like heroin.

   Help the foetus: folic acid; fish oils; regular but moderate exercise; a healthy, balanced diet.
2. Problems making mental connections; behavioural problems; lower intelligence and attention span; reduced ability to perform certain tasks.
3. a) B, then A, then C; B has the largest sample size; C has the smallest.

   b) *Case study A*: How many mothers were binge drinkers? What were the backgrounds of the children?

   Case study B: How much alcohol did the mothers consume during pregnancy? How many children came from poor backgrounds?

   Case study C: Were children from the same background tested, where the same number of mothers did not drink?

   What was the actual performance of the children in the tests? Could other factors explain why they did not do as well?

1.10.8 Communicating ideas about smoking in pregnancy

Lesson overview

Learning objectives

- Critique claims linked with the effects of smoking in pregnancy.

- Identify potential bias in sources of information.

- Give a reasoned opinion.

Learning outcomes

- Consider claims in adverts, including those about smoking in pregnancy. [O1]

- Explain what is meant by bias and relate it to claims about smoking in pregnancy. [O2]

- Give an opinion on smoking in pregnancy and support this with evidence and defence of the counter-argument. [O3]

Skills development

- Working scientifically: 2.16 Interrogate sources

- Developing numeracy: understand data in research summary

- Developing literacy: present ideas and assertions with supporting evidence (Q5)

Resources needed examples of adverts (on paper or electronic), aimed to sway the public; Worksheet 1.10.8; Technician's 1.10.8

Key vocabulary bias, opinion, justify, reasoning, evidence

Teaching and learning

Engage

- Show two or three adverts (either paper copies or electronic) selling a product, such as one for anti-wrinkle cream or shampoo. On first viewing, just ask students to watch with no prompts. Show the adverts again and ask students to **observe** the ways in which the advertiser tries to influence us. [O1]

- **Pair talk** Ask students to **discuss** how the advertiser tries to persuade us that the product is good. Take some feedback and draw out specific examples such as use of positive language, suggestion of a need for the product, use of research data (for example, '8 out of 10 testers said…'). [O1]

Challenge and develop

- Show some historical adverts specifically linked to smoking (e.g. in the Student Book or alternative examples). [O1]

- **Pair talk** Ask pairs to discuss the messages that the adverts give about smoking. [O1]

- Explain to the students that adverts promoting cigarettes were common on television before the mid-1960s. In the 1960s, restrictions were placed on advertising of cigarettes. If possible, show a video clip to show how smoking was used in films and was considered by many to be glamorous. Ask students to **suggest** why restrictions may have been placed on advertising. [O1, O2]

- Students **read** the 'Considering bias' section in the Student Book. Lead a discussion about why it took so long for some people to accept the danger of smoking during pregnancy, linked with advertisers' messages, for example the use of doctors in adverts. [O1, O2]

- Link back to the adverts used at the start of the lessons and ask students to **apply** what they understand about bias to **suggest** how other advertisers could have bias. [O1]

Explain

- Use questioning to recap with students the dangers of smoking in pregnancy from the previous lesson.

- In small groups, ask students to **read** the section 'Critiquing a claim about smoking in pregnancy' in the Student Book.
- Ask groups to **summarise** the information in only five bullet points. Circulate and informally assess the summaries or match up groups to share and compare their summaries.
- Ask students to **answer** questions in task 1 of Worksheet 1.10.8 to reinforce the meaning of the terms claim, evidence and opinion. [O1, O2]
- Provide information showing research studies on Worksheet 1.10.8 task 2.
- **Pair talk** Ask students to **discuss** the questions on task 2 of Worksheet 1.10.8. They should then work individually **write** full answers.
- As a check on understanding, ask the students to complete questions 3 and 4 in the Student Book.

Consolidate and apply

- Ask students to **read** the section on 'Justify an opinion' in the Student Book. [O3]
- **Pairs to fours** Ask the original pairs to form fours to **discuss** the success criteria for a reasoned opinion. Take feedback and, as a class, agree success criteria (e.g. give opinion, provide evidence, explain the reasoning, provide defences against counter-arguments). [O3]
- Students **plan** and **write** an answer to question 5 in the Student Book. Figure 1.10.8d can be used to help with planning. [O3]

  Low demand students could be provided with a writing frame to scaffold this task. They could also be provided with keywords to include.

- Pairs **peer assess** their partner's work, referring to the agreed success criteria and give feedback. Students then **improve** their work based on feedback. [O3]

Extend

- Students could provide a reasoned opinion on an issue such as drinking alcohol in pregnancy. This may require more justification, because a small amount of alcohol in pregnancy is acceptable to some. Students work independently to apply to processes of forming a justified opinion. [O1, O2, O3]

Plenary suggestions

The big ideas Ask students to pick out three main examples of learning from the lesson. In groups, they compare ideas and agree a list of the three most important aspects. [O1, O2, O3]

Answers to Student Book questions

1. That smoking can be beneficial to women, including pregnant women. Smoking is not harmful to an unborn baby.
2. The adverts are from tobacco companines, which did not want to reduce sales, and it was in their interest to persuade people that smoking is not harmful/is beneficial.
3. Smoking in pregnancy can increase the risk of babies born with low birth weight.
4. Suggestions similar to Table 1.10.8, linked with a study of a large sample of babies and weights when born to compare and show that they are more likely to be born weighing less if the mother is a smoker.
5. a), b), c). An opinion expressed with evidence to support opinion stated and reasoning given.

   d) Opposite opinion stated and some arguments against this opinion.

Answers to Worksheet 1.10.8

1. a) 1 c; 2 d; 3 a; 4 b   b) i Opinion; ii Claim; iii Bias because only shared a positive about the cigarettes; iv Evidence
2. a) i Smoking in pregnancy increases the risk of offspring becoming drug users, or similar.

   ii In monkeys, nicotine does not have an effect on birth weight of babies, or similar.

   b) i Suggestions such as: larger sample, similar numbers in sample and control.

   ii Suggestions such as: consider evidence in humans, identify sample size (and possibly increase sample size).
3. a) Sensible suggestions of a claim such as 'Enerise makes you feel less tired', 'Enerise makes you feel more energetic'.

   b) Suggestions of evidence that would support the claim such as: large group trials; control group that didn't drink Enerise as comparison; measures of e.g. amount of sleep over periods of time; difference in activity levels; way of comparing energy through a measured activity.

   c) Advert showing a claim and use of persuasive images and/or language and mention of evidence.

1.10.9 Checking students' progress

The *Checking your progress* section in the Student Book indicates the key ideas developed in this chapter and shows how students progress to more complex levels. It is provided to support students in:

- identifying those ideas;

- developing a sense of their current level of understanding;

- developing a sense of what the next steps in their learning are.

It is designed to be used either at the end of a chapter to support an overall view of the progress, or alternatively during the teaching of the chapter. The students can self-assess or peer assess using this as a basis.

It is helpful to encourage students to provide evidence from their understanding or their notes to support their judgements. In some cases it may be useful to explore the difference in the descriptors for a particular idea so that students can see what makes for a 'higher outcome'.

It may be useful with some descriptors to provide examples from the specific work done, such as an experiment undertaken or an explanation developed and recorded. If marking and feedback uses similar ideas and phrases, this will enable students to relate specific marking to a more general sense of progress.

To make good progress in understanding science students need to focus on these ideas and skills:

Students who are making modest progress will be able to:	Students who are making good progress will be able to:	Students who are making excellent progress will be able to:
Identify some features of different organisms of the same species.	Explain the difference between continuous and discontinuous variation	Use data to explain whether variation is continuous or discontinuous and to investigate correlations between varying features.
Identify examples of variation caused by inheritance and of variation caused by the environment in which the organism lives.	Explain how a mix of genes from our parents means that siblings are different.	Discuss the relationship between inherited features and the environment and describe how many features are caused by a combination, with examples.
Recognise that variation within a species can help that species to survive.	Use examples to describe how variation within a species can be an advantage if the environment changes.	Make predictions about changes within a species to changes to external conditions.
Name the main parts of the male human reproductive system.	Describe the structures and functions of the main parts of the male human reproductive system; describe how fertility problems may arise.	Explain how the male reproductive structure are designed for fertilisation; describe methods to combat infertility.
Name the main parts of the female human reproductive system.	Describe the structures and functions of the main parts of the female human reproductive system; describe how fertility problems may arise.	Explain how the female reproductive structures are designed for fertilisation; describe methods to combat infertility.
Recall the stages in development as a change from a single fertilised egg to an embryo and foetus.	Compare the growth of the foetus at different stages. Describe the role of the mother in protecting the developing foetus.	Describe the functions of different supporting structures of the mother.
Identify substances passed on from a mother that will either help or harm her developing foetus.	Describe how substances pass to and form a developing foetus and describe the effects of different factors on a developing foetus.	Apply knowledge of effects of substances on advice given to pregnant women, considering validity of evidence.
Identify bias in a claim and link it to claims about smoking in pregnancy.	Explain what it means to critique a claim and give examples of evidence to support a claim about the effects of smoking in pregnancy.	Justify an opinion about smoking in pregnancy using evidence to support the opinion and to defend against an alternative opinion.

1.10.10 Answers to Student Book end of chapter questions

This table provides answers to the Questions section at the end of Chapter 10 of the Student Book. It also shows how different questions assess attainment in terms of the focus and style of a question as well as the context. Question level analysis can indicate students' proficiency in approaching different aspects of scientific understanding and different types of answer.

Q	Answer	Marks available	Knowledge & understanding	Application	Evaluation of evidence	Objective test question	Short written answer	Longer written answer	Variation	Human reproduction
			Focus			Style			Context	
1	a	1	x			x			x	
2	Genetics and the enviromnent	2	x				x			x
			x				x			x
3	• A species with no variation is vulnerable if there is an adverse change (e.g. new disease, change in the environment)	4	x					x	x	
	• If organisms do not adapt to the change, the species will die out		x					x	x	
	• Variation means some organisms have a favourable feature		x					x	x	
	• This gives them a survival advantage		x					x	x	
4	a	1	x			x				x
5	b	1	x			x				x
6	Day 1: the lining of the uterus breaks down and first blood loss occurs	4	x					x		x
	Day 5: the lining begins to build up again; blood loss ceases		x					x		x
	Day 14: ovulation occurs; the egg moves from the ovary into the oviduct		x					x		x
	Day 21: the egg has now reached the uterus; if it is not fertilised, it will die and uterus lining will break down again		x					x		x
7	d	1		x		x			x	
8	Any disadvantageous feature for a predator (e.g. albinism; blunt teeth; poor sense of hearing and smell)	1		x		x			x	
9	Decrease variation (1) and if these roses are then grown in different soil, they won't grow well (1)	2		x			x		x	
				x			x		x	
10	c	1		x		x				x
11	d	1		x		x				x
12	Fertility – increases the number of eggs produced (1)	2		x			x			x
	Contraception – prevents ovulation (1)			x			x			x
13	a) 118	4			x		x		x	
	b) sizes 6 to 16				x		x		x	

Q	Answer	Marks available	Knowledge & understanding	Application	Evaluation of evidence	Objective test question	Short written answer	Longer written answer	Variation	Human reproduction
	c) Continuous				x		x		x	
	d) 11				x		x		x	
14	Large sample size	1			x		x			x
15	Sketch should be a bar graph	4			x			x		x
	• Smoker and non-smoker mothers on x-axis; weight of foetus on y-axis				x			x		x
					x			x		x
	• Higher bar for non-smoker mothers				x			x		x
	• Carbon monoxide passes across the placenta of smoker mothers and reduces the amount of oxygen reaching the foetus									
	• With less oxygen, the cells of the foetus do not grow as well									
	Total possible:	30								